THE GETHSEMANI ENCOUNTER

THE GETHSEMANI ENCOUNTER

A Dialogue on the Spiritual Life by Buddhist and Christian Monastics

Edited by Donald W. Mitchell
and James A. Wiseman, O.S.B.

CONTINUUM NEW YORK

1997
The Continuum Publishing Company
370 Lexington Avenue
New York, NY 10017

Printed in the United States of America

Library of Congress Cataloging-in-Publication Data

The Gethsemani encounter : a dialogue on the spiritual life by Buddhist and Christian monastics / edited by Donald W. Mitchell and James A. Wiseman.
p. cm.
ISBN 0-8264-1046-4
1. Christianity and other religions—Buddhism—Congresses. 2. Buddhism—Relations—Christianity—Congresses. 3. Spiritual life—Catholic Church—Congresses. 4. Spiritual life—Buddhism–-Congresses. 5. Monastic and religious life—Congresses. 6. Monastic and Religious life (Buddhism)—Congresses. 7. Catholic Church—Doctrines—Congresses. 8. Buddhism—Doctrines—History. I. Mitchell, Donald W. (Donald William), 1943– . II. Wiseman, James A., O.S.B.
BR128.B8G48 1997
261.2'43—dc21 97-24414
CIP

Contents

Foreword

It was a great source of happiness for me to join my Christian and Buddhist brothers and sisters in the Gethsemani Encounter. I was particularly pleased that we should meet at the monastery that was once home to Thomas Merton. Although we did not know each other very long, in his large-hearted faith and burning desire to know, I felt the inspiration of a kindred spirit.

For those of us who attended, this gathering of dedicated monks, nuns and lay spiritual practitioners was proof, if it were needed, that the purpose of religion is not to build beautiful churches or temples; it is to cultivate positive human qualities such as tolerance, generosity and love. Fundamental to Buddhism and Christianity, indeed to every major world religion, is the belief that we must reduce our selfishness and serve others.

Unfortunately, due to suspicion and misunderstanding, religion sometimes causes more quarrels than it solves. I believe that one religion, like a single type of food, cannot hope to satisfy all. Depending on their different mental dispositions, some people benefit from one teaching, others from another. All faiths, despite their contradictory philosophies, possess the ability to produce fine warmhearted human beings. Therefore, there is every reason to appreciate and respect all forms of spiritual practice.

Every religion and culture has its distinguishing characteristics. For Tibetans, the emphasis for many centuries has been on developing and upholding inner values such as compassion and wisdom. These are more important to us than acquiring material wealth, fame or success. We regard inner strength, gentleness, love, compassion, wisdom and a stable mind as the most important treasures a human being can collect in his or her lifetime. However, I am aware that this can lead to a kind of peaceful complacency. I feel that we Buddhists have much to learn from our Christian brothers and sisters. We are all aware of the inner peace that can be found in prayer and meditation, but our Christian friends may have a richer experience of bringing that inner peace to bear in practical ways in the generous service of others.

Gatherings of spiritual practitioners from different backgrounds, such as the Gethsemani Encounter, are of immense value. I believe it is extremely important that we extend our understanding of each other's spiritual practices and traditions. This is not necessarily done in order to adopt them ourselves, but to increase our opportunities for mutual respect. Sometimes, too, we encounter something in another tradition that helps us better appreciate something in our own. Consequently, I hope that Christians, Buddhists, people of all faiths and people without faith will approach this book from the Gethsemani Encounter with the same rigorous curiosity and courage for which Thomas Merton was renowned. It is my hope that readers of this book may find in it inspiration and understanding that in some way contribute to their own inner peace. And I pray that through that inner peace they too will become better human beings and help create a happier, more peaceful world.

His Holiness the Dalai Lama
January 1997
Dharamsala, India

Preface

The Buddhist-Christian encounter at Gethsemani will remain as a reference point for the future of interfaith dialogue. The success of this historic encounter depended upon two elements: the long history of interfaith contacts that led us to Gethsemani, and the deep spirit of dialogue that characterizes intermonastic encounters. At Gethsemani, we gathered the well-ripened fruits of a long interfaith collaboration. And the spiritual climate at the Abbey of Gethsemani during this week of dialogue left behind an understanding that such spiritual exchanges are not only occasions of mutual aid on the spiritual journey—in terms of mutual understanding, respect, and encouragement—but they are in and of themselves spiritual experiences that until the present were difficult even to imagine. Therefore, a long preparation, both historically and spiritually, was necessary to produce this profound quality of dialogue.

While undertaking his spiritual journey in Asia in 1968, Thomas Merton met with His Holiness the Dalai Lama. During his three days of conversations with His Holiness at Dharamsala, "a great affection" was born, as Merton noted in his journal: "I believe . . . that there is a real spiritual bond between us."[1] The Dalai Lama felt that Merton was his "spiritual brother," and called him a "Catholic geshe" (learned monk). From this friendship, His Holiness also developed a deep respect for all Christian monks and nuns.

One must remember, however, that during his lifetime Thomas Merton was not very well understood. Even five years after Merton's death, the Abbot Primate of the Benedictines, Dom Rembert Weakland, concluded at a monastic conference in Bangalore that very few monastics were engaged in interfaith dialogue. So it was necessary for Cardinal Pignedoli, President of what is now the Pontifical Council for Interreligious Dialogue in the Vatican, to write a letter to the Abbot Primate stating that intermonastic dialogue needed to be more systematically organized. Finally in 1978, ten years after the death of Thomas Merton, two dialogue commissions were created: what is now known as the "Monastic Interreligious Dialogue"

(MID) in North America, and the "Dialogue Inter-Monastic" (DIM) in Europe. With these commissions in place, the number of nuns and monks engaged in this path of interfaith dialogue grew in a sudden and remarkable way.

The wonderful fruits of this historic encounter of Christian and Buddhist spiritualities are presented in a talk in this book by Sr. Pascaline Coff, O.S.B. In brief, through the "Spiritual Exchange" in Europe since 1979, and the "Monastic Hospitality Program" in North America since 1981, Buddhist nuns and monks spent time living in Christian monasteries in the West, and Christian monastics were guests of Zen[2] and Tibetan monasteries in the East. This long history of profound experiences of shared spiritual life and dialogue brought us to the Gethsemani Encounter where an in-depth dialogue on the spiritual life was finally possible.

For Buddhists and Christians to make this historic step in our dialogue, MID needed years of preparation during which it drew on its long experience and its networking relationships in order to assemble at the Abbey of Gethsemani so many remarkable people trained in the spiritual life. Thanks to attentive organizing, this large gathering was able to unfold in monastic serenity, and to reveal in a remarkable way the profound communion that unites all seekers of the Truth.

However, it is important to remark here that the careful organization alone cannot explain the spiritual climate that we have known since the Gethsemani Encounter. This new climate of openness and unity is also the result of a process of interior evolution, a profound change in thinking, thanks to which the monastic orders, Buddhist and Christian, are now able to recognize themselves as forerunners of a spiritual unity that is prophetic for all humankind. So, let me say a few words about this evolution that brought us to Gethsemani; and then I will make some concluding remarks about the prophetic vision of the event.

In his 1974 letter to the Abbot Primate, Cardinal Pignedoli expressed the hope that he placed in the dialogue of Christian monastics with other religious. He made the remark that "the monk represents a point of contact and of mutual comprehension between Christians and Non-Christians. The presence of monastics in the Catholic Church is therefore, in itself, a bridge that joins us to all other religions."[3] However even with this great hope, during the first years of their existence the monastic commissions for dialogue had received, in effect, a mandate to limit their contacts to the level of religious practice in order not to risk errors at the theological level.[4] The ensuing exchanges at the level of monastic practice were enormously fruitful. Contacts were established, friendships built and the foundations of trust and respect were laid for future dialogue.

No matter what, dialogue had to evolve. Everyone in the early encounters recognized that the work was much more vast than anyone had anticipated. And fortunately, the spiritual dynamics that animate our monastic life raised up and guided this natural evolution. The concrete process of this change is very interesting to study. Little by little, it became clear that monastics are particularly well predisposed for dialogue. Humility, so central to monastic spirituality, provides them with protection against presumption, indifference, and a lack of openness to new ideas. There is above all the first word of the *Rule of Benedict, "Obsculta,"* which directly invites one to "listen" with an attitude of respect for the spoken word—the Word of God, the word of the spiritual leader, but also all other spoken words. This will to honor the words of all people explains, moreover, why Christian monastics in the Middle Ages contributed so much to the safekeeping of ancient culture.

Also, practice of *lectio divina,* taught early in the novice stage in the monastery or convent, formed the monks or nuns to discern the intention of God in the holy scriptures as well as in the unforseen events in our history—including our participation in interfaith dialogue. Finally, the monastic virtue of hospitality must be mentioned. Certain ancient traditions sometimes concealed this practice that risked troubling the contemplative quietude. But here again, St. Benedict allowed himself to be guided by the Gospel in demanding that monasteries offer unconditional welcome to guests. We should note that this hospitality is not practiced solely because of the goodness of the monastics, but it is also initiated by the hope the monastics place in meeting others. The monastics know, in faith, that the other could be a messenger of God who is carrying a providential word.

One can easily see that all these attitudes, so characteristic of monastic spirituality, provide an excellent school for dialogue. Indeed, while monastics are people of silence, they are above all people of spiritual experience. And this experience that surpasses words can nevertheless be placed in communication with persons who have similar experiences, thus establishing a dialogue in the deepest meaning of the word. This is what Thomas Merton expressed after his meeting with Chatral Rimpoche on November 6, 1968:

> The unspoken or half-spoken message of the talk was our complete understanding of each other as people who were somehow *on the edge* of great realization and knew it and were trying, somehow or other, to go out and get lost in it—and that it was a grace for us to meet one another.[5]

The greatest spiritual experiences do not produce insignificant words. And even the words that are used in the endeavor to realize such experiences are, in the monastic life, situated in relation to the mysterious reality that gives them their force. Therefore, interfaith dialogue most harmoniously opens up in the monastic context where the words are less explicit but more profound. To restate the image of Jean-Claude Basset, "It is here less a question of establishing bridges than of excavating an underground."[6]

As the communication evolved in the intermonastic encounters between Buddhists and Christians, the excavation of spiritual depth also progressed. Soon more and more monastics, both Buddhist and Christian, became involved in spiritual discussions. While the dialogue was always well rooted in their monastic lives, it became less and less restricted to only monastic topics. In allowing themselves always to be guided by their monastic *Rule*, the monks and nuns were brought so far on the journey of dialogue that they discovered that the encounter was itself a spiritual path. It gradually and naturally evolved to a profound discussion of the spiritual life in all its nuances as well as theological and philosophical implications for both traditions and, indeed, for all humankind.

Then with the Day of Prayer for Peace at Assisi in 1986, a point of no return was reached. The act of Pope John Paul II gathering together representatives of all religions for a moment of prayer proclaimed to the world that religious persons should gather together in spiritual engagement for the integral welfare of all humanity. This initiative of Pope John Paul II disarmed any possible Catholic resistance to interfaith dialogue.

Henceforth the spiritual dialogue of monastics, Buddhist and Christian, was able to be presented to the public. It was no longer considered to be reserved for only certain monastic specialists. Rather, it became known as representing the most authentic type of interfaith dialogue. It was seen as such an important endeavor in the exploration of the spiritual life that its findings were viewed as being of great value to all humankind. It was in this new context that Cardinal Arinze, President of the Pontifical Council for Interreligious Dialogue, explicitly invited the commissions for monastic interfaith encounter to continue and to deepen this dialogue concerning the value of meditation and prayer for today's world.[7] Because of this universal value of the spiritual life, monastics are not alone in endeavoring to pursue this "dialogue of spiritual experience," as the Pontifical Council for Interreligious Dialogue designated it since 1984.[8] All Christians are called to reach this level in their meetings with believers of other religions. While happily there are many who do this, monastics are probably the best prepared.

So, it was on the foundation of spiritual fellowship having evolved into spiritual dialogue, and with the encouragement of the Church, that MID organized and hosted the Gethsemani Encounter not just for itself but for the spiritual enrichment of all humankind. The spiritual talks presented here, as well as parts of and reflections on the actual dialogue about central issues in the spiritual life, are precious treasures offered to humanity from the rich heritage of centuries of monastic experience, East and West. These words—spoken from the silence of deep religious experience—are words of encouragement, light and peace for all people faced with the hopelessness, darkness, and violence that grip our modern world. After almost thirty years of evolution in the spiritual encounter of our traditions, now we have come together as Christian and Buddhist practitioners to share with one another and with the world the challenge, wonder and promise of the spiritual life.

There are other forms of dialogue such as the "dialogue of life," the "dialogue of works," and the "dialogue of theological exchange." While each one of these forms is indispensable, the "dialogue of religious experience" must remain at the horizon of all dialogue. We will never be able to formulate in an adequate way the mystery, the silence, the luminosity and the joy into which we journey. But communion in this spiritual journey defines dialogue's ultimate task. Our experience attests to the fact that when this journey of dialogue is pursued, this communion effects a remarkable renewal in our spiritual life. Through our sharing about and communion in the spiritual life, we progress as Buddhists and as Christians toward our own ultimate goals. But more than this, this communion presents us with something novel in the spiritual life. The participants of the Gethsemani Encounter were able to ascertain this surprising dimension of spiritual communion in the atmosphere of the event.

Given this shared experience, when we read—during a tribute to Thomas Merton—one of his famous statements made at a conference in Calcutta in October of 1968, we understand that his prophetic words were not a lyrical flight or a utopian dream. What only a few rare people could understand in 1968 was openly revealed at Gethsemani to all the participants, Buddhists as well as Christians. All were profoundly touched by Merton's description of the experience that we had lived during our days together:

[T]he deepest level of communication is not communication, but communion. It is wordless. It is beyond words, and it is beyond speech, and it is beyond concept. Not that we discover a new unity. We discover an older unity. My dear brothers, we are already one. But we imagine that we are not. And what we have to recover is our original unity. What we have to be is what we are.[9]

Pierre-François de Béthune, O.S.B.
Ottignies, Belgium
January 1997

Introduction

The inspiration for the Gethsemani Encounter happened at the Parliament of the World's Religions in 1993. Prior to the Parliament, Fr. Julian von Duerbeck, O.S.B., and Br. Wayne Teasdale proposed that the Monastic Interreligious Dialogue (MID) host an interfaith dialogue session at the Parliament with His Holiness the Dalai Lama and other Buddhist leaders. MID is the official monastic organization of the Catholic Church in the United States, Canada and Central America responsible for intermonastic dialogue with other religions. Its members are men and women monastics in the Benedictine, Cistercian and Trappist traditions. The MID Board accepted the proposal to host a Buddhist-Christian dialogue at the Parliament; and a morning dialogue session on "Emptiness and Kenosis" was designed by Sr. Katherine Howard, O.S.B., and Patrick G. Henry, who also moderated the event.

His Holiness the Dalai Lama participated in that dialogue, and later—during the Parliament—suggested that the dialogue be continued in a monastic setting. Discussions were then held by MID members at the Parliament, and the idea of a weeklong, in-depth intermonastic encounter on the spiritual life at Gethsemani Abbey—home of Thomas Merton—began to be formulated. The encounter was seen as an opportunity to bring together, for an extended period of time in a monastic setting, a small group of Buddhist and Christian monastics who are mature practitioners and teachers of spirituality. They would live, practice, and celebrate together; and in that contemplative setting, they would dialogue about the practice of the spiritual life and its value for the world today. While there had been local intermonastic hospitality exchanges and dialogues in different parts of the world in the past, this would be the first time an organized international monastic dialogue on the spiritual life would be held at this global level of encounter.

After the Parliament, the MID Board agreed to explore the possibility of holding such an ambitious international, interreligious encounter with

Buddhism; and Abbot Timothy Kelly, O.C.S.O., agreed to host the encounter at the Abbey of Gethsemani. However, first MID was committed to holding a meeting on Hinduism in the summer of 1994 for the MID "contact persons"—monastics appointed by their abbots or prioresses to be responsible for interreligious dialogue at their monasteries in Central and North America. So, it was not until the fall of 1994 that Wayne Teasdale traveled to Dharamsala, India, to meet with His Holiness the Dalai Lama and discuss arrangements for the Gethsemani Encounter. His Holiness was very supportive of MID's plans; so in the spring of 1995, Sr. Mary Margaret Funk, O.S.B., Executive Director of MID, asked Donald W. Mitchell to help organize the encounter as Patrick Henry had done for the Parliament session. The MID Board had used Mitchell's book, *Spirituality and Emptiness: The Dynamics of Spiritual Life in Buddhism and Christianity* (Paulist Press, 1991), to prepare for the Parliament dialogue.

Mitchell and Funk began designing a program and agenda for the Gethsemani Encounter during the spring of 1995. The result of their collaboration was taken to Dharamsala during the summer of 1995 by Funk, Sr. Pascaline Coff, O.S.B., Br. Aaron Raverty, O.S.B., and Fr. James Wiseman, O.S.B., who was the Chairperson of MID. His Holiness the Dalai Lama agreed to the encounter design and topics for discussion. Then in the fall of 1995, the program and agenda for the Gethsemani Encounter was finalized by the MID Board, and Mitchell began the task of selecting and inviting the Buddhist participants while Funk began to select and invite the Christian participants.

Theravadin Buddhist monastics were invited from the *Sanghas* in Sri Lanka, Thailand, Myanmar, and Cambodia; while lay practitioners were also invited from the newly emerging American Theravadin communities. Zen Buddhist monastics were invited from the traditions of Taiwan, Korea and Japan; while again lay practitioners were invited from the American Zen communities. Tibetan Buddhist monastics were invited from the Geluk lineage of His Holiness the Dalai Lama; and American lay practitioners were invited from both the Geluk and Kagyu lineages. All the lay practitioners had extensive monastic experience, and their presence blended new Western voices into the dialogue. Care was taken to include women's voices from each tradition. In this regard, a Buddhist nun from the Fokuangshan Buddhist Order was invited to represent the new wave of Buddhist women monastics in Asia. Most of the Buddhist participants were living in Buddhist communities in the United States; for example, in Los Angeles, San Francisco, Boulder, Minneapolis, Chicago, Atlanta and Washington, D.C. The hope was that the Gethsemani Encounter would sow the seeds for future local dialogues between

Buddhist and Christian spiritual communities in the United States and around the world.

The Christian monastics were invited from both the Benedictine and Trappist traditions in Europe, North America, Asia and Australia. Most of the Christian participants were MID Board members or MID advisors, who had years of experience in spirituality and interreligious relations. The Gethsemani Encounter was seen to be so important in the history of the Catholic Church and Christian monasticism that an invitation was extended to the Abbot General of the Trappist Order, Fr. Bernardo Olivera, O.C.S.O. Since the Abbot Primate of the Benedictine Order had recently died, his secretary, Fr. Jacques Côté, O.S.B., was also invited. Invitations were sent as well to the Vatican's Pontifical Council for Interreligious Dialogue, and to Fr. Pierre-François de Béthune, O.S.B., Secretary General of MID worldwide. Bishop Joseph Gerry, O.S.B., was invited to represent the National Conference of Catholic Bishops in the United States. Olivera, Côté and Gerry all accepted their invitations to the Gethsemani Encounter, as did Béthune, who also represented the Vatican. Among the MID advisors were also some priests, and lay practitioners—Catholic and Protestant—with experience in dialogue with Buddhism. In the end, 25 Buddhist and 25 Christian spiritual leaders, teachers and practitioners from around the world were invited to the Gethsemani Encounter by MID and His Holiness the Dalai Lama. We have included short biographical sketches of all the Buddhists and Christians involved in the encounter in the List of Participants section of this volume.

During the spring of 1996, the final touches were made to the encounter schedule by integrating rituals and practice sessions. Also, all the encounter participants were paired, Buddhist with Christian, in "dyads" that met once each day to allow for more intimate dialogue. In the final planning for the encounter, it was decided by the MID Board to allow interested contact persons, donors and media persons to attend as observers. The dialogue would be held at one end of the chapter room of the Abbey with the observers at the other end watching the proceedings. The observers would meet once each day to process the dialogue with the Buddhist scholar Robert Thurman and with Patrick Henry. A special session on the final day of the encounter was set aside for the observers to share their reflections with the participants.

It was also during the spring of 1996 that the Christian participants, who were to present talks at the Gethsemani Encounter, met at Our Lady of Grace Monastery in Indianapolis, Indiana, for a weekend workshop. At the workshop, Donald Mitchell presented lectures on the three forms of Buddhist spirituality that would be represented at Gethsemani, namely, the Zen, Theravadin, and Tibetan traditions. These are the three types of monastic Buddhism with which MID had intermonastic exchanges in the past. After Mitchell's presentations, the Christian talks for the Gethsemani Encounter were presented, and suggestions were made for how to make them more accessible to Buddhists. In this way, the Christian spiritual talks were crafted to express the experience of not just one person, but of a living spiritual tradition. It was felt that this workshop was instrumental in helping the encounter participants dialogue at a deeper level of engagement.

The first actual meeting of the Gethsemani Encounter was held during the evening of July 22, 1996. After dinner, there was a tree planting ceremony in the monastery courtyard, where a spruce tree was planted by His Holiness the Dalai Lama and Abbot Timothy Kelly. The evening program in the chapter room, which followed the ceremony, included a word of welcome and orientation by James Wiseman, and a talk by Pascaline Coff on the spiritual journey of dialogue leading to the Gethsemani Encounter. These presentations were followed by a "philosophical moment" during which Jeffrey Hopkins and Donald Mitchell presented the philosophical visions behind the traditions of Buddhist and Christian spiritualities. Both speakers presented what they felt persons in the other tradition should understand about their tradition's ideas and ideals as a prelude to dialogue. A closing blessing was then given by Abbot James Conner, O.C.S.O. We have included Coff's, Hopkins's and Mitchell's talks in this volume.

For the next five days of the encounter, our mornings began with sitting meditation in the Skakel Chapel at 5:45 a.m. Each sitting was followed by a Buddhist or Christian ritual at 6:15. Breakfast was at 7:00, with the first dialogue session starting at 8:00. The morning sessions included talks and dialogue on an essential element of the spiritual life as seen from two of the three Buddhist perspectives represented at the encounter. The sessions were followed by a Christian or Buddhist ritual at 11:00, and lunch at noon. After lunch, there was time for rest, sharing in dyads, or the meeting of the observers with Robert Thurman and Patrick Henry. The afternoon sessions on the Christian perspective concerning the spiritual issue being discussed for that day began at 2:30 p.m. ending with vespers in the church at 5:30. Dinner was at 6:00, with the evening session starting at 7:00. The evening sessions presented the third Buddhist view concerning the day's spiritual theme. The evenings ended at 8:30, with a closing blessing, or a special ritual for both Buddhists and Christians. On the final day, July 27, 1996, the encounter concluded with the morning session that finished with a final Christian blessing and Buddhist ritual.

Each of the different aspects of the week—the talks, dialogues, dyad encounters, rituals, periods of meditation, meals—were parts of an integral whole. They blended voices and silence into a unique and profound encounter experience in the contemplative atmosphere of the monastery. There were no "safe places," as Fr. Thomas Baima put it, into which one could retreat—we plunged into a deep engagement with each other and remained in that encounter for the full week. This may have been a bit demanding at times, but there was a sense that we were not there just for ourselves; but were in fact living and working together for the benefit of humankind. Hence, as Ewert Cousins remarked, there was a spiritual "treasure chest" that opened up right on the very first evening, and on the final day, it was "still there."

We have tried to share in this book the jewels of spiritual insight and advice that we discovered in the treasures of our spiritualities that have been mined for thousands of years by the great saints and mystics of our traditions. Besides the talks from the first evening, we have included the talks presented during the four full days of the Gethsemani Encounter at the morning, afternoon and evening sessions. The four daily topics for the encounter were: (1) "The Practice of Prayer and Meditation in the Spiritual Life," (2) "The Stages in the Process of Spiritual Development," (3) "The Role of the Teacher and the Community in the Spiritual Life," and (4) "The Spiritual Goals of Personal and Social Transformation." We have also included the talk by the Ven. Dr. Havanpola Ratanasara on the Buddhist view of interreligious dialogue given on the morning of July 24 in conjunction with a Theravadin ritual.

Each of these talks was intended to provide a short and insightful glimpse into the dynamics of Buddhist and Christian spirituality. These insights were then broadened and deepened in the context of the dialogue itself in ways that we hope will bring the encounter of our traditions to a new level, and will set the agenda for future spiritual dialogues for years to come. We have included an edited version of the dialogue as it explores the treasures of the spiritual life in both traditions. Also included are the tributes to Thomas Merton, offered by James Conner and His Holiness the Dalai Lama at a memorial service on the morning of July 25, and the final reflections given by the observers and others on the last morning of the encounter.

The chapters in which we have placed the talks, dialogues, tributes and reflections are all preceded by words of introduction—so we will not repeat ourselves here. However, we would like to note that the talks and dialogues led all of us in the Gethsemani Encounter into a spiritual adventure of discovery, both of each other and of ourselves. As monastic and lay practitioners, Buddhists and Christians, men and women, we felt that we were exploring the nature of our humanity as well as our spiritual potential as individuals and society. There was a sense that what we were discussing—and what was happening—at Gethsemani was relevant to the destiny of all humankind. There was an awareness that even with our differences, we were experiencing a dialogical movement from, in Merton's words, "communication" to "communion," from speaking with one another to being one with each other at the deepest level of encounter. We were not just speaking to each other about the spiritual life; we were, in the words of one observer, "giving birth to" a deep communion in our spiritual life together. This is a new spiritual possibility for humankind. So, our Gethsemani experience was, we think, an epiphany for all humankind: a profound unity, peace and harmony in the midst of the rich diversity of humankind is possible. And authentic spirituality can contribute to this evolution in the individual and social nature of humanity. We offer this book to serious spiritual seekers of all traditions as a contribution to spirituality seeking the realization of this vision of a more united and peaceful pluralistic world community.

There are many persons we would like to thank for their invaluable contribution to the Gethsemani Encounter and this volume. Besides the Christian and Buddhist participants, we would especially like to thank Abbot Timothy Kelly and the monks of the Abbey of Gethsemani for their wonderful hospitality. In this regard, special thanks to Fr. Paschal Phillips, O.C.S.O., and Grace Worthem, coordinator of the Gethsemani Guest House, who worked so hard before and during the encounter. We also want to thank Stephen Hays, who provided security for His Holiness the Dalai Lama and the encounter in general; Julian von Duerbeck and Sr. GilChrist Lavigne, O.C.S.O., who coordinated the rituals; Sr. Johanna Becker, O.S.B., and Br. Harold Thibodeau, O.C.S.O., who designed the dialogue environment; Michael Fitzpatrick and Patricia Day, who provided the music; Jacques Côté and Sr. Joann Hunt, O.S.B., who photographed the encounter; Gail Fitzpatrick-Hopler, Robert Thurman and Patrick Henry, who were responsible for the observers; Br. Wayne Teasdale, for his contacts; and Br. David Steindl-Rast, who was the moderator for the entire dialogue. Rinchen Dharlo, from the Office of Tibet, and Mary Margaret Funk deserve our deepest gratitude for their tireless efforts in helping us organize the encounter. For helping to bring the dialogue to a broader audience, we would like to thank Kate Olson, from the Public Broadcasting System; Karen Michele, from National Public Radio; John Buescher, from the Voice of America; and the following journalists: Dianne April, Fr. Murray Bodo, O.F.M., Judith Cebula, Jeffrey Cox,

Matthew Greenblatt, Fenton Johnson and Peter Smith. As for preparing this book, we want to extend our warmest appreciation to Doris Cross, for her transcriptions of the dialogue tapes; Gene Gollogly, for his support of our publishing project; Jeffrey Hopkins and Robin Mitchell for their translations; and Beth Turner, for her long hours of typing. Finally, we would like to thank the many generous organizations and people whose contributions were necessary to make the inspirations of a few people at the Parliament of the World's Religions a reality for us all—indeed for the world: the Fetzer Foundation, the Cudahy Foundation, Markell Brooks, Werner Mark Linz, Monique and Lester Anderson, Jane Owen, Tommy O'Callahan, Daniel Ward, Odette Baumer-Despeigne, and the Abbey of Gethsemani.

Donald W. Mitchell and
James A. Wiseman, O.S.B.

PART ONE

Talks on the Spiritual Life

1

Journey and Dialogue

One night, almost 2,000 years ago in the Garden of Gethsemani, Jesus Christ confronted the forces of darkness and death. During another night, about 500 years earlier, Gotama Buddha confronted those same forces at Bodhgaya. Now, centuries later, it was in the Abbey of Gethsemani that Buddhists and Christians confronted together the forces of suffering that still plague humankind. When one enters the monastery, one does not leave the world behind, but takes it into the monastery in one's prayer. So, as we gathered in the 150-year-old abbey, we were not only bringing the joys and hopes of our modern world, but also its anger, pain, divisions and violence. We brought all aspects of our shared world into our dialogue, our meditation and our prayer.

Jesus entered Gethsemani intending to pray, and Buddha entered Bodhgaya intending to meditate. We had come together intending to share with each other, as fellow pilgrims, the spiritual life we were leading. But then, as we opened our hearts to each other in deep and authentic dialogue, we found that, in the words of His Holiness the Dalai Lama, "We are all struggling with the same evil spirits." We identified these spirits as being such factors of the mind and heart as delusion and ignorance, greed and anger, hatred and revenge. And we identified their antidotes in clarity and wisdom, loving kindness and compassion, forgiveness and reconciliation.

As we shared these spiritual insights, and, more importantly, as we shared our spiritual lives, we found that—in the words of Thomas Merton—our "conversation" became "communion." We were all profoundly touched by this reality of spiritual communion; we even felt marked for life by this deep realization of unity. His Holiness the Dalai Lama said with joy, "God and the Buddhas are very happy with what is happening here. We are receiving many blessings from above."

But how did we get to this spiritual point? We had the sense that we alone were not creating this epiphany. Rather, we had entered a place that had been prepared for it by the lives of many who had gone before us. In her talk, that was given at the opening ceremony on the eve of the dialogue, Sr. Pascaline Coff, O.S.B., gives us a glimpse at what the journey of dialogue has been for those who prepared the way to Gethsemani.

On the Catholic side, a choice of dialogue was made over 30 years ago. Then, a seed was planted in 1968 in Bangkok with the death of Thomas Merton at the first intermonastic conference called to explore the way of dialogue with other religions. Organizations dedicated to interfaith exchanges and dialogues were founded, and the modern encounter of Buddhist and Christian monastics began. Eventually, based on heartfelt openness, spiritual friendship, and concrete collaboration, His Holiness the Dalai Lama suggested that we had reached the point for an in-depth encounter on the spiritual life. In her talk, Coff presents the hope that now, after such a long and inspiring road to Gethsemani, our communication can become communion. What better place for this prophetic vision of Merton's to be realized than at his spiritual home in the Abbey of Gethsemani?

The Ven. Dr. Havanpola Ratanasara delivered his talk at a morning program presented by the Theravada Buddhist delegation from Southeast Asia. In reading it, one might think that he was influenced in what he says by Coff's presentation. However, both talks were written prior to the dialogue. Ratanasara emphasizes the need today to realize, in the words of Pope John Paul II, "the unity that already exists." Dialogue, Ratanasara says, provides the environment in which such a unity can be realized.

But more than this, Ratanasara holds that this "unity" embraces the whole human family and must be recognized and realized socially for the benefit of all humankind. Since we came to Gethsemani from all over the world with our differences of religion, language, culture, etc., by the unity that we realize through our dialogue, we can show the rest of the world that this is possible for them as well. Ratanasara concludes by calling on our spiritual traditions to use their wisdom and counsel to teach the world to create "a truly harmonious existence" through choosing the path of dialogue and living together the spiritual values that unite us.

How We Reached This Point: Communication Becoming Communion

PASCALINE COFF, O.S.B.

This "point" where we are will unfold with all its richness and mystery as the next few hours and days together run their course. This point of spiritual exchange between Buddhist and Christian monastics began decades ago as "a preliminary experience in hospitality," "a prelude to in-depth dialogue," and "a mutually agreed ground-breaking first step." Over the years, this point has become, in the words of William Johnston, "Friendship, the crown of authentic dialogue." And now we have gathered together in this point of friendship to take the next step on the journey of spiritual dialogue. In the prophetic words of Thomas Merton, the very raison d'être for our presence here at Gethsemani is to realize "communication" that has become "communion."

The Journey Begins

Pope John XXIII was Pope only ninety days when he announced his surprise plan to convoke the Roman Catholic Church's 21st ecumenical council. When the prelates and bishops of the Church assembled in Rome and the council began on October 11, 1962, the pontiff was eighty years old. This council, known as Vatican II, was a gift to the whole human family in many ways. But according to Karl Rahner, one of the greatest theologians of this century, one of the greatest enactments of the Second Vatican Council was the document called *Nostra Aetate* (Oct. 28, 1965) on "The Relationship of the Church to Non-Christian Religions." In this document, for the first time in her history, the Roman Catholic Church publicly proclaimed that truth is to be found in other religions. A special secretariat was called into being (May 17, 1964) to promote the Church's relationship with other religions. It was the president of this secretariat, Cardinal Sergio Pignedoli, who wrote to the Benedictine Abbot Primate Rembert Weakland in 1974 to urge that Christian monks and nuns be invited to "pursue" being a "bridge and contact-point" for promoting mutual understanding between Christians and persons of other faiths. From that time forward, monasticism would have an essential role in this encounter.

Thomas Merton in Dialogue

In 1968, the world's Benedictine abbots sponsored their first Asian East-West Intermonastic Conference in Bangkok. It was this conference that brought Thomas Merton to the East and eventually to visit with His Holiness the Dalai Lama. It was a watershed beginning for East-West intermonastic dialogue. Two other Asian Conferences followed sponsored by Aide Inter-Monastères (AIM), an organization of the Benedictine Confederation which was given the responsibility to facilitate interfaith dialogue: Bangalore in 1973, and Sri Lanka in 1980. Thomas Merton, as many know, died during the Bangkok conference, just after he gave his own presentation on the second day. From his place beyond, he no doubt has had an influence on all that has transpired from then until now—on how we got to this "point." Indeed it has been said that "His [Merton's] death had the same effect of the seed, which in dying produces much fruit."[1]

The Founding of MID

In response to Cardinal Pignedoli's request to our Abbot Primate, in 1977 two groups of monks and nuns were invited by AIM to come together and discuss the future possibilities for East-West encounters. One meeting was held in Petersham, Massachusetts; and the second was in Loppem, Belgium. Then in January of the following year, at the invitation of AIM, a monastic organization was founded at the Rickenbach Center in Clyde, Missouri, choosing the name of "AIM's North American Board for East-West Dialogue." Later, this organization took the name "Monastic Interreligious Dialogue" (MID). Four of the six initial members invited by AIM are present today at this auspicious Gethsemani Encounter: Abbot Armand Veilleux, Sr. Donald Corcoran, Sr. Gilchrist Lavigne and Sr. Pascaline Coff. Some months later, a European monastic group met again at Loppem and chose the name "Dialogue Interreligieux Monastique" (DIM). The purpose of these working groups was to stimulate interest among Western monastics in the ideas and values present in Eastern religions, and to assist in the development of intermonastic dialogue, especially between Buddhist and Christian monastics. In 1979, MID cosponsored the ten-year Thomas Merton Commemoration at Columbia University in New York. This was the year of His Holiness the Dalai Lama's first visit to the United States.

The Naropa Connection

In 1980, MID was invited to co-plan an East-West conference sponsored by the Naropa Institute in Boulder, Colorado. Fr. Thomas Keating and Br. David Steindl-Rast, former members of MID, were invited subsequently to be speakers at the conference.

In 1981, the Naropa conference included His Holiness the Dalai Lama as one of its speakers. Two members of MID asked to be present at an audience with His Holiness. It was during this semiprivate audience with some thirty others that the secretary of MID asked His Holiness if he was willing to send his monks to our American Christian monasteries. He smiled, looked pensively, and said: "Yes, but I have no money." Abbot Lawrence Wagner spoke up and assured His Holiness that our American abbots would be happy to pool their resources in order to cover international airfare, and that the American monasteries would be glad to host Tibetan monks. And so began the Intermonastic Hospitality Exchanges between American Christian and Tibetan Buddhist monastics. We should also note that DIM has also hosted numerous exchanges with Tibetan and other Buddhist (especially Zen) monastics in Europe and Asia.

Exchanges and Dialogues

Phase I of the MID exchange was in 1982. One Tibetan monk (Ven. Kunchok Sithar) spent four months (July 25–November 22) visiting six Midwestern Christian monasteries. He came as Ven. Kunchok and left as "Brother" Kunchok. MID sent to each hosting monastery a *Source Book on Buddhism,* and also an "Outline of the Mass for Buddhists" written by Prof. Roger Corless.

Phase II in 1983 brought three Tibetan monks (Ven. Kalsang Damdul, Ven. Lobsang Choepel, and Ven. Lobsang Sonam) for five months (April 21–September 15) to thirty Christian monasteries and some convents in the United States. Then in 1985 in New Jersey, in preparation for the 100th anniversary of the 1893 Parliament of the World's Religions, four Tibetan monks and two MID monastics met together: Ven. Kunchok Sithar, Ven. Kalsang Damdul, Ven. Lhokdor, Ven. Sonam, Fr. Thomas Keating and Sr. Pascaline Coff.

Phase III in 1986 brought nuns more directly into the exchange. Six American Benedictines (Fr. Donald Grabner, Fr. Gabriel Coless, Fr. Timothy Kelly, Sr. Ruth Fox, Sr. Bede Luetkemeyer and Sr. Pascaline Coff) spent six weeks (September 1–October 15) visiting twenty-six Tibetan monasteries and four Tibetan nunneries in both north and south India. The dialogues with Buddhist monks in the Dialectic School and with seven Geshes in the Gyurme Tantric Monastery at Hunsur were challenging and rewarding. The highlight of the visits was an interview with His Holiness the Dalai Lama at his home in Dharamsala.

Phase IV in 1988 brought three Tibetan monastics (Ven. Kunchok Tsering, Acharya Ngawang Samten and a nun, Ven. Tenzin Dunsang) to the United States for two months (June 1–July 30) where they visited twenty-two American Benedictine and Cistercian monasteries and convents. At this point, His Holiness Pope John Paul II himself entered the encounter when he met these Tibetan monastics in Rome as they were returning home to India.

In 1989, His Holiness the Dalai Lama was awarded the Nobel Peace Prize on December 11. The announcement reached His Holiness in Newport Beach, California, on October 6 when MID was scheduled to have an interview with him to assure him of our support for his Five

Point Peace Plan which he had presented in 1987. The Dalai Lama and several members of MID were involved in the Contemplative Congress: Harmonia Mundi, which was being held there October 3–7.

In 1991, MID shared a press conference with His Holiness in Tesuqe, N.M., regarding the document on "Non-Violence and the Incompatibility of Religions and War." Members of MID present included: Fr. Thomas Keating, Sr. Katherine Howard, Sr. Johanna Becker and Prof. Wayne Teasdale, coauthor of the document.

Phase V in 1992 brought four American monastics (Fr. Kevin Hunt, Br. Harold Thibodeau, Sr. Katherine Howard, and Sr. Pascaline Coff) during six weeks (August 30–October 15) to twenty Tibetan monasteries and four Tibetan nunneries in India. Besides dialoguing with monks at the Dialectic School, the American monastics had several hours of intermonastic dialogue with five Geshes at the Library of Tibetan Works. Again, the highlight of the exchange and dialogues was the interview with His Holiness the Dalai Lama.

Based on these ten-plus years of contact, hospitality and friendship, a special intermonastic dialogue between His Holiness the Dalai Lama, other Buddhist leaders, and members of MID was held during the 1993 Parliament of the World's Religions in Chicago. The topic for this first organized dialogue was *kenosis*, or "self-emptying," in Buddhist and Christian spirituality. After this more formal encounter, His Holiness the Dalai Lama said that he felt the ground was prepared for a serious in-depth dialogue on the spiritual life in our two traditions. He suggested that we invite 25 Buddhist and 25 Christian spiritual masters to live together for a full week of shared practice and dialogue on the spiritual life. He also asked if it might be possible for our encounter to be held at Gethsemani, the home of his friend Thomas Merton. It was this suggestion by His Holiness that has led us to this gathering today at the Abbey of Gethsemani.

Phase VI in 1994 brought four Tibetan monastics (Ven. Geshe Damchoe Gyaltsen, Ven. Tsering Wangchok, and nuns Ven. Ngawang Chonzin and Ven.Tenzin Dechen) to the United States for four months (November 14–March 9). They were hosted in thirty American Benedictine and Cistercian monasteries and convents with more than one hundred public appearances. Interviewed on Voice of America, they were even heard by their own monastic friends back in Dharamsala.

Phase VII in 1995 followed on the heels of Phase VI. In the summer of 1995, four American Benedictine monastics (Fr. James Wiseman, Sr. Mary Margaret Funk, Br. Aaron Raverty, and Sr. Pascaline Coff) journeyed to Tibet and India for five weeks (June 15–July 28) visiting ten monasteries and three nunneries in Tibet, and dialoguing with monastics in twelve monasteries and three nunneries in the exiled Tibetan communities in north India. They reported challenging dialogues at the Dialectic School, Gaden Choeling and Dolma Ling nunneries as well as an enriching two hours at Bir in the Dzongzer Institute's monastic garden with five Tibetan professors. As with all of these American intermonastic hospitality exchanges and dialogues in India, the highlight was with His Holiness the Dalai Lama—sharing experiences in Tibet and preparing for this Gethsemani Encounter. The four Americans were given places of honor at two of the 60th birthday celebrations for His Holiness in Delhi and Dharamsala.

Finally in 1996, a new round of phases was created and begun between Tibetan Buddhist monastics in exile and Christian monastics in the United States. These new phases go beyond shared hospitality and friendship. They seek to concretely help our Buddhist brothers and sisters in exile in creative ways. For example, the new Phase I was an educational exchange. It brought six Tibetan monastics to the United States (Ven. Tenzin Tsepak, Ven. Tenzin Dhargye, Ven. Tenzin Choepel Rongpa, Tenzin Thutop, and nuns Ven. Tenzin Dechen and Ven. Tenzin Desel). This educational program has enabled these exiled Buddhist monks and nuns to study health care, computer skills and English within a Christian monastic context. This in-depth three month stay (March 1–May 31) was a mutually fruitful and enriching first step in a new and practical direction.

After many mountains, caves, harrowing Jeep rides, monsoons, landslides, soldiers, a one-eyed man/woman-eating mountain lion, giant spiders, hungry mice, and months of travel to monasteries and convents on both sides of the globe, we are here now at the Abbey of Gethsemani with His Holiness the Dalai Lama, MID Board members, advisers and contact persons from our monasteries—twenty-five strong—with twenty-five Buddhists, also strong, for a historic dialogue on the spiritual life. It will be the "longest and most demanding—yet most promising—dialogue on the spiritual life in the history of East-West encounter." We are at the "point" where, based on a long and rich history of friendship, Thomas Merton's prophecy of communication becoming communion may be realized. And at what better place than here at Thomas Merton's own spiritual home?

Dialogue and Unity: A Buddhist Perspective

VEN. DR. HAVANPOLA RATANASARA

In his recently published work, *Crossing the Threshold of Hope*, Pope John Paul II made some observations with which I, as a Buddhist, wholly agree: "What unites us is *much greater* than what separates us. . . . It is necessary . . . to rid ourselves of stereotypes, of old habits. And above all, it is necessary to recognize the unity that already exists."[1] The history of interreligious dialogue, extending over the past three decades, provides us with encouraging evidence that confirms the Pope's observation that there is indeed a "unity that already exists." Formal interfaith dialogue, however, does not materialize fully developed out of a vacuum. It evolves gradually in response to the needs and aspirations of the broader human community of which its participants are members. The "unity that already exists," of which the Pope speaks, is the very life of the human community. On the other hand, this preexisting "unity" must be recognized, and positive steps must be taken to build on it and to realize it in society. It is very encouraging, therefore, that the interfaith dialogue between Buddhism and Christianity that was begun some thirty years ago continues today with an increasing momentum.

A Brief History of Interreligious Dialogue

While in recent times interfaith dialogue has become not only national but international in its scope, I cite the experience of Los Angeles as but one example since it is the one with which I am most familiar. Almost from the very beginning, dialogue in Los Angeles included Buddhists, Hindus, Muslims, Jews, and Christians. Since it is unique in being a truly "global" community, Los Angeles provided an ideal environment for such dialogue. All major Buddhist traditions, each with its own language and customs, are represented in the dialogue.

Formal dialogue, however, required a catalyst and it was the Catholic Church which provided it. As early as 1964, in his first encyclical letter, *Ecclesiam Suam*, Pope Paul VI already emphasized the need for interreligious dialogue, an attitude which was further underscored in *Nostra Aetate* which set the stage for the beginning of genuine interreligious dialogue.[2] This decree encouraged interfaith dialogue and initiated a fundamental change in the way the Church views other religions.

For its part, the Catholic community in Los Angeles lost no time following the guidelines set by *Nostra Aetate*. In 1969, the Catholic Archdiocese of Los Angeles, together with representatives of the Jewish community, founded the Interreligious Council of Southern California (ICSC). In 1971, Buddhist communities joined, and this became the focal point of interfaith dialogue in Los Angeles. In 1974, the Catholic Archdiocese formed the Commission on Ecumenical and Interreligious Affairs (CEIA) to coordinate and expedite its relations with other religious communities. The work of both of these organizations continues, sponsoring ongoing dialogues, but also, and just as important, informal contacts among the various participating religious organizations. These activities have enhanced considerably our mutual understanding, and a lessening of conflicts among religious communities in the area.

Through the initiatives of both the ICSC and the CEIA, meaningful *informal* exchanges with the Buddhist community were begun. A highlight in this process was a visit by Pope John Paul II to Los Angeles in 1987. Then in 1989, the Los Angeles Buddhist-Catholic Dialogue began.[3] It marked the beginning of a *formal* Buddhist-Catholic communication, and was sponsored by the Buddhist Sangha Council of Southern California and the Catholic Office of Ecumenical and Interreligious Affairs.

What I think is most significant is that this formal dialogue in fact conferred recognition on what had already been happening, more informally, for almost twenty years. And this "informal" communication continues to the present day, alongside more formal or "official" dialogue. This suggests that the mandate for our dialogue, far from being "imposed from on high," is an expression of genuine respect and friendship. As a document prepared by the Vatican's Pontifical Council for Interreligious Dialogue puts it: "Dialogue does not grow out of the opportunism of the tactics of the moment, but arises from reasons which experience and reflection, and even the difficulties themselves, have deepened."[4]

Also encouraging is the evidence of international interreligious dialogue. In 1979, the World Council of Churches first published its *Guidelines on Dialogue with People of Living Faiths and Ideologies*. In the index to the fourth edition of that publication, I counted 75 major international meetings held between 1969 and 1989.[5] And most recently, in July 1995, the Vatican's Pontifical Council for Interreligious Dialogue organized a Buddhist-Christian Colloquium in Taiwan. It was attended by 10 Christian and 10 Buddhist scholars, four members of the Pontifical Council, many monks and nuns from the Buddhist monastery where it was held, as well as the Catholic Bishops in Taiwan. The attending scholars came from Japan, Taiwan, Sri Lanka, Thailand, Italy, and the United States. The very fact that an international colloquium at such a high level was taking place at all, seems to me a most auspicious development.

The Prospects for an Ongoing Dialogue

Perhaps the only mistake we can make now, is to allow our optimism to become complacency. While it is true that much has been accomplished by way of interfaith dialogue, there remain significant stumbling blocks to its longevity. *The first most enduring impediment to dialogue* is the view held by members of the various religions that by participating in dialogue they may be compromising their own beliefs. I would like to address this particular concern.

Pope John Paul II makes another point with which any Buddhist would find it hard to disagree, and which states an important principle on which dialogue can go forward: ". . . there is basis for dialogue and for the growth of unity, a growth that should occur at the same rate at which we are able to overcome our divisions—divisions that to a great degree result from the idea that one can have a monopoly on truth."[6] For a Buddhist, his or her faith is no bar to dialogue with other religions because Buddhism is neither a system of dogmas, nor a doctrine of "salvation" as that term is generally understood in theistic religions. The Buddha exhorted his disciples to take nothing on blind faith, not even his words. Rather, they should listen and then examine the teaching for themselves, so that they might be convinced of its truth.[7]

Once, when the Buddha was visiting a market town called Kesaputta, the local people, known as the Kalamas, sought his advice. Wandering ascetics and teachers used to visit the town from time to time and were not reticent about propagating their own particular religious and philosophical doctrine while disparaging the teachings of others. The Buddha advised them in this way:

> It is proper for you, Kalamas, to doubt, to be uncertain. . . . Do not be led by reports, or tradition, or hearsay. Do not be led by the authority of religious texts, nor by mere logic or inference, nor by considering appearances; nor by delight in speculative opinions, nor by seeming possibilities, nor by the idea, "This ascetic is our teacher." But rather, when you yourselves know [that] certain things are unwholesome and wrong, [that such] things are censured by the wise, and when undertaken, such things lead to harm, [then] abandon them. And when you yourselves know [that] certain things are wholesome and good, [that such] things are approved by the wise, and when undertaken such things lead to benefit and happiness, [then] enter on and abide in them.[8]

What the Buddha's teaching offers, then, is an aid that we may use until we are able to tread the path to liberation and enlightenment alone. The Buddha compared his doctrine, the *Dhamma*, to a raft which one uses to cross over a lake or stream but is left behind when one reaches shore. It would make no sense to continue lugging the raft about once it had served its purpose.[9] So attachment to doctrine for its own sake, be it religious, political, or ideological, is illogical from a Buddhist point of view. It follows then, that a Buddhist need not fear "losing" his or her faith by coming into contact with the faiths of others.

Now, as to engaging in dialogue itself, I would make two points. First, differences between faiths should not be overdrawn, or created where none exist. For example, in *Crossing the Threshold of Hope*, Pope John Paul II characterizes Buddhist soteriology as "almost exclusively negative," as leading to "a state of perfect indifference."[10] However, nothing could be further removed from the Buddhist attitude. In fact, it was out of *love* for the world that the Buddha spent 45 years of his life teaching. Nor was he reticent about involving himself in what today we would call "social issues." On one occasion, in fact, he intervened to prevent what started as a petty squabble over land ownership from developing into armed conflict. And many Buddhist traditions emphasize the *bodhisattva* ideal. This means that even one who has achieved liberation vows to remain in *samsara* (the cycle of birth and death), until all sentient beings have been enlightened. It is difficult, in Buddhist terms at least, to imagine an altruism more encompassing than this.

Secondly, we must be no less candid about our *differences* than we are sanguine about our *similarities*. Sometimes Buddhists who are highly regarded in the Buddhist community, and whose words therefore carry an aura of authority, lose sight of this principle. In a misguided zeal to promote an ecumenical atmosphere, they misrepresent the Buddhist position by making it seem more compatible with the beliefs of other religions than it actually is. Such attempts to water down basic Buddhist principles tend to have the opposite effect of what is intended because other participants will then express opinions on Buddhism, based upon what they have heard, believing that they have it on good authority. As a result, their remarks will appear to their Buddhist colleagues as ill-formed or disparaging of Buddhism.

What I am actually talking about here are canons of sound scholarship which all participants in the dialogue should recognize and try to honor. When non-Buddhists express opinions on Buddhism, they should take care to do their homework. Ill-informed comments not only engender ill feelings, but an attitude of condescension on the other side. Genuine dialogue, however, is possible only in an atmosphere of mutual respect, based upon a consensus that it is being conducted among equals. And this, obviously, should be no less true when Buddhists talk about Christianity or other religions. At the same time, it is necessary that all of us remain committed to an open forum, where the participants are free to express ideas and views without fear of recrimination. It may happen that certain religious communities that are only recently part of the dialogue and therefore new to its ways, will be unable to "find their tongue" when others make criticisms which seem to them unjustified or ill-informed. This is all the more reason why the representatives of each faith should be aware of the special needs of others.

As Buddhists, we cannot and do not close our eyes to the evil and injustice in the world. We are no less bound than our Christian friends to take a stand on it. The easy part, of course, is staking out a position when *we agree* with each other. The present Pope and his predecessors have issued encyclicals sternly condemning political and religious persecution, as well as reproving the oppressive excesses of all forms of economic systems: capitalist, socialist, or communist. And Buddhists would be the first to agree. The hard part is taking a stand *when we disagree* with each other. And this I identify as a *second potential stumbling block to interfaith dialogue*. Buddhists have often said what everyone knows, but is all too easily forgotten: that harsh words, once uttered, cannot be retracted. They remain "out there," to poison the ambience in which dialogue takes place; and they may, in the few seconds required to utter them, undo what has taken years to accomplish. On the other hand we cannot and will not always agree; and none of us can hope to enjoy the approval of everyone all the time. As the Buddha reminded us, "There never was, there never will be, nor does there exist now, a person who is wholly praised or blamed."[11] The very fact we are here, however, and expressing our willingness to talk to each other, suggests that we—all of us—must be doing *something* right!

Reflection on this second potential impediment to dialogue at once reveals a crucial reason why interfaith dialogue is important to everyone, including Buddhists in today's world. In the WCC's booklet, *Guidelines on Dialogue*, the author remarks that "[i]t is easy to discuss religions and even ideologies as though they existed in some realm of calm quite separate from the sharp divisions, conflicts and sufferings of humankind."[12] I wholly agree. But I and all Buddhists would also agree with the author when he suggests that "[r]eligions and ideologies often contribute to the disruption of communities and the suffering of those whose community life is broken."[13] Religious differences have often been the most deeply rooted and destructive of all. If *we*, as representatives of two of the world's major religions, can show the rest of the world that we can communicate with each other, they just *might* come to realize that there is no reason why they cannot do the same. Here is the real and pressing task of interreligious dialogue today. So, while we are gathered here to discuss the spiritual life, we must never forget the worldwide context in which we come together. It is a context of division and violence. It is a world that needs to realize the "unity" of which Pope John Paul II spoke.

In Buddhism, virtuous conduct (*sila*) includes "right speech." And by practicing the virtue of right speech in the context of dialogue, we will be setting an example for the larger world community to emulate. The many problems which beset our communities, indeed all humankind at the close of this century, include: the environment, international terrorism, human rights, urban violence, social justice, and the like. All of our religious communities are affected by these issues and are drawn into the fray. The only question is: Will we rise to the occasion? Will we choose the path of dialogue leading to a more united and peaceful world? I believe our gathering here at Gethsemani is a giant step on this path for the benefit of humanity.

In order to encourage our dialogue to move in this critical direction, I would like now to focus upon just one of these pressing issues—one, indeed, that must concern us as representatives of our religions—namely, religious intolerance and persecution. Not only has it not disappeared, but it is actually on the rise in many parts of the world and has shown itself in shameful incidents, even in our own country, and even within the last few weeks. For example, a recent spate of Christian church burnings has elicited a formal response from the White House, and has alarmed the public out of its characteristic lethargy. In fact, on the very day that I was working on this address, I happened to glance at the daily paper only to see on the front page a heart-rending picture of a 92-year-old black minister standing in front of what was left of his church in Boligee, Alabama.

As a Buddhist, who with great sadness must watch what is happening to his Christian brothers and sisters, I am reminded of the words of the Buddha: "Whoever harms a harmless person, one pure and guiltless, upon that very fool the evil recoils like a fine dust thrown against the wind."[14] When I see things like this happening, I find it difficult to forgive the perpetrators even though I know I must. The Buddha told his monks that "even if bandits were to sever you savagely limb by limb with a two-handed saw, he who gives rise to the mind of hate towards them would not be carrying out my teaching."[15]

As a Buddhist, I do not profess to know whether Christ ever really healed the sick, raised up a cripple, made the blind to see, the deaf to hear, or raised the dead. But, I do know that he never made anyone lame, or blind, or mute; nor did he ever put anyone to death. He was at the very least a good, compassionate, and virtuous human being; he was, indeed, everything that the Buddha was, and taught that we should be. Even though we (and I speak now not only as a Buddhist but as a human being) may wonder whether we can find it in our hearts to forgive those who harm us, who beat us, kill us, defame us, or burn our churches and temples, we must remember that Christ himself had no second thoughts about those who persecuted him, beat him, spat upon him, and even killed him. He forgave them from the cross; can we do less?

And *this* is why we must continue our dialogue; this is why we must talk! The only alternative to talking is the building up of resentment and anger, which in time must inevitably become open hostility and conflict. Nor can religions take the attitude that they will start talking when they have "settled scores." As the Buddha reminds us, "In those who harbor such thoughts as 'he abused me, he beat me, he defeated me, he robbed me,' hatred is not appeased."[16] In Buddhism there are few instances of "eternal truths," and so when the Buddha himself declares something so to be, we have to assume that he really meant it. In an often-quoted verse, the Buddha stated that "[h]atreds never cease through hatred in the world; through love alone do they cease. This is an eternal law."[17] And did not Jesus say, "Love your enemies and pray for those who persecute you"?[18] In Paul's letter to the Romans, we read: "Bless those who persecute you; never curse them, bless them . . . resist evil and conquer it with good."[19] So, now the question is: "What are the spiritual 'ways' that our traditions, Christian and Buddhist, ask us to follow so that we can tread in the spiritual footprints of our founders?" This is the spiritual wisdom we must give to the world today.

Concluding Note

Pope John Paul II's conviction that what unites us is greater than what separates us offers firm ground upon which to continue building a more united world in which all faiths can feel at home. I, as a Buddhist, believe that Buddhism is a "universal" religion in the sense that it is concerned with the fundamental human condition, and thus with the problem of suffering first and foremost.[20] The Buddha said, "It is suffering I teach, and the cessation of suffering." In this respect, Buddhism is like Christianity. For it too is concerned with the problem of suffering. As Pope John Paul II reminds us, "The cross remains constant while the world turns."[21] For Christians, this observation has led theologians to seek an answer to a most perplexing question: Since there is obviously evil in the world, how can God permit it? The Buddhist is no less aware of, and concerned about, the reality of evil and suffering. But for us, the question is not how *God* can permit it, but rather, what are *we* going to do about it?

In light of this question, we do not claim that everyone should become a Buddhist, but rather that, with respect to the fundamental problem with which Buddhism is concerned, everyone *already* is a "Buddhist," whether he or she accepts that name or not. Every spiritual tradition has wisdom to share concerning what we should do. For example, I must mention a comment by Francis Cardinal Arinze, President of the Vatican's Pontifical Council for Interreligious Dialogue. In one of the most gracious gestures by the Church in our memory, a letter was sent this year by the Cardinal to the Buddhist community extending his wishes for a "Happy feast of Vesakh." Vesakh is the day on which Buddhists commemorate the birth, enlightenment, and death of the Buddha. True to the spirit of its founder, Buddhism has been renowned throughout its history for its tolerance of other beliefs and values. But as the Cardinal reminds us, this is not enough. He points out that "the pluralistic society in which we live demands more than mere tolerance. Tolerance is usually thought of as putting up with the other, or at best as a code of polite conduct. Yet this resigned, lukewarm attitude does not create the right atmosphere for a [truly] harmonious existence. The spirit of our religions challenges us to go beyond this. We are commanded in fact [to] *love our neighbors as ourselves*."[22] And in the *Dhammapada* the Buddha exhorts us: "Conquer anger by love; conquer evil by good; conquer avarice by giving; conquer the liar by truth."[23]

Now, it seems to me that since we are so ready to embrace each other, and claim that we are already "honorary members" of each other's religion, there is good reason why in our dialogue we should address together the world's problems. We are alike in that we all suffer, and our primary concern in the spiritual life is the end of suffering for ourselves and the world; this is what we call liberation. As His Holiness the Dalai Lama has put it: "I am interested not in converting other people to Buddhism but in how we Buddhists can contribute to human society, according to our own ideas."[24] To this end, we Buddhists are ready to dialogue so that we may contribute thereby to the spiritual transformation of humanity that today's world so badly needs.

2

Ultimate Reality and Spirituality

The spiritual life is always being informed and guided by what we believe. What we hold as ultimate also provides the *telos*, the end point, toward which our spirituality leads. For the Buddhist, the goal may be the attainment of Nirvana as a holy one, an *arahant*; or it may be the attainment of Buddhahood for the benefit of all beings. For the Christian, the goal may be an intimate union with God in which we realize true selfhood, and the freedom in which we can work for a new creation, for the reign of God on earth. So, it seemed reasonable that we begin our time together at Gethsemani sharing what is the deepest reality in our hearts.

After the welcoming addresses and opening remarks on the eve of the Gethsemani Encounter, there was a "reflective moment." A Buddhist participant, Jeffrey Hopkins, shared with his Christian brothers and sisters what is truly ultimate in the Buddhist vision of the spiritual life. Then a Christian participant, Donald Mitchell, shared with his Buddhist brothers and sisters what is truly ultimate in the Christian vision of the spiritual life.

In his talk, Jeffrey Hopkins presents us with what he wants Christians to know about his Buddhist vision of life and how it guides Buddhist spirituality. Since he is speaking personally, he draws primarily on the traditions of Tibetan Buddhism. What is ultimate, at the very foundation of the spiritual life, is the Buddha-nature understood in terms of the mind of clear light and emptiness. Hopkins concludes that the ultimate goal of the process of spiritual growth is Nirvana and eventual Buddhahood where one realizes freedom from all bondage. In this freedom of full Buddhahood, one compassionately performs a "spontaneous altruistic display" for the benefit of all beings. Finally, in a more dialogical style, Hopkins discusses the similarities and differences between these Buddhist views and those of the Christian tradition.

In his talk, Donald Mitchell continues this dialogical approach in presenting what he wants Buddhists to know about his Christian vision of life and how it guides Christian spirituality. Speaking first to the Theravadin participants, he discusses the similarities and differences between their notions of *Nibbana* and dependent origination, and the Christian notions of God and creation. Then, Mitchell speaks to the Zen Buddhists present about the similarities and differences between their notions of emptiness and the mutual penetration of all beings, and the Christian trinitarian notions of a self-emptying God and the original communion of creation. Finally, Mitchell turns to the Tibetan Buddhists to discuss the similarities and differences between tantric and Christian spiritual transformation.

Nirvana, Buddahood and the Spiritual Life

JEFFREY HOPKINS

I am a Buddhist but not of a particular school, order or sect. I make use of whatever seems valuable among what I encounter in the various schools and national Buddhisms; and it is in this spirit that I am enjoying, more and more, the encounter with Christianity. My sources today are primarily, but not exclusively, texts and oral teachings of the Geluk and Nyingma orders of Tibetan Buddhism. I shall be speaking largely from their standard perspectives of the spiritual path; but much of what they say is shared with the other schools of Buddhism.

Buddha's focal teaching is the doctrine that all impermanent phenomena depend on their respective causes and conditions. The imagery used for Buddha is a physician who heals by teaching. The doctrine that a Buddha teaches is viewed as being like medicine for a diseased practitioner. Like a doctor, Buddha identified first the effect—the suffering of ordinary life. Suffering means the physical and mental pain which we all see as disease, but it also refers to ordinary pleasures. This is because if we partake of them too much, they show their nature of pain; they also become addictive—they do not have a nature of pleasure, we just think that they have a solid nature of affording pleasure. A deeper level of pain is the fact that our lives and our environment are not under our own control, but are subject to previous causes and conditions. This profound level of pain includes even neutral feelings. Just as a small hair in the palm of the hand is neglected but in the eye is excruciating, so the fact that our lives are under the influence of other forces does not bother someone who has not seen that this too is pain; but it is excruciating to those who have seen this fact.

Again like a physician, Buddha identified the cause of suffering. He said that this is craving—afflictive desire which itself gives rise to hatred of persons and factors that block the achievement of pleasure. Craving and hatred, in turn, depend upon ignorance. Ignorance is the absence of knowledge of how phenomena actually exist, as well as the active misconception about how they exist. The basic message is that we fool ourselves into suffering. Due to our own past conditioning in a beginningless cycle of rebirths, persons and other objects appear to have an exaggerated status. We assent to this false appearance, thereby drawing ourselves into afflictive desire and then into hatred. The Buddha's message is that our problems have a cause—ignorance.

Again like a physician, Buddha identified the effect of a cure—that there is a state of being cured from this disease. This is the ceasing of all defiling factors—the cessation of all processes that produce pain. This is called Nirvana—having passed beyond sorrow. Sorrow here is the three root poisons of desire, hatred, and their source, ignorance. The state of release from suffering is a time of life without error, without distortion, of markedly increased effectiveness. This is true also in those Buddhist schools that hold that the mental and physical continuum of an enlightened being is completely severed at the time of death; for there is a period of far more effective interaction with others, subsequent to enlightenment and before death, in a healed state of release. In the Mind Only School and the Middle Way School, the primary aim of *bodhisattvas* is to bring about the welfare of other sentient beings. The means to accomplish this is the *bodhisattva*'s own enlightenment, the gaining of authentic freedom where there is a limitless, unending, unhindered, spontaneous capacity to help others effectively. That is the best of cures.

Then like a physician, Buddha identified how to attain Nirvana. Based on insight into the causes of suffering, he taught that the effect, the attainment of Nirvana, depends upon its causes—namely, the cultivation of physical, verbal, and mental practices called the "path." The path is based on keeping sound ethical behavior as laypersons and as ordained persons in order at least not to harm others and preferably to help others. The stages in this process are first to control coarse activities of body and speech. Then, one develops profound love and compassion for each and every being—all six types of temporary lives in cyclic existence, these being humans, demigods, and gods as well as animals, hungry ghosts, and hell-beings. With such love and compassion, it is possible to generate an aspiration to Buddhahood for the sake of other beings—the aim being to attain the knowledge, compassion, and powers of a Buddha in order to benefit others.

This altruistic attitude is endowed with two aspirations. The first is for others' welfare and the second is for one's own highest enlightenment as a Buddha—the attainment of Buddhahood being seen as a means for accomplishing others' welfare. Even though one's own enlightenment must be accomplished before bringing benefit to others in a vastly effective way, in terms of motivation, service to others' and not one's own enlightenment is prime.

Having realized the effects of these two aspirations, a Buddha has omniscience and the capacity to emanate helpful forms. Those who heroically and altruistically strive to become Buddhas—called *bodhisattvas*—primarily seek to emanate physical forms. This is because it is through such forms that the welfare of others can be accomplished, since help is provided mainly through teaching what is to be adopted in practice and what is to be discarded in behavior. Though omniscience and emanations in forms necessarily accompany each other and thus are achieved together, a *bodhisattva*'s emphasis is on appearing in myriad forms suitable to the interests and dispositions of trainees and to teach them accordingly.

Some *bodhisattvas'* motivation is described as like that of a monarch. They see themselves as first becoming enlightened and then helping others. The motivation of other *bodhisattvas* is described as like that of a boatman. They want to arrive at the freedom of Buddhahood in the company of everyone else just as a boatman arrives at the other shore with all the passengers. Still other *bodhisattvas'* motivation is described as like that of a shepherd. They want to see others safely enlightened before they become enlightened, like a shepherd following the flock home.

This heroic effort to bring about others' welfare is conceived in terms of there being a basis for such purification and transformation within us that needs to be purified of adventitious defilements through practice, whereby a state of purification is achieved. Thus, there are four aspects to the spiritual life: (1) basis for purification and transformation within, (2) objects of purification, (3) paths that serve as means or causes of purification, and (4) the fruit or effects of that purification.

Basis of Purification

The basis of purification is the Buddha-nature, which is viewed in two ways. The first is the clear light nature of the mind, a positive phenomenon. The other is the emptiness of any inherent existence of the mind, a negative phenomenon. This mere absence of inherent existence of the mind is a precondition for its transformation. Both of these aspects are expressed in the famous statement from Dharmakirti's *Commentary on*

[Dignaga's] "Compilation of Prime Cognition": "The nature of the mind is clear light. The defilements are adventitious."[1] "Adventitious" here does not mean "uncaused." It means that the defilements do not subsist in the very nature of the mind. Since desire, hatred, and ignorance do not reside in the very basis of the mind due to the fact that the nature of the mind is clear light, all defilements can be removed without destroying the mind.

The clear light nature of the mind is described in certain *tantras* as the fundamental, innate mind of clear light. It is fundamental in the sense that its continuum exists forever—while one is afflicted and unafflicted. It has no beginning and no end in time. The mind of clear light is called the "all-good." It is also called the "basis-of-all" in that it is the basis of all phenomena, both of cyclic existence and of Nirvana. It may seem surprising that a system emphasizing suffering as much as Buddhism does should also have a doctrine of the basic goodness or fundamental purity of the mind. However, such a foundation is needed for the radical transformation of the condition of suffering into a state of freedom.

The second way of conceiving the Buddha-nature is as the absence of the inherent existence of the mind. This does not refer to the non-existence of the mind, nor does it suggest that the mind lacks definition or nature. Rather, it refers to the mind's not existing independently, under its own power. The mind is not established by way of its own character, from its own side. The emptiness of inherent existence is the true nature of all phenomena. All beings are empty of independent existence.

With respect to the mind, its emptiness can be realized by way of many approaches: examining its production by causes, its producing effects, its relationship with the beginning, middle, and ending of a moment of mind, and so forth. When, through any of these approaches, practitioners realize the emptiness of the inherent existence of the mind or any other phenomenon, they can for the first time with complete certainty understand that the mind and other phenomena are not what they appear to be. They appear to exist in their own right but do not. The distinction between appearance and fact is understood, and the endemic assent to the false appearance that underlies afflictive emotions is exposed.

From this point of view, all appearing phenomena are called *samvrti-satya,* which in this commentarial tradition should be translated as something like "truths-for-a-concealing consciousness." Our *concealing* consciousness is what obscures. It is only an ignorant consciousness, a concealing consciousness, that takes objects such as tables, mind, or any other commonly appearing object to exist the way it appears. In this context, an "*ultimate* consciousness" refers to a non-conceptual wisdom of emptiness, which is called "ultimate" because it has the power to overcome defilements from the root. However, this is not the "*final* consciousness." The final state of the enlightened consciousness of a Buddha is not mere realization of emptiness, but omniscience that provides the ground for a Buddha to altruistically and spontaneously help others.

Objects of Purification

Both the clear light nature of the mind and the emptiness of inherent existence of the mind are the Buddha-nature—the nature of the mind that allows for transformation into Buddhahood. They are the basis of purification and transformation. They are that from which defilements are removed. The defilements that are removed are primarily the two types of distortion just mentioned—afflictive obstructions and obstructions to omniscience. The afflictive obstructions prevent liberation from cyclic existence and are mainly the ignorance that conceives phenomena to exist inherently. But they also include unsalutary consciousnesses that such ignorance induces—desire, hatred, pride, enmity, jealousy, belligerence, miserliness, laziness, and so forth. These are called afflictions, or afflictive emotions, because they distort one's mind. An external analog is the distortion of the face that anger brings about. All of these depend on ignorance, for without ignorance they cannot exist. Ignorance is the basic affliction. It is the basic bondage, the basic distortion. From it, and entirely dependent upon it, the other distortions arise, seeming to be in the very fabric of life but actually not.

An even deeper distortion, the obstructions to omniscience, is the second type of object to be purified. It is described as the *appearance* of objects as inherently existent, and it can only be removed after the afflictive obstructions have been overcome. Since *bodhisattvas* are primarily motivated to help others, they mainly want to remove the obstructions to omniscience which prevent full knowledge of liberative techniques and prevent subtle knowledge of others' dispositions. Still, they must remove the afflictive obstructions before they can gradually do away with the basic false appearance of phenomena that prevents, obstructs, and hinders omniscience.

Means of Purification

Based on this twofold analysis of the nature of the mind—clear light and emptiness of inherent existence—it is held that these basic distortions can be removed. Discussion, dialogue, debate and internal reflection or reasoning are important aspects of many persons' gaining wisdom, but they are not sufficient. A powerfully concentrated mind is necessary.

Since the maintenance of ethics requires development of mindfulness in order to avoid negative activities, ethics is a foundation for the techniques of meditation because mindfulness and introspection are central to the process of meditation. Meditation requires that the mind become capable of staying one-pointedly on its object with clarity and intense alertness. This requires that the meditative mind become free from excitement, which in its coarser forms causes one to lose awareness of the object. Excitement in its subtler forms allows one to be constantly aware of the object, but also produces thinking about something else. Meditation also requires that the mind be free from laxity, which in its coarser forms causes the mind to be dark and dull. In its subtler forms, laxity produces a diminishment in the intensity of concentration. These problems are countered by applying antidotes that either loosen or tighten the mind, like tuning a guitar.

Meditation can be a case of concentrating on just one object; this is called stabilizing meditation. It also can be analytical; reasons behind attitudes such as universal compassion are contemplated so that egocentric emotions are undermined and, in a harrowing process, are replaced by cherishing others. Another type of meditation is to reflect on various levels and stages of the spiritual path, causing them to appear to the mind in order. This serves to establish predispositions that eventually will pull the mind into these very states. Since one is not capable of generating the mind into the actual state exactly as it is, a similitude of it is meditatively cultivated. Correspondingly, there is also meditation in which the mind is generated into the state of the path exactly as it is.

Another powerful mode of meditation is to cultivate wishes, as in wishing, "May all sentient beings have happiness and the causes of happiness," "May all sentient beings be free from suffering and the causes of suffering," or "May I attain the wisdom realizing dependent-arising," and so forth.

In order to empower wisdom to the point where it is capable of overcoming defilements from their root, it is also important to develop familiarity with the various types of interferences to meditation and with how to counteract those states. Then, the practitioner does analytical and stabilizing meditation on such reasons as "dependent-arising." This is to see the reliance of persons and other phenomena on their causes and conditions, and also to see that every single object depends upon its own parts. At a deeper level, one also sees that all phenomena depend upon a consciousness that designates them. Through reflecting on dependent-arising, it is realized that phenomena do not exist in their own right as they seem to—that all things are "empty" of such inherent existence. Let me reiterate that "emptiness" does not mean that an object does not exist at all; rather, it means that a phenomenon does not have the status of independent concreteness that it seems to have in our ordinary experience.

Alternation of stabilizing and analytical meditation is performed so that eventually the one serves to induce a greater degree of the other. When these two types of meditation become mutually supportive, a practitioner attains a greater degree of meditative stabilization called "special insight." Then, through cultivation of this state, totally nondual direct perception of the nature of things is gained. It is nondualistic in five senses: (1) there is no conceptual appearance; (2) there is no sense of subject and object, which are, instead, mixed like fresh water poured into fresh water; (3) there is no appearance of inherent existence; (4) there is no appearance of conventional phenomena—only emptiness appears; (5) there is no appearance of difference—although the emptinesses of all phenomena in all world systems appear, they do not appear to be different.

This degree of perception of dependent-arising and emptiness only removes artificially gained afflictive obstructions, that is, apprehensions of inherent existence gained through fortification by mistaken study, analysis, and systems of philosophy. This level of perception is profound, but is not yet sufficiently powerful to remove *innate* afflictive obstructions—the ignorance, desire, and so forth that even animals and infants have. For this type of liberation, repeated meditation on the reality already seen is needed; one must reenter direct perception of emptiness, the ground that makes all phenomena possible, again and again. Much like washing dirty clothing, the grosser levels of dirt are cleansed first and then gradually the more subtle.

Fruits of Purification

In time, all afflictive obstructions are removed, whereby eventually the cyclic creation of suffering is undone, and liberation—Nirvana—is attained. Since love, compassion, faith, and other virtues do not depend for their existence on ignorance, no matter how much they may at times become involved with ignorance and afflictive desire they have valid cognition as their support. Being qualities of mind, rather than of body, they can be developed limitlessly. Thus, even beyond this first level of Nirvana is the attainment of Buddhahood which can only be accomplished through conjoining wisdom with the most intense forms of love and compassion. The higher level of Nirvana—of having passed beyond *all* faults and limitations—is sought because of its effectiveness in helping others.

The attainment of liberation from the cycle of rebirth is not sufficient to remove the obstructions to omniscience. The wisdom consciousness can do this only when sufficiently empowered and enhanced through the *bodhisattva* practices of the altruistic deeds of giving, ethics, and patience in what are called "limitless ways over a limitless period of time."

Attitudes of altruism, and the concordant deeds that compassion induces, empower the wisdom consciousness so that it can remove the final layer of distortion—the false appearance of phenomena as if they exist independently, by way of their own character.

In this sense, altruism is in the service of wisdom, but also wisdom is in the service of altruism in that, concordant with a *bodhisattva*'s fundamental motivation, the full enlightenment gained through this more advanced type of wisdom allows spontaneous altruistic display. This altruistic display has forms more numerous than the grains of sand on this planet, to help all sentient beings in accordance with their interests and dispositions. This is freedom from all bondage, and freedom for authentic existence.

Considerations for Dialogue

Finally, I would like to raise some questions to help us begin our dialogue. The first question has to do with the "basis of purification": "Can emptiness and the mind of clear light be understood as creator?" One can say that while emptiness is not viewed to be a personal creator God, without emptiness nothing is possible whereas with it everything is possible. And the mind of clear light is creative in the sense of being the basic consciousness out of which all other levels appear. If this is so, the question arises, "Is Buddhist liberation experienced as something 'given' from emptiness, or 'bestowed' by the fundamental innate mind of clear light?" The presence of the Buddha-nature in every being is what makes Nirvana possible. Therefore, in many Buddhist traditions there *is* an emphasis on letting the liberation already within us manifest itself.

Following this line of thought, one can raise another question concerning the "means of purification": "Is there an experience of 'savior' in Buddhism?" Though the primary emphasis in Buddhism is on individual effort rather than on a savior, there are many references to the Buddha bestowing blessings that contribute to liberation. His Holiness the Dalai Lama once said that the more advanced one is, the more one can be helped from the outside. Perhaps we can say that Christianity has been taught for the most advanced disciples.

Another question has to do with the kind of love developed as a "fruit of purification": "Is emptiness, as the true object of wisdom, ever understood to be love?" Some Buddhists say that emptiness itself has an essence of compassion. Others says that compassion is the relational living of emptiness. Still, it is clearly said that one can realize the most subtle emptiness and not thereby be fully compassionate. Rather, realizing the emptiness of inherent existence of self and other can be used as a tool in developing compassion for others. Self-centered isolation can be broken through and other-centered compassion can be developed. Also, compassion is induced when one perceives that others' suffering is brought on by the unnecessary misperception of the nature of persons and other phenomena.

A last question might be, "In Buddhism, is there any sense of loving others because the highest being loves them?" His Holiness the Dalai Lama has spoken of valuing other beings by considering that they are the very beings for whom Shakyamuni Buddha became enlightened. Yet, we must remember that a deity's final nature and our final nature are understood to be the same in Buddhism. It is this fundamental innate mind of clear light that one must realize in order to love others as the supermundane beings do.

So while there are certainly differences between us, perhaps they are not as big as they sometimes seem before reflection. With this possibility in mind we can turn to our joint exploration of the spiritual life in Buddhism and Christianity.

God, Creation and the Spiritual Life

DONALD W. MITCHELL

On behalf of the Christian participants, I would like to thank Jeffrey for helping us gain a better understanding of the Buddha's *Dharma*. We certainly are all looking forward to hearing from our Buddhist friends about each of their tradition's spiritual journey toward the realization of this wonderful *Dharma*. I have also been asked to say a few words concerning the Christian understanding about God and creation that may help our Buddhist friends better appreciate the Christian spiritual journey that we will be exploring during these next few days.

God

Concerning our Christian understanding of God, I would like to begin by addressing our Theravadin friends. The Ven. Buddhadasa from Thailand has used the Buddhist distinction between the conditioned (*samkhata*) and the unconditioned (*asamkhata*) reality in a way that clarifies our Christian understanding of God. This distinction has been most helpful to dialogue because some Theravadins, when they hear Christian devotional theistic language about God, think that Christians worship a devalike god in hopes of this worldly benefits and rebirth into a devalike heaven. But to understand God in this way would be to see God as part of the conditioned world when, as Buddhadasa points out, God is to be more rightly understood in terms of the unconditioned. In our scripture, we too find references to such spiritual beings as "principalities, authorities, powers and dominions" (Eph. 1:21), which are part of the created order. On the other hand, God is the uncreated, unborn, unproduced Ground of this created and conditioned order of things.

We understand that for Theravada, the unconditioned ultimate is *Nibbana*. While this unconditioned reality is understood in nontheistic terms, these very terms remind one of the Christian experience of the Kingdom of God. For example, *Nibbana* is said to be a "refuge" that is "free from afflictions and harm," from any "disturbance" or "oppression." It is said to be an "abode of security" that is "peaceful and calm," indeed the very fullness of peace. It is a "place of rest" that brings "pacification of suffering," freedom from any "toil," "struggle" or "striving." It is a "supreme status" that is "pure," "blessed," a "consummation," the "complete truth," the "highest good," and the "final end."

In reading these descriptions of *Nibbana*, one is reminded of the prayer of St. Augustine: "Our hearts are restless until they rest in you."[1] For us to rest in God, to find his Kingdom here in our hearts, is to find an unlimited spiritual abode of perfect refuge, freedom and consummation. Further, in reading the description of the qualities of a person who abides in *Nibbana*—namely, compassion, loving kindness, sympathetic joy, and equanimity—one recognizes the qualities of a person who abides in the Kingdom of God. On the other hand, while *Nibbana* is primarily a state of consciousness, when we Christians gaze into the heart of our supreme refuge with the "mind of Christ," we find a personal God, who is "love" (1 Jn. 4:8). We also find that we have become children of God with his Holy Spirit in us calling out into this unconditioned refuge, "Abba," "Father" (Rom. 8:15). We will explore this personalistic notion of God in more detail later. But first let us turn from the unconditioned to the conditioned, from God to creation.

Creation

We understand that for Theravada, as for most Buddhists, the forms of the world originate in a process of "dependent arising." We Christians believe that the world is the creation of God. What do we mean by "creation?" Our Christian doctrine of creation is not a literal reportage on the cosmological beginnings of the universe. It is a statement of faith that God creates and sustains us in each moment of life by his power and in his love. While we recognize that there is a causal interdependence between the forms of life, and appreciate the Buddhist doctrine of dependent origination, we also recognize a "transcendent causation" that we call creation. This creation is not a past event at the beginning of time, but a continuing process (*creatio continua*), by which God conserves the cosmos in being (*conservatio*) and enables the interdependent forms of that cosmos to interact freely (*concursus*). Therefore, creation means that all interdependent forms of life are in a continuous relationship of dependence on God. God is the ultimate Ground of all being and action that stands to creation as its silent horizon.

This process of continuous creation is said to be *ex nihilo*. That is, the created forms of life emerge not out of a prior substratum, but out of their own nothingness. This creative formation is guided by the fact that all creation, from beginning to end, preexists in the infinite mind and loving heart of God. God's creative and loving power continuously pours forth, enabling the world to be in his love and to function in its freedom. This pouring forth of the creative Spirit of God takes place, our scripture says, through the Word of God that we find incarnate in Jesus Christ: "Through him all things come to be" (Jn. 1:3).

Elsewhere in our scripture it is also said that the divine Wisdom of God was "from everlasting . . . before the earth came into being" (Prov. 8:23). In a way that reminds one of Buddhism, this Wisdom is said to be:

> fashioner of all things. . . . For in her there is a spirit that is intelligent, holy, unique, manifold, subtle, mobile, clear, unpolluted, distinct, invulnerable . . . beneficent, humane, steadfast, sure, free from anxiety, all-powerful, overseeing all, and penetrating through all spirits that are intelligent and pure and most subtle . . . because of her pureness she pervades and penetrates all things. For she is a breath of the power of God, and a pure emanation of the glory of the Almighty. (Wis. 7:22–26)

Since God continuously creates through such beneficent power, all creation is inherently good and is a gift to be affirmed and loved. God calls us to care for all creation, especially the least, those in most need of our help. Evil is instead a distortion of this inherent goodness of our created nature. This distortion is caused by a fundamental misdirection of our free will that produces a self-centered consciousness and the unwholesome predispositions of the human heart. In response to this reality of evil, God's providence weaves the events of life, including the tragic that stem from our free will, into his loving plan for the universe. And, since God's creative Word is also "the true light that enlightens all men" (Jn. 1:9), it is through this Word that God enlightens and re-creates us in his image until we realize our true self.

Finally, in our vision of creation as God's gift of love, we also find that all beings are created in a single "communion" of love. When we say that all creatures are created in communion with each other, we are not speaking of a sentiment but of a fundamental disposition of "being for others." We exist for the benefit of others. As Thomas Merton says, all creatures are "created free in order to give themselves to others. . . . Love is the heart and the true center of that creative dynamism which we call life. Love is life itself in its state of maturity and perfection."[2]

To realize this fact of our communion, or the unity of creation in God, is to reach maturity in the spiritual life. In Christian spirituality, we journey from separation and alienation from others and God to a realization of communion with others in God. Our saints are like mirrors that reflect back to us our own true created nature of pure self-giving. Then upon death, we pass from creation back through the flow of God's luminous creative power into the heart of the Trinity, into full communion with God and one another in eternal paradise.

God and Creation

What more can we say about a triune God as the Ground of creation? Are there other notions in Buddhism that can help us in this regard? Here I would like to turn especially to our Zen Buddhist friends. I am aware of the great appreciation in your tradition for the vision of the cosmos developed by the Chinese school of Hua-yen Buddhism. One of the aspects of this vision, developed from the notion of emptiness or dependent origination that Jeffrey described for us, is that all things interact in a relationship of "mutual penetration."

What is implied here is that at the deepest level of life, there is a "mutual negation and affirmation between self and other," indeed between all beings. In this Hua-yen vision, at the deepest ontological level, each entity is negating itself and affirming all other entities. This negation and affirmation is mutual in that it is happening simultaneously between all beings. In this matrix of negation of self and affirmation of other, in this sea of self-giving, all creation is mutually and freely affirming each particular entity. In the freedom, or "mutual nonobstruction," of this fundamental being for others, a deep and compassionate harmony is realized.

This original or fundamental unity entails a "mutual entering" and a "mutual containment" of self and other. A Hua-yen metaphor for this compassionate unity is one of mirrors reflecting each other with no stain or shadow. We, like these mirrors, freely enter each other and contain each other in compassionate mutual interpenetration. In this unity of pure experience, the luminosity of our True Self, our Buddha-nature, shines with clarity as the true essence of all things. No matter how we enslave ourselves or others with defilements on the surface of life, this deeper harmony and freedom abides, waiting to realize itself in our experience and in our daily lives.

How does this Buddhist vision of mutual penetration help us understand God and creation? For us, God is a Trinity: Father, Son and Holy Spirit. The relationship between these three is said to be a total "mutual indwelling" (*perichoresis*). To use the Christian language of *kenosis* (self-emptying) in place of the Hua-yen language of negation and affirmation, all three persons are in a relatedness of kenotic love and unity. The Father empties himself out in total self-giving love into the Son. The Son does not cling to this loving affirmation but empties it back into the Father with total self-giving. Both the Father and Son are fully "in" the dynamic of this mutual love and unity which just is the Holy Spirit. The Holy Spirit does not cling to this mutual indwelling of Father and Son, but returns all to the Father and Son. In this way, all three abide in total nonobstructing freedom and mutual containment or indwelling.

Since God creates according to God's nature, we would expect that creation would display a similar kind of mutual indwelling. So, it is not surprising to us that the Hua-yen vision of the cosmos reveals a compassionate pattern of mutual negation and affirmation, of mutual entering and containment. However, for us, the cosmos is not self-enclosed, self-generating, self-maintaining and self-liberating. While the luminous and loving trinitarian nature of God is immanent, underlying creation, the Holy Trinity remains as its ultimate and transcendent Ground.

Finally, while our Christian theistic language may imply that God is an *object* of spiritual experience, God is also understood as the absolute *subject* of such spiritual experience. In the words of our scripture: "It is no longer I who live, but Christ within me who lives" (Gal. 2:19–20). While we do exercise our freedom and cooperate with God's grace, ultimately spiritual experience is not something we produce, it is produced in us by the Holy Spirit. The Holy Spirit is, as Merton says, living in us "as the ground of a totally new life and a new being."[3] Therefore, just as the original fact of the unity of life bursts forth in the Zen realization of the True Self, so too, the ultimate fact of the trinitarian unity of God at the Ground of life bursts forth in Christ's realization of himself in us.

God Transforming Creation

Turning now to our Tibetan Buddhist friends, let us look for a moment at how this realization of God in the spiritual life transforms creation. Given the dynamics of tantric practice, we sometimes find that Tibetan Buddhists think of the God of Christianity as a kind of mundane or supermundane deity. And Christian spirituality is sometimes seen as being similar to a common type of tantric practice in which one sees oneself in relation to an external, separate supermundane deity. In such tantric practice, one praises, confesses and makes offerings to this divine lord in front of oneself from whom one also receives blessings. Looking at Christianity from the outside, one could certainly get the impression that this is what we are about as well. And the conclusion could be drawn that there is nothing in Christian spirituality that is similar to the more advanced and interior forms of tantra.

On the other hand, consider for a moment the following scripture passage that deals with Christian transformation in God: "With our unveiled faces reflecting like mirrors the brightness of the Lord, all grow brighter and brighter as we are turned into the image that we reflect; this is the work of the Lord who is Spirit" (2 Cor. 3:18). Note here too that "God is spirit" (Jn. 4:24). For us the term "spirit" does not denote a subtle form of matter, as in some Asian traditions, but refers to the very pure and clear essence of consciousness—perhaps something similar to the "mind of clear light" as understood in the Tibetan traditions.

In the above passage from scripture, the point is that the spiritual "brightness of the Lord" is a luminosity, a clarity and purity of the Holy Spirit that transforms us in mind and body into what we receive: we become what we reflect in our spiritual life. In our liturgy, you may hear the priest say that in Jesus Christ, God took on our humanity so that we can share in his divinity. By sharing in the divine life of God, we become "divinized," to use a term coined by the early Fathers of our church. Therefore, as in the more advanced forms of tantric practice, we do not just worship the divine as an external deity. We become divine by sharing in that reality at the innermost core of our consciousness.

God's divine life of love and unity is realized in our life through our spiritual familiarization with and participation in it. In ways similar to some forms of tantra, we may use imaginative prayer forms to familiarize ourselves with the mind and heart of Christ. But as the above scripture passage states, the actual participation in God, the merging or union with God at the core of our being, is achieved through the work of the Holy Spirit within us. I assume that the experience of transformation in the mind of clear light in tantra is not ultimately achieved by the power of any particular meditation or visualization practice, but by the spontaneous power of primordial awareness itself.

As you will be hearing this week, our Christian transformation into the divine trinitarian life of God is not only facilitated by prayer, meditation and scripture, but also by our sacraments. As scripture says, Christ is for us a sacramental source of "living water" that "will turn into a spring inside [us] welling up to eternal life" (Jn. 4:10,14). This inner oasis of new life is nourished by the sacrament of the Eucharist we celebrate at Mass. When we receive the bread and the wine, signifying the body and blood of Christ, we receive a real and nourishing presence of God, refreshing, healing and sanctifying us in his divine life.

Taking within us this presence of God brings about a transformation on all levels of our being including our body. In highest yoga tantra, there are forms of spirituality, many of which are quite different from our own, that nourish the growth of a spiritual body in order to progress in the higher stages of the *bodhisattva* path. In our sacramental spiritual life, there is a nourishment of what we understand to be our resurrection body. Thomas Aquinas states that the Eucharist "is a cause of resurrection not only for souls but also of bodies."[4] Finally, divinized by the Eucharist, our physical bodies become "eucharist" for the transfiguration of the cosmos.[5]

In conclusion, I hope that these few words about God and creation will help point us in the right direction for our spiritual encounter during these next few days together. By sharing as fellow pilgrims on our common journey into truth, we can explore together the spiritual treasures of our traditions—the great heritages of Buddhist and Christian spirituality. Thereby, we can contribute to a deeper mutual understanding and appreciation between people East and West who are dedicated to the spiritual life for the good of humankind and the whole cosmos.

3

Prayer and Meditation

Over the main entrance to the walled garden in front of the Abbey of Gethsemani are the words "God Alone" inscribed in the stone archway. One passes under this archway and through the iron gate into the contemplative atmosphere along the inner garden path. In both Buddhism and Christianity, there are passageways into the spiritual life through which one journeys into freedom and fulfillment for oneself and others.

Prayer and meditation are passageways to the spiritual life in Buddhism and Christianity. But they are not just gates to be passed through and left behind. They are continuous passageways into ever deeper levels of insight and freedom, and love and compassion. For the Buddhist, meditation opens one to horizons in which one sees the truth about life and is enabled to live it for the benefit of all living beings. For the Christian, prayer opens up through meditation into contemplation that brings one into a life of intimacy with God lived for the service of all.

The three Buddhist talks on meditation practice are given by representatives of the Theravada, Zen and Tibetan traditions. The Ven. Dr. Dhammarakkhita from Myanmar (Burma) presents classic forms of meditation as they come to us from Theravada Buddhism. He emphasizes the practice of a breathing technique associated with mindfulness meditation, as well as the development of mind deliverance through loving-kindness meditation that can in turn have a liberating effect on society.

Zoketsu Norman Fischer presents the practice of Zen meditation understood through the writings of the great Japanese Zen Master Dogen. He explains the proper attitude needed for the practice of Zen meditation, namely, the acceptance of the genuineness of our life as it is. Following Dogen, Fischer sees such practice as a "backward step" to an undivided moment of immediacy where an original unity of experience is discovered. Through this discovery, we can appreciate our true genuineness and act for the benefit of others in a more enlightened way.

His Holiness the Dalai Lama begins his talk on meditation by pointing out that while we need spirituality today, we also need to practice the spiritual life with an attitude of respect for the different religious traditions of the world. He then shows how interfaith dialogue can further this ideal of mutual understanding and appreciation between the world religious traditions. With this in mind, he goes on to share with his Christian brothers and sisters the formative types of Buddhist meditation that he feels may be helpful to Christians as well.

His Holiness says in his talk that he is still unsure of what Christians mean by "contemplation." James Wiseman presents the contemplative life in the Christian tradition as one of graced attention to Christ. In this contemplative attention, one finds something more than an object of meditation. One finds the life of God to be lived. As in the Buddhist nondual meditation, described by His Holiness as a merging with the object or attitude on which one meditates, one participates through contemplation in the very life of God in Christ. Wiseman describes how this contemplative life is nourished by scripture into a fully integrated and holy life lived daily in the awareness of God.

Mary Margaret Funk describes *lectio divina* as a particular way of Christian practice that also nourishes the contemplative life. This ancient art of sacred reading moves organically from reading (*lectio*), through meditation (*meditatio*), to prayer (*oratio*), and finally into contemplation (*contemplatio*). Funk presents this spiritual journey in terms of the cultivation of the spiritual senses in the context of a contemplative community. She discusses its challenges and the difficulties that appear as the false self is peeled away and authentic integration of our person is realized in love for others in an ongoing "walking in the presence of God."

Mindfulness and Loving-Kindness Meditation

VEN. DR. DHAMMARAKKHITA

The Buddha said:

> O Bhikkhus [monks], there are two kinds of illness, what are those two? Physical illness and mental illness. There seem to be people who enjoy freedom from physical illness even for a year or two . . . even for a hundred years or more. But, O Bhikkhus, rare in this world are those who enjoy freedom from mental illness even for one moment, except those who are free from mental defilements [i.e., except the *arahants*, persons who attain *Nibbana* (Nirvana)].

The Buddha's *Dhamma* (teaching), particularly his way of "meditation," strives to produce a state of perfect mental health, equilibrium and tranquility. Lord Buddha has taught us the only way that leads to the attainment of purity, to overcoming sorrow and lamentation, to ending pain and grief, to entering upon the right path and reaching the realization of *Nibbana*.

The word "meditation" is a very poor substitute for the original term *bhavana*, which means "culture" or "development," i.e., "mental culture" or "mental development." Buddhist *bhavana*, properly speaking, is mental culture in the full sense of the term. Its aim is twofold. On the one hand, meditation aims at cleansing the mind of impurities and disturbances, such as lustful desire, hatred, ill-will, indolence, worries, restlessness and skeptical doubts. On the other hand, it aims at cultivating such positive qualities as concentration, awareness, intelligence, will, energy, analytical clarity, confidence, joy and tranquility. In the end, meditation leads to the attainment of highest wisdom which sees the nature of things as they are, realizes the *Dhamma* (Ultimate Truth), and achieves *Nibbana*.

The Buddha taught two types of meditation. First is the development of mental concentration (*samatha*), of one-pointedness of mind, by means of various methods. There are 40 objects of concentration and meditation that are prescribed in the early Buddhist texts. These practices can lead one to the highest "mystical" meditative states (*jhanas*) such as "the sphere of nothingness," or "the sphere of neither-perception-nor-non-perception." But all of these *jhana* states are, according to the Buddha, mind-created, mind-produced and conditioned. Just in themselves, these states have nothing to do with reality, the *Dhamma*, or *Nibbana*. The Buddha himself, before his Enlightenment, studied yogic practices under different teachers and attained these highest "mystical" states. But, he was not satisfied with them because they did not give complete liberation, they did not give insight into Ultimate Reality. The Buddha considered these states only as spiritual abodes for "happy living in this existence," or "peaceful living," and nothing more.

Therefore, the Buddha taught that the practice of mental concentration should ultimately lead one in another direction. So, he taught a second form of meditation known as *vipassana* or "insight" into the true nature of things that leads to the discovery of the *Dhamma*. This is essentially Buddhist "meditation," Buddhist "mental culture." It is an analytical method based on mindfulness, awareness, vigilance and observation by which we realize the truth about ourselves and our world in a way that leads to freedom, to *Nibbana*.

The most important discourse ever given by the Buddha on meditation is called the *Satipatthana Sutta,* "The Setting-up of Mindfulness." This discourse is so highly venerated in our tradition that it is regularly recited not only in Buddhist monasteries, but also in Buddhist homes with members of the family sitting round and listening with deep devotion. Very often, monks recite this *sutta* by the bedside of a dying person to purify his or her last thoughts. Many of us in Theravada Buddhism believe that the only way that leads to the attainment of purity, to the overcoming of sorrow and lamentation, to the end of pain and grief, to entering upon the right path and reaching the realization of *Nibbana,* is the way of mindfulness. Mindfulness deepens mental concentration (*samatha*) in the direction of meditation insight (*vipassana*). In mindfulness, the disciple dwells in contemplation of the body, feelings, and thoughts. Through being concentrated and mindful of these factors of our life, and by clearly comprehending through insight their true nature, the world of hate and greed, of sorrow and grief, is overcome and *Nibbana* is attained. With this description of the path of mental culture in mind, I would like to present a particular technique of mindfulness meditation, namely, "watching over in-and-out breathing."

Breathing and Mindfulness

You breathe in and out all day and night, but you are never mindful of it, you never for a second concentrate your mind on it. Now you are going to do just this. Breathe in and out as usual, without any effort or strain. Now, bring your mind to concentrate on your breathing-in and breathing-out; let your mind be aware and vigilant of your breathing-in-and-out. When you breathe, you sometimes take deep breaths, sometimes not. Breathe normally and naturally. When you inhale, the air will touch or strike at the "door" of your nose; and when you exhale, it will touch or strike at the same place. Before you start this practice, you must know that place exactly. This is the place where you must continuously watch over your in-and-out breathing. You must concentrate on this respiration process until a certain sign appears.

Now, to practice this mindfulness, first sit comfortably with legs crossed, body erect, and your eyes closed. Place your mind at the point of the nostril where the air touches and concentrate on the breath as it enters and leaves, noting mentally "entering" when you breathe in, and noting mentally "leaving" when you breathe out. In this first step, the beginner pays attention by saying mentally "entering," "leaving," "entering," "leaving." Try to do this for five minutes, and if you feel all right, continue for another ten minutes. As you sit in this way, first you will find it extremely difficult to concentrate your mind on your breathing. Your mind will run away, and you may be dismayed and disappointed. But if you continue to practice this exercise for fifteen minutes at a time, you will gradually, by and by, begin to concentrate your mind on your breathing.

With the second step, counting begins. When you breathe in and the air touches the nostril door, you must count "one" mentally. Do not count out-breaths. Automatically, the air will reenter and you must count "two." In this way, count every in-breath up to eight. When you reach eight, begin again with one. The counting and touching must be simultaneous for this is the secret of achieving mindfulness through this profound exercise. When counting, you become more and more mindful of the in-breaths and out-breaths as they enter in and issue out.

With the third step, you must count both the in-breaths and the out-breaths. When you breathe in and the air touches the door of the nostril, count "one" mentally. When the air goes out and touches the same place, count mentally "two." Again, touching and counting must be simultaneous. You must continue counting every in-breath and out-breath in this way up to eight. Then, you can begin counting again with one.

After a certain period, you will experience just that split second when your mind is fully concentrated on your breathing. You will no longer hear any sound from the external world. This slight moment of mindful concentration is such a tremendous experience, so full of joy, happiness and tranquility, that you will want to continue practicing meditation. If you continue practicing this method regularly, you may experience this mental state repeatedly and for longer and longer periods of time. This is the moment when you lose yourself completely in your mindfulness of breathing.

This leads to the fourth step, called "connection." This occurs when one stops counting and mindfulness becomes uninterruptedly established with one's in-breaths and out-breaths. Thereby, mindful consciousness becomes established by means of this absorption. With counting, one gives attention to the breaths with simultaneous counting and touching. However, in breathing with connection, attention to mindfulness occurs by absorption, attention is given directly to the connection of breathing and mindfulness.

Let us examine this process with the simile of a saw. A person places a tree trunk on level ground and cuts it with a saw. The person's attention is where the saw's teeth touch the tree trunk, but he or she pays no attention to the teeth as the saw cuts. The tree trunk represents mindfulness. The saw's teeth represent the in-breaths and out-breaths. Although the practitioner pays no attention to the particular breaths (the moving saw's teeth), this mindfulness is established where the breathing connects mindfulness (the teeth touch the trunk). Just as a person carries out the task of sawing and achieves the effect of cutting wood, in the meditation of connection, the task of breathing without counting effects deep mindfulness. Here imperfections are abandoned, thoughts are stilled, and fetters are released.

With this type of meditation, it is not long before signs arise as certain meditation states (*jhanas*) are achieved. As bodily disturbances are stilled by the gradual quieting of "gross" in-breaths and out-breaths, the mind and the physical body become light. The physical body at times may feel that it could leap into the air. And, as the practitioner continues with this type of meditation, a stage will occur when "gross" in-breaths and out-breaths have ceased and one becomes conscious of the sign of "subtle" in-breaths and out-breaths. Here the person's breathing will become successively subtler.

The practitioner must then fix his or her mind on the place normally touched by the breaths and mentally fix on the sign thus: "This is the place where they strike." The sign described here differs with individuals. For some, it may be a light touch like cotton, or silk-cotton, or a draft of air. For others, it can appear like a star or a cluster of gems or pearls. For still others, it may have a rough touch like silk-cotton seeds, a peg made of hardwood, a long bright string, a wreath of flowers, a cloud, a lotus flower, a chariot wheel, or a moon or sun disk. In any case, when any such sign appears, the practitioner should fix his or her mind on the sign and anchor the mind upon breathing in and out.

As soon as the sign appears, the five hindrances[1] are suppressed, mindfulness is established and consciousness becomes concentrated. If the practitioner continues fixing upon the sign, the first four meditation states (*jhanas*) may be achieved.[2] The fourth *jhana* is supreme because mental energy can be unveiled to benefit humankind. It is here that our Buddhist loving-kindness meditation can be added in order to channel this energy for the well being of all humankind.

Loving Kindness and Peace

In my spiritual workshops, I train all yogis to achieve up to the fourth *jhana*, and have organized a Peace Mission through the mind deliverance of loving kindness. Our group members meditate upon sending loving kindness to the eight geographical directions—east, southeast, south, southwest, west, northwest, north and northeast—and directions above and below. We send loving kindness to the entire world with our hearts filled with abundant and measureless loving kindness and wishing all to be free from enmity, affliction and anxiety. Our practitioners need to have achieved at least the first *jhana* to effectively send this type of loving kindness to humankind.

"Loving-kindness power" is the specific operational definition of my Peace Mission. If one has real loving kindness, one can radiate a noble, grand peace. Loving kindness breaks away all barriers which separate beings from one another. By loving-kindess power, I mean a special kind of supernatural power of consciousness. For those who practice the breathing meditation outlined above, loving-kindness power can be achieved easily. Through sending this loving-kindness power regularly, we can provide solutions to world problems not resolved by conventional means.

There is immense dissatisfaction (*dukkha*) almost everywhere today. Dissatisfaction creates ill will. Ill will creates hatred. Hatred creates enmity. Enmity creates war; war creates more dissatisfaction and ill will. Thus, a vicious cycle is created. *Why* is this cycle being created? Certainly because there is a lack of proper control over the mind. The Buddha taught that the world is mind-made, the mind predominates over everything. According to Buddhist meditation theory, training oneself first is the prerequisite for solving social problems. Since the state of the outer world is a reflection of our inner selves, individual perfection must be first so that the organic whole of humanity may be perfect.

The advanced stages of *vipassana*, or insight meditation, lead the Buddhist practitioner to this highest perfection. With the power of mind fully developed, the practitioner is trained to become sensitive to the atomic reactions which are ever taking place inside us. The course of training in *vipassana* involves an examination of the inherent tendencies of all that exists within ourselves in order to learn the truth of impermanence (*anicca*), suffering (*dukkha*) and no-self (*anatta*) as taught by the Buddha. Then, following a deep realization of the Four Noble Truths[3] taught by the Buddha, the practitioner breaks through to a state beyond suffering, enters the Streamwinner stage of spiritual life, and enjoys the fruit of his or her endeavors in the "*nibbanic* peace within."

The person who can always enjoy this *nibbanic* peace in all situations is the *arahant*, the Perfect Holy One. The *arahant* does not just enjoy the peace within as a "fruit" of the spiritual life. Rather the *arahant* attains a supermundane consciousness in full realization of *Nibbana* so that no negative feelings can be aroused through any of the sense centers. At the same time, the *arahant*'s body posture becomes strengthened (but both body and mind are at ease and gentle). In other words, the *arahant* is in a state of perfect physical and mental peace.

In my spiritual workshop, I always remind my yogis not to withdraw from society but to effectively serve struggling humanity when they attain the highest state. It is my earnest will always to serve humanity through the mind deliverance of loving kindness. Therefore, I would like to encourage you to meditate on sending loving kindness each day, using mindfulness and loving-kindness meditation. Thus, our thoughts, actions and words may be filled with loving kindness. From trained minds come the right thoughts, right actions and right words that can heal the world.

In conclusion, may I say that the changing of humankind's mental attitude through religion alone is the solution to the world's problems. What is necessary at this moment in history is the mastery over the mind, not just the mastery over matter. It is the Buddha's *Dhamma* (teaching) that should be studied by one and all for a new insight into the realities of the human mind. In Buddhism we have the cure for all mental ills that affect humankind. It is the "evil forces" of the mind (past and present) that are responsible for the present state of affairs all over the world.

There exists a great field for practical research in Buddhism. Buddhists in Myanmar are always eager to welcome those who wish to be free and experience the beauty of the mind. In the *Dhammapada*, the Buddha said: "A beautiful word or thought which is not accompanied by corresponding acts is like a bright flower which has no scent."

Therefore, may I sincerely suggest that you start practicing after listening to or reading this talk. Please come and see. Friends, you are welcome!

On *Zazen*

ZOKETSU NORMAN FISCHER

Here is how the great Japanese Zen Master Dogen (1200–1253) begins *Fukanzazengi*, his fundamental text on *zazen* (Zen meditation practice):

> The Way is basically perfect and all-pervading. How could it be contingent upon practice and realization? The *Dharma* vehicle is free and untrammeled. What need is there for concentrated effort? Indeed, the whole body is far beyond the world's dust. Who could believe in a means to brush it clean? It is never apart from one, right where one is. What is the use of going off here and there to practice?

Zazen is fundamentally a useless and pointless activity. A person is devoted to *zazen* not because it helps anything, or is peaceful, or interesting, or because Buddha tells one to do it—though we may imagine that it helps, or is peaceful, or interesting, or that Buddha recommended it—but simply because one is devoted to it. You cannot argue for it, or justify it, or make it into something good. You just do it because you do it. It is not even a question of wanting to, or not wanting to. *Zazen* for *zazen's* sake.

Birds sing, fish swim, and people who are devoted to *zazen* do *zazen* with devotion all the time, although there is no need for it. Our life is already fine the way it is. Everything that happens is already a manifestation of our original enlightenment even though we do not notice it. We do not need to enter another condition, or improve, or disprove anything. The gentle rain of the *Dharma* is falling all the time evenly and freely on everything; and each thing receives that rain and uses it in its own way, each in a different way. The whole world is unfolding in a beautiful and perfect interplay of forces.

We may have difficulty appreciating this, but, after all, we are only people and why would we not have difficulty? Our difficulty is this: that our minds cannot see difference without making comparisons, without making judgments and preferences. We want either everything to be the same as everything else, which it is although we cannot experience it that way, or if things must be different from one another, we have to struggle to rank them. So, we have this kind of difficulty. It is a difficulty that has to do with knowing and thinking, not with our actual being. As far as our actual being is concerned, whether we have a difficulty or not, we are just fine.

What, then, could be more foolish than the idea of religious cultivation, than the thought that we need to change our condition and become more holy, or more peaceful, or more wise? In fact, such thoughts only remove us from the holiness, peacefulness, and wisdom that are the actual essence of every moment of our lives. These qualities are with us wherever we are right now. What is the use in making efforts to acquire them? Such efforts could only lead us in the wrong direction. Someone once asked the famous Chinese Zen Master Yun-men (d. 949), "What does 'sitting correctly and contemplating true reality' really mean?" Yun-men said "A coin lost in the river is found in the river."

What I have said so far is very true, I think, and we need to appreciate it in order to do *zazen*. If we do not appreciate it, our *zazen* will be very acquisitive. Everything else in our lives is inherently acquisitive because our strong habitual sense of self always demands that we get some good out of everything we do—and we are exhausted by all this activity. But *zazen* is something different. If we do not appreciate its fundamental uselessness, which comes from the fundamental all-rightness of our life, we will turn it into something acquisitive and busy, just like everything else we do.

Another story from Master Yun-men: Once a monk asked him, "What is my self?" Master Yun-men said, "I, this old monk, enter mud and water for you." The monk said, "Then I should crush my bones and tear my body to pieces in gratitude." The Master gave a great shout. He said, "The water of the whole ocean is on your head right now. Speak! Speak!" The monk could not say anything. Master Yun-men answered for him, speaking from the monk's standpoint, "I fear that you, Master, do not think I am genuine."

The problem is that we actually are incapable of seeing *zazen* as useless because our minds cannot accept the fundamental genuineness, the all-rightness of our lives. We are actually very resistant to it, we hate it, because it is too simple and we persistently think we need more. This is not a detail or a quirk of our minds; it is not even a habit really; it is the very nature, deeply, of our minds. The Sanskrit word for consciousness is *vijnana*, which means "to divide," or "to cut." In order for us to have what we call experience, we have to divide or cut reality. Genuineness or all-rightness is wholeness, indivisibility, so it cannot be an experience for us. And even if we practice *zazen* and have an enlightenment experience, we will immediately confuse ourselves with it. Such an experience can be a promising beginning, but we have to be careful to let go of it, not to define it or name it, not to make it into a cherished memory, a hook for our identity.

Dogen goes on:

> And yet, if there is the slightest discrepancy, the Way is as distant as heaven from earth. If the least like or dislike arises, the Mind is lost in confusion. Suppose one gains pride of understanding and inflates one's own enlightenment, glimpsing the wisdom that runs through all things, attaining the Way and clarifying the Mind, raising an aspiration to escalade the very sky. One is making the initial, partial excursions about the frontiers but is still somewhat deficient in the vital way of total emancipation.

He then continues:

> You should therefore cease from practice based on intellectual understanding, pursuing words and following after speech, and learn the backward step that turns your light inwardly to illuminate your self. Body and mind of themselves will drop away, and your original face will be manifest. If you want to attain suchness, you should practice suchness without delay.

This "backward step" is a very famous saying of Master Dogen. It is the opposite of knowing or experiencing; or better, it is "prior to" knowing or experiencing. It is prior not in terms of time, but in terms of depth. In any case, all language fails us here because what I am trying to express does not have to do with space or time, and all our language is built on metaphors of space and time. In a seminar at Green Gulch, one student had a good image for it. He said consciousness is like cutting an onion. The edge of the blade of the knife comes into contact with the skin of the onion and immediately slices it so that the onion is divided. In every moment, we divide the world like this; and so we feel separate and lonely in it, divided from ourself, divided from everything, in exile, lost. And someone else in the seminar added, we cry because of this just as we cry when we divide the onion and release its juices into the air.

The "backward step" is that time when the edge of the blade of the knife touches the skin of the onion. At that precise instant, there is no division—not even between knife and onion, let alone within the onion. There is only one thing contacting itself, in touch completely with itself. This is how our life is in the present moment: one thing in touch with itself, not in the past, in the future, or in the present either. This is the backward step. Resting in the very beginning of the act of consciousness. When I say this, it sounds as if I mean that we should all carefully analyze our mind to watch every act of consciousness. Although this might be a useful exercise that can be done in the midst of and only after careful training in meditation, it is a fundamentally futile one. This is because it is an exercise based on a space-time notion of consciousness. They say in Zen that a fingertip cannot touch itself; and they say that a knife cannot cut itself. In fact, that first undivided moment of consciousness cannot be found in isolation: it pervades the whole of consciousness. The whole act of slicing the onion, even the tears, is the beginning.

Once a monk asked Master Yun-men, "What is my self?" Yun-men replied, "Your self is the one who, when a free meal is being handed out, rushes to get in line."

Again, what I am saying is, I think, true. But, there are two problems with it. First, you may find it hard to understand, and might imagine that someone who is not you understands it, and that someone who is you does not understand it. Thus, you will compare and reinforce your old habit of thinking that you are not all right the way you are. The second problem is that whether you think you understand it or not, what will you do with it? How will you live it?

To the second question, I would say this: just do *zazen* and pay attention to your life. Sit with the spirit of the uselessness of sitting. Enter it not as yourself, but as someone who is bigger than yourself and includes yourself. Do not assume anything about anything. Just sit, as Dogen says, "upright in correct bodily posture, neither inclining to the left nor to the right, neither leaning forward nor backward." Just be determined to be there without any idea of up or down, inside or outside, self or other, until the bell rings or you drop dead, whichever comes first.

And then when you get up and resume your life as a person, just be aware and simple. Know all the time, as you will have discovered laboriously in *zazen,* that what is going on in your mind is just what is going on in your mind, that thoughts and feelings are simply thoughts and feelings. What is actually also going on around you, events to which the thoughts and feelings seem to refer and define, is in reality unknown. Do not forget that, and when you do forget it, remind yourself many, many times. And be sure to keep your sense of humor. Do not get too tangled up in what happens, because while you are tangled up, something else is happening that you are missing. So, move through things as much as you can, just straight ahead, without too much deliberation. Master Yun-men once held up his staff and said, "When a monk sees this staff he just calls it a staff; when he walks he just walks, and when he sits he just sits. In all this, he cannot be stirred."

When we sit in *zazen,* we take care of our posture and try to pay attention to our breathing. When we breathe in, we know this is breathing in; and when we breathe out, we know this is breathing out. We give ourselves with great devotion, creativity, and love to our breath, and we let everything else go without denying anything or burying anything. When we forget our breathing, we remind ourselves and come back. But, we do not make the breath into something, and we do not make the fact of our doing *zazen* into something. There are no "big deals" in Zen, or in *zazen,* because everything in our whole life and in the whole wide world is a big deal. So, how could anything be a big deal? If everything is a big deal there is no such thing as a big deal. What we mean by a big deal is that something is a big deal and something else is not such a big deal. So, we do not worry about our *zazen,* and we do not think we are doing it right or doing it wrong. We just do it. My favorite Zen dialogue about *zazen,* which I quote whenever I have an excuse to do so, is the saying of Master Chao-chou. When a student asked him "What is *zazen*?" he replied, "It is non-*zazen*." The student said, "How can *zazen* be non-*zazen*?" Chao-chou replied, "It is alive!"

Again, in *Fukanzazengi,* Dogen says,

> The *zazen* I speak of is not learning meditation. It is simply the *Dharma* gate of repose and bliss, the practice-realization of totally culminated enlightenment. It is the manifestation of ultimate real-

> ity. Traps and snares can never reach it. Once its heart is grasped, you are like the dragon when he gains the water, like the tiger when she enters the mountain. For you must know that just there in *zazen*, the right *Dharma* is manifesting itself and that, from the first, dullness and distraction are struck aside.

"Ultimate reality" sounds like a pretty exalted idea, but actually where would ultimate reality be? Is it under my *zafu* (meditation cushion)? Is it buried deep within my brain? Is it in a cloud, or under the ocean? I think it is in all those places and everywhere else as well. So, sitting in *zazen* (and not sitting in *zazen*) is not preparation for something else. My *zazen*, Buddha's *zazen*, and your *zazen* are all the same. All are manifestations of ultimate reality. It is not a question of meditation, or nonmeditation. But, it is a wonderful thing because it is the one thing that is incorruptible. Traps and snares can never reach it. Reality is reality no matter what anyone does about it, or does not do about it.

You do not need to understand it, and you cannot understand it. All you need is confidence in it. Once you sit down and have real confidence in sitting down—not because it is something wonderful but just because it is nothing and useless, supremely useless—then you have real confidence in your life. Things certainly could fall apart tomorrow. You could be disgraced and humiliated and lose your job, your reputation, your husband or wife, or even your body. But, it would still be ultimate reality—it would still be real and genuine life—and you would be able to bear it, be with it, and see deeply into it for what it is.

We are living in a historic period in which we understand that it is necessary for all of us to be socially conscious and active in our world. None of us can ignore this call to action. And yet, if we do not practice *zazen*—whether we call it *zazen*, or whatever we call it and however we do it—we cannot act in any accurate way. There has already been plenty of action—too much action. What we need today is not *more* action, we need *enlightened* action. And this means letting go of action, so that, in the concluding words of Dogen's *Fukanzazengi*, "your treasure-store will open up of itself, and you will use it at will."

Harmony, Dialogue and Meditation

HIS HOLINESS THE DALAI LAMA

Spiritual brothers and sisters. At the beginning of my talk let me say something about my basic ideas regarding harmony between the different religious traditions of the world.

Religious Harmony

The need for spirituality is obvious. I think so long as there are human beings, some kind of spirituality is necessary. It may not be necessary for *all* human beings, but at least for millions of human beings. Therefore, there is today a very great interest and need for spirituality. At the same time, it is also clear that in the name of religious traditions there are more divisions among humanity, and in some cases even conflict and bloodshed. Not only in the past, but even today this is happening. This is very, very unfortunate! Therefore, on the one hand, there is still the value of religious traditions. But on the other hand, sometimes unfortunate things happen due to these religious traditions. So the choice must be made to maintain religious traditions while trying to minimize conflicts due to different contemporary situations.

Now, it is also quite clear that different religious traditions—in spite of having different philosophies and viewpoints—all have a great potential to help humanity by promoting human happiness and satisfaction. As a matter of fact, it is quite clear that given the vast array of humanity—of so many different kinds of people, of so many people with different mental dispositions—we need, and so it is far better to have, a variety of religious traditions. Religions are like medicine in that the important thing is to cure human suffering. In the practice of medicine, it is not a question of how expensive the medicine is; what is important is to cure the illness in a particular patient. Similarly, you see, there is a variety of religions with their different philosophies and traditions and the aim or purpose of each is to cure the pains and unhappiness of the human mind. Here too, it is not a question of which religion is superior as such. The question is, which will better cure a particular person.

As a Buddhist monk, a Buddhist practitioner, from my own Buddhist tradition I have learned the importance of the suitability of religions according to an individual's mental disposition. For example, in what we call Mahayana Buddhism, the *bodhisattvayana*, there are different views about reality. Also in the history of Buddhism there have been different interpretations of the *anatma* (no-self) theory. There are the interpretations of such schools as Vaibhashika, Sautrantika, Yogacara and Madhyamika. Also, just within the Vaibhashika School, there are eighteen different subdivisions. And also concerning the *Pratimoksha*, our monastic discipline, there are literally many differences as well.

Each school's interpretation is based on Shakyamuni Buddha's own words as recorded in certain sutras. So it may seem that the one teacher, Shakyamuni Buddha, himself creates contradictions for his own followers. This is certainly not due to his own confusion concerning his own viewpoint. Certainly not. We believe that Shakyamuni Buddha is enlightened, in full realization of the truth. Therefore, we must conclude that he deliberately taught different philosophies according to the different mental dispositions of his followers.

So from just our own tradition, we can learn about how important a person's mental disposition is for determining which religious tradition is best for him or her. It is not a question of determining that one interpretation of reality is true, and that since another is false you therefore should follow this first interpretation. You cannot say that. Even Buddha could not say that. So therefore from this experience it becomes very clear that for certain people, the way of approach, or the method, of Christianity is much more effective than others. For people such as the Muslims, their approach is more suitable. So we cannot say, "This religion is better, that religion is not good." That we cannot say. However on an individual basis we can say that a particular religion is good for us. For example, the Buddhist way is best *for me*. There is no doubt! But this does not mean that Buddhism is best for everyone. And even within Buddhism, Madhyamika philosophy, and particularly the Prasangika School of Madhyamika philosophy, is best for me. But I cannot say that this view is best for *all* Buddhists. We cannot say that!

So it is on this basis that it is extremely important to appreciate all the different religious traditions of the world, and particularly the major world religious traditions. I think that there are sufficient reasons to respect and appreciate all the major world religious traditions.

Interfaith Dialogue

Now, it was within this context that I met with the late Thomas Merton. As a result of meeting with him, my attitude toward Christianity was very much improved. It greatly changed. I always consider him a strong bridge between Buddhism and Christianity. So his sudden death was, I think, a great loss. Now while we remember him, I think the important thing is that we must fulfill his wishes. I think that with our dialogue today we are fulfilling one of his wishes.

I always tell audiences that interfaith dialogue can improve closer understanding between different religious traditions. One type of dialogue involves scholars meeting in a more academic way to clarify the differences and similarities between their traditions. The second type of dialogue involves a meeting between genuine practitioners of different religious traditions. This is to me very, very important; very, very helpful. An example was my meeting with the late Thomas Merton.

The third way of dialogue is pilgrimage by followers of different religious traditions. They can go together as a group in order to make a pilgrimage to the holy places of different religious traditions. The pilgrims should pray together if possible; if not, they can practice silent meditation. This is a very effective way to understand the value or the power of other religious traditions. I personally have gone on such pilgrimages. For example, as a Buddhist I have no particular connection with Jerusalem. But, because I believe that all religious traditions have great potential, with that belief I visited Jerusalem as a pilgrim.

The fourth kind of dialogue is a meeting like the "Day of Prayer for Peace" in Assisi in 1986. While there, religious leaders came together and exchanged a few nice words. That was also very helpful. In the eyes of millions of people, it was very, very helpful. I think our meeting here has a similar practical importance because this kind of work eventually creates a more positive grass-roots atmosphere wherein religious leaders can then discuss various crucial matters.

Now, I think that here the first two kinds of dialogue are actually taking place. Yesterday, scholars Jeffrey Hopkins and Donald Mitchell gave presentations. Mitchell's presentation about his Christian philosophy was really marvelous! Both presentations were very, very marvelous. They also spoke as practitioners; but the presentations were more on the academic level. This is very useful, very helpful.

And then today's presentations were on religious experience. And particularly many of the questions and answers were about how to face anger. That part of the discussion I really felt was a clear example of spiritual dialogue. The Christian practitioners and the Buddhist practitioners both realize that anger is something negative. We both have to work on that problem even if our methods are different. Christians have a faith in God, and through that way they try to work on the problem. Buddhists have another way. But it has the same objective, the same purpose. So, I think this way of exchange through questions and answers is the proper way of dialogue.

We have not come here to advertise our own religion, and certainly not for competition. But I think we should have one kind of constructive competition. The Buddhists should implement what we believe in daily life; and our Christian brothers and sisters should also implement their teachings in daily life. So on that field, I think, we should have some competition. Since each side would like to be better practitioners, there is no harm in such competition—it is really constructive. On the other hand, to say that my practice is better than anothers, I do not think that is of much use. So, that is my basic belief, my basic feeling about the encounter of our religious traditions.

Meditation

Now based on this kind of belief, I am now going to speak about the unique Buddhist practice of what you call meditation or contemplation. However, I do not know the exact meaning of contemplation. But I will try to explain something which can be useful and may be adopted by Christian practitioners. This can be, I think, a way to enrich one another. So, I am not going to talk about whether there is a Creator or not. This is too complicated; and anyway I think it is beyond our concepts. In that regard, it is better to follow one's *own* belief. Then you can achieve some kind of satisfactory result. Otherwise, the issue is too complicated. For centuries there have been great debates in India between Buddhist logicians and non-Buddhist logicians. The result is that the argument is still going on. So, it is better to follow according to one's own belief. To practice, to implement one's belief sincerely and seriously is the important point.

So now we will deal with Buddhist approaches to meditation. The Tibetan word for meditation is *sgom*, which appears in scriptures but is actually part and parcel of ordinary daily life. It means familiarizing yourself with certain particular objects or attitudes. In our daily life we normally engage in one or another kind of "meditation." Take for example when we feel emotionally afflicted from seeing a beautiful object or seeing an object that makes us feel unhappy. In both cases, we use some kind of analytical meditation that includes reasoning. The more we investigate, the more the afflictive emotion develops. And then, after each sort of analytical meditation, you will be able to come to a conclusion or a sort of conviction. You will realize, "Oh, this is something positive!" or "This is something negative!" This conviction of mind is a form of single-pointedness meditation. So, we always use analytical meditation and single-pointedness meditation in our daily life. The very purpose of meditation is to familiarize ourselves with any object or attitude we want to know more about. That is the meaning of meditation as familiarization.

This practice of meditation becomes important for the transformation of our mind. And this must also be true for the Christian practitioner. Of course you are seeking help or blessings from God. But spiritual transformation must also involve our own effort. For example, God's blessing is always present; God's grace is always there. But to the nonbeliever, you see, that blessing may not enter his or her life. Or, it may not enter easily because the level of effort from his or her side is missing. So Christian practitioners also need to practice some kind of personal effort in spirituality. And it is here that meditation is valuable.

For example, how can one develop faith in the proper way through meditation? Using our two types of meditation, first one can practice analytical meditation by thinking about how great God is, how merciful God is. After using these reasons in this analytical meditation, some kind of conviction is reached, "Now, yes, definitely this is the case!" Then, without further investigation, simply settle your mind in that belief, in that faith. This is single-pointedness meditation. These two forms of meditation from the Buddhist tradition must go together. So you see, faith is not just relying on words. Rather it combines one's own experience and the Gospel in developing a firm conviction. That is very important and even necessary in any religion.

There are also two other types of meditation that can be helpful. In the first type, you focus on a particular object and then meditate on it. In this case, you take an object of apprehension to mind. In the second type of meditation, you cultivate your mind in the form of an attitude of meditation. An example of the first type might be when the Christian practitioner is aware of the greatness of God. In that case you have a separate object as the focus of your meditation. An example of the second type would be when the Christian practitioner meditates to cultivate faith. In that kind of meditation, you cultivate your mind in the very nature of faith. In Buddhist practice, when we meditate like this on the attitudes of compassion or loving kindness, our mind transforms into that kind of mentality. However, in Buddhist practice, when we meditate on impermanence, or on *anatma*, we are doing the first type—taking an object to mind.

Now let us turn to the complicated topic of the different varieties of dualism and nondualism. The meanings of dualism and nondualism depend upon the context in which you use the terms. Nevertheless, let us take the example of the awareness of impermanence. Generally speaking, at the beginning this awareness is not through experience but relies on the scriptures or someone else's words. But then, one meditates on it using the kinds of analytical meditation and single-pointedness meditation we discussed before. After much thought and reflection, impermanence becomes familiar. Then, at a certain stage, you realize these reasons and reach a more full conviction concerning impermanence which you can now prove by these reasons with complete confidence.

At this stage of meditation, the awareness of impermanence is much firmer than one's previous awareness. Of course, one already thought that all things are impermanent, always momentarily changing. But then through reasoning in analytical meditation you develop a firm and full conviction. Then going further without anymore reasoning, there is a spontaneous realization of impermanence. Whenever you see something, without any effort there is a spontaneous realization or awareness of impermanence. In that uncontrived state of vivid realization and developed experience of impermanence, there is a kind of direct perception in which your mind is merged, as it were, with impermanence. From that point of view there is no dualistic appearance. This meditative process can have similar results with any religious subject. So, I think it can be useful for our Christian brothers and sisters to utilize also this kind of meditation technique.

Practical Advice

Diet is also important when we engage seriously in the practice of meditation. One should follow a light diet which is also very good for the body. One's daily routine is also important. As with Thomas Merton's routine, getting up early in the morning is very good. Some people, particularly in the city, do the opposite. They stay up very late at night and are very busy and fully alert. Then they are sleeping peacefully after the sun rises the next morning. For a practitioner, that kind of lifestyle is very bad. So, get up early in the morning: the freshness of early morning, the freshness of our mind. And for that you need sufficient sleep by going to bed early. I think that Thomas Merton's routine, read in Sr. Mary Margaret Funk's talk, is very good.

Then there is the question of posture. Generally this is also quite important. You should sit straight. The Buddhist justification for this posture is that if you remain straight then your body energy circulates more normally. If you sit one-sided then the body may not be so balanced. Therefore, you should consider this important. But, I do not think it is very important to sit cross-legged. For some people, instead of helping meditation it causes more pain. So, I do not think it is very important. You can find a more comfortable posture if you wish.

And then there is another thing. According to Buddhist tradition, sometime you may get some kind of extraordinary understanding or awareness. Take faith for example. Sometimes, without a particular reason, some kind of spontaneous feeling may occur. But from our tradition such an experience—while very positive—is not so reliable. One day, faith may be there spontaneously, but the next day it may not. Once we get that kind of spontaneous experience of faith, it is very useful *if* you maintain and sustain that faith through effort. So you should not rely too much on just spontaneous experience. It comes and goes, comes and goes. The other more sustained experience of faith, developed through continuous effort, is much more reliable.

One more matter concerning meditation practice. I think that in both analytical meditation and single-pointedness meditation the important thing is one's sharpness of mind, having a fully alert mind. This is very, very important. Now, in analytical meditation generally a sharpness of mind is essential for the analytical process. But in single-pointedness meditation, fully alert clarity of the mind must also be maintained. Otherwise, sometimes the experience of single-pointedness develops as a result of darkness. This is not at all helpful. You must remain fixed on the object of meditation with full alertness. Otherwise, there is the danger of mistaking a mental sinking for one-pointed meditation. You see, as your alertness reduces, so the movement of the mind automatically reduces. At that moment you may get the feeling that your mind is really focusing on the object. And you may also feel some kind of tranquility. That kind of tranquility is not positive and not constructive. If you cultivate this negative kind of tranquility, the sharpness of your mind will be reduced. This is very harmful. So, it is very, very important to keep a sharp and fully alert mind.

How can you keep full alertness? When your mental energy goes down, then an uplifted state of the mind does not occur. For example, when you start single-pointedness meditation, and if your mind at that moment is in a slightly sad mood, that mood automatically reduces the alertness of mind. So at that time you need to extend some effort in order to heighten the state or spirit of your mind. One method would be to think about God's grace or mercy, or these kinds of things, and to reflect on how fortunate we are. Thinking of these kinds of things, which make you feel happy with more hope and more self-confidence, will uplift your mind.

Sometimes you experience the opposite, namely, your mind may be too excited. That state of mind is also a great hindrance to single-pointedness. When you are about to do single-pointedness meditation and your mind is too distracted due to excitement, then think about the fact that because of this kind of mental attitude your spiritual practice, your spiritual experience, will not develop much. Think that because of this excited state, you will experience a failure of single-pointedness of mind. Then, you see, your mood will become a little reduced. When you see your mind come down a little bit, then with that cooler basis go on to meditate. So, these are methods for avoiding mental dullness and excitement in meditation. And this completes my reflections on the practice of meditation.

The Contemplative Life

JAMES A. WISEMAN, O.S.B.

Contemplation—the word has become so powerfully attractive among Christians of our era that numerous books, videotapes, and audiotapes refer to it in their very titles: *Contemplation and Love, New Seeds of Contemplation, Contemplative Meditation, Contemplative Prayer,* and many, many others. In earlier centuries the attraction of the term was not so widespread in the Church as a whole, but within Christian monasticism there has been hardly any word so frequently used to express the ideal of the monastic way of life. And since most of us at this dialogue are monastics, the majority of my reflections on the spiritual life will be drawn from this realm.

Even though all of us surely have a sense of what the word *contemplation* means, it might be helpful first of all to take a glance at its root meaning, and for this we must turn to ancient Rome. In that renowned city, and long before the coming of Christianity, there were persons known as *augurs* who were responsible for determining the will of the gods by interpreting certain kinds of signs, such as the direction of a flight of birds or of a flash of lightning. Since they needed a clear view of the sky for their augury, they would find an open space, which they called a *templum,* and then carefully mark its borders, an act designated by the verb *contemplor. Contemplatio* thus eventually came to mean any act of diligent, attentive observation, as in the case of an archer carefully taking aim at a target.

While few of the early Christian monks may ever have heard of this etymology, it nevertheless tells us something important about what they considered crucial to their calling. Of all the monastic sayings that have come down to us from the Egyptian and Palestinian deserts of the fourth and fifth century, my favorite is one in which an elder was asked by a younger monk what he could do to keep from being shocked or discouraged when he saw others leaving the monastic life and returning to the world. Rather than give an abstract, theoretical reply, the elder took an example from the world of nature to illustrate his point. He said the young monk should consider the case of a dog who sees a wild hare and sets off in pursuit until he catches it. Other dogs, seeing the first one running but not seeing the hare, will run after the lead dog for awhile but then give up and go back to where they were at first. The elder concluded with the following words:

> Only the one who has seen the hare follows it till he catches it, not letting himself be turned from his course by those who go back, not caring about the ravines, rocks and undergrowth. So it is with him who seeks Christ as Master: ever mindful of the Cross, he cares for

> none of the obstacles that stand in his way, till he reaches the Crucified.[1]

What I consider most noteworthy about this saying is the way in which it so imaginatively uses a simple, mundane example to sum up the lofty goal of the monks' *contemplatio*: Christ. Christ was the one they sought, holding him in view kept them faithful to their commitment, and this—or, more broadly, remaining mindful of God—was accordingly the heart of their contemplative life. A great deal of Christian spiritual teaching down the ages simply spells out in greater detail ways in which this can best be done. I want to talk about a couple of these ways, as they are found both in the spiritual, monastic tradition and in my own experience.

Finding Nourishment in the Scriptures

First, like devout practitioners of the other great world religions, all genuine Christians have a profound reverence for their scriptures. Sometimes we think of the early desert monastics as persons who tried to compete with one another in ascetical exercises like fasting, but at its best their bodily fasting was only a side effect of their finding far more substantial nourishment in biblical texts that were for them truly the word of God. Another of my favorite desert sayings is an account of a visit that one of the elders paid to another. These monks were always very careful to be hospitable, so the host prepared some lentils for them to eat and then suggested that they say a few prayers before beginning their meal. The saying concludes with the following words, which beautifully convey a sense of the rich nourishment that these men found in sacred scripture: "The first completed the whole Book of Psalms, and the [other] brother recited the two great prophets by heart. When morning came, the visitor went away, and they forgot the food."[2]

Since we will be having a separate talk on *lectio divina*, I do not want to dwell on this point at too great length, but it is important to note that the Bible could be so nourishing for these early monastics only because in praying it, whether by heart or by prayerfully meditating on the written text, they were convinced they were truly meeting their Lord and Savior. Holy Scripture was not there for some ulterior purpose, a mere means to some loftier end, but was itself life-giving. *This* is what these men and women were aiming for, *this* was a privileged moment of their ongoing *contemplatio*.

In my own experience, and despite the fact that I cannot recite any complete book of the Bible by heart as some of my monastic forebears could do, the scriptures have likewise been life-giving. In a special way this is true of the Psalter, that book of 150 Psalms which was the preeminent prayerbook of ancient Israel and has remained such for the Christian Church as well. Whether praying alone in my cell or with my fellow monks in choir, how nourishing and encouraging are such lines as the following from Psalm 103:

> As the heavens tower over the earth,
> so God's love towers over the faithful.
> As far as the east is from the west,
> so far have our sins been removed from us.
> As a father has compassion on his children
> so the Lord has compassion on the faithful. (vv. 11–13)

Such words not only confirm me in a sense of my lovableness despite an awareness of my own infidelities, but also engender a desire to show a similar love and compassion to others, even as the First Letter of St. John urges us when it says: "Beloved, if God so loved us, we ought also to love one another. No one has ever seen God; if we love one another, God abides in us and his love is perfected in us" (1 Jn. 4:11–12).

This scriptural teaching was well understood by the early monastics as well. How wonderful are those stories in which a wise, discerning elder is able to console another weighed down by a sense of sinfulness, or those other narratives when a monk gives to another what he needs to complete his work, as in the following account:

> It was said of a brother that having made some baskets he was putting on the handles when he heard his neighbor saying, "What can I do? Market day is near and I have no handles to put on my baskets." Then he took the handles off his own baskets and brought them to the brother, saying, "Here are these handles which I have leftover; take them and put them on your baskets." So he caused his brother's work to succeed by neglecting his own.[3]

Another of the early desert monks, in his concern for the poor, sold his one possession, a copy of the Gospels, and explained his action by saying that he had even sold the word that commanded him to sell all and give to the poor.[4]

Doing Everything with and for God

But have we here, with however laudable examples of care for others, strayed from the topic of contemplation? Not at all. At its best the Christian tradition has always recognized that the contemplative life is simply a fully integrated life, in which *all* our activities, whatever they may be, can be the occasion for, or can grow out of, that mindfulness of God which is the heart of contemplation. One particularly fine instance of this teaching can be found in a homily of St. Basil, that great legislator of the Eastern Church whose works St. Benedict recommends in his own *Rule*. After quoting the insistent words of St. Paul, "Whether you eat or drink, or whatever else you do, do all to the glory of God" (1 Cor. 10:31), Basil goes on in the following words:

> When you sit down to table, pray. When you take bread, give thanks to [God] who gave it. When you strengthen the weakness of the body with wine, be mindful of Him who gave you this gift to rejoice the heart and do away with infirmities. . . . When you put on your outer garment, let your heart swell with the love of God, who both winter and summer has given us suitable clothing which protects life and covers nakedness. And is the day done? Then thank God, who for the works of the day gave us the service of the sun and [gave us] fire for light in the night and to serve us in the other necessities of life. The night gives us still other reasons for prayer. When you look up into heaven and gaze upon the beauty of the stars, pray to the Lord of all things visible and adore God, the most excellent Creator of the universe who made all things in wisdom. . . . In this way you will pray without ceasing even though you do not [always] express your prayer in words, for by the whole conduct of your life you will unite yourself to God, and so your very life will become a continuous, uninterrupted prayer.[5]

The same contemplative ideal of a fully integrated life, all of it lived in awareness of God, can be found in early Celtic monasticism. In one of his last books, Thomas Merton quoted a beautiful poem composed by St. Columba, presumably at a time when the saint was living on the island of Iona off the west coast of Scotland. Part of it goes like this:

> That I might bless the Lord who conserves all:
> Heaven with its countless bright orders,
> Land, strand and flood,
> That I might search the books all—
> That would be good for any soul;
> At times kneeling to beloved Heaven,
> At times singing Psalms,

At times contemplating the King of Heaven, . . .
At times working without compulsion—
That would be delightful;
At times picking kelp from the rocks,
At times fishing,
At times giving food to the poor,
At times in my solitary cell.[6]

You will have noticed that St. Columba does once use the term *contemplating* in those verses—"At times contemplating the King of Heaven"—but the contemplative nature of his life is surely to be found in the entirety of such a day. Whether singing psalms, picking kelp, serving the poor, or sitting alone in his monastic cell, Columba was doing everything in profound awareness of the presence of God. There was here no disjunction between the secular and the sacred, for Columba's abiding awareness of his God helped sanctify and unify his entire day. *This is what contemplative life is all about in the best of our tradition.*

This is definitely what first attracted me to the monastic life when I was still in my teens, even though at that time I would not have expressed all this in terms of contemplation. It simply seemed to me that the monastic life, in colloquial jargon, "had it all together." Here was a way of living in which there were no great gulfs between the sacred and the profane, the eternal and the temporal, prayer and work. Everything fit together, and there were a number of persons of similar persuasion to support one by word and example.

Needless to say, one does not experience this deep integration all of a sudden. It is a matter of slow growth, with some inevitable backsliding, for it is all too easy to overlook the goodness of another and become irritated by his or her flaws, thereby falling into the judgmentalism that monastics from Abba Moses in the Egyptian desert to little Therese in her Carmel at Lisieux warned against so eloquently. There is also the danger, which I often experience, of becoming so caught up in one or another project that the essential symbols and practices of the life are unable to exercise their full power of fostering the mindfulness of God: I refer to such observances as the thrice-daily Angelus, the times and places of stricter silence, and in a major way the magnificent progression of the Church's liturgical year correlated so sensitively with the changing of the seasons. But if St. Benedict near the end of his *Rule* urges us to bear patiently the weaknesses of one another, it is just as important to be patient with ourselves and our own failings. The namesake of little Therese, St. Teresa of Avila, had it right when she wrote in her brievary the short poem commonly known as her "bookmark":

> Let nothing disturb thee,
> Let nothing affright thee;
> All things are passing,
> God only is changeless.
> Patience attains
> All that it strives for.
> Whoever has God
> Is lacking in nothing.
> God alone suffices.

Being Mindful of God in All Walks of Life

While most of my examples thus far have been taken from monasticism, I hasten to add in conclusion that this ideal of the spiritual life is one for all people. One of my favorite authors is a British medical doctor, Sheila Cassidy, who in her book *Prayer for Pilgrims* describes not only the way she sets aside a certain time each morning for prayerful meditation, but also the way in which she allows the rest of her day to be equally contemplative. She writes:

> I go to my work and to a different mode of prayer. Here my mind is fully engaged with the work in hand. I am a doctor and here in the hospital there are diagnoses to be made, problems to be solved, patients to be seen, relatives to be comforted, students to be taught. Here I sing no hymns, read no psalms, but work with and for my God. Christ's is the face I look for in the unconscious motorcyclist rushed in off the motorway, his the help I invoke as I struggle to set up thc blood transfusion, and it is he whom I thank when a brief flicker of an eyelid shows that consciousness is not far away and that this young man at least will be reprieved.[7]

What is this telling us? That whether hermit or doctor, nun or engineer, monk or postal worker, all Christians are called to live out those words of St. Paul that I quoted earlier: "Whether you eat or drink, or whatever else you do, do all to the glory of God." This is a charter statement of the Christian contemplative life. How it correlates with the life of our Buddhist sisters and brothers is something we will now be able to explore in our dialogue together.

Lectio Divina

MARY MARGARET FUNK, O.S.B.

St. Benedict prescribes in his *Rule* that we are to do *lectio divina* four to six hours a day.[1] While *lectio* is reading, *lectio divina* as spiritual reading is listening in that reading with the ear of our heart.[2] It is using our spiritual senses.[3] At the literal level of interpretative reading, one "names" historical or objective meanings. Thus, any serious Christian spiritual seeker must study the scripture and the commentaries to know about what she is seeking. But, the spiritual meaning of scripture is grasped only by the spiritual senses. The monastery is that school which is not for academic excellence, but is for the refinement of these spiritual senses in prayer, in the seeking of God. How does one cultivate the spiritual senses? How does one do *lectio divina*? That is the challenge of this little talk.

The Experience of Thomas Merton

First, let us look at a monk from right here at Gethsemani who actually did *lectio divina*. I would like to quote from a letter of Thomas Merton where he first shares his daily schedule, and then his actual process of prayer within that schedule. In this letter to the Sufi scholar Abdul Ch. Aziz, Merton gives this detailed account of his hermitage day:

> My Very Dear Friend, I go to bed about 7:30 at night and rise about 2:30 in the morning. On rising, I say part of the canonical office, consisting of the psalms, lessons, etc. Then I take an hour or an hour and a quarter for meditation. I follow this with Bible reading, and then make some tea or coffee . . . with perhaps a piece of fruit or some honey. With breakfast, I begin reading and continue reading and studying until about sunrise. Now the sun rises very late; in summer it rises earlier, so this period of study varies, but it is on the average about two hours.
>
> At sunrise I say another office of psalms, etc., then begin my manual work, which includes sweeping, cleaning, cutting wood, and other necessary jobs. This finishes about nine o'clock, at which time I say another office of the psalms. If I have time, I may write a few letters, usually short (today is Sunday and I have more time). After this, I go down to the monastery to say Mass, as I am not yet permitted to offer Mass in the hermitage. Saying Mass requires an altar, an acolyte who serves the Mass, special vestments, candles and so on. It is, in a way, better to have all this at the monastery. It would be hard

to care for so many things and keep them clean at the hermitage. After Mass, I take one cooked meal in the monastery. Then I return immediately to the hermitage, usually without seeing or speaking to anyone except the ones I happen to meet as I go from place to place. (These I do not ordinarily speak to as we have a rule of strict silence. When I speak, it is to the abbot, whom I see once a week, or to someone in a position of authority, about necessary business.)

On returning to the hermitage I do some light reading, and then say another office about one o'clock. This is followed by another hour or more of meditation. On feast days I can take an hour and a half or two hours for this afternoon meditation. Then I work at my writing. Usually, I do not have more than an hour and a half or two hours at most for this each day. Following that, it being now late afternoon (about four), I say another office of psalms, and prepare for myself a light supper. I keep down to a minimum of cooking, usually only tea or soup, and make a sandwich of some sort. Thus, I have only a minimum of dishes to wash. After supper, I have another hour or more of meditation, after which I go to bed. . . .

Now you ask about my method of meditation. Strictly speaking, I have a very simple way of prayer. It is centered entirely on attention to the presence of God and to His will and His love. That is to say that it is centered on faith by which alone we can know the presence of God. One might say this gives my meditation the character described by the Prophet as "being before God as if you saw Him." Yet it does not mean imagining anything or conceiving a precise image of God, for in my mind this would be a kind of idolatry. On the contrary, it is a matter of adoring Him as invisible and infinitely beyond our comprehension, and realizing Him as all. My prayer tends very much to what you call *fana* [*annihilation, kenosis*]. There is in my heart this great thirst to recognize totally the nothingness of all that is not God. My prayer is then a kind of praise rising up out of the center of Nothing and Silence. If I am still present to "myself" this I recognize as an obstacle. If He wills He can then make the Nothingness into a total clarity. If He does not will, then the Nothingness actually seems itself to be an object and remains an obstacle. Such is my ordinary way of prayer, or meditation. It is not "thinking about" anything, but a direct seeking of the Face of the Invisible. Which cannot be found unless we become lost in Him who is Invisible.

I do not ordinarily write about such things and ask you therefore to be discreet about it. But I write this as a testimony of confidence and friendship. It will show you how much I appreciate the tradi-

> tion of Sufism. Let us therefore, adore and praise God and pray to Him for the world which is in great trouble and confusion. I am united with you in prayer during this month of Ramadan and will remember you on the Night of Destiny. I appreciate your prayers for me. May the Most High God send His blessing upon you and give you peace.[4]

Over a year later, in another letter to Aziz, Merton further explains that while one has a lot of time for reading in the solitary life, it seems to be difficult to absorb more than a few pages before wanting to move to meditation and prayer. And we know that above all, prayer is a gift from God. This letter I have read from Thomas Merton is a precious disclosure. Written in 1966 here at Gethsemani, it humanly and humbly discloses one monk's gift.

Note the pattern of *lectio divina* in Merton's letter. He writes of reading scripture, meditating, praying the psalms, and sitting before the gaze of God, "being before God as if you saw Him." Here we see the pattern of *lectio divina*: reading (*lectio*), meditation (*meditatio*), prayer (*oratio*), and contemplation (*contemplatio*). Notice also that the centerpiece is the revelatory texts of scripture. Merton reports that only a few pages would suffice to call him to meditation and prayer. Notice here the reciting of the psalms, planting them ever deeper in the heart. Elsewhere, he speaks of praying without ceasing, being aware of God, as he makes his tea, builds a fire, walks in the woods. This contemplative awareness of God, of his "gaze," of "seeing" him, of being "called" by him to meditation and prayer indicates an awareness of the spiritual senses cultivated in the contemplative community, skilled in the practice of *lectio divina*. It takes a lifetime to learn and appreciate the monastic culture that provides the climate for *lectio divina*. For the sake of our dialogue, I would like to present a short teaching on *lectio* as we practice it in our monastic culture at Our Lady of Grace Monastery.

Our Daily Practice

Most sisters begin with reading scripture. This text is accompanied with readings from the patristic writers of the first Christian millennium. These saints provide an inspiring example of the fruit of their *lectio divina*. Some sisters use other classic texts such as *The Cloud of Unknowing*.[5] In this spiritual reading, one listens to the text with the *ear of the heart*. Thus, it is already a prayer of desire, a yearning that becomes thirst. This kind of "reading" has to be taught, since in our times we read only with our mind for information. *Lectio divina* is not functional, but personal. It is closer to ritual than intellectual activity because it is reading with one's body and soul.[6]

When done wholeheartedly, *lectio* is followed by "discursive meditation." This conceptual activity takes several forms such as (1) memorizing the text and reciting it during manual work;[7] (2) ruminating about the text;[8] (3) studying in dialogue with the text by using commentaries and study guides, footnotes, or cross references; (4) lingering on a text, setting it to music or another art form. This type of meditation is *about* the text and moves organically toward the *subject* of the text. In this spiritual movement, a relationship with God emerges.[9] And this emergence brings forth two kinds of response.[10]

The first response in meditation is *oratio*, prayer on the conscious level. The practitioner shifts from reading, that is listening with a grateful heart, to *oratio* prayer. In *oratio* prayer, the heart responds to the sacred Word in many forms of vocal or mental prayer. Prayer rises. The memory, filled with ancient texts, becomes one's own inner conversation. A dialogue happens with one passage, or a word literally lingers on in one's consciousness. Sometimes there are no words exchanged—just inklings are evoked from parallel situations one has read about in *lectio*.[11]

The second response in meditation shifts to a deeper silence—without words or any visualizations—where "spiritual resting" is nonconceptual. This experience slips beneath ordinary consciousness since it is without words and concepts. It is deep silence, which by God's grace alone may become *contemplatio*.[12] Contemplation happens.[13] St. Gregory the Great coined the classic description for this prayer as "resting in God."

The goal of the monastic journey is to find God. The challenge to the monastic is to order her life in such balance and harmony that contemplation can happen. In a Christian monastery we work and pray. All our work and prayer has as its end, contemplation. We order our day around the communal prayer of Divine Office and Eucharist, and the individual prayer of *lectio divina*. Our work is our prayer and prayer is our work.[14] The intention of prayer and practices of prayer can be done while we work, if we select works that are compatible with a recollected life. If we must serve in more demanding conditions, we consider this a privilege because the real fruit of contemplation is selfless service. Christ, the true center of contemplation, can also be found in the poor, the ignorant, and the sick.

In practice, most nuns I know do not do *lectio divina* in a single sitting; that is, first reading, then meditation, *oratio* prayer, and contemplation. Rather they speak of an all-day rhythm in which *lectio* plays a formative role. For example, one may start the day with a period of quiet sitting such as centering prayer. Then, one may do *lectio* for fifteen minutes, and reflection on the reading for another fifteen minutes. Some *lectio* and meditation are also done along with, or in preparation for, the readings of the Divine Office and/or the Eucharist. Other *lectio* is a sustained continuous reading of a book of the Bible or writings of the Fathers. Many do *lectio* during a holy hour before the Blessed Sacrament. Then they recite prayers all day long while walking, sitting, standing, doing manual labor, or just while waiting. This is the *oratio* time; literally, every waking moment is seen as depending on God's grace and faithfulness. And finally, another period of quiet meditation may conclude the day.

This all-day-long interior prayer, with individual periods of *lectio* and discursive meditation punctuated with the common prayer of the Divine Office three or fours times a day, and with the daily Mass as the center of the day, is the monastic life. This sacred culture nourishes our spiritual senses, and, thereby, our sensitivity to the abiding presence of God. So, St. Benedict was not too demanding when he prescribed four to six hours daily of *lectio divina!*

Difficulties on the Journey

A modern difficulty in the practice of the spiritual life is how to keep a steady practice and reduce the level of interior noise so that prayer happens. A meditation practice that calms the mind, stills the body, and awakens the interior spiritual senses is helpful, indeed, essential. This is why at our monastery, we teach the method of centering prayer, or sitting meditation.[15] Centering prayer is a contemporary form of the prayer of the heart, the prayer of simplicity, the prayer of faith, the prayer of simple regard; it is a method of reducing the obstacles to the gift of contemplative prayer and of facilitating the development of habits conducive to responding to the inspiration of the Holy Spirit.

We teach centering prayer as a little method to still the mind for contemplation. We practice two periods of 20 minutes each day. In and of itself, it is not strictly speaking prayer, nor is it *lectio divina*. Centering prayer is the little device of using the sacred word to signal our intent and consent to the presence of God. It can be used at any point along the process of *lectio divina* because it not only facilitates the "resting in God" as in contemplation, but it also prepares the mind to be clear for meditating on the Word, or it opens the heart to pray with zeal and attentiveness.

Another difficulty arises as *lectio divina* is practiced regularly and takes on a life of its own. When this happens, as with all spiritual practices, fidelity is tested. Resistance arises alongside the greater desire for union with God. Remembrance of sin and longing for God produces compunction of heart, sometimes accompanied with the *gift of tears*. Memories stored in the body arise and the psychological effects of repressed emotions peel off either gradually or suddenly as the false self is purified.[16]

During this purification, the classic eight thoughts rise to one's consciousness from personal or original sin (inherited consequences of the sins of others) that has been stored in one's unconscious. Through our practice we recognize gluttony, impurity, avarice, anger, sadness, acedia (despondency, depression, listlessness, a distaste for the spiritual life without any specific reason), vainglory, and pride. Once noticed, these thoughts can be redirected toward a deeper purity of heart and a more committed life of charity. *Lectio*, vigils, and prayer—these are the things that at this difficult time lend stability to the wandering mind.[17] Fasting and wakefulness are helpful to assist one in remaining faithful in prayer.[18] Ascetical practices, when done with the right motivation, remove obstacles to prayer so that prayer can happen.[19]

Listening to Scripture

As one's spiritual life is deepened through these difficult episodes, *lectio divina* leads the monastic to listen more profoundly to scripture with the spiritual senses.[20] Depending on which patristic source you study, there are generally four levels of scriptural meaning that are taught. The first refers to the literal, historical, narrative meaning of the text.[21] The allegorical sense is the second. This is often called the Christological sense of scripture and has as its main characteristic the act of reading the importance of the Christ event back into the scriptures. The third is the moral or behavioral sense, which challenges us not to be hearers of the Word without doing the Word.

Combine the moral senses with an allegorical storyline, and the reader takes the passage to heart: "That sinner is me!" or, "I have been that ignorant disciple!" I enter into the drama of salvation history, both as an individual on a journey to God, and as part of a collective, the ecclesial gathering we call "Church." Hence, many passages of scripture have a surplus of meaning.

The fourth level of reading scripture is the mystical, where God comes to abide in a contemplative indwelling: "You are my friends, remain in me" (1 Jn 4:16). This fourth sense is sometimes called the unitive, indicating that through *lectio* at this mystical level we are one with Christ. And since Christ is one with the Father and the Holy Spirit, we are one with the Trinity.

In this strictly spiritual reading of scripture, we borrow terms from the sensory world to convey the effect of the experience of union. When spiritual writers speak of this experience, or "nonexperience," they use a curious language of the five physical senses. It is "as if" there is sight, touch, smell, sound, taste but in fact there is no perception whatsoever![22] It is the practice of *lectio divina* that uses the spiritual senses to "hear," "taste," and "see" spiritual realities not immediately available to ordinary consciousness. As we contemplate this paradox, one wonders if we are talking about the reader's experience or the scripture's intended meaning. In *lectio divina* at this deepest level are we reading the intended meaning of the author? Or is the reader "hearing" levels of deeper consciousness? The answer is both. This interaction is *lectio divina*. It is an interaction between scripture and consciousness that continues throughout one's lifetime, always leading the reader deeper in the spiritual life.

The Fruits of Lectio Divina

In describing this spiritual journey of *lectio divina*, traditionally we use the language of relationship. Let me explain this to you by drawing on the four levels of *lectio divina* made famous by Guigo II in the twelfth century: *lectio, meditatio, oratio,* and *contemplatio*. We get acquainted with Christ through reading (*lectio*). We enter into a relationship with study and meditation (*meditatio*). The relationship becomes a friendship through an on-going dialogue of praying to God and listening to the ever-present impulses of the Spirit (*oratio*). Finally, it is through commitment that we enter into union with God through deep silence and adoration (*contemplatio*).

What is the "result" of the practice of *lectio divina?* The fruit of prayer motivates us to love one another. If we love the poor, we can be certain that our love is not for the self. The test of prayer, of the truth of our relationship with Christ, is to imitate Christ's love and service without return. Selfless service and compassion is not optional in the Christian spiritual life! That is why in Fr. Wiseman's talk the contemplative is characterized as being most of all a servant caring for the needs of others. For example, I witness a tireless effort among my sisters to work for the liberation of those oppressed by institutionalized violence. These sisters are articulate and ready to sacrifice personal comfort (and sometimes even risk financial support for our community). Our sisters work for justice as the fruit of their contemplation. They feel from their hearts an inner impulse to live for the good of others, to sow seeds of peace and justice in the lives of all they serve.

Other fruits of this practice include a renewed vigor in the spiritual life, a more profound insight and understanding of the scriptures, the sustained ability to study and even memorize scripture and spiritual texts, and the ability to relate to others and to carry out the actions of the day from the heart. In this more advanced spiritual life, there is an awakening to the fact that Jesus Christ lives in our minds and hearts.[23] In the language of relationship, Christ blesses us with an ongoing intimacy. Let me conclude, then, with an example in which we can "see," if we use our spiritual sense of sight, an example of this sacred intimacy. Once I was walking behind Sister Mary Robert going to Communion. She was 84. I told her that I hoped that when I was 84, I could walk with such poise and grace. She told me, "You will, when you know that you are walking in the presence of God!"

4

Growth and Development

On the eve of our dialogue, Buddhists and Christians gathered together in front of the monastery wall to plant a tree of friendship. When His Holiness the Dalai Lama joined us, he went directly to greet an elderly Cambodian monk, the Ven. Ghosananda, who is the Supreme Patriarch of Cambodian Buddhism. As he approached the Ven. Ghosananda, His Holiness bent over so low that his hands, pressed together in a gesture of reverence, seemed to brush along the tops of the grass. When they met and embraced, the smiles on their faces were radiant with joy and loving kindness.

Looking at the Ven. Ghosananda, one has the impression that not only his smile, but his whole body is radiant. It seems as if his skin has been washed so clean that it shines. One can only wonder what this man has seen, what he has experienced of the terrible killing fields in his home country. One thing however is obvious: whatever his experience has been, it has brought forth extraordinary growth in the spiritual life.

Having discussed types of prayer, meditation and contemplation in Buddhism and Christianity on the first day of our dialogue, the second day was devoted to presentations on the stages of spiritual development that we discern in our respective traditions. First, we heard from the Theravada tradition of Buddhism. The Ven. Dr. Vajiragnana from Sri Lanka speaks about the seven stages of purification through which meditators are guided in his tradition. From the ever deepening stages of moral excellence through the higher states of mental culture, the Theravadin is led to profound insight about the condition of existence, and, finally, to spiritual enlightenment and *Nibbana*. With *Nibbana* as a basis, one achieves a new lineage of awakened consciousness that evolves into holiness.

Eshin Nishimura, a Zen Master from Japan, presents the stages of Zen practice from the Rinzai perspective. Nishimura sees Zen practice as the reexperience of Buddha's self-inquiry. Starting with the Great Doubt concerning our suffering condition, with the guidance of a Zen Master one strengthens a Great Belief in the power of self-awakening, and a Great Effort from a deeper core of one's being. With the practice of *koans*, one then faces the great doubt mass which must break itself into the Great Awakening. This Awakening is then lived in its unique expression of one's life.

His Holiness the Dalai Lama presents the path to calm abiding. He discusses the factors that oppose such spiritual growth and their antidotes. In this regard, he describes certain kinds of meditation objects that he feels can be useful to all religious practitioners. He also discusses the use of mindfulness and the need to avoid such things as the scattering of concentration. His Holiness concludes by discussing the stages of spiritual growth that lead to calm abiding, as well as the stages of further spiritual growth that can develop from such calm abiding.

Pierre de Béthune discusses how, in Christian spirituality, prayer can be a lifework. Drawing on two-thousand years of spiritual research, de Béthune presents the three main stages of spiritual ascent to God that follow a trinitarian pattern. The first stage is one of awakening and reorientation of one's life toward God. The second stage is characterized by a following of Christ through meditation and communion. The final stage crosses a new threshold into overflowing joy and peace "inflamed" by the Holy Spirit. Here one finds freedom, embracement of all creation, and silent transformation under the "shadow" of the Spirit.

GilChrist Lavigne presents some of the spiritual phenomena that one experiences during the three stages that de Béthune describes. With regard to the first stage, GilChrist stresses the change of heart that takes place and leads from self-centeredness, through an often painful opening of self-knowledge, to simplicity and compassion for others. During the second stage, these virtues develop as one participates more and more fully in the very life of Christ. In this process of divinization, sometimes marked by further inner struggle, the qualities of Christ become one's own. Finally, in the third stage, a new inner harmony and unity that is found in God is reflected in one's actions and outward appearance. One may also have visions and supernatural abilities, but the true evidence of holiness is a life radiant with light, joy, peace and love.

Stages in the Buddhist Path of Purity

VEN. DR. M. VAJIRAGNANA

In the religious path of Theravada Buddhism, meditators are guided through *The Seven Stages of Purification*. These seven states of purification form the substructure of two later works that are both considered spiritual classics. The first is *The Path of Freedom* by Upatissa Thera; and the second is *The Path of Purification* by Buddhaghosa Thera, which holds the pride of place in the Theravada commentarial tradition. These seven stages are first described in the *Rathavinita Sutta* which is a dialogue between the Ven. Sariputta and the Ven. Punna Mantaniputta. The Ven. Sariputta, who was considered to have understood the *Dhamma* second only to the Buddha, questions his friend on the prominent features of living the holy life according to the Buddha's teachings. The striking replies highlight the stages of the Buddhist path, and still to this day are the essential guide for all would-be meditators in Theravada Buddhism.

One noteworthy feature of the instructions given by Ven. Punna Mantaniputta is his colorful simile of a relay of chariots. He made it clear that to advance on the Path of Purity one must follow the seven stages in sequence as a king would organize a relay of chariots to get from one point to a distant destination. He would mount the first chariot at point A and energetically drive to point B. At that time, he would fully understand the nature of both the horses and the vehicle. At point B, he mounts a fresh chariot to point C and so on until he arrives at the gate of his destination. Each stage must be energetically experienced and understood until one arrives at the goal—the seventh stage—*Nibbana*.

Both the first and second stages are likened to the roots of a great tree. These are the "Purification of Virtue" and the "Purification of Mind." The totality of the holy life pivots upon these two. Without both of these, there can be no success in any religious life. They must be fully appreciated and constantly nourished by the individual until they become implicit parts of the character of the aspirant.

The *Purification of Virtue* consists of ever deepening stages of moral excellence. Beginning with the basic five precepts—not to kill, steal, commit sexual misconduct, lie, and become intoxicated—through their expansion into the eight and then ten precepts, moral virtue reaches its full refinement in the Monastic Code (the *Patimokkha*). The role of shame and dread of moral transgression as the "Twin Guardians" of all vocal and bodily actions are given great prominence, for they lead to a mind free of the guilt and remorse that can be so destructive to the spiritual life. In this way, the necessary moral foundation is laid for the development of the five spiritual faculties of confidence, energy, mindfulness, concentration, and understanding.

The second stage is the *Purification of the Mind*. By this is meant the attainment of the eight meditative states (*jhanas*). There are listed forty meditation objects, but they can be selected according to the individual personality. Just as the earlier moral purification removed obstacles caused by immoral conduct, so the development of "tranquility meditation" (*samatha bhavana*) removes the more subtle obstacles within the mind. These are known as the "five hindrances" of sensual desire, ill-will, sloth and torpor, restlessness and remorse, and finally skeptical doubt.

In these meditative states, the mind is cleared of all impediments and the meditator develops confidence, the spiritual faculties, and the energy and concentration that are factors of enlightenment. On the other hand, these meditative experiences do not in themselves lead to the wisdom necessary for enlightenment. They are not final accomplishments, but momentary interludes. Therefore, there is a second method of meditation which leads not to the suppression of these defilements, but to their complete eradication. This is known as "insight meditation" (*vipassana bhavana*), and since it leads to spiritual enlightenment, it becomes the dominant form of meditation in the remaining stages of spiritual growth. It is generally understood that a combination of these two meditative methods—*samatha* and *vipassana*—produces the quickest results.

The first two stages are concerned with the purification of the person. First, on the moral level, there is a purification of speech and action. Second, at the level of mind, there is a purification of unwholesome mental and emotional defilements. The third stage is called the *Purification of View*. Here, the meditator begins to clarify his or her understanding of reality, opening up the way to deeper spiritual insight. The differences between the body and the mind, and their separate natures, are discerned. On the one side is the "aggregate" (*khandha*) of insentient matter, and on the other is sentient mind with its other four aggregates of feelings, perceptions, mental formations, and consciousness. This insight is important as it sets the meditator on the path of wisdom that will lead to the realization of the Buddha's teaching of "no-self" (*anatta*) which states that the human psychophysical organism does not constitute an unchanging substantial entity whatsoever. This also leads to an appreciation of the constantly changing and insubstantial nature of all animate and inanimate beings.

The next stage, the *Purification of Overcoming Doubt*, draws the understanding to the cause-and-effect relationship between the body and the mind. The meditator comes to realize that consciousness never arises unless there co-arises a particular sense faculty coupled with a sense object. (Here the mind with its emotions and thoughts is considered a "sixth sense.") One of the exercises used to draw out this understanding involves noting one's mental intention before an act (such as intending to walk), and an act (such as walking). This action arises dependent on the intentional thought. On the other hand, when the meditator becomes "mentally" aware of breath sensations at the nostrils, he or she realizes that this awareness arises dependent on those "physical" sensations. This relationship of cause and effect is then extended to one's understanding of the whole universe. All existing phenomena are understood to be in an interrelated process of cause and effect.

The fifth stage, the *Purification of Knowledge and Vision of What Is Path and Not-Path,* again changes the person's perspective. This time one observes the "three characteristics of existence," namely, impermanence (*anicca*), dissatisfaction (*dukkha*), and the insubstantiality of self (*anatta*). For instance, the meditator experiences the momentary nature of the breath and realizes that "All formations of existence ever and again arise as something new!" Insights such as this are a delight to the meditator who now begins to experience all sorts of wonderful states brought about by the purity and concentration of the mind. However, because these states all hold the danger of attachment and can be mistaken for enlightenment, they are known as the "ten impurities" of effulgence of light, knowledge, rapture, tranquility, happiness, determination, energy, awareness, equanimity, and delight. Abandoning such misunderstanding, the meditator comes to see them as "Not-Path." The way to *Nibbana* is not one of indulgence in any pleasure, not even in the most refined and ecstatic spiritual experiences. One learns not to be attached to anything, even spiritual experiences.

The meditator now enters into the insight knowledge stage of the *Purification of Knowledge and Vision of Path Progress* that leads through a process of nine lesser stages to the supramundane experience of *Nibbana.* In brief, they begin with the knowledge that comes from the "contemplation of the rise and fall" of things. Having abandoned the pleasures of the former stage, the meditator turns with added zeal and clarity to observe the three characteristics of existence, of which transiency (*anicca*) becomes uppermost. He or she attains a more direct experience of the momentariness of all phenomena in which the process of arising and disappearing is more clearly seen. From this point, the meditator suddenly realizes more prominently the vanishing of momentary phenomena. This is the knowledge that comes from the "contemplation of the dissolution" of things. Such experience of the continuing dissolution of the world also brings the meditator face-to-face with the insubstantiality of life (*anatta*).

Now the mood radically changes toward negative modes and the meditator experiences the terror, the danger, and the horror, of living in such an evanescent world. This knowledge from the "contemplation of the fearful," of "misery," and of "aversion" leads the meditator on to a great desire to escape. A great restlessness often accompanied by despair besets him or her. But just as in the fifth stage where the meditator realized that liberation does not come with indulgence in pleasure, so now in the "desire for deliverance" there comes the knowledge that liberation does not come with running away from suffering. Free of the desire to escape suffering, the meditator can reestablish the quality of his or her insight meditation and reach the "knowledge of reflecting contemplation." Here, the three characteristics of existence are once again penetrated and deeper insights are experienced. This is greatly encouraging and renewed energy and determination arise in the meditator. All the previous negative emotional reactions dissolve and the mind becomes more and more pure. This newfound mental stability and strength allows the meditator to continue to observe the nature of reality with calm awareness. This is called the "knowledge consisting in equanimity."

Again the meditator centers his or her attention upon the three characteristics of existence and delves deeper into the universal quality of the insubstantiality of selfhood—now more deeply investigated, penetrated, and realized with unruffled calmness. Finally, at its maturity, the "knowledge in adaptation of truth" arises naturally and leads immediately into the supramundane experience where the seventh and final stage of purification is begun.

This seventh stage, called the *Purification of Knowledge and Vision*, begins with what is called a "change of lineage consciousness." Here, the changing and conditioned world of cause and effect is finally transcended. One's understanding takes "as object the unconditioned, the standstill of existence, the absence of becoming, cessation, *Nibbana*." With *Nibbana* as the focus of this new lineage of awakened consciousness, there is the entrance into the first path to sainthood, to becoming an *arahant*. This first path to full sanctity is called the "Streamwinner Path." As a Streamwinner, one brings to an end the whole gradual progress of the *Seven Stages of Purification*. The Streamwinner Path to sanctity eradicates many of the unwholesome mental factors, such as destructive doubt and clinging, that bind one to the changing world (*samsara*). But the seven stages must be repeated in more and more profound depth until all the "fetters" which bind us are eradicated. Therefore, after the Streamwinner Path, one enters the Once-Returner and Never-Returner Paths where the more subtle fetters are utterly destroyed. Finally, the person reaches the *Arahant* Path, becomes an *arahant*, the Perfectly Holy One, and is freed from all attachments and ignorance. Here, one attains the Highest Goal of perfectly continuous and sustained *Nibbana*. So it is that through the *Seven Stages of Purification*, the spiritual goal of Buddhism, of full *Nibbana*, is realized.

The Path of Self-Inquiry in Zen Buddhism

ESHIN NISHIMURA

Great Doubt

Zen Buddhism requires one to reexperience in one's own life the Buddha's way of deep self-inquiry through lifelong practice. Therefore, Zen life should start with the "Great Doubt" concerning the suffering condition of the world with which the Buddha himself was confronted in his youth. Without having this existential doubt about suffering, this questioning struggle with one's suffering existence, there is no entrance into the Zen way of life. To say that the doubt is "Great" means that this is not merely an objective doubt about a particular thing or a particular question. It is rather a "great mass of doubt" itself where the distinction between the doubting consciousness and the things doubted no longer remains. In the writings of the Zen Patriarchs, this nondualistic doubt is said to be like an experience of "Darkness fully covering the world," or the "Great Death."

Great Belief

For the Zen person who wanders in such a dangerous condition of life, what is written in the scriptures is no longer useful. One's only hope is to be saved by a lifeboat that can be found only by his or her own effort. In this way, one finds himself or herself at the Gate of Zen Buddhism that is called the "School of Buddha's Heart," or the "School of Self-Power." What the Zen person believes in is therefore not something other than himself or herself. However, this "self-belief" is not an objective belief in oneself, but is a belief where there is neither one who believes nor one in whom one believes. Therefore, this phenomenon is called the "Great Belief" in Zen teaching. In this way, the Great Belief and the Great Doubt cooperate in the process of Zen Awakening.

Great Effort

To break through the dark state of the Great Doubt, one must go straight ahead in the way of self-power even at the risk of one's life. This going ahead entails what is called the "Great Effort." This effort, like the doubt and belief just described, is beyond our ordinary objective effort to do something. It is effort itself where any consciousness of making an effort does not exist.

The Zen Master

The Zen Master who leads a student through the Great Doubt with Great Belief and Great Effort, should be a genuine Master who is a qualified successor of the Buddha's *Dharma* (Truth) and who embodies the true Buddha-heart through existential experience. In the Zen tradition, therefore, the "lineage of transmission" is thought to be most important because the Buddha's way of meditation and his Great Awakening have only been transmitted from heart to heart, from master to disciple through the twenty-five centuries of Buddhism's history.

No matter how authentic and great a Zen Master might be, it is impossible to transmit certain answers directly to the student who is bound by the existential problem of the Great Doubt. Therefore, the Zen Master is a bit like the so-called Socratic midwife. The Master "leads" the student by staying with him or her and helping the student break through this existential stage of the Great Doubt by himself or herself. Thus the Master leads the student to the realization of his or her own Reality. In this way, the realization of Reality is transmitted indirectly from Master to student.

The Koan Method

Throughout the history of Zen Buddhism, the traditional Patriarchs have used their own techniques as midwives, and therefore they produced a rich variety of practical spiritual methods in China, Korea and Japan. For example, in Japanese Rinzai Zen Buddhism, the Zen Master Hakuin Ekaku created a so-called "*koan* system" in the eighteenth century. This koan system contains a systematically arranged collection of 1,700 anecdotes about Zen Masters and their students in the monasteries of ancient China. These *koans* are documents that record for us how Zen students were able by themselves to break beyond their dark stage of existential doubt through their daily dialogues with their Zen Masters. So today, Zen Masters offer these anecdotes one by one to their students according to the stage of development of the students' state of mind. Through this *koan* study, the Master leads each student to the most extreme state of darkness possible in their Great Doubt. It is only there that the student's mass of great doubt can be broken through by itself. By so doing, the student finally arrives at the great Realization of Reality (*Satori*). In this way, we are assured that the student's realization today has the same content as experienced by the Buddha and Patriarchs.

Going Beyond Tradition

For the Zen student who hopes to live his life with absolute freedom, the personal satisfaction that he or she finds in arriving at *satori*-realization is actually a restriction of his or her freedom. So the student still has to be freed from even this restriction, which is really just another shell of egoism. The student must take one more step beyond the goal. This is thought to be a most crucial and difficult final step in the whole journey of Zen life. With this step, the student must transcend the tradition and return to his or her own existential way of being, which has never been transmitted by any of the ancient Patriarchs. This is called "Training after the *Satori* Experience."

It is traditionally taught that this part of Zen training is only possible amid ordinary life in secular society. So, unlike as in Christian monasticism, the Zen student in Japan leaves the monastery after a certain number of years and returns to secular society. Here, he or she lives with ordinary people as a religious and spiritual leader. On the one hand, to live in secular society is generally thought to be indispensable to the role of the *bodhisattva* (the enlightened person of compassion) in Mahayana Buddhism. On the other hand, in Zen this is the most important part of the path of Self-inquiry which should be continued to the very end of one's life.

The Path to Calm Abiding

HIS HOLINESS THE DALAI LAMA

I will be speaking today about the development of a state of meditation, or *samadhi*, called "calm abiding"; and I will be speaking about it from Buddhist texts. However, this practice is common to both Buddhists and non-Buddhists; for instance, in India both Buddhists and non-Buddhists have practiced it. Therefore, I feel that our Christian brothers and sisters also could practice this form of meditation.

Faults and Antidotes

With respect to achieving the state of calm abiding, there are five faults, or five factors that oppose the development of calm abiding; and there are eight antidotes to those five faults. The first fault is laziness. The second is called "forgetting the advice," but what it means is to forget the object on which you are meditating. The third is laxity and excitement. The fourth is nonapplication of the antidotes; and the fifth is over-application of the antidotes.

Now with regard to the eight antidotes to the five faults: with respect to the first fault, laziness, there are four antidotes. These include faith, aspiration, exertion and pliancy. Faith here means faith in the qualities of meditative stabilization. Aspiration is the aspiration to attain meditative stabilization and is induced by faith. Exertion means to exert oneself to attain meditative stabilization. As for the last antidote, pliancy, at this point one does not have pliancy, but one can consider the advantages of pliancy.

Among these advantages are: that one's body, compared to the usual state, will be very light and pliant; and you will be able to set your mind in whatever virtue you want. Thus, as an antidote to laziness, you can contemplate—that is, you can reflect on, and you can be mindful of—the good qualities of pliancy that will be achieved through overcoming laziness.

With regard to the types of laziness, often there is the type in which you feel, "Oh, I am not capable of doing this; I am inferior; I could not possibly do this!" Although this attitude often is not mentioned explicitly, it is very important to counteract this psychological sense of inferiority. This can be done through reflecting on various encouraging tenets that are taught by the different schools. For example, one good way for a Buddhist to do this is to reflect on the Buddha-nature that is within everyone, and is therefore within oneself. Also, a Buddhist could reflect on the marvelous situation of leisure and fortune that is difficult to attain and that one has already attained. One has a human body with a lifetime that gives one enough time to practice—and the conditions to practice—the spiritual life. Through reflecting on this fact, one can realize what a good situation one is in, and thus overcome the laziness of feeling inferior. From a Christian point of view, one could reflect on the fact that God's grace is always present, that the blessings of God are always there ready to be received. With this point of view, one can overcome the kind of laziness which entails a feeling that "I cannot possibly do this!"

Objects of Meditation

Then the next fault, namely, the forgetting of the object on which you are meditating, is overcome through mindfulness. But before we examine this fault and its antidote, it will be helpful to mention some of the types of meditation objects in Buddhism. One type is called "an object for purifying afflictive emotions." What this means is that from a Buddhist point of view, over many recent past lifetimes, one has engaged in particular afflictive emotions with the result that in this lifetime one has a predominate afflictive emotion such as desire, hatred, confusion, pride, or discursiveness. Thus, one meditates on an object that will oppose one's predominate afflictive emotion. For instance, in the case of someone who has a lot of hatred, you would concentrate on love. In the case of someone who has a lot of desire, you would concentrate on ugliness. For someone who has a lot of confusion, you would meditate on the way that the cyclic round of suffering arises in the process of dependent arising. For someone who has pride, you would reflect on the five mental and physical aggregates or the other constituents of our existence. Someone who is dominated by discursiveness would meditate on the inhalation and exhalation of the breath. So you see, there are a variety of afflictive emotions. And for each afflictive emotion there are different objects on which to meditate in order to lessen these afflictions.

From among the different categories of objects of meditation, I would like to speak about the one that is called "pervasive objects of meditation." These objects are called pervasive in the sense that they are used for the development of both calm abiding and special insight. Within this category there are four types of objects. One type is called "an image together with analysis," and another is called "an image without analysis." The image without analysis is used in the process of developing calm abiding. The image with analysis is used in the process of developing special insight. And besides these two types, there are two others. The first of these other two is called "the limits of things" which refers to the varieties of phenomena and their final nature. The second is called "the purposes that one is seeking to accomplish"; these are the aims of meditation. I think that each of these can be subdivided with regard to the attainment of calm abiding and the attainment of special insight. And, I might add, calm abiding and special insight are also common to both Buddhists and non-Buddhists.

As mentioned in my earlier talk on meditation, analytical meditation is used for the development of special insight, and single-pointed meditation—stabilizing meditation—is used for the development of calm abiding. The difference between calm abiding and special insight is not determined by the respective objects of these different meditative states. Rather, the difference is determined by *how* one is engaging the objects. For instance, there is calm abiding that even observes emptiness; and there is also special insight that is observing the varieties of phenomena. For a Christian, for instance, there would also be both stabilizing and analytical meditation. For instance, there could be both stabilizing and analytical meditation with regard to developing faith in God. And there could be both stabilizing and analytical meditation with regard to developing love for fellow human beings.

So then, what are these objects that are appearing to the mind in these types of meditation? We are not speaking about appearances to our sense-consciousnesses; one does not achieve meditation through a sense-consciousness. Rather, there is an appearance to the conceptual mind, or interior mind, of objects that have been seen with the senses. These types of meditation are achieved with respect to these more internal images. That is why they are called nonanalytical *images* and analytical *images*. For instance, with regard to initially developing calm abiding, one could meditate even on a flower. This would not be the flower that you are seeing with your sense-consciousness—with your visual consciousness—but would be an image of that perceived flower that is in the mind. You would concentrate on that internal image. But to begin this process, one could look at the flower very carefully in order to develop familiarity with it. You could look at one detail and then see if you could imagine it. Then you could look at another detail and so forth. In this way, the internal image could be made very clear.

Mindfulness

Having said this about the objects of meditation, one can see how the function of mindfulness is to keep from being distracted to other objects. Mindfulness can only work on an object with which you are familiar, with which you have developed an acquaintance. Then, by developing mindfulness, it can serve its function of preventing distraction to other objects. It is mainly through developing the dexterity of mindfulness that one can achieve calm abiding.

To develop strong mindfulness, it is important to act mindfully in all aspects of one's behavior. Whether one is walking about, or one is standing, or sitting down, or even lying down, it is important to maintain mindfulness of what you are doing. In order to maintain mindfulness continuously, it is necessary to have conscientiousness. This is very important for *all* religious practitioners. And this is why it is necessary to have an ethical foundation in the development of calm abiding. That is, ethical behavior requires that one maintain mindfulness of what one is doing, and conscientiousness with respect to what one is doing. That mindfulness and conscientiousness developed in moral practice will also help in one's meditation.

Silence is also very, very important to the practice of mindfulness. The reason for this is that we have many different thoughts, many different ideas, that run through our minds. Those thoughts arise as if following after sounds. Language itself, therefore, induces a lot of different thoughts. But when one remains silent, in time this silence will gradually reduce the number of thoughts. In Dharamsala, there is a fellow religious practitioner who from time to time spends a month in total silence. But on Saturdays, he will talk. Sometimes that person engages in this practice for several months. So through supports such as these, the object of meditation is held by the power of mindfulness.

Scattering and Concentration

The antidote to the fault of "laxity and excitement" is introspection. If one has developed powerful mindfulness, introspection will come of itself. But the special way to develop introspection is from time to time to inspect what is happening with your body and your mind. With regard to laxity, its coarser form is like darkness in which one loses the object. In the subtler form of laxity, the object is clear enough but there is a lack of clarity in the subject. That is, the consciousness that is paying attention to the object is itself unclear. In this case, there is a great danger in confusing this subtle laxity with real meditation.

It is also true that "scattering"—that is, distraction—to any type of object is a serious fault to developing meditation. However, desire is singled out as an important cause of scattering because everyone has a great deal of distractions due to objects of desire. Thus, excitement, meaning here desirous excitement, is emphasized and is often mentioned in place of scattering. However, any type of scattering is harmful. For instance, if you are meditatively cultivating faith in God, and during that period you scatter to another object such as the cultivation of compassion, then that distraction is something that needs to be stopped *at that time*. Even though the meditative cultivation of compassion is something that in general you should do, it should be done at another time. The same is true with regard to meditatively cultivating compassion. If at that time you scatter to developing faith in God, then that faith-developing meditation needs to be stopped *at that time*.

As an illustration, what one is trying to do here is like starting a fire and keeping it going by adding fuel to it. If rather than doing that you do something else—even something good—you are letting the fire diminish or die down, and you are going to have to begin all over again. Similarly, when laxity and excitement arise, one's mind easily comes under their power. And it is a fault at that time not to apply the antidotes to laxity and excitement. This would be an example of the fourth fault, namely, the "nonapplication of antidotes." Furthermore, the antidotes to laxity are all within the class of raising the mode of apprehension of the mind. The antidotes to excitement are within the class of allowing the mode of apprehension of the mind to diminish a little bit. Now, when you have applied the antidotes to laxity or excitement, and whichever one of them is bothering you does in fact diminish, if you keep applying that antidote, then that activity itself turns into a fault. This is the fifth fault, the "overapplication of the antidotes." In this case, you simply have to stop applying the antidote. So, this is how one uses the eight antidotes to overcome the five faults in meditation practice.

Stages of Meditation

Let us now look at the experience that one goes through on the path to calm abiding by applying the eight antidotes to the five faults. First is the stage called "setting the mind," where one is trying to set the mind on the object of meditation. When through effort one is able to keep the mind set more continuously on the object, this stage is called "continuous setting." Then, through noticing scattering and putting the mind back on the object, one attains the point where two-thirds of the time one is able to stay concentrated on the object. This stage is called "resetting." When one is more effective with regard to applying the antidotes to coarse laxity and excitement, one attains the fourth stage which is called "close setting." Then, as one deals with subtle laxity and excitement and overcomes them, one passes through the fifth stage (called "disciplining"), the sixth stage (called "pacifying"), the seventh stage (called "thorough pacifying"), the eighth stage (called "making one-pointed"), and finally the ninth stage, which is called "setting in equipoise."

As it is stated in the Buddhist texts, when one reaches this ninth stage, one has reached a level of one-pointed concentration that is still included within the "desire realm." In Buddhism, we speak of there being three realms: the desire realm, the form realm, and the formless realm. Setting in equipoise is still categorized within the desire realm. While this ninth stage itself is not calm abiding, through continuous meditation at this stage, one develops calm abiding itself. Both Buddhist and Hindu sources present this calm abiding as the initial preparation for a level of meditation called the "first concentration" (*jhana*). Thus, calm abiding is called the "not unable" because through cultivating it, one is able to achieve the first concentration. Then through further continuous cultivation, one can achieve the second, third, and fourth concentrations. These four concentrations are included within the form realm.

Besides these four concentrations, there are also the four higher states called absorptions that are included within the formless realm. The objects of these absorptions include limitless space, limitless consciousness, so-called nothingness, and the peak of cyclic existence. For our Christian brothers and sisters, I think that the four concentrations and the four formless absorptions are not needed. What you need is the development of calm abiding, or the level of one-pointedness of mind that is included within the so-called desire realm. The purpose of developing such a level of meditation is so that you can have very firm qualities of mind, such as faith. The stability of this kind of meditation will make your faith very strong. The various types of faith, and other spiritual qualities of mind, can then be understood and described according to one's respective religious tradition.

Prayer as Path

PIERRE-FRANÇOIS DE BÉTHUNE, O.S.B.

Prayer is a path, a lifework. It develops necessarily like all that lives, and therefore it goes through various stages. Before describing these stages, I must situate the presentation I will give of them in the whole of this living world of prayer where a great biodiversity prevails.

The methods of prayer of today's Christians benefit in fact from the spiritual research made from the first centuries of Christianity and even earlier, since we are also heirs of the age-old tradition of Judaism. We must be grateful to the Fathers of our faith who have sharpened their experience of prayer. They have fashioned the practice of the Lord Jesus of Nazareth and we keep drawing from it abundantly. But since then, and throughout the history of the Church, the ways of spiritual life and prayer have never stopped growing in a remarkable way down to today. Also today, new encounters with the realities of our contemporary world challenge the faithful to renew the prayerful practice of their faith in Christ. One of the major encounters in the course of recent years is indeed the discovery made by Christians of the spiritual practices elaborated in Hinduism, Buddhism and other religions. This encounter is a new opportunity for an ever more lively practice of Christian prayer.

The fact is that a great diversity of schools of prayer exists today in Christianity, and it is clearly impossible to consider here the stages of prayer in these various schools. I will not be able to describe the Jesuit, Carmelite or the more modern methods of prayer that have evolved in the new Christian communities of Africa or Latin America. I will limit myself to the Western monastic tradition, with reference mostly to St. Benedict (d. 547 C.E.). But one must bear in mind that this presentation of the stages of Christian prayer describes a specific but highly significant school of the Christian tradition.

I will study three main stages, referring to the three persons of the Trinity: the Father, Son and Holy Spirit. Prayer indeed is nothing else but an initiatory path which introduces us into a divine movement which is that of God himself. In addition, I will follow the main lines of spiritual progress as St. Benedict has drawn them in chapter seven of his *Rule*. This is the chapter at the core of his spiritual doctrine where he recapitulates the whole Benedictine spiritual itinerary through the image of a ladder. This spiritual ladder has several steps of humility, that is of truth, by which the monk ascends toward God. The stages of prayer correspond generally to these steps, or degrees, of humility or truth.

I. "Truly Seek God"[1]

The first stage of a life of prayer is *conversion,* a reorientation of one's own life toward God.[2] It is a step one has to take again and again during one's spiritual life—and even at the beginning of each individual prayer. We see, for instance, how the Patriarch of Western monks, St. Benedict, while still a young student at Rome, all of a sudden drops his studies which might have secured him a good career. He withdraws to the solitude of Subiaco where for three years he lives in a cave "alone with himself, under the eyes of the Heavenly Witness," as his biographer St. Gregory writes.[3]

As a matter of fact, the reality of God had suddenly invaded his conscience and turned his values topsy-turvy. What seemed to him sweet and tasty until then had now become tasteless and meaningless. All that matters at present is the quest for the Truth of God that he had glimpsed as a student. The point of conversion is to break from a certain way of life and a certain logic. St. Gregory remarks that by retiring to Subiaco the young Benedict was *scienter nescius, sapienter indoctus:* "he chose intelligently to remain ignorant [of the ways of the world]; in his wisdom he remained unlearned."[4]

Do not all monks share in this initial conversion experience? Yes, all of us, whether Christian or Buddhist, have heard in one way or another Abba Arsenius's advice: "Run away [from this fleeting world], remain silent and seek peace" (*Fuge, tace, quiesce*).[5] This first stage in the spiritual life is an exit, an *exodus,* it is *leaving one's father's house,* it is a step which makes you "different from the world's way."[6]

If at the beginning of the spiritual life there is an experience of the Absolute strong enough to impel one to leave everything, still a good deal of time and effort will be necessary to "prepare our hearts and bodies" for a much deeper experience.[7] At this primary stage, prayer is mostly lived as a labor (*opus*)[8] and a duty (*pensum servitutis*).[9] The monk at this point can say with Psalm 72: "I am no better than a beast before you, yet I am always with you."[10] But in this way, little by little, the heart is "touched," even "hurt," by an acute feeling of the sacred that is awesome and fascinating.

In the *Rule of Benedict,* this stage is described as the "first step of humility." It consists in fully discovering the truth of one's own weaknesses, and—more importantly—in recognizing the presence of God in all of our life: "The Lord looks down from heaven on the sons of men to see whether any understand and seek God. . . . Then, brothers, we must be vigilant every hour."[11] Conversion is indeed an awakening, but it is still lived in semidarkness.

II. "Follow Christ"[12]

The first stage is often characterized by an acute awareness of the weakness of our human condition. But we cannot walk for very long on the spiritual path out of a sorrow for our own sorry condition. If the apostles gave up everything, it was because they were overcome by the fascinating person of Jesus and the taste for the Kingdom he announced. They were attracted to this new and more fulfilling condition of life. Then following after him they found themselves taken in a direction they had not foreseen: "They drank the chalice of the passion and became his friends" (cf. Mt. 20:22).[13] Whoever advances along the spiritual path from darkness into light must experience death in the midst of life. That is, one must assent to a still deeper purifying of heart and mind in order to have access to the new spiritual life he or she is seeking.

All spiritual paths know an "obligatory passage" through death to oneself into a new life lived joyfully for others. For us Christians, the figure of Christ is "the door" (Jn. 10:7), "the narrow gate" (Mt. 7: 13), our Passover ("passage" in Hebrew) to this new life. By participating in his death, mysteriously we have access to true life. The monastic tradition of the West has distinguished two degrees for this following of Christ (*sequela Christi*).

A. Meditation

First of all there is the meditative approach. The novice who enters the monastery is asked by St. Benedict before all else to devote himself or herself to *meditation* (in the Benedictine sense of the word) and liturgical prayer (*opus Dei*).[14] The aim of this practice is that one may become more familiar with the life of Christ and its transformative power to take us beyond death into this new life. In other words, the goal is that one "may know the Lord and the power of his resurrection, being made conformable to his death" (Phil. 3:10). To this end the *Rule of Benedict* provides for about three hours of "meditation" daily and four hours of divine office. The meditation referred to here consists of a meditative, prayerful reading of the Bible according to the method of *lectio divina*. Much time is also devoted to memorizing these texts. In the long run, such an assiduous practice makes the one who meditates somehow "dwell" in the world of the Bible to the point that his or her whole language is steeped in it. St. Bernard's sermons are but a collection of quotations from scripture.

This process of dwelling in the transformative Word of God is not without originality or personality. As St. Gregory says somewhere, "The Word develops in a new way as it incarnates itself in the reader" (*Scriptura crescit cum legente*). With his or her prayer, the monastic gradually offers to Christ, the Word of God, a new incarnation. The singing of psalms plays an essential part in this process, for psalms are not only a marvelous initiation into a life of prayer, but they also reveal to the Christian the life of Christ in solidarity with all human beings. Therefore, this process leads to a deeper transformation of the self in communion with Christ and in solidarity with all humanity.

B. Communion

In order that the first steps of *lectio divina* should not be confined to mere specular imitation or even mimicry at the psychological level, St. Benedict shows how it can become still more interiorized. This second degree of the following of Christ is achieved through learning obedience. Here obedience, in its more profound sense, means that one's life at its deepest core corresponds with, or conforms to, the object of one's meditation, namely, Christ.

"Listen" is the first word of the *Rule of Benedict*. Now, in Latin "listen" (*obaudire*) and "obey" (*oboedire*) are almost identical words. This means that obedience, conforming to Christ, is the normal outcome of listening to scripture in the meditation of *lectio divina*. The continuing steps of humility are steps of obedience in the following of Christ who "became obedient even to death."[15] From now on, one participates more and more deeply in the mystery of the death and resurrection of the Lord. At this stage, prayer introduces the Christian into an existential communion with this mystery. He or she goes in faith through what St. John of the Cross calls a "night of the senses and the spirit" to become ever more conformed with the Lord. St. Benedict also mentions the indubitable signs of this conformity to Christ: gentleness, kindness and loving forgiveness: "They bless those who curse them";[16] and "Out of love for Christ they pray for their enemies."[17]

These two degrees of the following (*sequela*) of Christ correspond to the two parts of the Mass. After a rite of introduction, which corresponds to what I described in the first stage of prayer as conversion, the "Liturgy of the Word" is a meditative celebration of biblical texts. It leads to the "Liturgy of Bread and Wine," in which the faithful associate themselves far more intimately with the Lord in Holy Communion. This communion is not just a rite. In the form of the sacrament, it realizes the fundamental process of the disciple of Christ. St. Benedict, while not saying much about the Eucharist, shows clearly how to realize its substance concretely—that is, to commune with the work of salvation in Christ.

It is not possible to mention here all the characteristics of prayer as it is lived when one reaches the apex of this communion with Christ. I will only say a word here about "the Jesus prayer," which has known a remarkable development in Eastern Orthodox monasticism and has always been practiced in the West as "continuous prayer." This form of prayer consists in repeating ceaselessly a simple formula, a Christian *mantra*, as for instance "Jesus Lord," or "*Maranatha*" ("Come, Lord!"). These words give form and express the essence of our prayer, namely, a continuous sense of the presence of the Lord. In this respect, St. John Cassian, to whom St. Benedict constantly refers, once said, "When we have reached this step, we have become so much attached to him [God] that our whole breathing, thinking, our whole utterance will be only him. . . . Then the whole movement of our heart becomes one uninterrupted prayer."[18]

III. "With the Joy of the Holy Spirit"[19]

On this high path of prayer, we can still discern a new threshold. As one's communion with Christ deepens into joy and peace, prayer becomes ever more intense and is finally "inflamed," set on fire so to speak, by the Holy Spirit. Having achieved spiritual simplicity, the heart is filled with "the light that comes from God."[20] It is this stage that St. Cassian describes in another Conference: "The heart is inflamed, it is rapt in the prayer of fire (*ignita oratio*) which human language is unable to express. The soul which has reached this stage of true purity pours out in pure, lively prayers which the Spirit himself breathes out to God with unspeakable groaning."[21] The descriptions of this state are always awkward, but the signs which testify to its presence are obvious. Two such signs are the "freedom" of the Spirit, and a "silence" under the shadow of the Spirit.

A. The Freedom of the Spirit

The first fruit of the Spirit received in prayer is being *beyond fear*. In the conclusion to his chapter on humility, St. Benedict remarks:

> After ascending all these steps of humility, the monk will quickly arrive at that perfect love of God which casts out fear. Through this love, all that he once performed with dread, he will now begin to observe without effort, as though naturally, from habit, no longer out of fear of hell, but out of love for Christ, good habit and delight in virtue. All this, the Lord will by the Holy Spirit graciously manifest in his workman now cleansed of vices and sins.[22]

One will notice in this description how, at the end of this long path, the person finds a new freedom and integration of self, recovers his or her former simplicity, and delights in a state of loving unity with God.[23] The beginning of the Christian spiritual journey was an *exodus*. But it now becomes a joyful *homecoming*, marked by a certain spontaneous and natural ease, and by "the joy of the Holy Spirit."[24] The long road following Christ has often been painful for the disciple, but now "he runs on the path of God's commandments, his heart overflowing with the inexpressible delight of love."[25] He or she apparently does nothing special, but the prayer which floods his or her heart overflows with love.

St. Cassian has transmitted to us a saying of St. Anthony, the first Christian monk, "a heavenly saying, and more than human," about the highest degree of prayer: "Prayer is not perfect if the monk keeps his self-awareness and knows he is praying."[26] Indeed, when the Spirit of Christ inhabits a person to this degree, that person no longer just *makes* prayers, he or she *is* now entirely prayer (cf. Ps. 108:4). And with this prayer overflowing with love, the person *is* love, is God's love for all creation.

B. A Silence under the Shadow of the Spirit

The Word received in meditation and obedience opens up a path to the silence of communion and consent. No one sees the Spirit, and "you do not know where he comes from and where he goes" (Jn. 3:8), but silence has been called the shadow of the Spirit, of the Spirit who overshadowed the Virgin Mary (Lk. 1:35), conceiving God in her.

Silence is often referred to in the *Rule*, but the monastic Fathers have always felt uneasy about making its contents explicit. Here, I will only quote Fr. Henri Le Saux, otherwise known as Swami Abhishiktananda:

> Finally the most intense, the most fruitful prayer, at least when the Spirit invites us, is the complete silence of the soul which has gone beyond the senses and the spirit even, collected in its source now and unable to say anything but *Abba*, Father, but without any word to pronounce it or thought to conceive it.[27]

Indeed the works of God, revealed by his Word, enable us to know what God is *for us*, but in silence God reveals what he is *in himself*, his very Being.

I want to add one last feature which characterizes the man or woman who is thus inhabited by prayer: with a heart enlarged by the love of God that embraces all of creation, he or she is spontaneously in communion with all those who suffer and all those who follow the spiritual life, whatever their religion. Ultimately, the prayer of the Holy Spirit that brings us into this communion is that of all humanity and even the whole creation which, as St. Paul says, groans and travails in pain (Rom. 8:23). Conversely, the opportunity to meet other fellow pilgrims stimulates us to deepen our prayer. Yes! I am convinced of it: this encounter at

Gethsemani is not just an occasion for speaking *about* prayer and meditation; it is a chance to progress in our communion with one another, each of us according to his or her path, on the way of meditation and prayer.

Spiritual Experiences on the Path of Prayer

GILCHRIST LAVIGNE, O.C.S.O

In this presentation, I will be describing some phenomena of spiritual experience that are associated with the stages of prayer from a monastic perspective. Many Christian writers, such as St. Teresa of Avila and St. John of the Cross, have given us wonderful accounts of their experiences, often in a more systematized manner. However, I am deliberately placing my focus on the monastic saints of the Benedictine-Cistercian tradition because it is the tradition with which I am most familiar. While I will focus on the past tradition, it is important to note that monks and nuns continue to experience what I am describing here. For example, here is a description of a more advanced stage of prayer written by Thomas Merton:

> The unitive knowledge of God in love is not a knowledge of an object by a subject, but a far different and transcendent kind of knowledge in which the creative "self" which we are seems to disappear in God and to know him alone. In passive purification, then, the self undergoes a kind of emptying and an apparent destruction, until, reduced to emptiness, it no longer knows itself apart from God.[1]

In this description it can be seen how a particular stage of prayer may be closely linked and associated with a certain experience. In this particular passage, if we were to identify the experience, we might speak of a new intuitive knowledge of God as well as an experience of emptiness and darkness. And yet, the sense of emptiness can at the same time contain the perception of fullness, that is, the self that no longer knows itself apart from God. So the darkness can also at times be apprehended as light. Such opposites, like yin and yang, frequently characterize the interior and exterior experiences that are related to prayer.

Furthermore, experiences that may seem to be associated with one stage of prayer could also be linked to another stage. For example, a beginner in the spiritual life might be given an experience of unity with God that is usually associated with a much later stage. But this experience encourages the person to move forward and persevere in her journey to find God. Another example is that some of the perceptions of light experienced by those advanced in prayer are quite different from the perceptions experienced by someone who is just learning to meditate and sees some shimmering lights. Yet both the beginner and the proficient are describing their experiences in terms of light. So, we cannot make too many radical or rigid distinctions. There is movement backward and forward, since this process is fluid and dynamic rather than static or clear-cut. At times words can be misleading, but good spiritual guides should know how to discern and interpret the experiences of those they help.

Christians all through the ages—including monastics, both monks and nuns—have experienced a great variety of spiritual phenomena. This list could include such categories as visions, lights, locutions, clairvoyance, the ability to read hearts, discernment of spirits, spiritual senses, and the gift of healing. Often, these are the experiences that come to mind when we think of spiritual phenomena. However, in the monastic tradition there are also other phenomena of spiritual experience that are considered equally, and in some cases, even more significant. These include self-knowledge, compunction of heart (which is a sense of sorrow for sin and self-centeredness), inner freedom, joy, gratitude, compassion, single-heartedness, simplicity, inner radiance, and loving kindness.

Some of these words—*purity of heart,* for example—describe stages as well as the phenomena that accompany them. Other terms, such as *loving kindness,* do not really refer to particular phenomena. Loving kindness, or charity, is a gift of God. It is God's love dwelling in the person; and this love is the matrix for various behavioral manifestations deriving from it. So, when describing these behavioral phenomena in the monastic tradition, it becomes artificial to try to speak of them apart from this matrix of charity. To give an example, in prayer a monastic may become aware of an infusion of God's love. In turn, this love brings about many changes in that person. There may be a felt sorrow for one's self-centered behavior leading to a change of heart, more simplicity, and compassion toward others.

If examples from this second group of phenomena are not clearly manifested in a person (e.g., self-knowledge, single-heartedness, and compassion), then one would seriously doubt the authenticity of any visions, lights, or locutions—which are not important in themselves and could even be manifestations of an unhealthy and disintegrating personality. This is not to say that visible and audible phenomena are always bad. Some of the greatest Christian saints, such as St. Paul and St. John of the Cross, have "spoken of such experiences as gifts of the Spirit, though they always add a note of cautious reserve."[2]

In taking a closer look at some of the experiences mentioned above, it may be helpful to link them with the three main stages of prayer outlined in the talk by Fr. Pierre de Béthune. These stages are inserted within the context of the degrees of humility found in the seventh chapter of the *Rule of Benedict.*[3]

To Truly Seek God

The first stage of prayer described in the fifty-eighth chapter of the *Rule of Benedict* is the experience of conversion, or, in Benedict's words, "to truly seek God."[4] We know that conversion is not something that happens only once in a person's life. It is ongoing—it is a process—and after many years in a monastery, a monk or nun may experience conversion at a much deeper level which may even completely reorganize the personality. Or, as is most often the case, this conversion process occurs little by little over the years, bringing various parts of the personality into more unity, and perhaps changing the behavior of the person as one cooperates with God's graces. In our own Benedictine tradition, monks and nuns make a "vow" of conversion. This implies a daily effort to live the monastic life in a manner more harmonious with the gifts of God.

One of the most predominant phenomena experienced in the conversion process is compunction of heart. This is expressed at times in symbolic language as a "puncturing" or "piercing" of the heart. The heart which previously had been "cold" or "lukewarm" (that is, given over to superficial concerns, vanities and sophistication, and self-centeredness) now becomes "pierced," so to speak. The monastic feels acute sorrow accompanied with a desire to change his or her way of life, thus becoming more focused on God and spiritual values. But even though one may be given the gift of conversion and of compunction, this grace must be accepted and nurtured. One of the desert Fathers in the early centuries said the following regarding compunction, or *penthos* as they called it:

> One day, seeing his disciple weighed down from eating, he took him aside, "Do you not realize that *penthos* is a small lighted lamp? Unless you shelter it carefully, it will go out in an instant and its flame will disappear. Excessive eating puts it out, as do prolonged sleep, evil speaking and gossip. In a word, every relaxation of the flesh chases it away, makes it disappear."[5]

Another desert Father explains:

> If you really wish to weep for your sins, be watchful over yourself and die to the eyes of every man. . . . Cut off these three things: your will, self-justification, and human self-satisfaction. Then com-

> punction will come in all truth, and God will shelter you from every evil. . . . Be watchful over yourself, rejoicing when you are struck, reproved, insulted, punished. Keep the dove's simplicity together with prudence, and the Lord will come to your aid. This is the way of salvation.[6]

As alluded to in the above text, sometimes the experience of compunction is also accompanied by the gift of tears. This is especially true in the Eastern Church, where the gift of tears has been regarded as highly desirable, and sometimes even as essential. Evagrius of Pontus, a fourth century monk from a monastery on the Mount of Olives, felt that the gift of tears was necessary in all the stages of the monastic life. He explained that a person who had reached perfection might no longer need to practice severe asceticism, but that it would be an illusion to think there would be no further need of tears. "If it seems to you that you no longer need to weep in prayer for your sins, consider how far you have gone from God."[7] In the twelfth century, one of the English Cistercian Fathers, Gilbert of Hoyland, speaks also of the gift of tears. He writes: "Their silent tears flow copiously . . . so that if perhaps those who sit near are cold [of heart] themselves, they may catch fire from the sparks of their neighbors."[8]

Certainly the gift of compunction is not the only one experienced by the person going through conversion. However, some of the other phenomena will also appear in other stages of prayer. These would include: zeal for living the monastic life, greater simplicity and single-heartedness, an awareness of God's love, and, in turn, a deeper love for God and neighbor.

Following Christ

In the second stage of prayer, the following of Christ, we read in the *Rule of Benedict* that persons should not love their own will nor take pleasure in the satisfaction of their desires, but rather imitate by their actions that saying of the Lord: "I have come not to do my own will, but the will of him who sent me."[9] As we see here, following Christ involves partaking in his life and destiny, and sharing in his free and loving obedience to the will of the Father.[10]

Some of the phenomena characteristic of this period include a deeper self-knowledge, mindfulness, modesty, simplicity of life, and concern for what benefits the neighbor. These are experienced in the context of love and a following of Christ that is not just an imitation of the life of Jesus, but a real participation in his life. In the words of St. Paul, it is a "putting on Christ," a becoming Christ so that Christ is the reference point of all one is and lives. This is not a question of practicing humility by necessity alone, but out of love.[11]

Gilbert of Hoyland wrote that "modesty does not wantonly boast of its blessings but speaks sparingly, content with a gentle hint when need demands. Good Jesus, what modesty there is everywhere in your speech!"[12] In this passage, we see how Gilbert wishes to be modest because Jesus was modest. He desires to follow Jesus not just by reading about his life, but by living it in his own person. The qualities and attitudes of Christ became one's own.

Following Christ out of love brings one to a love that is all-embracing. Saint Lutgard, a thirteenth-century Flemish nun, felt called to undergo a seven-year fast:

> At the end of her first seven years of fasting, it was revealed to Lutgard that she must now fast on behalf of sinners. The obedient Lutgard again took only raw vegetables and bread, seven years in succession. Meanwhile, the Lord granted her another vision: before her eyes appeared the wounded Jesus standing before his Father and interceding for sinners. Jesus spoke to Lutgard: "You see, I totally surrender myself to my Father to save sinners, and you should do the same."[13]

St. Gertrude, a famous thirteenth-century mystic who lived the *Rule of Benedict*, came to a true inner freedom resulting from her desire to follow Christ. This desire expressed itself in small practical ways. For example, she would be ready at a moment's notice to change her occupation as the need arose: "She was equally at peace whether she prayed, wrote, read, instructed, reproved or consoled."[14] The secret to this inner equilibrium was her one-pointed concentration on the heart of God as a "single outward movement of the heart in the direction of God which becomes possible when outward clamor recedes."[15]

However, following Jesus to the Cross, expressed in an inner journey to the heart, is not as easy as it may sound here. Certainly in our Christian spiritual experience there is alternation between light and darkness, joy and difficulty, inner freedom and anxiety or restlessness. In other words, there is a profound struggle that is felt more keenly at certain times along the journey. There are many stories or anecdotes to exemplify this struggle to go beyond the false self, to move from self-centeredness to selfless love. St. Bernard, a mystic and founder of many monasteries during the beginnings of the Cistercian Order in the Middle Ages, wrote to his monks:

> . . . . When you feel weighed down by apathy, lukewarmness and fatigue, do not yield to cowardice or cease to study spiritual truths, but look for the hand of the one who can help you, begging like the bride, to be drawn, until finally, under the influence of grace, you feel again the vigorous pulse of life. Then you will run and shout out: "I run the way of your commandments since you have enlarged my heart."[16]

Not too long ago, a Cistercian monk who died in Spain during this century was beatified, a process used by the Church to state that someone may some day be declared a saint. This simple monk, Br. Raphael of San Isidro, knew very well the struggle of the spiritual life. However, the life of Christ gave him the courage and perseverance he needed to continue forward. In his diary, Br. Raphael left us a detailed account of one of his struggles. It is a simple incident where he is asked to peel a turnip:

> Patience and waiting. They have handed me a knife and in front of me have put a basket containing a species of very large "white carrots" called turnips. . . . What can be done . . . but to peel them. Time goes slowly, and my knife too. . . . That I've left my home to come here in the cold to peel those ugly old things! There really is something rather ridiculous about this peeling of turnips with the gravity of a funeral director.
>
> Deep inside of me a very subtle little devil is getting at me, and with honey tongue reminds me of my home, my parents and brothers, my freedom, all that I've left in order to shut myself up here among lentils, potatoes, cabbages and turnips. It's a dreary day. . . . What am I doing? . . . Peeling turnips, peeling turnips. What for? And the heart with a leap answers half wildly: "I am peeling turnips for love, for love of Jesus Christ!"
>
> I can say nothing that will be understood clearly; but this I will vouch for, that within, deep within the soul, the confusion which I felt earlier was replaced by a great peace. I can only express the one thought that the smallest actions in life can be made acts for love of God . . . that the peeling of some turnips for real love of God can give Him as much glory, and ourselves as much merit.[17]

We can smile at this simple story, recognizing in it our own small struggles at the beginning of the monastic life, and even sometimes later in our life, but it is precisely these smaller moments which prepare us for the larger ones. Several times in this century, Cistercian and Benedictine monastics have suffered persecution and death on account of their religious beliefs (and here in this assembly, we know that this has been true for monastics all over the world and continues right now in Tibet, Africa, and other countries). We have personal testimony that in many of these situations, the monks or nuns, knowing that they were in grave danger, responded by living their simple daily lives more intensely, in a dedicated way with attention to the present moment. One example concerns some Trappist monks who were killed at the monastery of Consolation in China during the Communist takeover. The most recent instance was the murder of our seven Cistercian brothers at the monastery of Atlas in Algeria earlier this year. We know that for these brothers, the small moments of their daily life were their preparation for the crossover into ultimate reality.

Just as Jesus struggled during his forty days in the desert, and in many other moments of his life, sometimes the inner struggle of the monk or nun becomes acutely painful and is not readily resolved. Thomas Merton wrote:

> The only full and authentic purification is that which turns a man completely inside out, so that he no longer has a self to defend, no longer an intimate heritage to protect. . . . The full maturity of the spiritual cannot be reached unless we first pass through the dread, anguish, trouble, and fear that necessarily accompany the inner crisis of "spiritual death" in which we finally abandon our attachment to our exterior self and surrender completely to Christ.[18]

He adds:

> Only when we are able to "let go" of everything within us, all desire to see, to know, to taste and to experience the presence of God, do we truly become able to experience that presence with the overwhelming conviction and reality that revolutionize our entire inner life.[19]

St. Gertrude referred to herself as a "vessel emptied of self but filled to overflowing with God."[20] However, a person may not necessarily experience the presence of God. This may remain hidden for years, keeping one in total darkness or with perhaps very brief interludes or moments of light. Sometimes there can be a breakthrough to another level, but often only after a crisis and perhaps acute pain. St. Benedict, in discussing the fourth degree of humility, speaks of the monastic who "quietly embraces suffering and endures it without weakening or seeking escape . . . for the Lord's sake."[21]

Another good description of this stage, with its experience of inner storm that may eventually lead to repose, comes from the thirteenth-century Flemish nun Beatrice of Nazareth's *The Seven Manners of Loving.* She describes the fifth manner in the following way:

> The crisis point of the relation between love and knowledge occurs in the fifth manner. The experience of love is no longer fully delightful but is mixed with sorrow. The disproportion between love and knowledge leaves the soul frustrated. . . . Love awakens in the heart like a storm—a tempest so violent . . . that it threatens to break the heart. The storm bears the soul outward into expressions of love and then returns the soul into the heart of the sea. At its most riotous moment the storm carries the soul outward into occupations of love. When the storm breaks, love falls back to its source. . . . Yet in its phase of tranquil repose the soul is not inactive. Though resting in the embrace of love—as in a quieted sea—the soul with all its powers is intensely focused: it is fully energized, strong in spirit, conscious of itself—in fact, it seems to be all activity at the moment of its greatest quiet.[22]

In the Joy of the Holy Spirit

In the third stage of prayer, St. Benedict speaks of the one who does everything "in the joy of the Holy Spirit." Here, we have a picture of the monk or nun whose life has become integrated and full of the gifts of the Holy Spirit. Fear is cast out by perfect love of God. Through this love, all that was once performed with dread, will now begin to be observed without effort, as though naturally, from habit.[23]

One of the phenomena experienced at this stage is that often even the person's outward bearing reflects his inner harmony and unity. St. Bernard comments on this in Sermon 85 in his commentary on the Song of Songs:

> When the spiritual light of beauty has filled all the depths of the heart with its abundance, it must necessarily shine outwardly. . . . It erupts and its rays appear in the body, reflection of the soul. . . . This beauty spreads through the limbs and senses until the whole body manifests its brilliance: the way of acting, of speaking, the look. . . . The movements of the whole body and of the senses in their gestures . . . will show the beauty of the soul.[24]

At this stage it seems that often the phenomenon of light is used to express divine realities. Our Father St. Benedict had the following experience:

> Long before the Night Office had begun, the man of God was standing at his window, where he watched and prayed while the rest were still asleep. In the dead of night he suddenly beheld a flood of light shining down from above more brilliant than the sun, and with it every trace of darkness cleared away. Another remarkable sight followed. According to his own description, the whole world was gathered up before his eyes in what appeared to be a single ray of light.[25]

It is also said of an old desert Father: "A brother came to the cell of Abba Arsenius at Scetis. Waiting outside of the door he saw the old man entirely like a flame."[26] And St. Seraphim, a nineteenth-century Russian hermit who was a monk of the monastery of Sarov, heard the complaint of one of his disciples: "I cannot look at you, Father, because lightning flashes from your eyes. Your face has become brighter than the sun, and my eyes ache."[27]

A closer examination of the life of St. Seraphim reveals many other phenomena proper to the advanced stages of the spiritual life: the gift of healing, levitation, clairvoyance, many visions, deep peace, joy and compassion, a development of the spiritual senses, etc. While he had periods of extreme asceticism and did not speak to anyone for many years, toward the end of his life he felt called by God to be a spiritual guide. He had a happy disposition and would call people: "My Joy." There is a beautiful story about Seraphim and it is recounted by the abbess of a monastery of nuns under his direction. The abbess writes:

> Although he did not allow evil talk or anything bad, he never forbade anyone to be merry. He would ask me sometimes: "Well, Good Mother, do you join the sisters when they have their meal?" And as I answered No, he would exclaim: "How now, good Mother! my Joy, if you are not hungry, do not eat; but never fail to sit at table with them. They may come in tired and depressed, but seeing you at their table, full of gaiety and gentleness toward them, and of good cheer, they too will regain their courage and gaiety, and will eat more and with greater enjoyment. For gaiety is no sin, good Mother. It drives away fatigue and fatigue breeds accidie [despondency]."[28]

There are many accounts of visions and raptures among monastics, but perhaps more impressive is the fact that some of these visions led to a new way of life or a deep unification of the person. This was certainly true for St. Gertrude, whose whole attitude was transformed after a vision of Christ: "All places now seemed sacred to her; all times and activities holy, not only those involving worship."[29] Another such example was Mother Louise de Ballon, a seventeenth-century nun who was the first superior of the Bernardine reform. Her visions led her to organize her life around the theme of simplicity. After beholding the simplicity of God and of the angels, she introduced simplicity as a reform and way of living the religious life.[30]

Ida of Nivelles, a Flemish Cistercian nun born in 1199, although not highly educated was full of charismatic gifts. Among those listed in Ida's life "were knowledge of things past and future or present happenings far away, and clairvoyance."[31] But her mystical life also brought her a deep sense of compassion:

> Her charity and cheerfulness were in evidence throughout her life. If in the monastery, she noticed a sister looking sad, she would sit beside her "and let the cheerfulness of her own sunny face blow away the clouds on her sister's countenance." She remained sensitive to the needs and sorrows of others, sometimes to the extent that her delicate health was affected. Her compassion also expressed itself in prayerful intercession for others—an intercession that she lived out.[32]

Again, it is important to remember that the stress here is not so much on the visions or the ability of the saints to do miracles, but on the gift of love, compassion, peace, and joy. These are the true signs that persons have received the gifts of the Holy Spirit and that their lives are given over to God who acts in and through them. It implies their total surrender to God. This would be the criterion for the authenticity of any spiritual phenomenon. They are like fingers pointing to the moon. Here the moon would represent a life in Christ Jesus, to see Jesus as the manifestation of the life of God and to receive a communion of life with him.[33]

Using other words, Thomas Merton described the reality of this life of God within us in lyrical tones shortly before his death:

> At the center of our being is a point of nothingness which is untouched by sin and by illusion, a point of pure truth, a point or spark which belongs entirely to God, which is never at our disposal, from

which God disposes of our lives, which is inaccessible to the fantasies of our own mind or the brutalities of our own will. This little point of nothingness and of *absolute poverty* is the pure glory of God in us. It is so to speak His name written in us, as our poverty, as our indigence, as our dependence, as our sonship. It is like a pure diamond, blazing with the invisible light of heaven. It is in everybody, and if we could see it we would see these billions of points of light coming together in the face and blaze of a sun that would make all the darkness and cruelty of life vanish completely. . . . I have no program for this seeing. It is only given. But the gate of heaven is everywhere.[34]

5

Community and Guidance

The silence of Gethsemani speaks volumes about the spiritual life. As we moved through and kept that silence, we understood that it provides a spiritual openness, a place in which to dwell and explore with deeper awareness what is truly within and around us. This spiritual atmosphere is something that takes the full community to create. It is not the result of persons not speaking, but of persons silently working, walking, eating, serving, caring, suffering, offering—fully living with gentle attention to living fully.

When we, Buddhists and Christians, gathered in a small chapel to meditate together in silence as the sun was rising in the morning, we also realized that this quiet space was opening us to a deeper experience of our own being and of our being together. Again, this experience of depth and unity is not something that one person could create, it took the full community of persons dedicated to the spiritual life. It also nourished our sense of solidarity as fellow pilgrims, which in turn enriched our dialogue and daily life together.

There are moments of silence and places of silence on the spiritual journey. Then there are the times and places when and where it is necessary to process what is happening on the journey, to speak to others about one's heart and mind, to seek guidance from wise elders. In those times and places, it is important to share one's journey with a spiritual guide. So, after speaking about the stages of growth and development on the spiritual journey, it seemed appropriate to discuss the importance of community and guidance in this process of spiritual transformation.

The Ven. Dr. Chuen Phangcham presents the role of the *Sangha* (monastic community) and the teacher in the Theravada practice of meditation. He discusses in some detail the *Dhamma* (teaching) of the Buddha and shows how the Buddha is a role model for Buddhist teachers of a *Dhamma* that calls for moral, meditative and wisdom training. Phangcham then presents the kind of Buddhist community that contributes to this training by providing a spiritual and meditative atmosphere. In that context, he also discusses the role of the meditation teacher in the process of spiritual development that produces mindfulness, cultivates the inner spiritual faculties, brings awareness of things as they really are, and leads to *Nibbana*.

The Ven. Dr. Yifa speaks about the great success of the Buddhist nuns' communities in Taiwan today. Reflecting her own experience as a nun of the Fokuangshan Buddhist Order, she explains why this vocation is so attractive to thousands of women in Taiwan. Inspired by their master, the Ven. Hsing Yun, her fellow Buddhist nuns have developed a youthful and energetic community life that has enabled them to advance in spiritual development, and also to enter the world with "a transcendental spirit" in order to make religious, educational and social contributions to society.

Another talk from the Chinese tradition presents six characteristics of a Ch'an (Zen) Master. The Ven. Dr. Sheng-yen's talk, delivered by his disciple the Ven. Guo Chou, tells how the Ch'an Master first masters himself or herself. Then he or she must possess correct views and attain valid practice and realization or enlightenment. With this realization in a true *Dharma* lineage of transmission, a Master also receives a proper sanction for his or her awakening and permission for teaching. Then, a Master must have the ability and conditions for teaching, such as students and community support. Finally, the Ch'an Master develops skillful methods for teaching students that will make him or her successful in transmitting awakening.

His Holiness the Dalai Lama discusses how the monastic community keeps the Buddha's teachings alive. He presents the Buddhist understanding of celibacy and the importance of monastic rules for the spiritual life. He shows how the guru—who is learned, disciplined and has a good heart—can provide a role model for practitioners on the basis of respect and the spiritual qualities of their student-teacher relationship. His Holiness then shows how the attainment of Nirvana depends on the nature of the mind as clear light, and on the removal of mental defilements such as ignorance. He concludes by discussing Nirvana, God, higher beings and the practice of deity yoga.

Sr. Donald Corcoran presents a Christian understanding of spiritual guidance. While the spiritual guide in Christianity is not responsible for a person-to-person transmission of realization, he or she plays more of a midwife role in the spiritual formation of a Christian's life. The real guidance comes from the Holy Spirit working in the person's mind and heart. This ongoing passage from being self-filled to being spirit-filled shows forth in love, compassion, wisdom and prophetic insight. In the monastic community, the *Rule* is itself a teacher. It produces a spiritual culture, a spiritual atmosphere, in the context of which the monastic guide helps the monks or nuns discern the work of the spirit within them as it heals, integrates and expands their hearts and minds with purity and charity.

Armand Veilleux has given us a very moving presentation of the role of the community in the contemplative life as it can be seen in the monastic community of Our Lady of Atlas in Algeria. All but two of the monks of this Trappist monastery were recently martyred. The Testament of Dom Christian de Chergé gives us a glimpse into the contemplative foundations of their communal existence. Their radical freedom, poverty and purity of heart lived out in daily communal life gave them the eyes to see God in the "shining beauty" of their Muslim neighbors—and even in the faces of those who took their lives: "Contemplative life has no frontiers."

Teaching Meditation in the Buddhist Community

VEN. DR. CHUEN PHANGCHAM

Araham Sammasambuddho Bhagava,
Buddham Bhagavantam Abhivademi.

> The Blessed One, far from mental defilements,
> the Perfectly Self-Enlightened One, the Awakened One, I bow down to the Blessed One.

Svakkhato Bhagavata Dhammo,
Dhammam Namassami.

> The *Dhamma*, the Law of Reality, the Noble Doctrines,
> well-expounded by the Blessed One,
> I pay homage to the *Dhamma*.

Supatipanno Bhagavato Savakasangho,
Sangham Namami.

> The *Sangha*, the Noble Disciples of the Blessed One, who have practiced well, I pay respect to the *Sangha*.

In this reciting, we see the three constituents of Buddhism: namely, the Buddha, the *Dhamma* (what the Buddha taught) and the *Sangha* (the order or community of disciples of the Buddha). These three essential elements of Buddhism are known as the Three Gems (*Tiratama*). Let us look at each of these Gems as we explore the role of the teacher and the community in the practice of Buddhist meditation.

Who Is the Buddha?

The Buddha was a human being born about 566 B.C.E. to King Suddhodana and Queen Maya in Royal Park, Lumbini, which is now southern Nepal. The prince was named Siddhartha Gotama. He married Princess Yasodhara at the age of 16, renounced the world and became a monk at the age of 29, and attained enlightenment at the age of 35. Since then he has come to be known as the Awakened One, the Buddha. He spend 45 years teaching the *Dhamma* to the people and establishing his *Sangha*. He passed away from their eyes at the age of 80. He left us with his most valuable and enduring teachings in which we find the way to the truth, enlightenment, real happiness and peace. Buddhist followers pay respect to the Buddha not as a god, but as the Perfect One, a human being who has a perfect and pure mind, the greatest teacher of the great teachers, the Blessed One. By his example, the Buddha left us a perfect model for being a teacher of Buddhism. He also left us the *Dhamma* to be used in the teaching of Buddhism, as well as the *Sangha* structure in which these teachings can best be conveyed to the people.

What Is the Dhamma?

The *Dhamma* is what the Buddha taught, namely, the true law of reality discovered by him, the noble doctrines well expounded by The Blessed One, Gotama Buddha. This *Dhamma* is taught to have the following seven characteristics: (1) it is to be seen here and now, (2) it is experienced as timeless, (3) it invites all people to come and see, (4) it leads inward, (5) it can be seen by the wise, (6) it protects those who hold to it from falling into miserable worlds after death, (7) it is the destroyer of the darkness of ignorance.

In the first sermon of the Buddha, he taught his first five disciples to avoid the extremes of sensual indulgence and self-mortification. The former retards one's spiritual progress and the latter weakens one's intellect. The Buddha himself put into practice both of these extremes before he found the way to enlightenment. He lived the first when he was a prince living in his father's palace before he renounced the world. He lived the second as an ascetic in the forest prior to his enlightenment. Hence he realized their nature and discovered that only self-conquest in moderation leads to the ultimate goal of a perfect and free mind, of enlightenment and *Nibbana*.

The Buddha then taught his disciples the Four Noble Truths, namely, the Noble Truths about suffering, the cause of suffering, the extinction of the cause of suffering, and the path leading to the extinction of the cause of suffering. Thus, the Buddha explained to his new disciples the causes of suffering and how to put them to an end. After his talk, one of the five ascetics, the most senior named Kontanya, realized the truth of the Buddha. He became witness to the Buddha's enlightenment and thus became the first monk in Buddhism. Later, he and his four friends, Vappa, Bhaddiya, Mahanama, and Assaji, received ordination from the Buddha, practiced meditation according to the Buddha's instruction and realized the *Dhamma*. They then became *arahants*, enlightened followers of the Buddha. Here we see the goal of Buddhist teachers, namely, to lead their students by teaching and meditation training toward an enlightened realization of the *Dhamma*.

It should be noted here that the *Dhamma* realized by the Buddha is the law of reality. It is the truth about ourselves and the world, that is both a means of deliverance from suffering, and deliverance itself. Whether the Buddhas arise or not, the *Dhamma* exists for all eternity. It is the Buddha that realized the *Dhamma* which lay hidden from the ignorant eyes of humanity until he, the Enlightened One, came and compassionately revealed it to the world.

The Buddha once said,

> Whether the *Tathagatas* [Enlightened Ones] appear or not, O monks, it remains a fact, an established principle, a natural law that all conditioned things are transient [*anicca*], suffering [*dukkha*] and that everything is selfless [*anatta*]. This fact the *Tathagata* realizes, understands, teaches, proclaims, establishes, discloses, analyzes and clarifies: that all conditioned things are impermanent, suffering, and that everything is selfless.

Given this suffering element of conditioned existence, the Buddha also said: "One thing does the Buddha teach, namely, suffering and cessation of suffering." For the cessation of the causes of this suffering—namely, craving, hate, and delusion—the Buddha introduced the Noble Eightfold Path that will lead to the end of suffering.

The Eightfold Path consists of: (1) Right Understanding or Right View, (2) Right Thought or Right Motivation, (3) Right Speech, (4) Right Action, (5) Right Livelihood, (6) Right Effort, (7) Right Mindfulness, and (8) Right Concentration. This Noble Eightfold Path can be divided into three levels for Buddhist training: (1) Right Speech, Right Action and Right Livelihood are classified as the moral level of training; (2) Right Effort, Right Mindfulness, and Right Concentration are classified as the meditative level of training; and (3) Right Understanding and Right Thought are classified as the wisdom level of training. Because Buddhism is a way of living, not merely a theory about life, training in this path is essential to self-deliverance. Cease to do bad deeds, learn to do good, cleanse your own heart (through meditation practice). This is the teaching of the Buddhas. Therefore, the Buddhist teacher must be able not only to teach the doctrines of the Buddha, as a teacher he or she must also be able to guide the student in moral, meditative and wisdom training. And this training takes place in the *Sangha*, the spiritual community.

What Is the Sangha?

The *Sangha* is the order or communities of disciples of the Buddha. Another definition is a community of persons who believe, trust and follow the Buddha's teachings in order to realize the truth of reality, the *Dhamma*. There are three levels of the *Sangha*, namely, the Noble *Sangha*, the Ordinary *Sangha*, and the community of lay disciples of the Buddha:

1. The Noble *Sangha* refers to those Noble Disciples of the Buddha who attained enlightenment. When we pay homage to the *Sangha*, we refer to the community of these Noble Disciples of the Buddha and their virtues. They preserved the *Dhamma* and transmitted it to us. They were responsible for spreading the *Dhamma* and ensuring that the teachings of the Buddha endured. The Noble Disciples, having realized the *Dhamma*, remained to instruct others and help them attain enlightenment too. They are the treasures of the *Dhamma*, and by their practice and teaching of the *Dhamma* to others, the Buddhist tradition continues today.

2. The Ordinary *Sangha* is the community of fully ordained monastics, both male and female, who observe at least 227 precepts in their daily life. These monastics leave their families and become homeless as they search for the *Dhamma*. They practice the *Dhamma* and guide people by training them to avoid bad deeds, to cultivate good deeds and to cleanse their mind of impurities. These monastics shave their heads, dress in robes and work for the benefit and happiness of humankind without expecting any return or reward. Today in the United States, you may find many of them walking in the streets of cities like Chicago, Los Angeles, New York and Washington, D.C.

3. The community of Buddhist lay followers study, learn and practice the *Dhamma* in daily life. They practice the *Dhamma* in many ways, such as being kind and compassionate to all living beings, respecting others and honoring all people from all walks of life. In their treatment of others, they disregard social, economic, religious, and family background. In the broadest sense, it can be said that people who follow the Eightfold Path in order to train for their own enlightenment and for the benefit of all humankind are members of the *Sangha*.

Teachers in the Sangha

The Buddha once said to his monks: "O monks, to attain the enlightenment or freedom of mind you have to work out your own salvation by your own effort. One depends on oneself; the *Tathagata* is only a teacher." So, we consider the Buddha to be a teacher of the *Sangha*. He is the model for all teachers in the *Sangha*, and it is his *Dhamma* that we teach. In the monastic *Sangha* of Theravada Buddhism, the teachers are male and female monastics. But in the *Sangha* in general, there can be both monastic and lay teachers. Monastic and lay teachers have both played significant roles in Buddhist communities in all parts of Asia. The handing down of the *Dhamma* has been dependent upon the compassion and hard work of many teachers in the *Sangha* who follow the example of the Buddha. These monastic and lay teachers have studied, learned, lived, and taught the *Dhamma* to people, helping them to understand and training them to pursue their practice in order to realize the full truth and real happiness.

As for the monastic teachers, not only have they played leadership roles in the teaching of doctrine and the practice of meditation in the monasteries, but they have also been leaders in the fields of social, cultural and economic development throughout the centuries. Sometimes their role has been to be judge and mediator, helping to find a compromise in disputes concerning the family and social problems of lay followers. The monastic teachers have also been good role models for a simple and peaceful life-style. In addition, the monasteries are not closed to the people, and even the temple grounds are often used as playgrounds for families, including children.

Teachers of Meditation

The word "meditation" is a translation of the Pali word *bhavana*, which means "to develop," "to improve," "to cultivate" mindfulness and awareness so that the mind can become healthy and strong. Meditation is the way to cultivate the mind so it becomes calm, clear, peaceful, stable, bright, light and pure. And ultimately this way of meditation leads to the cessation of suffering by enabling the meditators to *"see things as they really are."*

Meditation is the way to psychologically train the mind to develop the tools of "mindfulness" and "insight," enabling meditators to realize inner peace and enlightenment. The development of mindfulness, or awareness, is the very heart of Buddhist meditation. The "Four Foundations of Mindfulness" were emphasized by the historical Buddha. He once said: "There is one way, O monks, for the purification of beings, for overcoming of sorrow and lamentation, for disappearance of suffering, grief and pain, for winning the Noble Path, for realizing enlightenment, *Nibbana*, that is to say, the Four Foundations of Mindfulness." These four include: (1) mindfulness of the body, (2) mindfulness of feelings or sensations, (3) mindfulness of thinking, and (4) mindfulness of the mind's objects.

By mindful awareness of all aspects of our being, we can discover the causes of our unhappiness. Unhealthy mental and emotional patterns can be exposed to a powerful meditative insight that brings freedom and happiness. Therefore, particular meditation techniques taught by Theravada teachers include both *samatha bhavana* and *vipassana bhavana*, or "tranquillity meditation" and "insight meditation." In teaching meditation, Buddhism lays great stress on the need for both inward stillness and penetrating insight through the process of spiritual training in morality, mental culture, and wisdom. This training leads in time to the development of the inner spiritual faculties and enlightenment.

As Buddhists, we believe that human beings should at all times be mindful and self-possessed in order to be free from mental and emotional attachments to worldly life. This freedom is achieved by developing an increasingly mindful attitude to our inner and outer circumstances while meditating. This helps the practioner to keep his or her reactions always under control. Therefore the spiritual life, with periods of quiet for inner spiritual training, is essential for a balanced and peaceful life. For this purpose, meditation teachers train practitioners to apply Right Effort, Right Mindfulness, Right Thought, and Right Concentration from the Noble Eightfold Path.

Let us take Right Effort as an example. There are four kinds of positive effort described by the Buddha, namely: (1) effort to prevent new evil thoughts from entering one's mind, (2) effort to remove all evil that exists already in the mind, (3) effort to develop whatever good is in one's mind, and (4) effort to acquire still more good unceasingly. This effort involves the right use of one's energies, so a good teacher trains one to secure the maximum results with the minimum expenditure of force. This training also demands a knowledge of the whole field of modern psychology on the part of the teacher in order to identify and eliminate mental-emotional factors and patterns that result in inner friction and consequent loss of energy and power. In today's world especially, experienced teachers with a knowledge of the *Dhamma*, the techniques of meditation, and modern psychology are needed to guide people in the process of inner healing and mental development.

Expert Buddhist meditation teachers give instruction, interviews, and offer guidance to meditation practitioners in a step-by-step process of mental culture. This is done on an individual basis or in a group in a calm, quiet, natural atmosphere in both forest and urban monasteries. Without experienced teachers, meditation practitioners may go in a wrong way that will be harmful to their practice as well as a waste of time. And without the *Sangha* environment, meditation practitioners may not have the meditative atmosphere needed to progress in the cultivation of a spiritual life. In the Theravada tradition, therefore, experienced teachers and the *Sangha* are needed. Teachers in the *Sangha* are called "good friends" of their students, just as mothers and fathers are in many ways good friends of their children. In Thailand there are many male and female meditation teachers giving instruction to practitioners today. They work actively with different centers throughout the country and also here in the West.

Conclusion

Dear *Dhamma* brothers and sisters. We have shaved our heads and donned the robes, be it of any tradition, and we carry with us the message of the Enlightened Ones. We have left ourselves behind, and now go forth representing the *Buddha*, the *Dhamma*, and the *Sangha* to be a refuge for ourselves and for others.

Think of what the Buddha said to his first group of 60 disciples before he sent them out to be teachers of the *Dhamma:* "Go monks, not two of you in one direction, proclaim the *Dhamma* beautiful in the beginning, beautiful in the middle, and beautiful at the end for the benefit and happiness of many out of compassion and loving kindness."

May all beings be free from enmity, be free from ill-treatment, be free from suffering, and may all beings be happy. May all of us be successful in our duties and responsibilities for the peace of communities and peace for the world as a whole.

The Women's *Sangha* in Taiwan

VEN. DR. YIFA

The phenomenal growth of Mahayana Buddhism in Taiwan today is something unique in recent history. Why is Buddhism flowering so fragrantly in Taiwan? One reason is the significant contributions of the Buddhist nuns which have also greatly benefited Taiwanese society. I have been asked to address the role of the religious community in the formation of its members. Therefore, I would like to present an example of a prominent *bhiksuni Sangha*, or nuns' Order, in the Mahayana tradition in Taiwan. I will also show the important role Master Hsing Yun has played as a modern teacher in its development. A better understanding of the *bhiksuni Sangha* will provide us with a vehicle for exchanging ideas among our religious traditions.

Present Status

More than 2,500 years ago, as a result of the pleas of Mahaprajapati Gotama with 500 other women, and the support of the elder disciple Ananda, the Buddha accepted nuns into the Buddhist monastic Order. This was the formal establishment of the *bhiksuni* Order. However, the *bhiksuni* Order in the Theravada tradition did not continue after the year 1017 C.E. As Buddhism traveled to the East, there were also women who took vows to become nuns. In 433 C.E., there were eleven Sri Lankan nuns who came to China and transmitted the *bhiksuni* precepts. This was the first transmission of *bhiksuni* precepts which was in accord with the disciplinary teachings of the Buddha. From that point on, the Mahayana Buddhist nuns' Order was able to transmit its practice generation after generation.

Due to the Chinese Communist government, since 1949 religious freedom and activities have been suppressed. Many Buddhist monastics fled to Taiwan; and in 1953, Chinese Buddhist monastics transmitted the Buddhist precepts to Taiwan for the first time. Thus, the Buddhist nuns in Taiwan have inherited the Chinese transmission of the *bhiksuni* Order. With an emphasis on monastic moral discipline and practice, the nuns' Order in Taiwan is one of virtue and chastity.

Presently, there are about 21 million people in Taiwan. Of this population, one-fourth (5 million) are Buddhist practitioners. There are many Buddhist temples and over 10,000 monastics with a ratio of one monk to four nuns. The better known established *bhiksuni* Orders are Hsiang-Kuang Monastery and Chen Fo Shan. However, in the Fokuangshan Buddhist Order alone—which is the largest in the Republic of China—there are well over 1,000 nuns.

In Taiwan, Mahayana Buddhist nuns receive higher education, establish temples, give Buddhist lectures, conduct research, transmit Buddhist disciplinary precepts, manage temple economics, as well as manage and participate in various charitable programs such as free medical care, child care and services for senior citizens. These nuns have not only reformed the old traditional Buddhist monastic system, but have also proved to be equal with the male Buddhist practitioners. Consequently, in addition to advancing within the monastic hierarchy, the nuns have made many religious, educational and social contributions to society. Thus, they have helped to propel Buddhism into people's daily lives and thereby to purify Taiwan society.

While working in these ways to create a Pure Land on earth, the Buddhist Order of nuns at Fokuangshan has some special characteristics.

It upholds the Mahayana Buddhist ideal of benefiting and serving society by "entering the world with a transcendental spirit." Therefore, while the nuns serve and work among the people, they also cultivate this transcendental spirit in themselves in many ways. Nuns of this Order deem the career of spreading of Buddhism to benefit others to be a "family" undertaking. So as sisters, they wholeheartedly invest their efforts together in cultural, educational, charitable, and religious activities.

Reasons for its Success

The founder of the Fokuangshan Buddhist Order is Ven. Master Hsing Yun. When he first set out to build his monastery 30 years ago, he received great assistance from many female lay Buddhist disciples. He later accepted into the Order those women who wished to be monastics, thus creating a permanent supporting force within the Order. Then, to establish a sound Buddhist educational system, Buddhist nuns were sent to Japan to study. In recent years, some Buddhist nuns of Fokuangshan have received their degrees from universities in the West. After graduation, greater responsibilities were given to the nuns so that they no longer played simply a supporting role in the temples. Soon, they conducted religious activities and became abbesses. Also, Buddhist nuns may give teachings to students in university lectures. A recent Yale graduate, I myself am now serving as the Dean of Academic Affairs at Hsi Lai University in Los Angeles. All of these new roles enable nuns with talent to demonstrate their abilities and take on leadership positions in ways that are not found in the older conservative Buddhist traditions.

These kinds of opportunities appeal to many young women in Taiwan. So, they enter the Buddhist educational system to gain education and also to explore the possibility of becoming a nun. Students with a high school or lower educational background are placed in the Eastern Buddhist College and the Tsung-Lin Buddhist University where they learn the basic doctrines and practices of Buddhism. Advanced level students may choose their major, and special foreign language education (English and Japanese) is available. Therefore, this Buddhist educational system not only develops Buddhist women's talents, it also serves as a means to discern the possibility of entering the Buddhist Order. When lay female students enter the Buddhist College to study, they gain a certain understanding of Buddhist monasticism and have the option to join the Order as nuns. If they do so, all tuition and resident fees are waived for the duration of their study.

Because of this system, over half of the nuns at Fokuangshan have received university or higher education. About three-fifths of the nuns are between 20 and 40 years of age. Therefore, this monastic Order is a young and energetic one—which makes it very attractive to young lay women. In addition to the members of the nuns' Order living and serving in Taiwan, there are hundreds serving in the Fokuangshan nuns' Order who are from America and Europe. Presently, the Fokuangshan nuns' Order also offers free long-term monastic education and training to promising young women from Nepal, Ledakh, Indonesia, Thailand, Malaysia, and Sri Lanka. With the goal of developing human talent and spiritual aspiration in service to the world, the Fokuangshan nuns' Order continues to train and encourage women as equal partners with male monastics.

Another aspect of our monastic life that appeals to young Asian women is its objective fairness. The advancement system upholds the laws of discipline taught by the Buddha and also follows the teachings of harmonious living. In Fokuangshan, nuns follow the monastery's personnel advancement program. Everyone is placed into this program according to education, age, expertise, and ordination seniority. Every year, there is an evaluation based on religious practice as well as academic and career achievement. With this healthy personnel system, the nuns of the monastery are encouraged to demonstrate their talents and abilities, and to practice with diligence. They follow the Buddhist concept of "relying on the *Dharma* (teachings) and not on individuals." In this system, all monastics, monks and nuns, are given equal opportunities. The Order is managed by a collective leadership assembly of monks and nuns known as the Religious Affairs Committee. The chairperson of this committee can be male or female and is elected by secret ballot.

One final reason for the success of our nuns' Order is the Ven. Master Hsing Yun's personal charisma and wise leadership. Many a disciple is enlisted and provides her or his ardent support for the internationalization and modernization of the Fokuangshan Buddhist Order due to the inspiration of Master Hsing Yun. One cannot underestimate the significance of the Master for the success of the Buddhist monastic Order. Over 1,000 women disciples have followed Master Hsing Yun into monasticism. As a remarkable educator, Master Hsing Yun recognizes the potential of the *bhiksuni* and provides equal opportunity for both his male and female disciples. In him, disciples, male and female, have a living model of an outstanding dynamic Buddhist Master.

Outlook for the Future

The teachings of the Buddha are "humanistic." That is, the Buddha emphasized the importance of human practice in order to gain liberation. More than ever before, people living in modern society need humanistic Buddhism. It is the duty of all Buddhists to bring this message of our true human potential to the world. Nuns in the Order will play an important role—in terms of the leadership, support, and organization—in such an international effort.

For example, to propagate Buddhism to the world, in 1992 the Ven. Master Hsing Yun founded the Buddha's Light International Association (BLIA). There are now over 100 chapters established on five continents. The purpose of this organization is to mobilize lay Buddhists and encourage them to be active throughout the world so that Buddhism may further penetrate and influence its social development. In realizing this ideal, nuns play a leading role in organizing activities and mobilizing resources. BLIA in Taiwan has received the "National Award for Social Achievement" for three consecutive years. This was due to the excellent leadership of the Ven. Tzu Jung, a Buddhist nun.

The future of Buddhist women's monasticism in Taiwan is bright indeed! With the modernization of Taiwan's multifaceted society, women in Taiwan society in general are courageously breaking free from their traditional molds. They seek the fulfillment of individual ideals. Moreover, with education easily accessible to everyone, women can now proclaim economic independence and demonstrate their talents and abilities. In Buddhist Orders, women are provided with a vast opportunity to develop and exercise their creativity, pursue personal spirituality, learn and teach the *Dharma*, and work together for the benefit of humankind. This breakthrough in the history of traditional Buddhism was made possible by the inspiring leadership of the Ven. Master Hsing Yun.

The Role of Ch'an Teachers in China

VEN. DR. SHENG-YEN

As many of you probably know, tradition has it that Ch'an Buddhism was transmitted into China from India. In India we cannot find anything we could properly call a Ch'an School of Buddhism. The heart of Ch'an is from India, but the form of Ch'an is really a Chinese development. Of course, Zen in Japan and Son in Korea later contributed to Ch'an Buddhism, and Americans today are surely joining the ranks of contributors to the development of this important form of Buddhism in the West. In all these traditions, the Ch'an Master plays a central role. In what follows, I will present six characteristics of a Ch'an Master.

Masters Oneself through the Practice of Ch'an Methods

The first aspect of being a Ch'an Master is to develop the use of Ch'an methods, and to master oneself through these methods. One can say that a Ch'an Master wants to develop the content of Ch'an, wants to understand and develop Ch'an methods, theories, and forms, and wants to train in these to master oneself.

However, properly speaking this self-mastery alone does not really constitute a Ch'an Master. It really constitutes someone who is a Ch'an practitioner. When we hear and speak of Ch'an Masters, we normally think of someone as being a Ch'an teacher. Being a Ch'an teacher, one has to have disciples, and among those disciples there must be disciples who are accomplished. Of someone who does not have accomplished disciples, disciples who have gained some sort of Ch'an realization, it would be difficult to speak of that person as being a Ch'an Master.

Possesses Correct Views

The second point is that a Ch'an Master must possess and develop correct views. What precisely do I mean by correct views? Here I want to make three points. First of all, one must have an understanding of moral causes and conditions, understood as karma and its workings, as a basic, guiding principle. This is essential: it is one of the criteria for developing "Right View" in Buddhism.

Second, one must take this understanding of the world as operating by causes and conditions as one's point of view or one's outlook on all things. And thirdly, based on this understanding, one must make as one's goal the realization of the emptiness of self, the emptiness, the marklessness, the featurelessness of things.

Regarding the topic of causes and conditions, there is a text credited to Bodhidharma, the First Patriarch of Ch'an. The name of this text is roughly translated as "The Two Entrances, and the Four Approaches to Practice." In effect, the "Two Entrances" mean the two entrances to realizing the content of the core of Ch'an. These two entrances are as follows. The first is called the "Entrance by Principle," or the "Principle of Absolute Reality." This entrance by Principle in the Ch'an tradition is the notion of sudden or instantaneous enlightenment or awakening. The idea here is that one does not use any deliberate effort or method, but comes to a realization instantaneously.

The second entrance is "Entrance by Practice," and is in fact the Four Approaches to Practice. In these approaches we find correspondences to the understanding of the world in terms of causes and conditions. For example, the first of the four practices tells how to respond to enmity, anger, or aggression from others with an open and accepting mind. That corresponds to my notion of taking karmic causes and conditions as a basic principle. Thus, one deals with anger with this principle by understanding the anger in terms of causes and conditions, of karmic connections, and so forth.

The second of the four practices follows the outlook that everything transpires or comes to us through the operation of multiple causes and conditions. Thus, if fame and fortune come to us, it is not only a result of one's own doing or one's own efforts. It is a contribution of past lives, of one's encounters and relationships with many other people. The same is true when bad things happen. The idea behind this is that events and circumstances come and go in relation to many karmic causes and conditions. These events are not something over which one has absolute control.

Finally, to have a correct view, one must have as one's goal the realization of the emptiness of self and the marklessness or featurelessness of reality. This means that nothing has absolute permanent existence. Nothing is unchanging. By mark or feature, I mean something which defines the existence of something. The idea of marklessness means that there are no absolute, unchanging, permanent features or marks that define the factors of existence, since everything is constantly changing. This includes people as well as things. People and things are really all events that are influenced by changing causes and conditions. The lesson of understanding marklessness is not to be attached to any phenomenon or any event, to realize that it is only a product of causes and conditions. The term "emptiness" used here is also sometimes difficult to understand. It does not mean that things are absolutely nonexistent. It emphasizes, again, this idea that everything is a product of multiple causes and conditions so that everything is "empty" of any absolute permanent existence.

On the other hand, some people believe that this attainment of nonattachment implies that Ch'an Masters are free to do whatever they want—that because of their enlightenment they are not subject to the karmic retribution that ordinary people experience. This misunderstanding may result from some unusual teaching techniques that a Master may have used once in a lifetime. For example, Nan Ch'uen once killed a cat to show some monks how their attachment was ruining their practice. Even if his mind was free, he certainly suffered karmically for this action. Ch'an Masters are subject to the law of karma, and they must follow the rules of the monastery and the society at large. They may not do whatever they please in ways that breed desire in themselves and in those around them.

Experiences Practice and Realization

The third criterion is that one must have experience of two things—practice and realization. By practice, I mean religious practice, and by realization I mean enlightenment. Without these two things you cannot be a Ch'an Master. If you do not practice, you really cannot be a Ch'an Master, because Ch'an is an experience. We can also divide practice and realization into three parts. These are three very traditional aspects to practicing Buddhism. The first one of these is that one must have a very stable and normal life-style and approach to life guided by moral principles. The approach to the development of this kind of life is what we call Buddhist precepts. When it comes to precepts, for a person to practice effectively in Ch'an, it is absolutely necessary for one's life to be morally very stable, very regular, very routine. This is an important prior condition.

The second aspect of the practice and development of enlightenment in Ch'an is meditative concentration, or the mental stability developed by meditation. This is necessary to ease us from the influence of external surroundings, of the environment. Meditative concentration is developed by sitting in meditation, as a form of practice.

Finally we come to the third aspect, namely, the experience of awakening and enlightenment itself. This awakening and enlightenment involves two aspects—wisdom and liberation. If you do not have enlightenment experiences that involve liberation, and if you do not have enlightenment experiences that involve wisdom, you are not really a true Ch'an Master. If you do not have wisdom, and if you do not have true experiences of liberation, you cannot develop genuine compassion. If you do not have compassion and teach students, you will probably do them a lot of harm.

Possesses a True Dharma *Lineage*

The fourth criterion for becoming a Ch'an Master is that one must have a true or correct *Dharma* lineage. There are three aspects to having correct *Dharma* transmission. One must have the guidance of an illumined teacher, a teacher who has a high degree of realization and understanding, who can recognize your progress in Ch'an and can lead you through the different stages of Ch'an practice. This is very important for becoming a Ch'an Master. Secondly, one also must have the recognition or sanction of a bona fide Ch'an Master. Only a person who is already enlightened can recognize enlightenment and awakening in another person. This is the idea of transmission in Ch'an: the Ch'an Master must approve your awakening. The third aspect is that one must have permission to teach from a bona fide Ch'an Master. There can be a number of people who receive sanction of their awakening, but being able to teach Ch'an is something different.

This need for an awakened or enlightened teacher poses something of a problem. One really has to have awakening oneself to be able to know if a teacher is enlightened and capable of functioning as a really good teacher. For a student of Ch'an, it is impossible to know if you are in fact studying with the right teacher. And there are many people around who consider themselves Ch'an teachers.

The idea of a sanction or approval of one's experiences is also very important. One needs to go to an experienced and enlightened teacher in order to know if you have achieved what you feel you have. A teacher can tell by your speech and behavior whether your experience is genuine or not. For the most part, what people feel are Ch'an experiences are really false enlightenment experiences. In fact, to receive a genuine sanction is not easy. The word for "sanction" in Chinese means a "seal" or a "stamp." There is a famous saying from Ch'an masters of the past: "A seal made of pure gold is a difficult thing to find." There are many seals (or sanctions), but very few are made of gold.

You also need approval to go out and spread Ch'an teachings and to train other persons and disciples. This is not a simple matter. Can a person with the sanction of enlightenment really be a teacher without the formal approval of his or her teacher? There are circumstances under which it is permissible. It depends on a number of factors. For example, if a student was practicing hard and received sanction for his or her enlightenment but did not get approval to teach before the Master passed away, it might be that in a short time thereafter that student's capability could mature enough to be able to be a Ch'an Master.

Possesses Meritorious Influence

There is a fifth criterion that is necessary if one is to be a Ch'an Master. On top of having sanction for one's awakening and having permission to teach, one must really possess the influence or power of merit. By influence or power of merit, I mean three things. First, I mean literally the time and space to teach. For example, in China during the Cultural Revolution, there was no way that one was able to teach. The circumstances were impossible.

The second criterion of possessing the power or influence of merit is that one must have people to teach who are truly interested in learning about Ch'an. And finally, while one might have time and a place to teach at one's disposal, and might have an audience to teach, one also needs to have a patron or support from individuals in the community. This could be material support as well as human resources. Without these resources, you really cannot teach.

Possesses Skillful Methods in Teaching

The sixth criterion is that one needs skillful means, skillful methods, and skillful knowledge of methods with which to teach students. I have in mind here four things. First, one really needs an intellectual knowledge of Buddhism. Second, one needs worldly knowledge, knowledge of the world as it is. Third, one needs powers of observation. And fourth, one needs the power to respond appropriately to various circumstances.

You have probably heard the saying that Zen (Ch'an) does not depend upon words and letters. Zen involves direct realization of one's true nature. Many people who hear or read of this type of saying would think that a Ch'an Master does not need to have a formal knowledge of Buddhism. All a Ch'an Master has to do is curse and beat people and that is enough for enlightenment. However, it is a rather ironic fact that in the history of Chinese Buddhism the school that produced the most literature is Ch'an. Actually the expression "not depending on words and letters" does not mean that one does not read about Buddhism. It means that one does not *ultimately* depend on language, or discriminating knowledge based on language, to reach enlightenment. So, for someone who does not have any knowledge of Buddhist teaching, it would be very difficult to be a *Buddhist* Master. It is also true that if one does not have knowledge of worldly affairs and worldly matters, one really cannot act effectively in sympathy with one's students. One cannot be in accord with students under certain circumstances, and so it would be rather difficult to help them in Ch'an training.

The third item under the category of skillful knowledge and methods, the powers of observation, deals with the ability to observe with respect one's students or disciples. This is a very important matter. It is the power of observing and thus knowing their mental state. One must be able to clearly observe their behavior, and know what that behavior expresses about their inner mental state. This ability is needed to guide students, to meet their needs.

The fourth item, the ability to respond to circumstances, especially circumstances of a student in training, is also important. Simply put, it means that when a student needs reproaching, you should give the student a reprimand. When a student needs shouting, you should give the student a shout. If a student needs kind encouragement, one should give that student encouragement. In other words, one must be able to adapt one's responses to each student according to the student's needs at the moment.

As for shouting and things of that sort in Ch'an training, these methods should not be used at all times or under all circumstances, nor at any time you casually feel like doing it. The point is that it must serve a purpose and must be done at the appropriate time. The deciding factor is whether at that moment it is going to benefit that student. When done under the appropriate circumstances, the student will be very grateful. An analogy for this situation is a hen and her egg. In hatching the egg, the hen first sits on it and nurtures it for a long time. At about the time the chick is ready to hatch, the chick will start to peck its way out of the eggshell. At the same time, the mother hen may peck from the outside to help the baby chick to hatch and come out. But, if the mother hen pecks at the egg all the time before it is ready to hatch, the pecking does no good.

Being a Ch'an Master

Finally, in looking at these six characteristics, we can see what it means to be a true Ch'an Master. If one were to perfect certain aspects of some of these conditions well, but not necessarily all of them, one might be able to function as a Ch'an Master, there is no question about it. However, in order to be a really effective Ch'an Master, it is necessary to perfect the entire range of these conditions.

Spiritual Guidance and the Attainment of Nirvana

HIS HOLINESS THE DALAI LAMA

I would like to begin by talking about the role of the guru in the Buddhist spiritual community.

The Spiritual Community

There are two types of Buddhist teaching: scriptural teaching and realizational teaching. These teachings are approached by way of explanation and by way of practice. And it is in connection with these approaches to teaching that the *Sangha*, the spiritual community, is important. In Christianity also, and in Catholicism in particular, the spiritual community is very important. In Buddhism, it is on the basis of the full functioning of a certain number of monastics that you can determine whether the Buddha's teaching is a living practice or not. When the monastic community observes the three basic monastic practices, then we can say that the Buddha's teaching is still alive.

After Buddha was enlightened, he began setting forth the rules of discipline beginning with telling the five ascetics who were accompanying him that they should wear their lower robes in a level way, that is, not letting them sag. Eventually, Buddha taught the *Pratimoksha* of the

Mulasarvastivada, which is our *Vinaya* lineage of monastic precepts. According to this *Vinaya* lineage, the fully ordained *bhiksu*, or monk, has 253 precepts. According to the Theravada system, there are 227 precepts. However, the differences between these *Vinaya* systems are very minor.

Celibacy

Now with this in mind I would like to say something about celibacy. This is a common practice for both Buddhist and Catholic monks and nuns. However, we have different ideas concerning the practice of celibacy. In Buddhism, our goal is *moksha* (liberation) or Nirvana. What is Nirvana? It is the complete elimination of afflictive emotions. Among the afflictive emotions, according to all Buddhist schools of thought, desire or attachment is one of the key factors which bind the person in the cyclic existence of suffering. In this regard, sexual desire is one of the more serious sorts of attachment. And since our goal is the overcoming of these attachments, the practice of celibacy becomes important. This is the Buddhist understanding of the practice of celibacy.

The Christian concept of celibacy may be different, but the result is the same. Both say that the monastic should not engage in sexual practice. The reasons do not matter; what is important is that the practice of celibacy in both traditions is similar. Now concerning this practice, sometimes it may appear as if it were against human nature. This is because sexuality is a natural biological force and critical for human reproduction. Therefore, celibacy is not easy. But at the same time it is spiritually very important. So, in practicing celibacy we need a firm determination on the basis of an awareness of the disadvantage of sexual practice and the advantage of celibacy.

I think that in order to gain this awareness it is useful to examine the layperson's life-style. For example, look at those couples who have no children and worry a great deal about having a child. On the other hand, if they begin to have children, they have another worry, namely, they worry about having too many children. So, then they worry about birth control. That too is very difficult: birth control, and worst is abortion. This also brings mental troubles, mental burdens. And once you have a family, half of your freedom is already lost. So, maybe people with families or those who have love experiences have a life that is very colorful. But I think that this kind of life has too many ups and downs.

So while our life may be less colorful, our mental stability is much more steady. And in the long run, that is also good for one's health. I think it is very useful to think of the value of celibacy along these lines. Even in the short run there are advantages, such as mental stability, to a life-style with celibacy. In the long run, celibacy is a great help in the Buddhist way to achieve freedom from cyclic existence. And in the Christian way, celibacy also is helpful to developing greater devotion to God and other aspects of the spiritual life. Here, it need not be mentioned that celibacy is helpful in the long term; and it even makes a difference in the short term.

Monastic Rules

In Buddhism, there are general rules that are for all monks and nuns, and there are also rules that are specific to particular monasteries. The same is true in Christianity where there are general rules that all monks and nuns keep, and there are also particular rules that are kept by certain monastics. For example, in this monastery I noticed that after one finishes the meal at lunchtime, each monk washes his own spoons and forks. This for me is a new experience! It is very, very important to have strict rules in monastic life. This is not a matter of imposing rules by force. Rather one first examines himself or herself to see if, because of certain reasons, there is an attraction to becoming a monk or nun. Then when one makes up his or her mind, voluntarily he or she takes on this discipline.

These rules are very important aids to pursuing the spiritual life. Since some aids are more essential to cultivating the spiritual life than others, in our type of discipline generally there are practices that must be kept tightly, and others that can be kept more loosely. Some monasteries are more strict than others. I prefer to be more strict. I think that choice is very good because when one becomes lax in the spiritual life, then it is something like a small crack and the laxity eventually becomes greater and greater. So, it is very important to be more strict right from the beginning. Here, it is not a question of the quantity of monastics but their quality. From this we can see the importance of the spiritual community in both traditions.

The Spiritual Teacher

Now about the spiritual teacher. For there to be a good and strong spiritual community, there must be teachers who teach the path well, and for that, they must provide proper role models. Teaching about spiritual matters does not just take place on the intellectual level. The teacher must also show what is taught to his or her followers by example. The teacher must provide an example for the eyes of his or her followers. Then the students will develop a genuine appreciation or respect. If the teacher says one thing and does something else, how can the students develop genuine respect? And without that respect, how can the teacher lead the students in the spiritual life? True spiritual leading is not done by force, but arises from respect and devotion freely given. So to have a teacher or abbot of the highest quality—such as Thomas Merton—is extremely important.

In the Buddhist texts, they speak of three different qualities that the teacher must have: the teacher (1) must be learned, (2) must be disciplined, and (3) must have a good heart. Regarding the first two, as was said in an earlier Tibetan tradition, one must have learnedness that does not hinder the discipline, and one must have discipline that does not prevent learnedness. One needs to have a union of both learnedness and discipline. But, even though one has both learnedness and discipline, if one does not have a good heart then one cannot help on a vast scale.

The relationship between the teacher and student is also very important. Since the relationship between the student and the teacher is developed within a religious context, it has an impact on the implementation of practice. Teachers in some sense are not appointed. It is the student who chooses a teacher, who makes that person into his or her guru, because the teacher has certain spiritual qualities. So the status of guru is not an appointed one because for someone to have that status, he or she needs disciples. Therefore at the beginning, the student's side of the relationship is absolutely crucial. It is necessary for the student to watch, to check, to investigate whether a person has the proper qualities to be a guru—whether that person is really reliable or not. At the beginning, that kind of examination or investigation is extremely necessary. Otherwise, if you just hurriedly accept a person as your guru without much investigation, as time goes on you may find some fault in that person. Then, you could lose your respect and that is not good for a spiritual practitioner.

Because the qualities of a good teacher in the student-teacher relationship are of such great importance, Buddha himself spoke very clearly about the different types of qualifications that various levels of teachers must have. For example, Buddha spoke in great detail about the qualifications for a teacher of laypersons, of those receiving novice ordination, and of those receiving full ordination. At all these levels in the *Sangha*, the true guru—with learnedness, discipline and a good heart—guides practitioners with instruction and by personal example. In this way, one progresses toward the spiritual ideal of liberation in the community with the guidance of a guru.

The Attainment of Nirvana

Having said this about the role of the teacher and the *Sangha* in the attainment of liberation, I would like to say something about what it is that makes the attainment of Nirvana possible. There are two factors that make liberation possible: one is that the nature of the mind is clear light, and the other is that the defilements of the mind are adventitious, superficial. With respect to the fact that the nature of the mind is clear light, we can say that the basic nature of the mind is that it has the capacity to know, to cognize objects. It does not have a nature of *not* having the capacity to know objects. Therefore, since the mind itself has a nature of cognizing objects, ignorance of objects is not due to the nature of the mind but is due to some other obstructive factor. For instance, if you put your hand over your eyes, you will not see anything. That absence of sight is not due to the fact that the eye does not have a nature of seeing or capacity to see. It does have a nature of seeing, but something is obstructing its sight.

So then, what are these obstructing factors? In the scriptural collections of the *bodhisattvas*, there are descriptions of two types of obstructions: (1) those factors that are afflictive emotions and prevent liberation from cyclic existence, and (2) those factors that prevent knowledge of everything. Also, in the phenomenology of the *Treasury of Manifest Knowledge* tradition, there is a description of two types of ignorance. One is an afflictive ignorance, and the other is a nonafflictive ignorance.

Among the Buddhist systems there are many ways of identifying what these two types of obstructions are. I am going to give one description based on a text by Nagarjuna (ca. 150–250 C.E.). As it is said in Nagarjuna's *Seventy Stanzas on Emptiness*, that which views what arises from causes and conditions as existing as its own reality is ignorance. And from it, the twelve links of dependent arising, of a lifetime in cyclic existence, arise. Thus, Nagarjuna is saying that a consciousness that views what arises from causes and conditions as being produced in its own right, as existing from its own side, is ignorance.

So then, what is ignorance? Ignorance is a type of consciousness that does not know the actual mode of being of objects, and instead conceives the very opposite of the actual mode of being of objects. As Aryadeva (ca. 170–270 C.E.) says in his *Four-Hundred Stanzas on the Bodhisattva Deeds*, the seed of cyclic existence is consciousness, and objects are its sphere of activity; so when selflessness is seen in objects, the seed of cyclic existence ceases. The first part of the passage literally says, "The seed of cyclic existence is consciousness." If by "consciousness" Aryadeva meant that consciousness in general—or consciousness as such—is the seed of cyclic existence, there would be no way of overcoming cyclic existence. This is because consciousness itself has the nature of luminosity and knowing, and there is nothing that can act as a counteragent to consciousness having such a nature of luminosity and knowing. Thus,

Aryadeva's intention here is to refer to a specific type of afflictive consciousness as the seed of cyclic existence.

This becomes clear when Aryadeva says that since objects are the sphere of the activity of consciousness, if one sees selflessness in objects, the process of cyclic existence will be ceased. What then is this selflessness of objects? As Nagarjuna says in his *Treatise on the Middle,* "Those which are dependent arisings are said to be empty." That which arises in dependence on other factors arises relative to something else. That it arises dependently, or relative to something else, is a sign that the object does not exist under its own power. Therefore, what is ignorance? Ignorance is a consciousness that views what is not inherently existent, or existent under its own power, as existing inherently or under its own power.

So, in sum, when external and internal objects appear to us, they do not appear to be relative. Rather they appear to exist in their own right, or from their own side. That objects exist in their own right is not factual but is susceptible to refutation by reasoning, and it is not suitable to assert what is contradicted by reasoning. Thus when objects appear to exist in their own right, in fact they do not. That objects do not exist in and of themselves can be ascertained through reasoning and can be realized. One can develop greater and greater familiarity with this realization, due to which the conception of nonrelative existence is harmed since these two modes of apprehension are contradictory. Hence, it is said that ignorance has an antidote. Because there is an antidote to ignorance, ignorance is removable. This is why ignorance is called adventitious, superficial. Thus, it is by way of these two factors that it is shown that liberation is possible, that liberation is attainable: (1) the mind has a nature of clear light, and (2) defilements of the mind are superficial.

What then is Nirvana? Different Buddhist schools of thought have different interpretations of Nirvana. According to Nagarjuna and particularly Chandrakirti, Nirvana is something like a quality of mind. But then, what is that quality? It *is not* a quality of realization; it *is* a quality of having separated from defilement. It is the state of having separated from defilements through the application of the antidotes to those defilements. And then, when you look to see what that is, it is the final nature of the mind itself. Thus, the final nature of the mind exists as long as there is the mind, namely, from beginningless time. So, even though this final nature of the mind is of itself with us from the very start, when it becomes endowed with the quality of having separated from defilements through the power of their antidotes, then that final nature of the mind is called Nirvana.

The very basis, the foundation of Nirvana is always with us. It is not something that is sought from the outside. Therefore, some Zen practitioners say that Buddhahood is not to be found outside; it is already inside. A further distinction is found in the statement that cyclic existence (*samsara*) and Nirvana are the same. This means that the *final nature* of all phenomena, not just the mind, is the same. From the point of view of the objects that have this quality of a final nature, those objects are many and various, good and bad. But from the point of view of their final nature itself, the final nature of all of them is of the same "taste." Thus, it is said that the one taste is diverse, and the diverse has one taste. From this point of view, cyclic existence should not be looked at as bad and Nirvana as good. Rather, the nature of cyclic existence and the final nature of Nirvana is the same. This position is stated in the sutras and in the tantras. It is also particularly stressed in the Great Completeness System of the Nyingma School.

God and Deity Yoga

Finally, I would like to add that when I speak of God in the sense of "infinite love," Buddhists also can accept that kind of interpretation of God. Here I think is one common point: Buddhists also accept higher beings. We consider Buddhas, *bodhisattvas*, and *arahants* as higher beings. However, the difference between them and God is that those higher beings were not in their higher status right from the beginning. They became higher beings by pursuing the spiritual life. Compared with us, these beings are considered higher beings. To some extent, we can appeal to these higher beings through prayer. Also, there are certain influences that are blessings from these higher beings. But, we place a greater emphasis on our own spiritual effort. According to Buddhist traditions, even these higher beings also became higher beings through their own practice. So, we place our main emphasis on our own effort and practice.

With this emphasis in mind, let me conclude by saying something about deity yoga. The main purpose of deity yoga is not worship, nor seeking some blessings, nor things like that. The main purpose is to create a union of motivational method and wisdom. How is this to be done? It is acheived by taking the wisdom realizing emptiness itself and using it to appear as an ideal being, that is to say, as a deity. Then, the main purpose of the highest tantric yoga is to minimize the grosser level of consciousness, and to manifest the innermost subtle mind. Once that subtle mind becomes active, it can be transformed into wisdom which understands emptiness. This transformation of the subtle mind is important because of the following reason. A coarser level of consciousness that realizes emptiness—the emptiness of the inherent existence of phenomena—can act as an antidote to defilements. But if one is able to utilize this subtler level of consciousness and turn it into a wisdom consciousness that realizes emptiness, then since that subtle level of consciousness is more powerful it has a far greater effect in removing these obstructions. And it is by this removal that one progresses in the attainment of Nirvana.

The Spiritual Guide

SR. DONALD CORCORAN, O.S.B. CAM.

"When the Paraclete comes, whom I shall send you from the Father, he will remind you of everything and teach you all truth. Even as no one knows anyone's secret thoughts except that person's own spirit within him, so no one comprehends the mysteries of God except the Spirit of God. Hasten therefore to share in the Holy Spirit."—William of St. Thierry, *The Mirror of Faith*

". . . in the secret of my heart teach me wisdom."—Psalm 51

"If these are the first fruits, what will the full harvest be?"—St. Basil the Great, *Treatise on the Holy Spirit.*

The Book of Sirach counsels that one should seek a person of understanding, cleave to a person who is wise, then go to that person who is wise, letting one's feet wear away the steps of their door (Sir. 6:36). Saints beget saints, an old saying goes. Another anonymous proverb comments: "There is no greater charity than to lead another person to God." The importance of the master-disciple relationship is one of the fundamental commonalities of the great spiritual traditions. To be a disciple of a master is the spiritual means *par excellence* in many traditions.

Yet, the spiritual teacher, mentor, or guide is not as central in Christianity as in many other traditions. The Christian tradition has always emphasized that Christ or the Holy Spirit is the true guide of souls. In its conflict with the early heresy of gnosticism, the Church's theological tradition emphasized that true Christian teaching is present in the whole community of the Church, therefore being public and exoteric rather than private and esoteric. The spiritual master, in the sense of an extraordinary spiritual teacher responsible for person-to-person transmission, is very rare in Christianity. However, there are two sub-traditions, as it were, that somewhat approximate this phenomenon: the early monastic desert Fathers and Mothers, and the Russian *startsi* of the eighteenth and nineteenth centuries.

While there is no semi-institutionalized person-to-person line of spiritual transmission in the Christian tradition, certain individuals have stood out as great guides of souls. And much of the great spiritual literature of the Christian tradition deals with the guidance of the soul, at least in an indirect way. In the early monastic centuries (fourth-to-sixth centuries), a type of literature consisting of sayings and stories witnesses to a highly charismatic and directly personal manner of spiritual teaching. This literature, called the *Apophthegmata Patrum*, is a genre similar to Hasidic tales, Sufi stories, and Zen *mondos*.

In early Christianity, a more charismatic and deeper sense of the care of souls stressed the pneumatic element (the role of the Holy Spirit). For this reason, Dom Odo Casel commented that the monk *par excellence* is the *pater pneumatikos* (the spirit-filled elder), and St. Benedict, he said, was the prime example. Despite Jesus' counsel, "call no man father," this more charismatic form of the care of souls has often used the term *spiritual father* or *mother*. The relationship of master to disciple in this case was so generative that it was called spiritual fatherhood or motherhood, though in a precise sense it was a kind of spiritual midwifery. The early Christian monastic guide was called *pneumatikos* or *pneumataphore*—that is, spirit-filled or spirit-bearer. The guidance of the soul was called the "art of arts and the science of sciences" by St. Gregory Nazianzen—and also by St. Nil and St. Gregory the Great.

Historically, spiritual direction as a self-conscious pastoral function increasingly became the province of ordained clergy. The notion of more formal spiritual direction emerged in the late Middle Ages. Because of the link to sacramental confession, it often tended to have a strong moral emphasis, especially in the last several centuries. In France, for example, the spiritual director was called *le directeur de conscience*.

There is in our day a widespread revival of interest in spiritual direction. The model of friendship—the spiritual director as friend of one's soul—seems to be one of the favored models for the director-directee relationship. The ancient Celtic tradition, for example, called the spiritual guide *anamchara*—the friend of one's soul; and Buddhism refers to the spiritual guide as "beautiful friend." Jesus Christ also spoke of his relationship to his disciples in terms of friendship: "And now I call you friends, because I have shared with you all the things I have received from my Father" (Jn. 15:15). Today, spiritual direction tends to be understood as a branch of practical ministry. It is a skill which can be acquired, and there are even training programs for spiritual directors. But the classic sense of spiritual guidance always reminds us of the strongly pneumatic and charismatic nature of the teacher-disciple relationship.

The Holy Spirit as Guide

The purpose of the Christian life, succinctly put, is what St. Seraphim of Sarov, a nineteenth-century Russian monk and famous spiritual guide, called "the acquisition of the Holy Spirit." In the Acts of the Apostles, the early Christians were continually spoken of as "spirit-filled" people. The grace of Christ transforms us continually—if we are receptive—so that we are transformed "from glory to glory" (2 Cor. 3:18). To deepen our identity in Christ, to become ever more deeply immersed in the Paschal Mystery, is to become increasingly spirit-filled. The Paschal Mystery is the archetype or pattern of Christian transformation. Thus, St. Paul prays: "All I want is to know Jesus Christ and the power of his resurrection and to reproduce in myself the pattern of his death" (Phil. 3:10). This ongoing passage, from our false self to our true identity in Christ, is a transformation which will show in love, compassion, wisdom, and prophetic insight. Thus, St. Paul describes being spirit-filled as being "life-giving spirit."

It is the Spirit, promised by Jesus Christ, who will "teach you all things." This is the reason the Christian tradition has always emphasized that Christ or the Holy Spirit is the true guide of the soul—the human teacher being a vehicle of grace, as it were. So, for example, in the sixteenth century, when spiritual direction was becoming widely fashionable because of the spread of Jesuit influence, Benedictine monk Dom Augustine Baker reacted with the strong assertion: "God alone is our only master and director." We truly become a new person in Christ through the action of the Holy Spirit. Twelfth-century Cistercian William of St. Thierry puts it this way:

> . . . the Holy Spirit is the light that enlightens the poor in spirit, the love that draws them on, the sweetness that attracts them, their access to God, the love of the loving. The Spirit is devotion and piety. From one degree of faith to the next, the Spirit reveals to believers the justice of God, so that grace follows grace, and the faith that comes from hearing gives place to a faith enlightened by understanding.[1]

The Spirit can come to us in many ways—through the teaching of Christ (the Gospel), the sacraments and liturgy, nature, other persons, and the like. A medieval saying speaks of three books by which we are guided in the spiritual life: the book of Holy Scripture, the book of nature, and the book of the deep self. In one sense, the privileged access to God is the deep self. The oldest spiritual anthropology of the early and patristic centuries—and the one that dominated through the medieval monastic centuries until the rise of scholasticism—is summarized by the term *imago Dei*, image of God. All human beings are created in the image of God and thus have a divine indwelling. Even sin does not destroy this presence of God in the depth of the self. But the image can be distorted in our human existence so that we need to be healed, restored, re-created by Christ's redemptive grace. This healing process by the spirit of God is the passage from being self-filled to being spirit-filled (*psychikos* to *pneumatikos*), from containing the image of God to being in the likeness of God (*imago Dei* to *similitudo Dei*).

The Guide in the Monastic Context

St. Benedict's spiritual way of life is itself a great teacher. It teaches us how to be open to, and receptive of, the guidance of the Holy Spirit. In this regard, a French Benedictine nun said to me once that: "the *Rule*, she is one big yoga." Fidelity and perseverance in this spiritual way of life expand the heart (*dilatatio cordis*). Benedict says in the Prologue to the *Rule*: "As we run the way of God's commandments our hearts expand." St. John Cassian, a major influence on Benedict, described the *immediate* goal of monastic life as "purity of heart," or "charity." This is the Latin equivalent of the Greek *apatheia*. *Apatheia* is difficult to translate into English, but it certainly means, as St. Augustine said, that the soul is "re-ordered in charity." It is healed, restored, integrated, and thus becomes characterized by tranquillity (*hesychia*) and a contemplative disposition (*quies*). In other words, the immediate goal of monastic life is to refine the vessel of the heart in order to become ever more receptive of the Holy Spirit. Therefore, St. Cassian describes the *ultimate* goal of monastic life as "the Kingdom of God"—which, I believe, certainly refers to heaven but can also be read as the acquisition of the Holy Spirit.

Monastic life is an immersion in a sacred culture. Benedictine life is a total experience of sacred place, symbols, and rituals that shape and nourish the contemplative disposition with tranquility. As the monk or nun is healed and reintegrated in this sacred culture, the person finds himself or herself more and more filled with the grace of the Holy Spirit. *Lectio divina*, or sacred reading, has traditionally been a principal factor in this formation of a sacred culture. *Lectio* is an inculturation into scriptural-liturgical-monastic culture. It is not so much a discrete spiritual practice as a total outlook and symbol system. Formation in the monastic way of life is not so much a one-to-one charismatic transmission, as it is an exposure to wise teaching, to a lifetime of spiritual discipline, and to the support and example of the community. The abbot or abbess plays an important role as far as teaching, but he or she is not a guru for each member of the community. While there are always wise "elders" in a typical monastic community who give spiritual guidance to other members of the community who are in need, in general, formation happens through the action of the Holy Spirit aided "generation to generation" by a disciplined life "under a Rule and an abbot," and by the total spiritual environment.

Discernment of Spirits

A final word about discernment of spirits. A Christian expects to be guided by the Holy Spirit in the spiritual life (Gal. 5:18; Rom. 8:14). But how does one discern the presence and action of the Holy Spirit? This was a critical question for St. Paul, who had to deal with some unacceptable behavior and claims among his early followers. Thus, over the centuries Christianity has evolved a teaching and practice called the "discernment of spirits." Practical guidelines for discerning the Spirit's presence were elaborated, for example, in Ignatius of Loyola's "Rules of Discernment." Ignatius's teaching (in the sixteenth century) is a summary and refinement of the teachings on "discernment" from the previous centuries. Fundamentally, one's interior condition, reflected upon in a prayerful state, will be an indication of the Spirit's presence. The presence of the Spirit is indicated in one's inner state by light, peace, and charity. But the ability to discern and judge this presence of the Spirit in others is itself a special gift of the Spirit, one of the charismatic gifts (1 Cor. 12:10). Some of the monastics and saints over the centuries, who were famous for their discernment ability, even had another special gift by which they could read and know the interior dispositions of others. These gifts of the Holy Spirit indicate to us that the practice of discernment is an indispensable part of the spiritual guidance of others.

I would like to conclude with a quotation from a desert Father of Gaza as a kind of prayer over all of us. Barsanuphius was asked about the meaning of pure prayer and tranquility (*hesychia*). He describes it as receiving the Holy Spirit overflowing into love and wisdom (reminding one of Buddhism) that transforms us in the very trinitarian life of God. It is this dynamic of the Holy Spirit that provides the Christian with his or her true guide and teaching. Barsanuphius says:

> May the Lord Jesus, the Son of the blessed God most high, empower and strengthen you for the receiving of His Holy Spirit, that He may come and by His good presence teach you about all things, and may He enlighten your hearts and guide you in all truth, and may I see you flourishing as palm trees in the paradise of my Father

and God: and may you be found as a fruit-laden olive tree in the midst of the Saints, and as a fruitful vine in the divine plan, all true.

And may the Lord count you worthy to drink of the Well of Wisdom—for those who have already drunk from the Well of Wisdom have forgotten themselves and are all outside the old man; and from the Well of Wisdom they have been guided to another well, the Well of Love which never fails. And having come to the Well of Love and Wisdom they have attained to the unwandering and undistracted measure, becoming all mind, all eye, all living, all light, all perfect, all Gods.

They have toiled, they have been magnified, they have been glorified, they have been clarified, they have lived, since first they died to self. They are gladdened in the indivisible Trinity—and they make glad the Heavenly Powers. Desire their rank, run their race, be zealous for their faith, obtain their humility, their endurance in all things, that you may be found with them in the good things that none can utter, where eye hath not seen nor ear heard, neither hath entered into the heart of man, what God hath prepared for those that love Him.

But as to the quiet—for the present train thyself a little, and God works his mercy. God will enlighten your heart to understand the meanings herein contained. For they are hard of understanding to him who has not come to their measure. Forgive me, and pray for me, that I may not fall short of this measure, unworthy though I be.[2]

Community, Church and the Contemplative Life

ARMAND VEILLEUX, O.C.S.O.

The word "contemplation" is a beautiful and rich word. It is also an ambiguous one because of the various ways in which it has been understood in the Christian tradition. The expression "contemplative life," used in the title of this talk, does not have the same ambiguity. It expresses very well what I consider to be the most important dimension of contemplation. Contemplation, as I see it, is not an isolated act, some kind of peak experience attained on some rare occasions. It is a way of life.

As Christians, we have our spiritual roots in the religious experience of Israel. The main characteristic of the religious experience of the people of Israel was to have perceived God as someone present to its life—its victories and its defeats, its joys and its suffering. A contemplative person is not only someone who sees God—that is, who sees God in everything and in everyone—but is also a person who sees everything and everyone with God's eyes. The contemplative person is the one who, in this way, is deeply present to everything she or he lives and experiences.

The God of the Bible and the Father of Jesus Christ is neither someone far distant in heaven who cannot be reached by human beings, nor someone who deals with isolated individuals. Our God wants to establish a deeply personal relationship with each one of us, but always reminding us that we are part of a people, of a family of believers, of a family of nations. The God of Abraham, Isaac and Jacob is the God of Jesus Christ, who is the firstborn of a multitude of believers. Therefore, it is through this communal vision of God that the contemplative sees himself or herself in relation to others.

For that reason, there is an essential relationship between the contemplative life and the experience of community and church. Christ is the sacrament of salvation, because he is the perfect visible manifestation, the perfect incarnation of the Father's desire of salvation for the whole of humankind. The Church, that is, the community of those who believe in Christ, is the visible manifestation of that same reality under the sign of a visible and active communion in love, faith and hope. To receive Christ's message is to be called to follow him with others and to embody his message of universal love in our life of service, worship and universal compassion. A monastic community is a particular way of realizing that mission and that sacrament. This, of course, can be lived in various ways. So, I will speak from the experience of a coenobitic monastic tradition that follows the *Rule of Benedict* and that has been handed down to me through the Cistercian way of life.

The only way to speak about the contemplative life is to speak from experience. I could speak from my own experience, sharing with you my desires, my trials and my failures, but also my ongoing commitment to this contemplative search. I could also speak from the experience of all those who—through their teaching and their writings—have shared with us what they have tried to live. And the body of Christian and monastic literature on the contemplative life is very large. I have rather chosen to present to you the experience of a concrete community of Christian monks who have recently achieved, through their martyrdom, the ultimate realization of their contemplative community experience. They developed that experience through several years of common life, and showed its authenticity by facing death together. What they lived was particularly well expressed in a short text written by one of them.

You may have already understood that I am talking about the community of Our Lady of Atlas, in Algeria, and about Dom Christian de

Chergé's Testament. That small monastic community was a typically Christian community; that is, it was not a group of people who had chosen each other. Rather it was a group of persons who had chosen the same vocation, or rather who had all been called to the same mission. The history of the community is complex. Founded as a refuge by a group of monks from Slovenia in 1934, it soon became a regular foundation of a French abbey when Algeria was still a French territory. The monastery survived Algeria's war of independence and the departure of almost all the French people from Algeria. At some point, the Order thought of closing it, but then decided to maintain it as a Christian contemplative presence in a Muslim society. The community was then refurbished with monks coming from various communities and different monastic traditions. They were all strong people who had chosen to come to Algeria. It was only through dialogue, prayer and contemplative attention to the manifestations of God's will that they attained a deep and amazing unity that kept them joyfully courageous during the dangerous last three years of their life together.

Let us now look at some aspects of their experience seen through some passages of Dom Christian's Testament (which was a text written on the day when the first threats against their life were made):

> If it should happen one day . . . that I become a victim of the terrorism which now seems ready to engulf all the foreigners living in Algeria, I would like my community, my Church, my family to remember that my life was *given* to God and to this country.

There are several elements of great significance in this short sentence. Dom Christian wants his community, his Church, his family to remember something. His life has not been a solitary relationship between him and God. He is aware of belonging to a community ("my community"), to a Church ("my Church") and to a natural family ("my family"). All those relationships were very important for him. But more important was the fact that his life did not belong to him. It had been given. And it had been given not only to God but also to this country, that is, to Algeria. Everything here is very incarnated. He does not own his own life; he does not own his community, his Church, and his family. He has renounced all of them; but they remain important for him. He is, therefore, a free man, a man who is poor and pure of heart who can see God.

That radical detachment was not something done one day once-and-for-all, and it was not done alone. It was a common experience that he had done with the rest of his community. In their last circular letter, sent in

December 1995, the brothers of Atlas—speaking of a possible death—said, "the violent death of one of us or of all of us together would be simply the logical consequence of all the forms of renunciation we have already done: of family, country, community in order to follow Christ. . . ." Because of all these encompassing forms of renunciation, the real community of Dom Christian and his brothers was made up not only of the twelve monks of Tibhirine and Fès, but also of the members of their natural and ecclesial families, and of all the Algerian people whom they loved.

Dom Christian loves the Algerian people so much that he cannot desire martyrdom, since this would be to desire that someone whom he loves should commit a terrible crime against the God of love:

> I do not see, in fact, how I could rejoice if the people I love were to be accused indiscriminately of my murder. To owe it to an Algerian, whoever he may be, would be too high a price to pay for what will, perhaps, be called, the "grace of martyrdom," especially if he says he is acting in fidelity to what he believes to be Islam.

Someone who has reached that level of purity of heart is a real contemplative. For at that level, there is the deep relationship between community life and contemplative life.

We must now read the most important section of Dom Christian's text:

> . . . my avid curiosity will then be satisfied. This is what I shall be able to do, if God wills—immerse my gaze in that of the Father, and contemplate with him his children of Islam just as he sees them, all shining with the glory of Christ, the fruit of his Passion, and filled with the Gift of the Spirit, whose secret joy will always be to establish communion and to refashion the likeness, playfully delighting in the differences.

In everything that has been said and written about interreligious dialogue, I do not think there is anything whatsoever that has reached such a depth. On the one hand, there is this contemplative attitude that wants to see through God's eyes and contemplate all his children of Islam (of Buddhism, of Hinduism, of Judaism, etc.) as he sees them, in all their shining beauty. On the other hand, there is this beautiful vision of a playful God who takes a secret joy in establishing communion, refashioning in each one the original likeness—God's image and likeness—playing with the differences.

Then, Dom Christian thanks God for his life:

> For this life lost, totally mine and totally theirs, I thank God who seems to have willed it entirely. . . . In this *thank you,* which sums up my whole life from now on, I certainly include you, friends of yesterday and today, and you, my friends of this place. . . .

Finally comes the most mysterious thank you and the most beautiful part of the text. To appreciate it properly, we should note that at the beginning of the Testament there was a kind of subtitle: "Quand un À-Dieu s'envisage"; or "When a farewell is contemplated." The French word "À-Dieu" is much stronger than the English equivalent "Farewell." Meaning "to God," it corresponds to the original meaning of "Good-Bye." Then there is also a play with the French word *"en-visagé,"* which means "envisaged," or "contemplated." But it can also mean, in the line of thought of Levinas, something that has received a visage, or has been given a face. So this subtitle could be read, "Contemplating when God has been given a face."

With this in mind we can understand the final part of the message where Dom Christian speaks to the person who might take his life:

> And also you, the friend of my final moment, who would not be aware of what you were doing. Yes, I also say this *Thank You* and this *"À-Dieu"* to you in whom I see the face of God.

This capacity of seeing God's face, God's incarnation, in the person who is slitting your throat is certainly the fruit of a profound contemplative life lived in deep relationship with a group of brothers, with a Church and with the whole human family.

The community of Our Lady of Atlas was an ordinary small monastic community, living a life of solitude, prayer, work and silence. When it became dangerous for foreigners and especially for Christians to stay in Algeria, and when they were all invited to leave, several people said to the monks: "You should leave. We understand that missionaries want to stay in order to continue their work of evangelization; but there is no reason for you to stay here, since you can continue your life of prayer in any other place. To pray here or to pray in France is just the same thing." Such reasoning did not make any sense to these monks. Because they had lived that life of prayer for so long together in that place, not only had they become deeply united as a community, but they had created deep bonds with the whole local Church and also with a group of devout Muslims, especially a Sufi community, that regularly came to the monastery to reflect and pray with them. They had also developed deep bonds of friendship with the local people, to the point of letting the local Muslims use a building of the monastery as the village mosque.

Does all of this have anything to do with the contemplative life? Of course it has. It was their presence, not as individuals but as a Christian community in a Muslim world, that gradually enabled them to see God. The God they saw is not an abstract God, but a God who had been "envisagé," that is, who had assumed a face in each one of those Muslim brothers and sisters, including the one who might slit their throats. And this story has not stopped with their death. Because of what these very humble and simple monks lived, and because of the way they died, millions of people, including millions of Algerian Muslims, have also seen something of God's face in them. Contemplative life has no frontiers.

6

Spirituality and Society

Sometimes when we passed through the guest house at Gethsemani Abbey, there would be persons in the lobby who were from the area around the monastery. One might think that they came to visit one of the monks for spiritual advice, or to inquire about the possibility of attending a retreat. But in fact, these people were there to ask for financial help. The work the monks do each day not only provides for their simple needs, but also enables them to share something with their neighbors.

What is the relation between personal spirituality and social action, between the spiritual transformation of the person and of society? This was the final topic of the Gethsemani Encounter—one that Thomas Merton would have considered essential to the future of spirituality East and West. No longer can the spiritual life be the treasure of those behind monastery walls. All humankind desperately needs a new spiritual foundation as it seeks unity and peace in the face of division and violence.

The Ven. Maha Ghosananda speaks to us from the experience of this search in Cambodia. Speaking of human rights, the human family, peacemaking, freedom and justice, he invites everyone to join in a journey of loving kindness and compassion toward all—even one's enemy. Ghosananda teaches the *Dhamma* in terms of "love for all beings and the uplifting of ignorance into light." To live this reality, he says that Buddhists must leave their temples to enter the "temples" of the modern world that are so filled with suffering.

The Ven. Samu Sunim, speaking from the Korean Son (Zen) experience, presents us with a picture of Asian monastic Buddhism facing the many challenges of modern social change. In response to this situation, he raises the distinction between the worldly and unworldly *bodhisattvas* and how this split has been played out in Korea. Samu Sunim then explains how the life of the Korean worldly monastic can be helpful in defining the relationship of Western Buddhism to modern society with all its social problems. He concludes with describing the true heart of the *bodhisattva* and how it can be expressed in social engagement.

His Holiness the Dalai Lama presents his view of the role of Buddhism in modern society as a bridge between more faith-oriented religions and modern science. He also discusses the particular practices of the *bodhisattva* as they relate to social engagement and the attainment of wisdom realizing emptiness. His Holiness gives a wonderful teaching about the understanding of emptiness in Buddhism, and then speaks about the teaching role of the *bodhisattva*. Finally, he addresses one of the most pressing of issues for modern Buddhism, namely, the need to reinstitute the practice of women's ordination in Buddhist Orders.

Joseph Gerry presents the Christian notion of holiness as a contemplative ideal. He describes how such a holiness is a trinitarian participation in the very holiness of God, in Christ, by the Holy Spirit. Then, he tells how the ways of monastic spirituality provide an atmosphere in which one can be transformed in Christ free from fear, motivated by Christ alone, and delighting in goodness and virtue. Living in the presence of God in wholeness, openness and peace is an ideal that one sees in Christian holiness. The holy person, finding God's presence everywhere and in everyone, is a "worker" for God using his or her energy with love and generosity joyfully for the benefit of others.

Finally, Ewert Cousins relates contemplative spirituality in the Christian sense to building the reign of God that encompasses the entire human community in all its spiritual, material and social aspects. He sees this encompassment as entailing a new integration of contemplation and action within a global interreligious context. Cousins describes the change in human consciousness that took place in the Axial Period and then became the basis of subsequent civilizations. This change brought a new individual consciousness, but also a loss of organic relatedness that was characteristic of the earlier tribal consciousness. Cousins believes that we are entering a Second Axial Period wherein a new form of global consciousness is emerging that can in turn become the basis of a new global community. He proposes that the rich spiritual traditions of monasticism, Buddhist and Christian, can provide the spiritual tools to build such a new and more united and peaceful world community. This vision of new beginnings is a good place for our Gethsemani Encounter to conclude.

The Human Family

VEN. MAHA GHOSANANDA

During his lifetime, the Buddha lobbied for peace and human rights. We can learn much from a lobbyist like him. Human rights begin when each man becomes a brother and each woman becomes a sister, when we honestly care for each other. Then Cambodians will help Jews, and Jews will help Africans, and Africans will help others. We will all become servants for each other's rights. It is so even in my tiny country. Until Cambodians are concerned with Vietnam's right to exist and be free, and with Thailand's rights, and even with China's rights, we will be denied our own rights.

When we accept that we are part of a great human family—that every man and every woman has the nature of Buddha, Allah, and Christ—then we will sit, talk, make peace, and bring humankind to its fullest flowering. I pray that all of us will realize peace in this lifetime and save all beings from suffering!

Peacemaking is at the heart of life. We peacemakers must meet as often as possible to make peace in ourselves, our countries, and the whole world. And real peace will not favor east, west, north, or south. A peaceful Cambodia will be friendly to all. Peace is nonviolent, and so we Cambodians will remain nonviolent toward all as we rebuild our country. Peace is based on justice and freedom, and so a peaceful Cambodia will be just and free.

Our journey for peace begins today and every day. Making peace is our life. We must invite people from around the world to join in our journey. As we make peace for ourselves and our country, we make peace for the whole world.

Who Is the Enemy?

In 1981, the United Nations held a conference to discuss the future of Cambodia. During that time, we held a Buddhist ceremony for peace. At the end of the ceremony, a Khmer Rouge leader came up to me very cautiously, and asked if I would come to Thailand to build a temple at the border. I said that I would.

"Oh!" thought many people, "He is talking to the enemy. He is helping the enemy! How can he do that?" I reminded them that love embraces all beings, whether they are noble-minded or low-minded, good or evil.

Both the noble and the good are embraced because loving kindness flows to them spontaneously. The unwholesome-minded must be included because they are the ones who need loving kindness the most. In many of them, the seed of goodness may have died because warmth was lacking for its growth. It perished from coldness in a world without compassion.

Gandhi said that he was always ready to compromise. He said, "Behind my noncooperation there is always the keenest desire to cooperate, on the slightest pretext, even with the worst of opponents. To me, a very imperfect mortal is ever in need of God's grace, ever in need of the *Dharma*. No one is beyond redemption."

I do not question that loving one's oppressors—Cambodians loving the Khmer Rouge—may be the most difficult attitude to achieve. But it is a law of the universe that retaliation, hatred, and revenge only continue the cycle and never stop it. Reconciliation does not mean that we surrender rights and conditions, but rather that we use love in all of our negotiations. It means that we see ourselves in the opponent—for what is the opponent but a being in ignorance, and we ourselves are also ignorant of many things. Therefore, only loving kindness and right mindfulness can free us.

Gandhi said, "The more you develop *ahimsa* [nonviolence] in your being, the more infectious it becomes, until it overwhelms your surroundings and by and by, it might oversweep the world!" We are each individually responsible for our own salvation and our own happiness. Through our service, we find a road to salvation. This service is nothing but our love for all beings and the uplifting of ignorance into light.

Peace Is Growing Slowly

There is no self. There are only causes and conditions. Therefore, to struggle with ourselves and others is useless. The wise ones know that the root causes and conditions of all conflicts are in the mind.

Victory creates hatred. Defeat creates suffering. The wise ones wish for neither victory nor defeat. So, we can oppose selfishness with the weapon of generosity. We can oppose ignorance with the weapon of wisdom. We can oppose hatred with the weapon of loving kindness.

The Buddha said, "When we are wronged, we must set aside all resentment and say, 'My mind will not be disturbed. Not one angry word will escape from my lips; I will remain kind and friendly, with loving thoughts and no secret malice.' " Peace begins in the mind. Yes, we show loving kindness, even for the oppressor.

After a great darkness, we see the dawning of peace in Cambodia. We are grateful for the Buddha's compassion and light, his realization of peace, unity, and wisdom. We pray that this unity, the heart of reconciliation, the Middle Path, will be present at every meeting and dialogue of Cambodia's leaders. We seek to learn and teach the skills of peace. When we live the *Dharma*, we develop inner peace and the outer skills needed to make peace a reality. With peacemakers of all faiths, we can accept no victory except peace itself. We have no need for personal honor, title, or glory.

Loving kindness is alive in every heart. Listen carefully. Peace is growing in Cambodia, step by step.

We Are Our Temple

Many Buddhists are suffering—in Tibet, Cambodia, Laos, Burma, Vietnam, and elsewhere. The most important thing that we Buddhists can do is to foster the liberation of the human spirit in every nation of the human family. We must use our religious heritage as a living resource.

What can Buddhism do to heal the wounds of the world? What did the Buddha teach that we can use to heal and elevate the human condition? One of the Buddha's most courageous acts was to walk onto a battlefield to stop a conflict. He did not sit in his temple waiting for the oppressors to approach him. He walked right onto the battlefield to stop the conflict. In the West, this is called "conflict resolution."

How do we resolve a conflict, a battle, or a power struggle? What does reconciliation really mean? Gandhi said that the essence of nonviolent action is that it seeks to put an end to antagonism, but not the antagonists. This is important. The opponent has our respect. We implicitly trust his or her human nature, and understand that ill will is caused by ignorance. By appealing to the best in each other, both of us achieve the satisfaction of peace. We both become peacemakers. Gandhi called this "bilateral victory."

We Buddhists must find the courage to leave our temples and enter the temples of contemporary human experience, temples that are filled with suffering. If we listen to the Buddha, Christ, or Gandhi, we can do nothing else. The refugee camps, the prisons, the ghettos, and the battlefield will then become our temples. We have so much work to do.

This will be a slow transformation, for many people throughout Asia have been trained to rely on the traditional forms of monkhood. Many Cambodians tell me, "Venerable monks belong in the temple." It is difficult for them to adjust to this new role, but we monks must respond to the increasingly loud cries of suffering. We only need to remember that our temple is with us always. We *are* our temple.

Worldly *Bodhisattvas*: Zen Awakening and Social Transformation

VEN. SAMU SUNIM

Buddhism today faces unparalleled challenges stemming from both internal and external causes. While most would believe that the main problem Buddhism faces has to do with conflicts between traditional Buddhism and modern social change, or Westernization, there is an internal issue which presents just as difficult a problem. At its core is a challenge that has resulted from the Buddhist failure to deliver the vital nondual message that all beings are Buddhas, fully capable of emancipation. This failure has resulted from a division which occurred in Buddhism slowly—over hundreds of years—and has created two very different definitions of a *bodhisattva*.

Traditional Buddhism in Asia is still predominantly monastic and is based on renunciation of the worldly life. The purpose of the "homeless life" of monks and nuns is to devote oneself to imitating, as best one can, the life of Siddhartha Gotama when he was a *bodhisattva*, namely, from his renunciation to his enlightenment through meditation under the Bodhi Tree. So, Buddhist monastics spend most of their life in meditation practice and training. Often, they end up spending their entire life in training so that the ministry of Buddhism, the ministry of the post-enlightenment Buddha, is out of reach for them.

When one becomes a practicing Mahayana Buddhist, or sets out on the Buddhist journey toward enlightenment and liberation for all, one changes one's life direction from *samsara* to Nirvana. That is, when one turns from the life of violence based on the three unwholesome "roots" of greed, hatred and delusion, to the life of nonviolence based on the six *paramitas* or the four divine states of mind,[1] one is transformed from an unenlightened sentient being into a *bodhisattva*. A *bodhisattva* is a sentient being with a "great heart" who has discovered his or her intrinsic Buddha-nature and has made a vow to save all sentient beings from their suffering. *Bodhisattvas* incorporate into their lives the two connected roles of "seeking full enlightenment above and helping all beings below," or "awakening oneself and others." Since it is their vow to help others while helping themselves, they embody both wisdom and compassion.

As a result, the caring and service aspect of a *bodhisattva's* life is often emphasized over the seeking of full enlightenment—so *bodhisattvas* voluntarily postpone their full enlightenment in order to devote themselves to helping others. They vow not to attain complete enlightenment until all living beings are liberated from the cycle of *samsara;* or they vow to attain enlightenment with all beings at the same time. The bottom line here is a belief that our own enlightenment and emancipation are not complete without the enlightenment and emancipation of all. This is because all beings are one body, we are all an interrelated whole.

In the Asian tradition, contrary to this spirit of the Mahayana Buddhist movement, over time the pursuit of the *bodhisattva* path and the attainment of Buddhahood became the monopoly of the monastic compounds for monks and nuns. Further, monastics divided the two connected roles of their vocation into a quest for full enlightenment first, and service to others later. On the one hand, there are *bodhisattvas* seeking full enlightenment; on the other, there are *bodhisattvas* engaged completely in such things as social service for the liberation of all beings. The former is the unworldly *bodhisattva,* who, with an awakened heart, strives for the highest enlightenment. The latter is the worldly *bodhisattva* using as a role model the transformation body of Buddha who appears in the form of a *bodhisattva* for the purpose of helping and saving all beings. Here is the basis of the split between training in the monastery as a pre-enlightenment Buddha working solely for one's own enlightenment, and living one's life in the world focusing on the post-enlightenment Buddha working for the salvation of all beings. This critical schism still survives to this day. The justification for the distinction between seeking full enlightenment and being of service to all was based on the disparity between the ideal and the real world, on the lack of worldly role models, and on canonical descriptions.

The Korean Experience

The history of Buddhism in Korea provides a case study which allows us to understand this split more clearly. With the rise of the Choson Dynasty (1392–1910), Buddhism fell out of favor with the state, and was replaced by Confucian ideology in both official and public life. Different schools of Buddhism were abolished or merged into each other, and the number of temples was also reduced. Members of the ruling class were banned from attending temple functions, and eventually Buddhist clergy were expelled from fortified cities where members of the ruling literati class and petty officials resided. Buddhism in Korea suffered severe oppression.

Outside the walled cities, the Buddhist clergy met peasants and people of the "lower and despised class." This encounter with oppressed people, and the need of the Buddhist clergy to regroup under a new structure, led to a division of the monastic *Sangha* into the *Ip'an-sung,* or "unworldly monastics," and the *Sap'an-sung,* or "worldly monastics." Originally, the "unworldly monastics" devoted themselves entirely to sutra study and meditation practice. *Son* (J. Zen) monks and nuns belong to this category. The "worldly monastics" were, and still are, involved in administration, cooking, gardening, maintenance and farming needed for the monastery to function. Also, the monastics who perform social functions such as rituals, ceremonies and counseling for lay people belong to this category. They are called "support *bodhisattva*" monastics who, because of the nature of their work, practice socially engaged Buddhism.

Initially, worldly and unworldly monastics deeply appreciated each other as representing the two aspects in the pursuit of the *bodhisattva* path. In reality, they needed the support of each other. The unworldly monastics set an example for what a homeless monk or nun does in spiritual cultivation, thus serving as inspirations to all. The worldly monastics quietly fulfilled their support roles as *bodhisattva* monastics and transferred their merits to the benefit of all beings. Frequently, both were good *Dharma* friends, or *Dharma* brothers and sisters, who took turns in changing their roles in order to support each other in attaining their Buddhahood.

However, this mutual relationship began to change under the impact of the government's suppression of the Buddhist monastic system. The unworldly monastics, on the one hand, moved farther away from the world into the remote mountains. Driven away from cities and towns, they refused to stay in the same monastery with the worldly monastics. So, they became more reclusive, more austere and more single-minded in their spiritual pursuit. The worldly monastics, on the other hand, became full-time workers. As a means of supporting themselves many specialized in the production and manufacture of paper, shoes, noodles, sesame oil, dried persimmon, tofu and so on. Others helped villagers during planting season and harvest times, and did volunteer work such as digging wells and building bridges. Therefore, as time passed, these worldly monastics looked more and more like people on the fringe than people in the monastery.

But, the real question is, were they simply fallen monastics, or were they *bodhisattvas* working with awakened hearts to save all beings? Did they try to transcend the division between the unworldly life of a pure monastic, and the worldly life of a lay person? One thing is clear: they pursued the nondual path of liberation and sought enlightenment by involving themselves in the world.

Buddhism Moves West

What can we learn from this Korean experience? Zen Buddhism in the West is predominantly a lay *Sangha* with quasimonastic training. The

Buddhist clergy or spiritual teachers of the lay Zen *Sanghas*, called "centers" or "temples," offer monastic training geared for the laity. This practice originated largely from *zazenkai*, usually a 5 or 7 day *sesshin* conducted by a *Roshi* (Zen Master) who may be a lay person or a married monastic. In spirit and life-style, the Western Zen Buddhist communities resemble the Korean communities of worldly *bodhisattva* monastics. These worldly monastics embody: (1) the Buddhist principles that all beings are Buddhas and that ordinary everyday life is the Way of the Buddha (the nondual gate of liberation); (2) that we are all an interrelated whole (the mutual nonobstruction and perfect harmony of all phenomena); and (3) that truth and liberation do not discriminate (the all-inclusive teachings according to one's capacity and need).

These are the kinds of principles that are held by Western Zen Buddhists. Like the Korean worldly monastics, who discovered the dynamic aspect of their *Dharma* life in the secular world, the majority of Western Buddhist practitioners pursue their *Dharma* life actively engaging the world while also being seriously involved in Buddhist spiritual practice. Like Korean worldly monastics who were socially engaged but lacked clear role models, socially active Western Buddhists also suffer from a lack of role models to inspire them, and to provide encouragement and guidance to their Buddhist journey.

However, the similarities between the tradition of Korean worldly monastics and Western Buddhism end here. The Buddhist movement in the West is largely a nonmonastic grassroots movement based on the teacher-disciple relationship. There are many sincere men and women in the West who are drawn to Buddhism and seriously commit themselves to Zen practice. Many of them come to Zen Buddhist practice in a search for the truth and for spiritual emancipation. They are motivated by this twofold spiritual aspiration: to *experience* the truth directly, and to *embody* the truth in their daily lives. For them, Zen awakening and social engagement go hand in hand.

Another difference between the Korean and Western experiences is found in the fact that there are as many women practitioners and teachers as there are men practitioners and teachers in American Buddhism. These women enjoy equal rights and equal opportunities. In our Buddhist Society for Compassionate Wisdom we have two women teachers, a priest and a *Dharma* teacher, who are single mothers. They have raised their children all by themselves while managing the temple and working full time. They are *Dharma* heroes of American Buddhism today! This is something that has been missing in Asian monastic Buddhism for a long time. In South Korea, Buddhist nuns outnumber monks. In recent times, more nuns and women *Dharma* teachers have been playing greater roles in a number of social areas. However, while there is nothing in the contemporary Korean Buddhist practice that discriminates against women, many female lay devotees and nuns still tend to be subservient, mainly due to the legacy of Confucian customs and the male-dominant Korean society.

These differences aside, I think that the Korean worldly *bodhisattva* life in the broad sense can serve as a model for Western Buddhism. One could live as a worldly *bodhisattva*, regardless of whether one is a monastic or a non-monastic man or woman. In any case, the focus is clearly on living in the world as a *bodhisattva* cleaning up the mess and removing confusion both from one's own mind and from the society in which we live. This is the model Western Buddhism needs right now in order to create a *Dharma* revolution. Already, there are Buddhist social activism and liberation movements growing from Zen centers throughout the West. The Buddhist Peace Fellowship, the AIDS Hospice of the Zen Center in San Francisco, Bernard Glassman's Zen activist community of New York, the Greyston Foundation, and the Friends of the Western Buddhist Order in England with its Aid for India and Right Livelihood Business projects are wonderful examples of these Western socially engaged Buddhist movements.

Worldly Bodhisattvas

The *Dharma* work in the world today requires *bodhisattvas* with boundless hearts. The worldly *bodhisattvas* are ordinary persons with "great hearts," who involve themselves enthusiastically in world affairs. The main ingredients of a great *bodhisattva* heart are wisdom, vow power, nonretrogression and daily practice of the six perfections. With such great hearts, they bring charity to the needy, peace and calm to the troubled, comfort to the afflicted, smiles and forgiveness to the angry, and clarity and wisdom to the confused and perplexed. These worldly *bodhisattvas* are care givers. They love and care. They care right now, not later. They care everyday. It does not matter whether one is Buddhist, Christian, Jewish, Muslim, agnostic or atheist, communist or capitalist. They love, care and honor all. They love them as sentient beings. They honor them as Buddhas and Christs. All sentient beings are not only potentially Buddhas, they are in fact Buddhas. Worldly *bodhisattvas* believe that all beings are originally Buddhas, so they honor them. This is how worldly *bodhisattvas* help all sentient beings to enter the nondual gate of liberation and attain Buddhahood.

Now, what about those who do not have such a "great heart"? Zen meditation practice is self-help, self-empowerment and spiritual awakening. So, people who do not have a great heart can begin to practice meditation in order to help themselves. In meditation you learn to trust and believe in yourself as a living embodiment of wisdom and compassion. First, you feel inadequate and uneasy about believing in yourself. You also suffer from the dualistic conditioning you have received, and so you have difficulty developing a nondualistic faith in yourself. In nondualistic faith, the subject and object of your faith are identical.

Then you begin to realize that you may be a Buddha, and that originally there is nothing wrong with you. In other words, you realize that your original mind remains pure and untainted in spite of your confusion; and that your awakened heart is there right in the midst of your delusion. It is just like the failure to see the sun on cloudy days. It does not mean the sun is not up there. It is just that you cannot see it because of the clouds. So, you begin to trust yourself and develop faith in your innate Buddha-nature.

Still, you are stuck in your old-habit energy and delusion. It is like the case of ice. You know that ice is made up of water, but you are stuck with ice until you get sunlight, or another source of heat, that can melt the ice into water. Based on this "understanding of awakening," you practice Zen meditation. This regimen for beginners is called the "Four Foundation Stones:" faith, understanding, cultivation and realization. Often, the Four Foundation Stones are reduced to two stones: faith and cultivation. You cultivate a strong faith in yourself as a living embodiment of the *Dharma*, and develop concentration through meditation and practice of the six perfections in daily life. This path leads to Zen realization of our true Buddha-nature.

However, Zen is an endless journey where there is no goal aside from the daily living of our life responsibly and full-heartedly. As the new travelers acquire *Dharma* habits and begin to lead a mindful life, an awakening of the "great heart" begins. The *bodhisattva* compassion and wisdom develop, and a new peace of mind and gratitude take hold—the traveler's life begins to be transformed. The presence of such a transformed traveler among us has an impact. A good *Dharma* friend is such a traveler who helps us with her or his example, and whose presence enhances our very being in the world.

The peace and happiness we experience inside through personal transformation must find an expression outside through social transformation. Therefore, Zen awakening and social transformation must begin with each traveler who sails out into the open sea of the spiritual life. We are a universal family, and as such, we depend on one another for peace, harmony and equilibrium. We all participate in the unity of this family, and this unity diversifies itself into the many. This is somewhat like the relation between the ocean and its waves. The manifold movements are always unified in the unity of the ocean, in the totality of all things. This is certainly a dynamic and vibrant relationship! Therefore, the awareness of this unity through Zen awakening also helps us awaken to our global responsibility and planetary consciousness.

Centuries ago, Buddhism traveled north from India into China, Korea and Japan. Now, it is struggling to transplant itself into Western soil. Never before in her long history has Buddhism encountered a civilization and society permeated with such a high level of sophistication and scientific and technological advancement, yet beset with so much tension and conflict. It is bewildering and fascinating at the same time. However, as we Buddhist teachers have found, there is a cost to living and working in an automated city where the culture of desire and consumerism predominates. It takes a new awakening, a new wisdom and a new vision for Buddhism to do *Dharma* work for the West. In this regard, it is crucial for Buddhism to understand the Christian tradition and its social engagement for the successful implantation of Buddhism in the West. Buddhism in the West would fail without proper understanding and appreciation of Christianity. We do not know yet what form Western Buddhism will take and what message it will develop. But it must communicate the *Dharma* in a way that speaks to the modern Western need for spirituality and social engagement. Buddhism must speak the language of the worldly *bodhisattva*.

The *Bodhisattva* and Society

HIS HOLINESS THE DALAI LAMA

At the beginning of my talk, I want to present my views about Buddhism and the role of Buddhism in the future.

The Role of Buddhism in Modern Society

It seems to me that we can divide humanity into three groups. One group—which is the majority—has no interest in religion. These persons are simply concerned about daily life—especially about money. Then there is another group which has a very sincere religious faith and practices some type of religion. Finally, the third group is intentionally very much opposed to any religious ideas. Looking at these three groups, we see that they all are the same in that they all seek happiness. Here, there is no difference. But differences do arise concerning how to achieve happiness. The first group believes that money alone can bring happiness. The second believes that it is through religious spirituality that we can attain happiness. And the third group not only believes that we benefit from money, but also that religious ideas are actually very poisonous to human happiness. They believe that religion is used by the ruling class of older societies as an instrument to exploit the masses.

During much of this century, there has been competition between this antireligious group and religions. Recently it seems that the value of religion is becoming clearer to more and more people. Still, today there are radical materialists, some of whom even deny the existence of the mind. And on the other hand, there are some religious believers who see religion as a matter of faith, and therefore do not value the use of human intelligence. Now, it seems that Buddhism is in between these two positions. It is different from those religious people who are concerned most about faith and not with using human intelligence. These persons consider the skeptical attitude not to be good. From the viewpoint of the Buddhist system, particularly the *bodhisattvayana* or Mahayana system, at the beginning one should be skeptical even toward Buddha's own words. You have to investigate whether they are valid or not. If you find some contradiction between Buddha's own words and scientific findings, then you should follow the scientific findings. We should accept scientific findings rather than Buddha's own words because Buddha himself made it clear that, "My followers should not accept my teachings out of respect, but rather based on investigation and personal experiment." This gives us the liberty to test Buddha's own words.

So, you see, Buddhism seems not to belong completely to the religious group which is mainly concerned with faith and which feels that a skeptical attitude does not go well with such a spiritual faith. Also, while Buddhism has some things in common with the radical atheists there are of course some big differences. So, sometimes I feel that some faith communities look at Buddhism as being a kind of atheism. But then the atheists see Buddhism as something spiritual. In fact, Buddhism seems to be in between.

This being the case, I think that in the future, Buddhism can be a kind of bridge between the spiritual world and the materialist world. Perhaps Buddhism can even contribute to bringing them together. I have found that in some occasions my Buddhist views have actually helped my Christian brothers and sisters in their own faith. And on other occasions—when meeting with scientists mainly in the fields of cosmology, neurobiology, physics (including subatomic and quantum physics) and psychology—we have found common things between Buddhism and science.

On quite a number of occasions when meeting with scientists, mainly from these four fields, at the beginning some of the scientists thought the meeting was going to be wasteful because Buddhism is a religion. They thought that in a discussion or dialogue between science and Buddhism as a religion there would not be any common ground. But as the discussion developed, some of these scientists became more and more eager to learn what the Buddhist concept is about subtle particles, or about the relationship between mind and body or the brain. This shows that there is the possibility of mutual understanding between science—at least the soft sciences—and Buddhism. In this regard, there are already contacts and communication taking place.

Bodhisattva *Practice and Society*

For somebody who has an interest in the *bodhisattva's* attitude and a *bodhisattva's* deeds or activities, it is important to understand that it is necessary for the *bodhisattva* to have concern for the welfare of society and a strong relationship with society. In a *bodhisattva's* practice, there are the six perfections, among which the first is the perfection of giving, of charity. Within giving there are three types: (1) giving material things; (2) giving the *Dharma*, or the religious teaching; and (3) giving "non-fright," that is, relieving beings of fear. Now, all three of these, the giving of material things, the giving of teaching, and the giving of non-fright, are necessarily connected with society. Our Christian brothers and sisters are also implementing these forms of giving in the fields of social service, education and health care.

In order to serve effectively in the community, you have to live in society. Because of this, there is also a danger that this social involvement may weaken your own spiritual practice. Therefore, during the initial period of the spiritual life, the important thing is to develop strong mental qualities according to the *bodhisattva* teaching. Once you gain the necessary inner strength and self-confidence that can maintain your spiritual life under difficult circumstances, that is the right time to involve oneself in society. While in society carrying out service in daily life, one should also spend time on one's own spiritual practice. This is just like recharging a battery. Then, you can use that charge as power for the rest of the day. I think this is very important. Our Christian brothers and sisters should follow this same pattern. Although you may be involved fully in the field of education or the field of social welfare, in the meantime there is no point in neglecting one's own spiritual practice. Social activities and spiritual practice go side by side.

Among the six perfections of the *bodhisattva* life, the second is the practice of ethics. The main idea in the practice of ethics for *bodhisattvas* is to restrain concern only for oneself. Then the third perfection is the practice of forbearance or patience. There are three types of patience: (1) not being concerned about any harm that might come to oneself, (2) voluntarily accepting hardships, and (3) the patience or forbearance involved in ascertaining the doctrine.

With regard to a selfless ethics, to accepting hardships and to lacking self-concern, we find a complete similarity with the practice of our Christian brothers and sisters. Your monastic way of life deliberately fosters simplicity and contentment. Even your food is simple. In fact after an exchange program, one group of our monks returned from their tour in the United States. I met with them and they really enjoyed the visit to your monasteries. They gained a lot of experiences, and—most importantly—their attitude toward Christianity was also very much changed. Their only complaint was that in some monasteries they remained half-hungry after meals; and through some of their friends they tried to get some biscuits! So, I think that your genuine practice of poverty, even in your meals, is very important for reducing greed or attachment. Also, there is no doubt that you practice tolerance. If somebody hits you on one cheek, you turn the other. That is the gospel, and it is clearly the same practice as ours.

In Buddhism, there is also forbearance with respect to ascertaining the meaning of the doctrine. Here too the basic pattern is the same for both our traditions. For the Buddhist, in considering very difficult subjects such as emptiness, at the initial stage one might find it difficult to accept or understand. In that case you need patience. Similarly with regard to Christian belief or faith in God, sometimes you may experience doubt. In that case, you need this forbearance with respect to ascertaining the meaning of having faith in God.

Then we come to the fourth *bodhisattva* perfection, which is effort. Every religious practitioner needs effort. By effort, we mean an enthusiasm for the practice of virtue. On the positive side, this means to pay attention to what needs to be achieved. On the negative side, it means to overcome the forces opposing such effort, that is, the various types of laziness. One type of laziness is attachment to the meaningless activities of worldly life. Another is the laziness of thinking, "I could not possibly do this!" This is really a matter of having low self-esteem. The other form of laziness is procrastination. Since these are problems faced by all religious practitioners, the practices of effort are also for everyone.

The Wisdom of the Bodhisattva

The fifth perfection is of concentration, about which we have already spoken in another talk. So let us go on to the sixth perfection, namely, the perfection of wisdom. Among the types of wisdom, there is the wisdom knowing the varieties of phenomena, and the wisdom knowing the mode of being of phenomena. Between these two, the latter—the wisdom knowing the mode of being or the final nature of phenomena—is more important. This wisdom is the wisdom realizing emptiness.

So, what should be understood by the word "emptiness"? There are many different ways of positing the meaning of emptiness. On one level, it means understanding that the person is not permanent, unitary and self-powered. Within Buddhism, all schools agree on this type of understanding of emptiness. Then, a subtler level is the emptiness of the self-sufficiency of the person. By self-sufficient personhood, we mean that the person has a nature, and that the mind and body have natures other than the nature of the person. This is like a lord and two subjects; that is, the lord (person) is distinct in nature from the subjects (mind and body). Emptiness means that there is no personhood (lord) separate from the mind and body (subjects)—that there is an emptiness of this type of personhood. Then there is another level of misconception of the nature of the person in which one sees the person and the mind and body as of the same essential nature, but still conceives of the person as being like the boss and the mind and body as being like subjects that are bossed around.

In the Mind-Only School and the Middle Way School of Buddhism, they also speak about a misconception of a "self-of-phenomena," and an emptiness of a "self-of-phenomena." The Mind-Only School speaks of two types of basic misconceptions in this regard. One is the misconception that subject and object are different entities. The other is the misconception that phenomena exist by way of their own character as referents of our words and our conceptual thoughts about them. Thus, the Mind-Only School teaches that there is an emptiness of these two types of status.

In the Middle Way School, they speak about the misconception that phenomena truly or ultimately exist. Since that is taken as what is to be negated, they also speak of an emptiness of the true or ultimate existence of phenomena. Then, within the Middle Way School, further distinctions are made. One tradition, the Autonomy School, holds that the phenomena that appear to a nondefective consciousness—a consciousness that does not have any superficial types of errors—do indeed truly exist conventionally. Thus, what do they posit as true existence when they say that phenomena are empty of true existence? For this tradition, the false status is that phenomena are not posited through the force of appearing to a nondefective consciousness, but are established by way of their own unique mode of being. This status is the true existence that is being negated.

Then in the other Middle Way School, called the Consequence School, the final thought of Nagarjuna is described by Buddhapalita, Candrakirti, and Shantideva. In this final system, the way phenomena appear to nondefective consciousness—as if they exist in their own right—is itself taken as what is to be negated in emptiness. Phenomena actually do not exist in that way; they exist only nominally. Thus, emptiness is the absence of this exaggerated status of phenomena—as if they exist from their own side. So, the emptiness of such inherent existence of phenomena is the subtlest selflessness of phenomena.

Now, both of these systems—the Middle Way School and the Mind-Only School—have their sources in Buddha's own words, in the *sutras* of the Buddha. This is what I meant when I said earlier that one teacher set forth many different views. For instance, those who propound that objects truly exist say that the view of those of the Middle Way School has fallen into an extreme of nihilism. And those in the Middle Way School argue that the view of these proponents of the true existence of phenomena has fallen into an extreme of superimposition.

The Bodhisattva *as Teacher*

Not only does the *bodhisattva* affect society in his or her practice of the six perfections, but also as a teacher and role model of this way of life and its wisdom. According to the *bodhisattva* vehicle, a *bodhisattva's* practices are twofold. First, one must perform the practice of the six perfections in order to ripen or mature his or her mental continuum. Then with respect to teaching others, that person should also have what are called the four means of gathering students. First is to give material things to students. Second is to speak pleasantly—giving greetings and showing concern. Third is to teach students what is to be adopted in practice and what is to be gotten rid of in their behavior. Fourth is to practice oneself what one teaches to others. As it has been said, when a guru teaches a student how to behave, if the teacher is not practicing what he or she teaches, then the student will say, "Well, you should be doing it first! You should practice these yourself!" And finally as Aryadeva says in his *Four-Hundred Deeds of the Bodhisattvas,* a teacher should interact with students so as to determine first of all their predominant afflictive emotion. Whether this be pride, or belligerence, or lust, or confusion, the teacher should respond correspondingly. Therefore, he or she should treat some people very softly, and other people more strongly; scolding some for instance, and praising others a lot. The teacher should respond accordingly, and always out of a motivation of altruism.

Women's Ordination

With respect to the topic of the *bhiksuni*—the nuns'—ordination, in general the ordination that came to Tibet stemmed from the Indian teacher Shantarakshita, and the particular type of vow is that of the Mulasarvastivada. In this transmission, the way that a nun is ordained requires a head officiant who is a nun, and other officiants who are males. Thus, there are both women and men involved in conducting the ordination ceremony itself. Now as it turned out, no fully ordained Indian nun ever made it to Tibet; and due to this, the transmission of the nun's vow never spread to Tibet. However, in other systems of the transmission of the rule of how vows are given, it is possible that the head of the ordination be a man. Therefore, there are histories or biographies of male Tibetan masters in which it is said that they gave nuns full ordination. But, the Indian scholar Gunaprabha says about the Mulasarvastivadin tradition of vow transmission that if the person performing the nun's ordination is a fully ordained monk, the transmission will not be completely without fault. Therefore, if one proceeds on the basis of the transmission of the Mulasarvastivadin School, it is necessary to have a nun as the head officiant.

This is in regard to the Tibetan tradition. Today, fortunately, the *bhiksuni* lineage exists among the Chinese and Korean Buddhist traditions. It is very important and necessary to restore that lineage in traditions where it presently does not exist. Actually, twenty years ago we started doing some research on this subject. And now we have already fully prepared material on this matter. So I am hoping that some kind of monastic conference, with participants from all Buddhist traditions and countries, can provide a thorough discussion and then reach a resolution or decision on this matter. Through this process, the decision will be very authentic. The conference will be like one of the early three councils that were held after the Buddha's passing away, so the *bhiksuni* lineage will be very authentic. I think that one system alone cannot decide the issue, since this is something connected with the *Vinaya* (discipline) which should be very pure and authentic. That is very important. If at a good conference with good participants a decision is reached, I think that will be a great service for the Buddha *Dharma*.

Christian Holiness

JOSEPH GERRY, O.S.B.

We have heard talks on spirituality, on prayer and meditation, on contemplation, on the spiritual teacher, and on spiritual transformation or growth. For Christians, the goal of such a spiritual life is holiness. But we believe that holiness is not coterminous or interchangeable with what is called spirituality or contemplation. In reflecting on these matters, I recalled, perhaps with a certain amount of wry humor, the adage of St. Benedict: "Do not aspire to be called holy before you really are, but first be holy that you may more truly be called so."[1] As spiritual—or even contemplative—as we may be, is anyone really willing to lay claim to personal holiness? And, if so, what would that really mean?

All Christians are drawn by God in the spiritual life to prayer. And all Christians are invited by God to the deeper contemplative life. In fact, in the early years of this century some theologians of spirituality claimed that contemplation was for the few; while others—led by the Benedictine Abbot Cuthbert Butler and the Dominican theologian Reginald Garrigou-Lagrange—supported the view that every Christian was invited and graced to be able to achieve that state which everyone admitted was high indeed. Needless to say, it was the "universalists" who won that battle. Then, Vatican II clearly stated that all Christians are called to a life of holiness. Therefore, given the vast diversity of Christian living, any normative definition of holiness must be somewhat open-ended, or at least broad enough to include a rather full range of Christian ideals. However, while recognizing that Christian holiness may be realized in individuals through a variety of spiritual paths, I shall speak principally of that ideal as it has been lived and spoken of in the Western monastic tradition. Therefore, I will be emphasizing its personal contemplative dimensions and presupposing all that leads to those dimensions.

Holiness and God

We are all aware that the Christian monastic tradition has always viewed itself in terms of a continuation of the life lived by the earliest church communities in Jerusalem. This is the view of St. John Cassian, who was responsible for bringing the early traditions of Eastern monasticism to the West. It was he who claimed that the very first monks were cenobites and that they were the successors of the members of the original Jerusalem Church.[2] Whether this is historically correct or not does not concern us at the moment. Rather, what I wish to emphasize is the theological point that monastics are members of the Church and that they are Christians before they are monks. It follows from this that the "holiness" to which they may aspire is an "ecclesiastical" holiness. Monks, as well as all other Christians, profess that they both believe in, and are members of, a Church which is "holy" itself. But what can this mean?

In the New Testament, the word for "holy" is the opposite of that which is "profane," or that which lies outside the holy area. The holy is that which God himself has set apart. Human activity is not primarily involved here; what matters is the sanctifying will and word of God. And thus we read: "God chose you from the beginning to be saved, through sanctification by the Spirit" (2 Thess. 2:13); and again: "But you were sanctified, you were justified in the name of the Lord Jesus Christ and in the Spirit of our God" (1 Cor. 6:11). Therefore, Christians are "saints" insofar as they are sanctified by God, in Christ, and through the Spirit. There are no self-made saints; only through divine sanctification can people become holy in the sense in which we read: "As he who has called you is holy, be holy yourselves in all your conduct since it is written: 'You shall be holy for I am holy' " (1 Pt. 1:15).

All of this is spelled out in detail by the Second Vatican Council in its *Dogmatic Constitution on the Church.*[3] What does the Council tell us? It presents us with the following line of thinking: First, God alone is holy; and he calls men and women to share that holiness. In our days, that call is issued by and through his Son, Jesus Christ, who is the exemplar and cause of that holiness. Second, the holiness of God is made operative through the working of God's Spirit in the hearts of those who believe in Christ. Therefore, Christian holiness is a trinitarian holiness: that of the Father, in the Son and by the Holy Spirit. Third, the sanctification of individuals results in their becoming a "communion of saints" in the Church—in being "anointed in the Spirit" as Christ himself was anointed in the Spirit. This holiness of the members of the Church is not a static, but a dynamic holiness. That is, it is intended that it shall grow, progress, advance and reach out toward a goal which lies beyond this life. Finally, this is a holiness which is at variance with the spirit of this world and sets one apart from it. Its root and foundation are faith, and its core and culmination are love of God and of neighbor.

In this trinitarian perspective, holiness is, as Augustine would call it, the result of sheer grace. That is, it is an undeserved and unmerited gift of God our loving Father, of Christ who loved us and gave himself up for us, and of the Spirit who is the bond of love between the Father and the Son. These persons of the Trinity make their abode and dwell in the depths of our very being, renewing and re-creating our hearts at each moment of our lives. This renewal is, as the Fathers of the Eastern Church would describe it, the divinization of the human, the making of each of us to be and to act as the triune God is and acts. The result, then, is to be holy as God is holy. And only God can effect such a holiness that is, ultimately, his own.

Holiness and Spirituality

What is the art and the spiritual discipline that a person uses that helps him or her to live this divine life? What, in other words, are the ways in which one can cooperate with the sanctifying grace of God in order to live in the presence of the Lord, enwrapped by the Lord who is everywhere? God is always present and revealing himself to us. Vatican II, in reflecting on faith as it exists in the person, describes it as the response a person makes to God when God reveals himself to that person. Note here that for a person who believes in a Creator, when is God not revealing himself? Certainly creation sings loud and clear of God's presence, beauty and grandeur. Certainly our fellow human beings are a further revelation of the Lord, as is Jesus and his Church. And we ourselves, if we would only realize it, are reflections of the presence of the majesty which dwells within us.

We might say that monastics live lives of response to, or if you prefer, disciplined fidelity to the divine call to God's presence. Progress in that vocation becomes evident as monastics become increasingly aware of the living God in every situation of life and are willing to respond to him. Their life is, in a sense, a continual opening of the self to the presence of God in order to permit the divine to enter evermore fully into all areas of their lives. As the Eastern Fathers would put it, they let themselves become divinized. Self-gratification and independence are categories that have less and less meaning, and less and less driving force in their motivation. This divinization is nurtured by the monastic's attention or response to the diverse forms under which God presents himself, and by the monastic's progressive self-distancing from alternative objects of affection. It is a matter of consenting to be transfigured by consciously surrendering to the "presence," the "call," or the *memoria Dei* (the remembrance of God), and by allowing that reality to overflow into one's life in all its aspects and actions. Call it prayerfulness, call it presence, call it a contemplative spirit, call it what you will, but gradually God's presence pervades the monastic's entire existence, wherever he or she is, whatever he or she does.[4]

It is important to note that this condition of life is not so much the result of "saying prayers" as it is the outcome of a life open to God's grace, directions and promptings. But this can come about in whatever degree it actually comes about only when one has entered through the "narrow gate," and trod the arduous path of the "fear of the Lord" in obedience to the Gospel and self-forgetfulness. It means that God must be allowed to be God, while we remain the creatures that we are rather than trying to put ourselves in God's place.

Those who seek God in this way choose to persevere in the attempt to live in accordance with the teaching of the Gospel. At the heart of this quest is the voluntary gift of self "for love of Christ" and not the search for the enjoyment of spiritual gifts. It is the search for the "Giver" of all gifts and not the "gifts of the Giver." Thus their energies are used primarily to deepen their openness to the presence and call of God in all the circumstances of life. This openness is reflected in their daily turning to God in prayer. For it is from this openness that results the integration of monastic life, and the consequent unity of monastic prayer and action. So much is this the case that, as the Trappist author Michael Casey puts it, "a monk who is dissatisfied with his prayer needs to make use of that feeling to motivate himself to greater daily fidelity to grace rather than to attempt to alleviate his pain by techniques for altering consciousness."[5] The monastic emphasis on the unity of prayer and daily life is at the very heart of what it means to be whole and at peace. It means to be in harmony with God, self and creation; and to be in solidarity with one's brothers and sisters. In short, the monastic prays, as do others, from the same "center" from which he or she lives.

Holiness and the Rule

We might ask again, this time confining ourselves to those who have embraced the monastic life under the *Rule of Benedict:* what is the art and spiritual discipline that the monastic uses that helps him or her to live in the presence of the sacred, or to live from that core of his or her being which is the gift of God? Indeed, Benedict wants the monastic to be unremittedly aware of God, of his presence, and of his enduring love. Thus, he focuses on cultivating, both by day and by night,[6] that awareness of the presence of God. For Benedict knows that the monastic's life is largely dependent on a continued response to a living God, a response that is both complete and joyful.[7]

A cursory glance at the *Rule* reminds us that "First of all, every time you begin a good work, you must pray to him most earnestly to bring it to perfection."[8] Thus would Benedict have the monastic ever conscious that he or she lives in the presence and under the eyes of God; and that God's grace is needed both to begin and complete all that he or she undertakes. Wherever one is, there is God; and whatever one does, it is done in him, with him, and unto his glory. This is not a question of the superficial position of some kind of contrived or pseudo-presence, but of growing in the ability to see and taste the genuine presence of God always, everywhere and in everyone.

Acknowledging and being drawn into the very presence of God, with mind and heart and bodily response, is, we might say, the basic atmosphere of monastic life. The *Rule* intends that the life of both the community and the individual should become an integral whole in that spiritual atmosphere. The presence or absence of that integrity will surface not only in daily relationships, but also in the hours of the daily liturgy. When it is present and reaches a certain degree of completeness, for the monastic it results in that "purity of heart" that enables one to become transformed in Christ. Therefore, the work of the monastery is to provide this atmosphere that enables the monastic "to put on Christ" (Rom. 13:14), and to experience in life the words of St. Paul: "I live, no longer I, but Christ lives in me" (Gal. 2:20).

If we cannot serve two masters (Mt. 6:24) it becomes clear that we cannot serve both God and the self-will whose urgings the *Rule* commands us to "hate."[9] The monastic must respond to God and his commands and not to the whims of desire or self-will. By so doing, and by God's grace, one is led beyond one's self-limitations into the freedom and holiness of the life of God. In this regard, the *Rule* summarizes its teachings in the quiet but deeply meaningful words: "All this the Lord will, by the Holy Spirit, graciously manifest in his workman now cleansed of vices and sins."[10]

I ask you to reflect upon these words, for they have much to tell us about holiness. In the first instance, they focus on God's action ("by the Holy Spirit") within each individual. Benedict holds firm to the notion that it is God within us who is responsible, in the ultimate sense, for all those actions which can be called "good," or "holy":

> They praise the Lord working in them, and say with the Prophet: "Not to us Lord, not to us give the glory, but to your Name alone." In just this way, Paul the Apostle refused to take credit for the power of his preaching. He declared: "By God's grace I am what I am." And again he says: "He who boasts should make his boast in the Lord."[11]

In the simplest of terms, it is God who makes the monastic to be free from fear, motivated solely by the love of Christ, delighting in goodness and virtue, and, finally, cleansed from vice and sins. In short, the monastic becomes holy because he or she lives the life of the holy God.

Next, we might note that this transformation takes place in one who is designated as God's "workman," God's "*operarius,*" or—having in mind the twentieth chapter of St. Matthew's gospel—God's "day laborer." This reminds us that we have agreed to be "workers." Each day brings us our agreed-upon task and Christian holiness implies that we shall be diligent in performing it. While we can use all the resources which God places at our disposal, we must also contribute our own energy and effort. We must also accept as part of this task the discomfort or the unpleasantness brought by the heat of the day or by the difficulties of the labor in hand. Because of these difficulties that come with serving God in a world of suffering and injustice, the *Rule* emphasizes a "patience" through which we share in the sufferings of Christ, who, in this as in all else, is our model and exemplar.[12] But in the end, the reward will be more than we expect, more than we deserve, even though it may not come until the end of the day.

Again, we may note that the agent of this transformation is "the Holy Spirit." St. Benedict does not have much to say about the Spirit, but what he does say is significant. In the chapter on Lent, he speaks of the monk offering to God something over and above his usual measure of service. He characterizes the attitude with which he wants this to be done as "with the joy of the Holy Spirit."[13] There is here a reference to 1 Thess. 1:6 with its description of the reception of God's word "in much tribulation," but also "with joy inspired by the Holy Spirit." What is important here is to note that the spiritual life should be lived in joy. That joy not only arises from an appreciation of God's gifts to us, but is a joy which, in the midst of trial and tribulation and perhaps real suffering, comes from that center of our being where dwell the Father, the Son and the Spirit. If the cleansing of our hearts is painful to us (and surely that is the case), still there arises from within us the joy of the Spirit. As in the case of Lent, which for Benedict is the desired prototype of the monastic life, we look forward to our personal Holy Easter and Resurrection with joy and spiritual longing.[14]

Christian Holiness

It is and should be a cause of joy that our souls are being cleansed; that we are coming more and more under the influence of God's presence and less and less under the influence of our own smallness of spirit and selfishness. How can we not rejoice in the newness of life which is the work of the Spirit, through whom we are made to be a new creation in the Lord and become sharers of the divine nature? It is when we become partakers of the divine nature that we may begin to speak of holiness. This is not a holiness which is of our own making, but a holiness which is from God and is of God. It is a holiness which is based on the presence of God within us, which through the cleansing presence of the fire of the Holy Spirit purifies our hearts and minds so that we may attain to that charity which casts out fear and fills us with the love of sons and daughters for a gracious and loving Father. It is a holiness which illumines as it purifies and which enables us, because we have become pure in heart, to "see God" (Mt. 5:8).

In short, it is a holiness which brings us to the contemplation of God: a contemplation which in this life is in faith: "for now we see as in a mirror, dimly, but then face to face. Now I know in part, then I shall understand fully even as I have been fully understood" (1 Cor. 13:12). But it is also a holiness which makes us to be like the God we contemplate: "Beloved, we are God's children now, it does not yet appear what we shall be, but we know that when he appears, we shall be like him for we shall see him as he is" (1 Jn. 3:2–3).

Building the Reign of God

EWERT COUSINS

In speaking of the reign of God, or the kingdom of God, we touch one of the central themes of Christianity. The coming of God's kingdom was the explicit and direct focus of Jesus' teaching. There can be little doubt that the term goes back to Jesus himself. The phrase, in several variations, is pervasive in the gospels of Matthew, Mark, and Luke. It appears in the first of the beatitudes in Jesus' Sermon on the Mount and is explicated in many of his parables.

In English the term "reign" is often preferred to "kingdom," which suggests a political institution. Since this latter concept is by no means the import of Jesus' message, there is reason to use the noun "reign," which suggests God's rule, power, and presence. Through the centuries, the meaning of the reign or the kingdom of God has encompassed a broad spectrum of meanings: (1) from an inner spiritual dimension of the individual, (2) to the inner spiritual dimension of the members of the Christian community or the Church, (3) to the social, economic, and political dimensions of the lives of Christians. For example, liberation theology, especially in Latin American countries, has criticized the past for focusing on an exclusively spiritual interpretation of the kingdom.

At the present time there is abundant reason to see the reign of God as encompassing the entire human community in all its spiritual, material, and social aspects. It is with this latter sense that I will develop my topic: "Building the Reign of God." To formulate it another way, I believe that we are witnessing a transformation and new integration of contemplation and action within a global interreligious context—a transformation that is bringing about a new global consciousness.

At this time all the religions—and all the peoples of the world—are undergoing the most radical, far-reaching, and challenging transformation in history. The stakes are high: the very survival of life on our planet; either chaos and destruction, or creative transformation and the birth of a new consciousness. Forces, which have been at work for centuries, have in our day reached a crescendo that has the power to draw the human race into a global network, and the religions of the world into a global spiritual community. Our individual and collective responsibility is to build this global spiritual community. This, I believe, from a Christian perspective and in continuity with Christian origins, could be called building the reign of God.

Axial Period

In order to understand our present situation, I suggest that we look back in history to another great transformation. From the period between 800–200 B.C.E., peaking about 500 B.C.E., a striking transformation of consciousness occurred around the earth in three geographic regions, apparently without the influence of one on the other. If we look at China, we will see Lao-tze and Confucius, from whose wisdom emerged the schools of Chinese philosophy. In India the cosmic, ritualistic Hinduism of the Vedas was being transformed by the Upanishads, while the Buddha and Mahavira ushered in the religious traditions of Buddhism and Jainism. If we turn our gaze farther west, we observe a similar development in the eastern Mediterranean. In Israel the Jewish prophets—Elijah, Isaiah, and Jeremiah—called forth from their people a new moral awareness. In Greece, Western philosophy was born. The pre-Socratic cosmologists sought a rational explanation for the universe; Socrates awakened the moral consciousness of the Athenians; Plato and Aristotle developed metaphysical systems.

It was Karl Jaspers, the German philosopher, who forty-seven years ago pointed out the significance of this phenomenon in his book *The Origin and Goal of History.*[1] He called this period from 800–200 B.C.E. the Axial Period because "it gave birth to everything which, since then, man has been able to be." It is here in this period "that we meet with the most deep-cut dividing line in history. Man, as we know him today, came into being. For short, we may style this the 'Axial Period.' "[2] Although the leaders who effected this change were philosophers and religious teachers, the change was so radical that it affected all aspects of culture, for it transformed consciousness itself. It was within the horizons of this form of consciousness that the great civilizations of Asia, the Middle East, and Europe developed. Although within these horizons many developments occurred through the subsequent centuries, the horizons themselves did not change.

Prior to the Axial Period, the dominant form of consciousness was cosmic, collective, tribal, mythic, and ritualistic. This is the characteristic form of consciousness of primal peoples. The consciousness of the tribal cultures was intimately related to the cosmos and to the fertility cycles of nature. Thus there was established a rich and creative harmony between primal peoples and the world of nature—a harmony which was explored, expressed, and celebrated in myth and ritual. Just as they felt themselves part of nature, so they experienced themselves as part of the tribe. It was precisely the web of interrelationships within the tribe that sustained them psychologically, energizing all aspects of their lives. Their spirituality was organic and holistic.

The Axial Period ushered in a radically new form of consciousness. Whereas primal consciousness was tribal, Axial consciousness was individual. "Know thyself" became the watchword of Greece; the Upanishads identified the *Atman*, the transcendent center of the self. The Buddha charted the way of individual enlightenment; the Jewish prophets awakened individual moral responsibility. This sense of individual identity, as distinct from the tribe and from nature, is the most characteristic mark of Axial consciousness. From this flow other characteristics: consciousness that is self-reflective, analytic, and that can be applied to nature in the form of scientific theories, to society in the form of social critique, to knowledge in the form of philosophy, to religion in the form of mapping an individual spiritual journey. This self-reflective, analytic, and critical individual consciousness stood in sharp contrast to primal mythic and ritualistic tribal consciousness.

Although Axial consciousness brought many benefits, it involved loss as well. It severed the harmony with nature and the tribe. Axial persons were in possession of their own identity, it is true, but they had lost their organic relation to nature and community. They now ran the risk of being alienated from the matrix of being and life. With their new powers, they could criticize the social structure and by analysis discover the abstract laws of science and metaphysics, but they might find themselves mere spectators of a drama of which in reality they were an integral part.

The emergence of Axial consciousness was decisive for religions, since it marked the divide in history where the major "world" religions emerged and separated themselves from their primal tribal antecedents. The great religions of the world as we know them today are the product of the Axial Period. Hinduism, Buddhism, Taoism, Confucianism, and Judaism took shape in their classical form during this period; and Judaism provided the base for the later emergence of Christianity and Islam. The common structures of consciousness found in these religions are characteristic of the general transformation of consciousness effected in the Axial Period.

The move into Axial consciousness released enormous spiritual energy. It opened up the individual spiritual path, especially the inner way in which the new subjectivity became the avenue into the transcendent. It allowed the deeper self to sort out the difference between the illusion of the phenomenal world and the authentic vision of reality. On the ethical level, it allowed individual moral conscience to take a critical stand against the collectivity. And it made possible a link between the moral and spiritual aspects of the self, so that a path could be charted through virtues toward the ultimate goal of the spiritual quest. One of the most distinctive forms of spirituality that became available in the Axial Period was monasticism. Although it had roots in the earlier Hindu tradition, it emerged in a clearly defined way in Buddhism and Jainism at the peak of the Axial Period and later developed in Christianity. Monasticism did not develop among primal peoples because their consciousness was not oriented to sustain it.

The Second Axial Period

If we shift our gaze from the first millennium B.C.E. to the present, we can now better understand the transformation of consciousness I described above. It is so profound and far-reaching that I call it the Second Axial Period.[3] Like the first it is happening simultaneously around the earth, and like the first it will shape the horizons of consciousness for future centuries. However, the new form of consciousness is different from that of the First Axial Period. Then it was individual consciousness, now it is global consciousness.

In order to understand the forces at work in the Second Axial Period, I would like to draw upon the thought of the paleontologist Pierre Teilhard de Chardin.[4] In the light of his research in evolution, he charted the development of consciousness from its roots in the geosphere and biosphere and into the future. In a process which he calls "planetization," he observed that a shift in the forces of evolution had occurred over the past hundred years. This shift is from divergence to convergence. When human beings first appeared on this planet, they clustered together in family and tribal units, forming their own group identity and separating themselves from other tribes. In this way humans diverged, creating separate nations and a rich variety of cultures. However, the spherical shape of the earth prevented unlimited divergence. With the increase in population and the rapid development of communication, groups could no longer remain apart. After dominating the process for millennia, the forces of divergence were superseded by those of convergence. This shift to convergence is drawing the various cultures into a single planetized community. According to Teilhard, this new global consciousness will not level all differences; rather it will generate what he calls creative unions in which diversity is not erased but intensified.

Although we are moving toward a global community, we are still conditioned by the forces of millennia of divergence. In this situation we face what seem insurmountable obstacles: ecological disaster, economic injustice on a worldwide scale, widespread warfare. Against these forces, we must individually and globally devote ourselves to "building the earth," as Teilhard says, that is to building the reign of God. In order to do this, we must develop the global consciousness of the Second Axial Period.

Paradoxically, it may seem, the development of such a global consciousness necessitates that we rapidly reappropriate the forms of consciousness of the primal peoples of the pre-Axial Period. Having developed self-reflective, analytic, critical consciousness in the First Axial Period, we must now, while retaining these values, reappropriate and integrate into that consciousness the collective and cosmic dimensions of pre-Axial consciousness. That is, we must recapture the unity of tribal consciousness by seeing humanity as a single tribe; and we must see this single tribe related organically to the total cosmos. This means that the consciousness of the 21st century will be global from two perspectives. First, from a horizontal perspective, cultures and religions must meet each other on the surface of the globe, entering into creative encounters that will produce a complexified collective consciousness. It is here that religions have had a special role to play, since for over a hundred years a number of their followers have pioneered in the development of interreligious dialogue.

Second, from a vertical perspective, they must plunge their roots deep into the earth in order to provide a secure base for future development. They must develop a new spirituality of the earth and of the material aspects of human existence. This new spirituality must be organically ecological, supported by structures of justice and peace. The voices of the oppressed must be heard and heeded: the poor, women, racial groups, and other minorities. These groups, along with the earth itself, can be looked upon as the prophets and teachers of the Second Axial Period. This emerging twofold global consciousness is not only a creative possibility to enhance the 21st century; it is an absolute necessity if we are to survive.

The Christian World View

Having examined the common human experiences of the First and Second Axial Periods, I would now like to view them from inside the Christian world view. In this I will again follow Teilhard de Chardin, who was not only a scientist, but a theologian and mystic. Teilhard views evolution as a process of Trinitization. By this he means that all the energy systems of matter and spirit operate according to a dynamic of differentiated and interrelated unions. In this way they share in the dynamic, creative interrelatedness of the inner life of the Trinity. Thus the whole of the universe shares in and manifests the presence and reign of God. Building the reign of God, therefore, entails giving social form—in unity with the whole cosmos—to this trinitarian interrelatedness.

In addition, Teilhard sees the evolutionary process—from the geosphere to the biosphere to the sphere of consciousness—as being energized and guided by the Cosmic Christ, whom he calls the Omega or goal of evolution. This is the universal divine presence drawing the entire cosmos to its fulfillment. The cosmic Christ, who is simultaneously the incarnate divinity and the eternal Son of the Father in the Trinity, is the immanent source of all energy, guiding the cosmos on its spiritual journey into a trinitarian unity in God.

Monasticism in the Second Axial Period

What, then, can monasticism offer to the Second Axial Period? Although I will address this question from a Christian point of view, my remarks will have obvious resonance with Buddhist monasticism. As monasticism was central for the First Axial Period, so can it be for the Second. Out of the womb of monasticism, the new global consciousness can be born, and monasticism can be the midwife for its birth in our culture as a whole. At this time of transition, we need a vision and a prophetic voice—like that of Hildegard of Bingen in the twelfth century and Thomas Merton in the twentieth. We need a vision of an organically interrelated global community that is spiritual at its core and at the same time grounded in the natural world and the cosmos. This is what Benedictine and Cistercian monasticism has provided for centuries through its cultivation of contemplation and literally through its cultivation of the land, and through the cosmic symbols of its liturgy which harmonize the community with the cycles of nature. This rich spiritual tradition must be fully retrieved and reinterpreted for the transformation into the global consciousness of the Second Axial Period, and made available for the human community as a whole.

I will close with a comment on the Monastic Interreligious Dialogue between Buddhists and Christians as it has developed over the last fifteen years. This may be the best example of the emerging global spiritual community with its accompanying dialogic consciousness. Finally, I believe that the major prophetic witness to the world in this time of radical transition is the suffering monastic communities of Asia, and the nonviolent teaching of the Ven. Maha Ghosananda and His Holiness the Dalai Lama.

PART TWO

Topics in the Spiritual Life

7

Mind and Virtue

At the center of the Gethsemani monastic complex is a cloistered garden surrounded by the walls of the three-story monastery buildings. As one walks through the buildings, one can see the inner garden through the narrow windows of the hallways. But the passageway that leads into the garden area is not easy to find. When you do enter the interior garden, you are struck by the stillness caused by the high walls surrounding it. This stillness seems to shut out the outer monastic world with the monks coming and going so that the clarity of this inner place is greatly enhanced. The many flowers and plants seem even more clearly to present themselves to our senses.

As one passes through the corridors of the inner monastery of the heart, one can sometimes catch a glimpse of an even more interior place of extraordinary stillness and beauty. When one is able to find the passageway into that center cloister of the heart, one finds the bare ground of our being from whence our innermost thoughts and feeling arise. There one finds the plants of our caring dispositions as well as our unhealthy inclinations, the flowers of our virtues along with the mind weeds that seem to choke our ability to bring happiness to ourselves and to others. One soon understands that whatever conditions—positive or negative—there are in the monastery and the world outside its walls, those conditions arise from this inner place in the hearts of all humanity.

In our dialogue, we addressed such questions as: What is the inner life of the mind, and what are its levels? How do the dynamics of our inner life affect us and the world around us? In what ways can such mental forces as anger and hate be considered mind weeds, and how can they be dealt with? Can such mental factors ever be considered something positive? Is it possible to purify the mind of these negative factors? What are the stages of such purification; what are the stages of spiritual growth? Does this growth imply a denial of ourselves? If so, what about the value of love of self, or a healthy sense of self-worth? How is this love of self related to love of others? How is a positive love of self related to the virtue of humility, so important in the spiritual life?

Mind

KEVIN HUNT: As a Christian monk, when I study Buddhism or hear Buddhist teachers talk they often focus on the reality of realization in a way which is very different from our tradition. They often use the term "mind." When you speak of mind, I am not too sure what you mean because in the Western Christian tradition mind would not be ultimate. Mind is a part of the conscious self—what we would in general call soul—and it is basically where consciousness, the thought process and rationality, take place. Could you just help us focus in a little more on what Buddhism means by mind?

LOBSANG TENZIN: I want to address the question that Brother Kevin raised: the emphasis on mind in Buddhism and what the mind exactly is. I think that it would be important first to see the mind in terms of how Buddhism views being. From the Buddhist point of view, a being is made up of various aggregates. A human being is made up of five aggregates: the aggregate of material form as well as the mental aggregates of sensations, feelings, dispositions and thoughts. Therefore, the mind as defined in Buddhism is an entity that engages with its object through sensation, feeling, volition and thought. And in this respect, the mind plays a very important role because of a being's subjective experience of suffering or happiness, comfort or discomfort in regard to the objects of its experience.

It is in this context that Buddhism sees that certain mental experiences, desires, and emotional or perceptual misconceptions are in a way harmful. For example, hatred, attachment and ignorance cause serious discomfort. These are known as the "three poisonous states of mind." When we experience these states, there is certainly discomfort in one's life. On the other hand, if these states are the causes of life's problems, then their solution must be found in transcending or transforming them by eliminating or purifying them. That transformation also has to take place within the realm of the mind. Therefore in Buddhism, mind-training, the cultivating of positive states of mind and the purifying of negative states of mind, is highly praised. And therefore when the Buddha says in the *Dhammapada* that all phenomena are the nature of mind, that mind is primary and mind precedes every phenomenon, it is in that context, I think, that the emphasis on the nature and the function of mind and its development make sense in the Buddhist context.

HAVANPOLA RATANASARA: In Buddhism, followers are advised not to depend on anybody else but oneself. So based on this principle, individuals are asked to develop themselves. What are we to develop? Our mind. In Buddhism, mind and matter govern everything. This truth is compared with a trip undertaken by a crippled person and a blind person. That is, the body cannot function well without the mind; so the mind directs everything and the body follows. So, as was just mentioned, Buddha said that the mind is the forerunner of everything. If the mind is not properly developed, not carefully cultivated, one will be groping in the darkness. This is where the stress is laid in Buddhism: you are the protector, you are responsible for yourself.

This view is substantiated by the theory of karma. Volitional actions are called karma. Influenced by karma, individuals construct their existence. The question given in Buddhism is, "Is life as we construct it a comfortable thing? Is it satisfactory at all times?" The answer that Buddha gave is that life is full of suffering. Under ordinary circumstances people do not understand their suffering condition. So, we are always unsatisfied. We yearn for many things, but once we achieve them, we want something more. Therefore this unsatisfactory race, this rat race we are running, has to be stopped. Since it is the mind that creates our unsatisfactory condition, it must be the mind that can bring us freedom. So, cultivate your own mind and do not depend on anybody else to do it for you. This is the message of the Buddha.

LHUNDUP SOPA: Our mind is like an elephant. An elephant is huge and if he is not tamed, he becomes very dangerous and can destroy many things, harming both self and others. If that much harm can be done by a physical elephant, how much more harm can be done by a mental elephant? The mental elephant is much more powerful and can do much more harm. If the mental elephant, or mind, is not tamed, not controlled, not subdued, then from within, it creates ignorance, hatred, anger, violence and war in which millions of people die.

The mind has two aspects: negative and positive mental states. Usually our mind is dominated by negative mental states, starting with ignorance, then attachment, hatred, and other poisons. In Buddhism, there are eighty-four thousand mental "delusions" to be reduced and purified. If this is not done, the mind becomes like an untamed mental elephant and will suffer in this life, and by its karma will suffer in future lives.

However, if these delusions are removed then instead of ignorance you will have wisdom that understands reality. Instead of hatred and anger you will have love and compassion. All of these positive mental states are developed through practicing meditation. Then when you achieve our goal, Buddhahood, there will be no obstacles of delusions, attachment, hatred, ignorance—all these negative states will be removed. They will be replaced with perfect wisdom and perfect compassion and love. This final goal cannot be achieved by external action. First, you must tame the mind and then your actions will be purified as well. That is why mind is the most important thing in the spiritual life.

We are born with three poisons and our whole life is always being affected by them. Therefore, this negative condition of mind looks like our essential mental nature. But these are temporary mental qualities and can be wiped out like stains on metal. The true nature of the mind is pure and so the goal of pure Buddhahood is possible. But if the mind is not purified, there is no way of achieving this perfect goal. That is why the mind is so important in the Buddhist way.

EWERT COUSINS: The question that has been raised touches us very much in the modern world because the term *mind* in Western culture has a very thin meaning. But if we look back into our own tradition, the equivalent term—*mens*—as reflected upon by St. Augustine seems to connect, from my point of view, with the Buddhist understanding of mind. I think it also connects with Don Mitchell's talk last night because, first of all, there are many, many levels of mind. There are the superficial levels in which we have negative attachments, distortions and illusions. But the deeper level of mind is the pure image of God in the soul.

In theistic terms, the ultimate reality of God is the transcendent and unbounded ground of all the other levels of mind. These other levels can be found in three faculties. First is what we call "memory," which is certainly not just our everyday memory, but the deeper memory by which we remember, or bring to mind, the ultimate. Second is "intelligence," not that by which we just know abstract things, but also intuitive, mystical intelligence by which we know the ultimate divine mind—the unlimited, absolute ocean of divinity. And then there is "affectivity," not merely the way we contact and love objects, but the way we come in contact with that boundless love, that self-communicating, compassionate love of God. And all of these are imaged in the depths of our being.

The only problem is that we have forgotten ourselves, our true selves where we find the remembrance, knowledge, and love of God. We use our faculties only to remember, know and love the things of this world.

So, with our memory we have forgotten our true self; with our intellect we reflect wrongly on ourselves; and with our love we love the wrong things. Therefore, our spiritual traditions also call for a purification of these levels of mind through which we discover our true self in the knowledge and love of God.

BASIL PENNINGTON: Your Holiness, could you speak a little bit about the distinction between the levels of the mind?

HIS HOLINESS THE DALAI LAMA: The division of mind into various levels of consciousness is not done in terms of the basic entity of mind which is luminosity and cognition. Rather, it seems that these divisions are made in terms of a subtle energy on which the mind rides. There are three categories of such consciousness: coarse, subtle, and very subtle. Now what are the coarse levels of consciousness? They are the consciousness of the sense organs. What are the subtle levels of consciousness? They are the different levels of mental conceptions. And then what are the very subtle levels of consciousness? From the point of view of the Quiasamatra system, there are four such levels called the four empties. These empties do not refer to the emptiness of inherent existence. These four empties are so called because of their being empty or devoid of the subtle energy that serves as the basis of the coarser levels of consciousness.

When the levels of conceptuality—which are specified as being of eighty different types—cease, then the four empties begin. And within the four empties the latter ones are more subtle than the earlier ones; thus the most subtle is called the "all empty." Why is it called the all empty? Because the earlier levels of subtle consciousness have ceased. The earlier levels are called "the vivid white appearance," "the vivid red or orange increase of appearance," and "the vivid black near-attainment." The all-empty level is called "the mind of clear light," which for us is the ground of all mental life. It is difficult to get a sense of what these levels are, but it can be done through the power of yogic meditation. It can also be done sometimes in the midst of some severe illness or accident where the earlier levels of consciousness dissolve. It happens also in the process of death.

JINWOL SUNIM: About the mind in Zen, for us what is truly important is the "mind of wisdom." I think that people misunderstand the practice of Zen meditation. They think that sitting in quietness is Zen, or that getting some insight is Zen. But how to behave in our life freely, that is the real purpose of Zen. This purpose is realized by the mind of wisdom.

GUO-CHOU: Zen people say, "If you see the Buddha, kill the Buddha!" To kill the Buddha means to live the Buddha. For example, knowledge itself is not important, but wisdom is knowledge used in living. While we have our minds, to truly know the *Dharma* in a "great thought" means "great enactment." Great enactment means to be a Buddha. Here is the true potential for our mind.

SHOHAKU OKUMURA: I am from the Soto Zen tradition that is based on the teachings of the Zen Master Dogen. About enlightenment, Master Dogen said that to convey ourselves to all beings, to all things, to all existence, such a practice of enlightenment is a delusion. All beings, all things, all existence, carry out the practice of enlightenment through our body and mind. This enlightenment is an interrelationship between the self and all beings. So there is no attainment. We attain nothing and we lose nothing. By practicing we keep letting go of our egocentric self and keep being illuminated, or enlightened, by all existing things in this whole universe. This should be manifested or actualized in our day-to-day activities. That is our main practice.

BLANCHE HARTMAN: Like Okumura Sensei, I am also from Soto Zen. Dogen equated *zazen*, Zen meditation, with realization. He made one word of it. His great burning doubt was: if we are Buddha from the beginning, why do we need to practice? He investigated that question and he pursued that great doubt through the practice of *zazen*, and his realization was that *zazen* and realization are not two. Suzuki Roshi said once that human beings practicing true human nature is our *zazen*. Our true human nature supports our practice of *zazen*, and our practice of *zazen* supports the realization of our true human nature.

Anger

JUDITH SIMMER-BROWN: I want to ask a very practical question. One of the very powerful and effective things that is presented in Buddhist meditation is how to work with anger. I am wondering about what is available, or what instruction there is in Christian meditation and how you specifically work with anger.

JAMES WISEMAN: In the Christian tradition, and I should almost say traditions because there is not great unity on this point, you will find some authors speaking as though anger in all respects and in all circumstances is wrong and is to be done away with. If anger is welling up in your heart, it is something that should be gotten rid of as quickly as possible. There is however another strand of the Christian tradition, represented by St. Thomas Aquinas. He points out that anger, rightly understood, is the proper response to injustice, and that it is only out of the energy that anger arouses that grave injustice will be fought against. So in this respect, there would have to be a distinction between anger that is appropriate, limited, and rightly directed at situations that are genuinely unjust; and, on the other hand, the anger that arises only because one is perhaps immature, or unable to accept criticism, etc. In this second sort of anger, a spiritual director would be necessary to help guide the person to a more profound understanding of his or her anger and then to an experience of healing and inner peace.

BASIL PENNINGTON: There are many spiritual traditions in Christianity. I would just share what I use in my own life for anger, and what I teach in the way of centering prayer, prayer of the heart. What we use depends on the degree of the anger. If it is an anger that is just kind of smoldering there but not really interfering with the way that I would ordinarily want to function as a Christian person, then I let the anger just be there to be taken care of in the process of daily meditation. I do so knowing that the anger will be cleaned up in time, but also knowing that some remnants of anger take a long time to be cleaned up, especially if the unjust state which is causing the anger is continuing. But if the anger is so intense it is interfering with my being able to function the way I should, then I go to my room, sit down, and start centering. Using my prayer-word, constantly I just keep going back to the Lord and letting that anger dissipate itself. And if the Lord is good to me, and I have enough time, I will stay with it until I pass into a state of contemplation which can be completely healing. But at least I will stay until it is sufficiently dissipated so that I am able, with relative peace, to return to my ordinary activities as I should.

GILCHRIST LAVIGNE: In our spirituality, when anger is something that comes up, we observe it, and we let it go. It is not something to cling to. It is not in itself something evil. It is only an emotion. Emotions are not evil in themselves; they are evil when you act them out. If the anger is a strong emotion, it may be very difficult not to be absorbed by it. It might take a long time to let it go, but that is what must be done.

CHUEN PHANGCHAM: I am very happy to hear from Sr. GilChrist about how we can deal with anger. This is a very common question that you often hear. Anger is a very great influence in the world today. The world is burning, the world is crying, because of anger. The world is lamenting, sorrowing, because of anger. In many traditions, especially in the Eastern ways of practice, anger can be compared to a snake, the poisonous cobra. So, Sr. GilChrist is right not to pick it up, not to hang on to it, not to attack it, not to welcome it. Since anger is like a poisonous snake, we should not welcome it into our small house. We should lock our door and let the anger snake go away.

How can we lock our house? As Fr. Pennington said, without contemplation we cannot know the real danger of anger. So, we need to meditate on the anger to know its danger. Then we need to develop mindfulness. Mindfulness helps us to maintain all aspects of the mind so we can close the door of our house to protect it, so anger will not master the mind. On the other hand, when anger becomes the master, the body is burning because the mind is burning. That is why the world is crying today. It is burning from anger. So, we need to get rid of this anger, to let go of this anger. Meditation and contemplation can help us do this.

PANDITH VAJIRAGNANA: No one can give anger to another person. Anger is an emotion in the minds of all of us; no one can say I do not have anger. In ordinary beings who are not saints, this is one of the emotions that we all have—to lesser or greater degrees—in our minds. Unless there are conditions present, it does not come out; it just stays there in a dormant state. When the conditions are present, suddenly it starts manifesting itself in different forms. When the anger comes up to your mind, it changes your entire appearance. Any beautiful person can immediately become ugly. It has such a negative power over us.

There is no way in Buddhism that we accept anger as a good thing. Under no circumstances is it accepted as a good thing. Besides anger, at the root of our mind is also selfish love or attachment. The mind does not remain empty; there is always an object in it. Sometimes it is a good object, giving peace to the mind; and sometimes it is a bad object, disturbing it because of our nonunderstanding. Therefore, in our Buddhist teaching, these three main things—attachment, aversion, and ignorance—are considered as roots of evil. All evil things are committed by people because of these three roots. Because of our attachment, anger and ignorance, we do unwholesome things. If you look at society, at all the crimes from petty quarrels up to wars, all are committed by the people because of selfish attachment or anger based in ignorance. In this way, all unwholesome things are committed by people because of these evil roots which they have in their minds.

LHUNDUP SOPA: We are talking about anger and hatred. These poisons have their antidotes in love and compassion. But they arise from an ignorance that is an egotistic point of view. From this point of view, we like people who benefit ourselves, our friends, relatives, etc. Then from this same point of view, there are other people we do not like, who do not benefit us. From our egotistic view, when bad things happen to them we may even enjoy it. But then if someone helps these people, we feel they are our enemy and get angry. Without this egotistic view, or self-centered view, you do not have this anger. If you have an egotistic view, you will always have anger. Once you have anger, Buddhists say it is like a fire. The nature of fire is burning. So, your anger first burns yourself. You burn inside; and then your body burns with shaking and your speech burns with anger. But anger not only burns you, it burns your friends and relatives, and then your town and country. When the fire catches our society, we even have war that burns uncontrollably. This fire cannot be controlled superficially by social laws, it must be extinguished individually by extinguishing its cause in selfish attitudes, in egotistic points of view. Ignorance is the most powerful source of all evils including anger. That is the Buddhist teaching.

DONALD MITCHELL: Oftentimes, we hear from our Buddhist friends that anger is a negative defilement; it needs to be rooted out since it comes from ignorance and there is a certain selfishness that is at its core. As James Wiseman said, there is also a kind of anger that arises over injustice. This seems to me to be an anger that does not come from self-centeredness or ignorance, but out of compassion. If I see an adult abusing a child, or if I see rich people exploiting workers, I am correctly seeing an example of injustice and am feeling compassion for the victims. There is some kind of unjust situation going on, and the anger that I feel indicates that this phenomenon is inappropriate and that it needs to be addressed.

One can distinguish between the feeling of anger and what one does with it. In Christianity this is very important. The anger focuses our attention on what in fact needs to be addressed. But then, we have to decide what we are going to do to address it. If we address it just out of anger, then we have got the problem Geshe Sopa mentioned. But there are constructive ways to address injustices that come from a more reflective or contemplative source. Social engagement that comes from a source of loving kindness and compassion, for example, does not add more flames to the fire. Such actions brings about peace and reconciliation. But, in order for there really to be forgiveness and reconciliation, we have to be able to speak the truth. We have to be able to say, yes, this is really wrong. Otherwise it is not true reconciliation or peace, it is just a kind of sweeping things under the rug. So, anger itself does not have to be negative. It can also play this positive role as long as it leads to deeper self-reflection and a response from a deeper center rather than from the anger itself.

Joseph Goldstein: I would like to respond to the Christian view that anger is at times a useful response to injustice. It seems to me that injustice could cover the spectrum including very great violence on the one hand, and personal injustices in our various relationships on the other. If we focus on the unjust action, that attention very easily gives rise to anger or rage. But if we focus on the ignorance behind the unjust action, it seems to me there is a greater possibility of keeping the heart compassionate. I do not think this implies a withdrawal from response. Rather, our action in response to the injustice would come from a very different space in the heart.

With respect to righteous anger—anger in the face of injustice—the Buddha gave a teaching which necessitates a great subtlety of discernment. He talked about what he called the *near enemy* of wholesome states of mind, that is, qualities of mind that look like wholesome states but are not. These get to be very subtle distinctions which take a great deal of awareness and discernment to disentangle. For example, the *near enemy* of compassion is sorrow. So, we may come face to face with suffering and feel this tremendous sorrow and think that it is compassion. Yet, because it is not—although it may feel like it and look like it—negative consequences will come in the kinds of actions we take.

The distinction is made between sorrow and compassion in that sorrow contains aversion and ill will toward the situation. And one might think, "This is a bad situation and I should have ill will toward it." The purity of compassion is that it can hold and embrace and connect with injustice free of the feeling of aversion toward it. And that is why often in our experience the very greatest people we know who are involved in situations of terrible suffering actually feel very joyful. As they are holding the suffering, it is not from a place of ill will, it is not from a place of aversion. So this brings us to something else that is mentioned in the teachings that I think in some way encapsulates our whole spiritual path: everything rests on the tip of motivation.

Norman Fischer: On the question of "righteous" anger, I passionately feel the importance of speaking out and not remaining silent. But I also feel that righteous anger has problems with it. I prefer to think along the lines that anger itself can actually be a source of energy for compassion. But as soon as we call it "righteous," then we open ourselves up to the possibility of a subtle self-identification with the situation. I know that when I was righteously angry, my effectiveness was tremendously reduced by my self-identification. For example, one of the most intimate things we self-identify with is our own religious tradition. On the other hand, we are taught that Buddhism, like everything else, is empty of any inherent nature. So if on a subtle level I take Buddhism into myself and defend it with righteous anger, then I have lost my tradition because it is really empty of any inherent nature to defend. If we all understood this about our own religious traditions, we would not have the kind of religious intolerance and violence that happens in Korea—where Christians today are burning down ancient Buddhist temples—and elsewhere.

BLANCHE HARTMAN: My own experience with righteous anger over injustice is very long and deep. I was a communist before I met Suzuki Roshi. My turning came when I discovered during the Vietnam War that I was fighting for peace. The contradiction in fighting for peace hit me very hard. This discovery happened when I was at a student strike at San Francisco State University. The first day of the strike had been very violent; the police tactical squad had attacked the students. So, members of the community were invited to come to the campus to interpose themselves between police and students. I came all ready to do battle! I watched the striking students and others in violent confrontations here and there around the campus. By that time I had become something of a pacifist, so I was standing there watching and wondering where my side was. Then, I interposed myself between some police and some students. I was face to face with a riot-squad policeman who, until that moment, had been the opposite of me. But suddenly we made eye contact and I had this sudden, overwhelming experience of identity, for which I had no conceptual interpretation. It was just a pure experience.

Knowing that this "not-me" and "me" were completely not separate, that there was no boundary, really changed my life. I had to find out who understood this. Meeting Suzuki Roshi and looking into his face, I realized that he saw me in that way. That is how I came to be a Buddhist. Now, before us we have two examples of people—the Dalai Lama and Maha Ghosananda—who have taken this practice to such a point that they can meet incredible injustice that touches them deeply, and clearly not meet it with anger. They meet it from something else that we see and respect even though we do not fully experience or understand it.

But I think it is not righteous anger, and I do not think that there is anything to be gained from righteous anger. I was very righteous; I was also very angry.

LOBSANG TENZIN: Of course, anger is one of the major problems in our society. So, we must speak about it in order to understand it and make peace with ourselves and come to some resolution. I think that in dealing with anger there is a level that is very personal, and also a level that is more social, dealing with the larger community. I think it is very important that we examine what is inside our hearts when dealing with our own anger. But anger often involves other people or other situations. Sometimes we may become angry at ourselves, but it is related to some situation. In those situations, I think that while we talk about anger coming from ignorance and so forth, what is important is to look at the larger situation and the other people involved in it.

I will give one example that happened in my own personal life. When I moved to Atlanta, two older ladies knocked on my door. They asked me if I had been saved, and I told that I did not think so. They asked if I would like to know something about Christianity. I said, "Of course, yes, I would." Then they gave me some books and asked for a donation. I gave them a five-dollar donation. Later, my landlady said that these people will come again, and asked why I did that. But this was not troubling for me personally, because I trusted in their faith. I felt that these people were genuinely concerned about me because of what they believe.

PANDITH VAJIRAGNANA: People have different temperaments, and one of those temperaments is informed by anger. Anger is in us all, so we need to recognize it. Then, what to do? The Buddha very clearly said that anger cannot be appeased by anger. It is to be appeased by love. So, we must practice love.

JUDITH SIMMER-BROWN: There is some very specific advice in the Tibetan tradition about bringing anger into our practice. The important thing is to purify our anger so that the energy of our anger can be transformed into positive and skillful action for others. There are specific trainings that you use for transforming your anger into genuine compassionate motivation to benefit others. Without that transformation, anything that you do will be polluted by the anger and will simply be promoting further anger. There are a few slogans we use that I wanted to share with you.

The first one is: "Drive all blame into oneself." What this means is that whenever you encounter an angry situation, rather than being swept up in it, just take the blame. This does not mean becoming a victim yourself, but with your confidence as a *bodhisattva,* it means that you have the responsibility and the power to handle the blame. Pragmatically speaking, when you are in a situation of anger, whether it is yours or someone else's, if you take the responsibility then you immediately transform the situation such that then you can actually go on and do something of benefit.

The next slogan says: "Be grateful to everyone." This is a slogan which suggests that your enemy is your greatest friend because by arousing your own anger, your enemy has given you the chance to unveil your deep-seated aggression and to transform it on the spot. The third slogan I want to share is: "Three objects, three poisons, three virtuous seeds." When you experience anger and you have an object of anger before your mind, you literally drop the object of the anger. You drop the object of the anger and feel just the anger itself. When you have no object for the anger and you just feel the energy of the anger itself, the anger transforms into compassion. The energy of anger itself is completely pure, so if we can give up the dualistic quality, that energy becomes compassion which can then benefit others. Anger then has a positive outcome.

ARMAND VEILLEUX: When Judith mentioned the three slogans I was thinking of something related to what I said. In my talk, I spoke of that beautiful text of Fr. Christian of Algeria and I mentioned his meeting with the six armed men who came to the monastery on Christmas, 1993. After that, Fr. Christian started praying every day for the terrorists in the mountains: "Lord, disarm them." Then he realized that he could not say that if he had any form of violence in his own heart. And so his type of *mantra* everyday for the next three years of his life was: "Lord, disarm them, disarm me."

Purity

LEO LEFEBURE: I would like to pose a question to our Buddhist friends about the completeness of the eradication of defilements. This, for me, is one of the more difficult things to understand. The Catholic tradition has a deep sense of the fragility of our own self-knowledge, that at no matter what stage of our spiritual growth, we are liable to deceive ourselves and to get caught in ever more subtle temptations. We believe that, apart from a few saints given revelation, none of us can know our own final disposition before God. And we believe that at every stage of our lives, we depend upon the grace of God—and we need the grace of God to take the next step. And yet you speak about the complete eradication of defilements.

PANDITH VAJIRAGNANA: There are many defilements, but all are reduced to three: attachment, anger, and delusion. A person who is going to gain enlightenment has to eradicate those three. And this can be achieved through attaining wisdom.

SHARON SALZBERG: It is important to make the distinction between purification of mind and purification of view. Purification of mind refers to meditative experience born of concentration and the unification of mind, which can be extraordinarily wonderful and blissful. And yet it is considered that these states and these kinds of experience just temporarily suppress defilements. Only wisdom actually has the ability to cut through or uproot defilements. So, any meditative experience within the context of this description may be purifying, but it is not liberating. What has been important for me personally in not clinging to meditative experience but moving on to the greater development of understanding, has been going back to my motivation for practice. That is, remembering that I am practicing not just for myself but for the sake of all beings. The compassion of that motivation has actually broadened my path.

Also, this path of purification within the Buddhist tradition is not just the evolution of wisdom but also the evolution of faith. We have a very "initial faith" that allows us to be even interested in practicing morality and ethical behavior. And then there comes what is called "bright faith," which is the exhilaration and delight that we have when we experience rapture, joy and so on in our practice. This is a very exciting and uplifting time, but not very reliable either. And then there are times of dissolution and difficulty. My personal experience of this was that it was like a crisis of faith. That time was extremely difficult and I felt as though everything were dissolving continuously—it was quite unremitting. It was very frightening and, in fact, it was only the thought of my teachers and of the Buddha that helped me to go on. It seemed there was no way to go back, and so it was because of that faith that I went on. Then in the discovery that there is nothing that one can hold on to, and that there is also no one to be holding on, I found some peace and equanimity. With that understanding, there is a "verified faith" that is not just based on an experience, but is based on one's deeper seeing of the truth. Finally comes "unshakable faith," where there is a realization that there is no going back—there is no returning—because one has seen much more deeply for oneself some sense of truth.

NORMAN FISCHER: I also want to speak for just a second about the issue Reverend Brother Leo raised. I agree with what you said about the

Catholic tradition, that there is no end to the confusion that can come up in the mind. As you said, with the exception of a few great saints we are all working with this fact. And yet my experience is that the mind arises in different configurations and with different tones and feelings. For me, it seems like the idea that I am confused, or that I am only a weak human being, and so on is extra. Naturally, something is going to happen. It might be good, or it might be bad. It might be an example of my own confusion from the past, or it might be an example of my own enlightenment right now. Whatever it is, I am going to try my best to face it with what I know and where I am at, and with all the help that I can get from those around me.

LHUNDUP SOPA: Based on Mahayana teaching, how are we able to get rid of our delusions, misery, suffering and all undesirable things? Everybody is seeking liberation, freedom and something perfect like everlasting peace. While people seek perfection, imperfection is everywhere—in body, speech, and mind within the individual and society. How can you change what is imperfect into what is perfect? Can impure things became pure? Let us take our individual mind for example. According to Buddhism, when the mind becomes perfect, everything will become perfect. If the mind is imperfect and full of delusions, then there is no freedom or peace no matter what you try. But that kind of freedom, how is it possible? Everybody wants to attain the highest peace and happiness. Not only religious persons, but everybody seeks those two things. Many people seek these ideals in temporary little things. Now the spiritual religious goal is to attain permanent freedom, peace and happiness. But is this possible?

Now, the Buddhist point of view is that it is possible because essentially our mind is pure. Now it is full of many delusions, attachments and hatred. But these are like stains on metal, or the sky filled with clouds. The stains can be removed, the clouds can be dispersed. Then how can we get rid of these mind stains? The cause of these stains is ignorance, and wisdom is its powerful antidote. When ignorance is pulled out from the root, then Nirvana is possible, an enlightened human being is possible, obtaining union with God also may be possible—maybe, we have to think about that. What does ignorance mean? That is a very deep issue in Buddhism. But the point is that it can be rooted out and peace and happiness can be attained.

SAMU SUNIM: I would like to say something about sudden awakening in regard to the question of delusion and purity. In our tradition,

Buddhahood is already inherent in us, it is not something outside. For example, say that this room has been in the dark, has never seen light. Perhaps this has been true for three-hundred years, or four-hundred years, or just three days or three weeks—it does not really matter. But today—in this very moment—if I light a candle, then it is light and the darkness is gone. So, you may wonder, "Where did the darkness go? The darkness that has prevailed here all this while, where did it go?" But the fact is it did not go anywhere: the darkness is simply transformed into light. So that means that even when this room was in the dark, the light potential has been in the dark all that time. That is the relationship between ignorance and enlightenment.

Stages

A Monk from Gethsemani: Is it absolutely necessary that one pass through all the spiritual stages in Buddhism?

Pandith Vajiragnana: It is not absolutely necessary to pass all the stages; Buddha never explained things in this way. The later teachers systematized these things in the form of stages. A meditator does not try to pass these stages one by one in sequence. We use two types of meditation—calming meditation and insight meditation—to realize the truth about impermanence, suffering and selflessness. That truth can come to a person quickly, or it may take some time. Along the way when they practice meditation these stages pass naturally, possibly even without one's knowledge. The teachers explain that one should not think that one has to pass all these stages or you might become disheartened.

Joseph Goldstein: In terms of the stages, I wanted to present a metaphor. The stages are like what happens when a person jumps out of an airplane. First, there is the tremendous exhilaration of free fall, which is like when one is really seeing the arising and passing of all phenomena and that there is no substantiality in life. There is just tremendous exhilaration and happiness. And then the falling person realizes after some time that he or she does not have a parachute. The person then goes through stages of tremendous fear and terror because there is no parachute—no security—and things do not look too good. But at a certain point, after realizing there is no parachute, the person also realizes that there is no ground. In a similar way, the practitioner settles into a place of great equanimity in which real spiritual insight matures.

DONALD MITCHELL: One of our topics of dialogue has been the need to address unwholesome states of mind and to cultivate wholesome states of mind, to address negative predispositions and to cultivate positive predispositions. We talked about this in regard to anger. But now, as we are looking at the process of dealing with these kinds of things, we are not just talking about particular states of mind, but about life itself. You are saying that our whole condition of life is changed as we understand the nature of life itself, when we understand the truth about its impermanence, suffering and selflessness. When you described the fearfulness that is involved in this realization, I wondered, "What exactly is that like? What is it like to realize that I do not have a parachute? What is it like to realize that there is no ground? And, what is it like to settle into that new reality of *Nibbana*?"

PANDITH VAJIRAGNANA: When the person examines the nature of life and its continuity, realizes its impermanency which causes unsatisfactoriness, and sees the insubstantiality of life, fearfulness arises and the person wants to get rid of the fear. When the person continues to practice and the concentration deepens, gradually the person sees the arising, the changing and ceasing of all existence. Then the person sees that in this life process there is nothing to be taken as substantial, to hang onto, everything is insubstantial. When the meditator sees that there is nothing eternal or unchanging in life, that everything changes and that change brings us unhappiness, then when that realization starts coming into him, the person feels evenmindedness toward everything. There is no longer attachment to one thing nor aversion to another thing. The person feels evenmindedness, equanimity, toward everything. And that gives the meditator some peacefulness and encourages him or her to continue.

When he or she continues along that path, peacefulness, realization, understanding—all these things start coming in. Some of the obstacles, the fetters, of the mind disappear. When these are eradicated the mind becomes very light, very clear and concentrated. The person starts feeling at a distance the real nature of *Nibbanic* bliss. This is the first entrance to the stream of sainthood, and that encourages the person to continue. When the person starts seeing reality more clearly, the strong fetters which bind us disappear and gradually the person progresses toward that *Nibbana*.

NORMAN FISCHER: Regarding the idea of stages of the path, it reminds me of the saying that the map is not the territory. So, my opinion is that while all maps of the path are very useful, if you mistake the map for the territory, you miss the actual path.

BASIL PENNINGTON: Some days in daily practice I find that as soon as I sit down, immediately what is happening in that day comes up: the fears, the joys, the plans, the worries, the problems and cares. Then, I have to use my prayer word just to keep cutting through until it dissipates and freedom comes. Then I can really rest deeply in the presence. Other days I sit down and immediately I am there, and sometimes that is the way the whole meditation is. And on other days I sit down and I am there, but then—all of a sudden—at some point there comes up from the depths of the memory one of those "knots" that is down in there. Again, using the prayer word, by just letting it go the healing of the memory takes place bit by bit in that way. It is a very simple process which sort of paces itself.

And I am profoundly convinced that if *anyone*, if any layperson busy in the world is faithful to meditating twenty minutes twice-a-day, they will come to that transformation of consciousness. Eventually they will come to true freedom. Or as we put it in the Christian tradition at times, they will die to the false self—to that construct that is made up of what I have, what I do, what other people think of me, what things I am hanging onto or worrying about, and so on. We die to all that and we find our true self in God and the tremendous freedom that comes from that.

Jesus said we judge a tree by its fruit. Those fruits that St. Paul speaks of in his Epistle to the Galatians in our Christian scriptures—the fruits of the spirit—are love, joy, patience, kindness, compassion and chastity. These fruits grow in our lives in God. I was a very self-centered, ambitious and angry young man, and I chopped people's heads off with some frequency. But I can remember the time when suddenly I realized I had not been angry for so long I could not remember the last time I was angry. The healing takes place if we are faithful to practice. We do not have to keep an eye on it, we do not have to judge it, keep a measure on it or mark its stages. We just need to live the practice and be faithful to practice, and it will take care of itself.

ESHIN NISHIMURA: People have been talking about climbing up some stages as if one were climbing up a ladder. But I think that when you arrive at the top of the ladder, that is a very dangerous place, isn't it? In Zen teaching, we are very, very strongly taught that you have to take one more step, a small step, from the top of the ladder. Do you have such a teaching in Christianity?

PIERRE DE BÉTHUNE: Of course the images of stepping always higher are just images, and we must always correct them by other images. Otherwise if we cling to those images, there will be confusion. In my own early life of Christian prayer, I "stepped" during many years in this way of climbing. When I encountered Zen Buddhism, I began another journey to go down, always more profoundly, in order to correct the ladder image. In this way, my Zen meditation practice gives me a good equilibrium. It balances my culture of the word with a culture of silence. I am very indebted to Zen Buddhism for having helped me to go much deeper in this experience of silence. And I think that when we have both experiences of silence and word, both can really improve very much.

JAMES CONNER: I was struck by the use of the image of climbing the pole and stepping off because, if you remember, in the very last talk that Thomas Merton gave in Bangkok he alluded to that same image when he said, "Where do you go from the top of a thirty-foot pole?" He was using it to refer to that plunge of faith that we have to make, a plunge of faith into trust in ourselves, trust in the spirit within us. This makes me think of the image that Joseph Goldstein used of jumping without a parachute and finding that there is no ground on which you are to land. So maybe that is where the climbing goes, to that plunge of faith.

ARMAND VEILLEUX: When the desert Fathers speak about prayer, one thing is very important for them. Their only concrete teaching about prayer, one that we find in the New Testament, is not that we should pray so many times a day, or so many times a week—it is that we should pray "unceasingly." This continuous prayer is the only thing that we are concerned about. And then, those who begin to reflect a little more about this matter become concerned about the goal of prayer, which is the perfect union of love with God. Then, they also become concerned about all the cleaning up that has to be done in us to arrive at that goal. And when people start reflecting about what they were living in their developing relationship with God, they start analyzing the various things that happened in them in the development of that relationship with God. Here we find mention of stages as steps. Sometimes those steps are numbered as in St. Benedict's different degrees of humility. But people take steps in different degrees and in different orders. So, I do not think we should be too concerned about the various steps. They are important, but most important for Christianity is the perfect union with God.

JINWOL SUNIM: I felt from Fr. Wiseman's talk that in communion with God one is so one with God that one's whole present thinking will be only him. Then the whole movement of one's heart becomes one uninterrupted prayer. In our Zen religion, we keep doubting and practicing until at last, suddenly, you have a breakthrough. Suddenly, darkness disappears and there is awakening or enlightenment. So now, I know that through non-dual prayer of communion, by just praying in that way, something happens at the end of that process. Sr. GilChrist quotes Thomas Merton as saying "The gate of heaven is everywhere." In this case heaven does not mean where you go after you die, but as "everywhere" it means the Kingdom of God, or as for the Buddhist, a kind of Pure Land. In our tradition, the Pure Land is in our mind. The important thing is that the gate of heaven is everywhere so you can get in the gate everywhere.

DAVID STEINDL-RAST: By saying that heaven is everywhere, Thomas Merton also meant that the spiritual journey does not just consist in putting one foot in front of the other and making many, many steps. The spiritual journey also consists in opening your eyes and seeing that you are already there. This is not an either/or matter, but one can look at it from two different sides.

Love

SHARON SALZBERG: I have two questions. One is perhaps more theoretical and it has to do with our own lovableness, our lovability. This seems to be in contrast to what St. Augustine said about loving oneself as presenting the face of stupidity. There seems to be a very different meaning of love, or a very different meaning of oneself in that regard. One type of self-love is very limiting and egotistical, and the other is freeing. The practical aspect of that distinction has to do with how we relate to the defilements that arise in our minds. Jeffrey Hopkins alluded yesterday to the Buddhist teaching that the mind is naturally radiant and pure—it is naturally shining. Our problems are because of the visiting forces known as defilements. These defilements are simply visiting, they are adventitious, they are not inherent to our being.

I have seen however in my own practice and in my teaching that it is very difficult to recognize this fact and have faith or confidence in it. Therefore, one of the greatest tools we have is actually the practice of loving kindness toward ourselves. In the Theravada Buddhist tradition, when we begin loving-kindness practice we begin with ourselves, which often seems rather shocking in a spiritual pursuit. It seems as if this would be selfish or limiting in some way. But in fact, it is considered the beginning or first coming close to that sense of the natural radiance and purity of our minds. It also implies having a relationship to defilements such as anger so that these defilements are less identified with who we actually are. So if you could, please just comment both on the appropriateness of seeing one's own lovableness, and also if there are actual practices or techniques that strengthen that sense.

JAMES WISEMAN: I deeply appreciate Sharon's question. I would start my answer by pointing out that in the very first book of the Bible, and in the very first part of that first book of the Bible—the Book of Genesis—when it talks about creation and goes through all the different things that the Lord God made, the refrain is, "and God saw that it was good." Then on the sixth day of creation, when human beings were created, it even adds, "and God saw that it was *very* good." I think a verse like that is truly foundational for our understanding of who we are. Deep down—at the deepest level—we have been made good. Therefore, all that goes wrong would be, in your terminology, these adventitious defilements. We tend to speak a little more in terms of sinfulness and imperfections, but I am not certain that there is a vast gulf of difference of meaning here. Those of you who would be more skilled in psychology than I am would know better than I, but at least I know the most harmful thing that can ever be done to a child is constantly to put the young boy or girl down, to say, "You are no good!" If you have ever read the life of Jean Genet you will see how horribly negative that kind of treatment was in his early life, and what it did to him in adulthood.

So, I fully agree with Sharon that just as you in your tradition would teach loving kindness first toward oneself, we would do the same. I would point out that when Jesus says, "Love your neighbor as yourself," he assumes a healthy self-love. St. Bernard, in his great *Treatise on the Love of God*, speaks of four steps of the love of God. The very first one, he says, is love of self for one's own sake. If you only read that far, you would assume that when he finally gets up here to the apex of love, it would be some pure form of the love of God. But for Bernard, the highest form of love is to love all—including oneself—for God's sake.

In terms of how one instills this, I completely agree with Pope John Paul—and with so many other people in our country and in our world today—who points out that the breakdown of the family is about the most tragic thing happening. So what you need first of all are loving mothers and fathers to instill that self-love in their children, and that sense of goodness and deep self-worth. If that goes wrong in the early years, I would say that the kind of practice of meditation and prayer that you have talked about would be very helpful.

EWERT COUSINS: Since I spoke about Augustine this morning, perhaps I should comment further. It is true that Augustine puts primacy on self-transcending love, and he does speak about the alternative being the image of stupidity. But in this context, it means that if that is all you have, that would be the image of stupidity.

I think that you can find in the West a kind of polarity which is natural to the human experience. On the one hand, there is healthy self-reflective estimation, authentic esteem for ourselves as creatures of God; or as St. Bernard says, we love ourselves for our own sake in the first degree of loving God. On the other hand, there is self-transcending love. We have a famous example of that in Richard of Saint Victor, the twelfth-century theologian–mystic who, perhaps better than any other person, has formulated this when he speaks about the perfection of charity. He quotes Gregory the Great, one of the greatest of all monastic writers, and he says this: If we are asking about the perfection of charity, *caritas*, or love, we do not say that a person has the perfection of love if he or she has *only* love for oneself. If a person has love for oneself, we would not say that he or she achieved a perfection of love. There is a kind of instinctual, spontaneous resistance to saying that. But nevertheless, according to Bernard, and Augustine too, it is indeed necessary to have love that is self-esteeming. In the Christian tradition, that is grounded in the very fact that we are creatures of God.

HIS HOLINESS THE DALAI LAMA: I want to mention something in the Buddhist texts that I think is very appropriate for our Christian sisters and brothers. This is the importance of cultivating an altruistic intention to develop oneself spiritually for the sake of others. In this cultivation process, one realizes that one has self-cherishing and lacks the cherishing of others. Then we should reflect on the disadvantages of cherishing oneself, and the advantages of cherishing others. Through this process of meditation, self-cherishing is diminished and the cherishing of others is developed. In this case, one is developing what is called a neglecting of yourself and an emphasis on the welfare of others. But, this does not mean that you should neglect your own situation entirely. In order even to develop a sense of cherishing others, you have to know what it means to cherish yourself. So, selflessness does not mean just to forget oneself. Rather what one must reduce is any selfish feeling which leads one to exploit the other or to harm the other. But generally, low self-esteem is very negative. I think that low self-esteem, or hating yourself, is really sad. It is not good at all.

So you see here, when we deal with different mental emotions, we have to know precisely what is positive and what negative. For example, there are two kinds of desire. The desire to have more happiness, or the desire to be close to God, these kinds of desires are very constructive. Other desires, like wanting all sorts of things, eventually lead us to disappointment and disaster. Also, there can be two kinds of anger. One form of anger, which is motivated by compassion, is in a real sense very constructive. But anger which eventually develops into hatred, that kind of anger is absolutely negative. So we have to make distinctions. Then also the ego feeling, the sense of a strong self, is also of two kinds. One is the feeling that, "I can work hard in order to serve others! I must dedicate myself for the welfare of others!" In order to develop such a willful determination, we need a strong sense of self that is very positive. The other kind of ego feeling leads to harming another with no hesitation. That kind of strong ego feeling is very negative. Again, we have to make distinctions when we deal with different emotions in developing love and compassion.

I would like to suggest that to cultivate compassion, one can take as an object of meditation sentient beings who are full of suffering, and then wish that they become free from suffering. To cultivate love, one can take as one's object of meditation beings who are bereft of happiness, and then develop the wish that they become endowed with happiness. In both cases, you should be unbiased. Usually, because of our feeling toward our own close friends, we may have some kind of natural concern about their welfare. That is not necessarily true compassion because it is mixed with attachment. So, that is a biased feeling that is directed only toward a limited number of persons. Also, because our friends' attitude toward us is positive, as a response we feel compassion or a close feeling. This is not genuine compassion. Genuine compassion does not regard what kind of attitude the other has toward you. Rather, on the basis of realizing that others are just like oneself—they too want happiness, they too do not want suffering, and they also have the right to overcome suffering—on that basis, one can develop a true sense of concern. That is genuine compassion which is not biased and even extends toward one's enemy.

Now, how can you develop that kind of concern or compassion? The way to develop compassion is first of all to visualize a being whose level of suffering is such that, to our ordinary mind, we feel we cannot bear it. We just do not even want to look at it. But take that person to mind and reflect on the qualities of his or her suffering. Then reflect on the fact that he or she is similar to yourself in terms of wanting happiness and not wanting suffering. Through time, you will very strongly feel a sense of concern for that other person. That is how compassion is developed. Then move your meditation to other persons who are close to you one by one. Eventually work on your enemies, one by one, taking them to mind and seeing that they are similar to yourself in wanting happiness, not wanting suffering, and having the right to be free from suffering. Thus, you can develop the same strength of concern with respect to them. It is important that we emphasize developing compassion with respect to those beings who are hard to love. In the Gospels, there is also the same message about the need to develop patience and forbearance in loving one's enemies.

Humility

JOSEPH GOLDSTEIN: As I was listening to the wonderful Christian talks this afternoon, there was a word that jumped out at me and which I began to think about in terms of a Buddhist understanding. This was the word "humility." When I was thinking about Christian humility, it seemed very connected with an idea in Buddhism which is often seen as opposing the Christian view of things. This Buddhist idea is selflessness. But the Christian understanding of humility seems to come together with the Buddhist understanding of selflessness. This is expressed by an Englishman named Wei Wu Wei where he says that true humility is the absence of anyone to be proud. So, I feel that humility in its deepest understanding is a realization of selflessness.

GUO-CHOU: I too was glad to hear about Christian humility. In the Chinese Ch'an or Zen tradition, especially according to the teaching of my master, Ven. Master Sheng-yen, humility is very important for practitioners. Very often we find that during the process of practice we will encounter obstructions. For many intelligent people after they study the *Dharma*, or teachings of Buddha, and even after they practice the *Dharma* they really cannot merge with the *Dharma*. They cannot really make themselves one whole with the *Dharma*. So, at this time we need this practice of humility. In this practice, we calm our mind with contemplation of the earth which is very impressive and very supportive to all human beings, to all living beings. In a sense, the earth is very down to earth, it is very low, beneath every living being. But at the same time it is very supportive—it is willing to support everything without any conditions.

By this contemplation, to a certain degree we open our hearts because of this humility. We realize what we have done wrong in the past, and we see all sorts of shortcomings in our character. Usually in Western languages "humility" has a negative sense. But from our viewpoint, we actually form a very positive ground for practice because through humility we really understand ourselves better. And then from that self-understanding, we can be humble, modest, down to earth and return back to our practice with a newborn mentality. So, with this sense of humility, we are really affirming ourselves. From there, we continue our practice and we can really start dissolving the ego, the self-centeredness, so as to merge with the *Dharma*.

SAMU SUNIM: The Ven. Guo-Chou spoke of the importance of humility in Zen. Personally, I have found many Zen teachers to be proud and arrogant. But growing up in a Korean Zen monastery, one of the senior monks who did my novice training used to tell us that to know who is really an authentic Zen Master is to see whether he has the novice mind or not. All the great Zen Masters always carry the novice mind, being nobody, the pure mind.

PIERRE DE BÉTHUNE: I would like to say that humility is the human face of emptiness. Emptiness is very great, but humility is when somebody has been grasped by emptiness. Then he or she is modest and has a very simple way of living. In Christian spirituality, humility is the same thing as emptiness. We see this in the Bible where it is said in Latin that Christ "humbled" himself. The Greek text states that he "emptied" himself. This self-emptying, or *kenosis*, is crucial for Christian humility, for our becoming like "little children" in the Kingdom of God.

ESHIN NISHIMURA: A beautiful story of humility just came to my mind. This humility comes out of great wisdom and compassion through long, long Zen training. I know a lovely Zen monk who used to live alone in a hermitage at the foot of a mountain near Kobe in Japan. Right after World War II, because of the bombing there were many, many children begging and sleeping homelessly. When this monk went to Kobe, he brought children back whenever he found them. Soon his poor hermitage was full of boys and girls, even babies. Then after the war, one of my students, who was studying at my university, lived at the hermitage of this monk. One day, this student was picking up frogs in the small pond near the hermitage. At that moment, the monk came back to the hermitage and happened to find the boy putting the frogs into a bucket. The monk asked, "What are you doing?" The student answered, "Well, these frogs are so noisy they disturb my study. So, I am going to put them on the other side of the mountain." The monk said, "Well, be sure not to forget that you are staying here for only four years. The frogs stay here their whole life."

8

Method and Experience

The inner cloistered garden is tended by an old gardener monk. He seems to have a green thumb—everything he touches bursts into new life. He walks slowly, humbly and quietly throughout the garden, tending to each plant only according to its needs. He seems to spot the weeds even before they break through the ground, removing them with a gentle and respectful motion of his hands. His hat gives shade to his eyes so he can see what needs to be seen. His tools seem to be extensions of his body as they work the soil, pulling out the weeds and fortifying the flowers. Sometimes the gardener goes to the well at the center of the garden to draw water for the plants. The water is brought up from a deep underground watercourse that passes below the monastery as it flows under the hills and valleys of the surrounding countryside. The water drawn by the old monk comes from the same source from which the monks drink and the farmers use for themselves and their crops.

The inner cloister of our heart needs to be tended with care, removing the mind weeds, and giving the flowers of virtue room to grow. We can each learn to do this task from the teachers of spiritual gardening, from their words and their example. There are many ancient traditions of spiritual gardening, each with its own methods and goals. But besides the techniques, there are the necessary spiritual nutrients from the ground of our being and the water of life that springs forth from that ground which are both needed for real spiritual growth. A true spiritual lineage must provide access to the inner passageway that leads to the ground of our being. And it must also be able to draw from the water of spiritual life within that ground for true spiritual growth to take place. One can judge a spiritual lineage from the fruit it bears, from the flowers it produces.

In our dialogue, we addressed such questions as: What are the types and roles of teachers in the spiritual life? What are the signs of spiritual maturity? What is the value of words in the lineages of spirituality? In what way are the words of scripture spiritually transformative? What are methods that can be used for spiritual cultivation? What experiences and habits of the heart develop in the spiritual life? What are the means of discernment that are used to validate true spiritual experience? Where in this process is there room for spontaneity? Is there the experience of blessings, or grace, or a deeper source of spiritual transformation?

Teacher

PASCALINE COFF: In our Christian scriptures, we have not only the words of Jesus Christ but also his example to aid in our discernment concerning how to live. So, if we are going to teach meditation on compassion, we would first have someone meditate on how Jesus was compassionate. Do Buddhists ever meditate on the life of the Buddha for an example of how to live?

PANDITH VAJIRAGNANA: We also have exactly the same method, especially for our spiritual teachers. The teacher in our Buddhist tradition should always be an ideal person. He or she should always be an example not only by teaching, but also in behavior and in words. A teacher should not only have knowledge, but he or she should also have the discipline to be able to do his or her job properly. This is especially important because in Sri Lanka, Thailand, Burma, Cambodia, Laos—in these Theravada Buddhist countries—the normal practice is to ordain people at a very young age. The average age is between twelve and fifteen. At such a tender young age, the young monastic needs a teacher who can play the role of a parent. The youth needs the love of a mother and a father. So, the teacher should have knowledge about the feelings of that youth, and also the teacher should be able to play the role of a mother as well as a father toward that youth. In this regard, the teacher always takes the Buddha as an example of how to be kind and loving toward disciples.

JULIAN VON DUERBECK: In the *Rule of St. Benedict,* the monk or nun is called a son or daughter of Christ. And it is because the abbot or abbess represents Christ that they are referred to as father or mother. I have noticed in Thailand that monastics are referred to as children of the Buddha. So, when you or we perform the roles of mother or father, we are actually imitating the actions of Christ or Buddha. It is in these actions that we understand the virtues of our founders.

ESHIN NISHIMURA: Let me introduce two types of teachers in the Japanese Zen monastery. One is a softer type and the other is a harder type of teacher. Both are very effective even though their methods are different. Here is a story about the soft type. When the Master went out of the monastery on some business, a young monk who just came to the monastery thought that this was a chance to take a nap in the corridor at the back of the Buddha Hall. Unfortunately, the Master came back to pick up some things he had forgotten to take with him. So the disciple, with no chance to run away, pretended he was sleeping. When the Master came to where the disciple was sleeping, he just passed by his feet making a deep bow as he did so. After that, the disciple felt very much ashamed. In the end, this gentle action was a great encouragement to this young monk.

Now here is a story about a hard teacher. When a young disciple was walking the narrow corridor behind the Buddha Hall, he was frightened because the walkway was very high up. At that moment, the great Master came by. For a young disciple, to meet the Master privately is an awful thing, you know. So doubly frightened, the disciple stood along the wall. When the Master passed by the young disciple, this Master gave him a blow. The disciple could not understand why he was given a blow in spite of giving him room to pass by. So he went to the Master's room where he was having a meal and asked, "Why did you give me blow at that time?" The Master replied, "Why did you let me walk along the dangerous side?" This disciple was shocked, but he was also stimulated and opened his mind to the importance of carefulness.

JOSEPH GOLDSTEIN: The essence of the heart of the practice of awakening is awareness. The teacher plays a very critical role in helping the students free themselves of obscurations to that awareness. I would like to tell two very brief stories—not quite as colorful as Zen stories—that also show the power of simplicity, of making the mind very simple. Once, when I was doing a retreat with my teacher I had judgments in my mind about everyone including myself. So in my interview with my teacher, I reported what was happening in my mind—that there were all these judgments. He just looked at me and said something very, very simple. He said, "Be more mindful." I had heard those words tens of thousands of times, and I thought that he was not really understanding me. But as I went outside and started doing walking meditation, I thought that maybe I would try it. So, I actually became more mindful in my walking. And lo and behold, in the care that I was taking to be more mindful, there was no room for the judgments to arise! In this I learned something very useful: even in practice we can go through the day only kind of mindful. That is what my teacher was pointing out to me. Sometimes a very simple instruction actually reveals something very important about the nature of practice.

Another time, I was practicing at a monastery in Burma and it was incredibly noisy. In Asia, it is not uncommon to have loudspeakers in the villages blaring music. Also, there was construction going on at the monastery right outside my window. So I was thinking, "Here I came all the way to Asia to get enlightened and they are making all this noise. Why can't they stop it!" So again I went to my teacher and reported that all this noise was disturbing my practice. And again he said something very, very simple. He said, "Did you note it?" To note it means to be mindful of it. I thought that he was just trying to make the best of an unfortunate situation. But as I practiced, I realized he was talking about something much, much deeper. He was pointing to the truth that, from the perspective of awareness, it does not matter what is arising in the mind. The nature of the mind, this luminous and clear nature of awareness, is not affected by whatever is arising. It can be the most unpleasant noise or the most unpleasant sensation, and this mirrorlike wisdom of the mind is always present. I feel that this is a very important role of the teacher in a student's practice, to help him or her see the ways we get hooked in misunderstanding and the ways to free ourselves in the moment.

PANDITH VAJIRAGNANA: I am very happy with what our friend Goldstein has said about how the teaching of the teacher depends on the mentality of the students. We come across students who are very young and also some mature ones as well. So, the teacher should be skillful in judging their mentality, their capabilities, where they are mentally.

JAMES WISEMAN: Your Holiness, we know that ever since the time of your discovery as a young boy, you have had many special teachers. Could you say something about your teachers and your relationship to them?

HIS HOLINESS THE DALAI LAMA: In my case, I have had seventeen gurus from different Buddhist lineages. There were two official tutors from whom I received teaching for the longest period of time. One gave me *bhiksu* ordination when I was about six or seven. Then he took full responsibility for my education. I remember that when I was small, he very rarely smiled. I was really very much afraid of him, and on a few occasions he scolded me. That, of course, is the Tibetan tradition. Sometimes the teacher even uses a whip. For the young Dalai Lama there is a particular whip. When I started my study my immediate elder brother was also with me. So, my teacher prepared two whips—one for me and one for him. The only difference was that my whip was yellow. Except for the color the whips were the same so the pain was the same. The color did not make any difference! My teacher always kept that whip beside him; but, fortunately, he never used it on me. However, on a few occasions he threatened to use it. My poor elder brother did receive the blessing of the whip on a few occasions.

Now I realize that when I was a very young student I did not think properly. So my tutor's sternness was suitable. A story will show why. When I was small, one lama from the search party was—at the initial stage—an acting tutor. Since he was very jovial and very peaceful, we became very close friends. When he came to give me my lesson, instead of reading or reciting, I would ride on him and tell him, "You should chant! You should read!" I was that kind of student. So, I think my tutor's sternness was very appropriate. Also, he always had a caring attitude, and gradually when I grew up that tutor's attitude toward me became much softer. He never made any negative comments, and he fully trusted me—always smiling and laughing. It has been now more than ten years ago since he passed away. Still, very often in my dreams he comes and gives me some inspirations. He was a great teacher and a top scholar. At the same time, he never showed off his knowledge. He always remained very humble. If you asked him something, he would say "I don't know; I don't know." If you insisted, he would explain his knowledge with experience. It was something marvelous!

ARMAND VEILLEUX: In Christianity, we have an eremitical tradition and a communal tradition. We bring these together under the name of one monastic tradition. But, in fact, they are two different traditions. In the tradition of the desert, you have the role of the spiritual father and mother which is very similar to the role of the guru in the East. But when monastic communities appear, a large part of the role of spiritual father or mother of the desert is transposed to the community. What the guide in the desert was doing was transmitting his own experience. Now, that experience is embodied in a way of life, in the *Rule*, of the community so that the experience is transmitted from generation to generation. So, the abbot or abbess of a monastic community has responsibility for the communion, for the cohesion, for the quality of life of the community. He or she may play the role of spiritual father or mother to some monastics, or others in the community may also play this role. In this way we maintain those two traditions in monastic life. But I must add that when we have tried to transpose on the communal abbot or abbess the role of the charismatic father or mother, it has been a recipe for disaster.

NORMAN FISCHER: I have always been impressed that in the Mahayana tradition it says that the purpose of practice is to bring about mature beings, for people to really become mature individuals. And I assume that in the Christian tradition this is pretty much the same if by maturity you mean really living in the fullness of God's love—God's grace—and that most of us are not so mature. Since we are really immature, I like the Christian quotation I just heard, namely, that those who think that they can be their own spiritual director are being directed by a jackass. Just because we are so deeply immature, to make the journey to true maturity requires not only luck, the Holy Spirit, and everything else, but probably a mature guide with whom we can work.

However, the problem that I have seen is that sometimes the relationship to the teacher can stand in the way of the student really becoming mature. You may get a lot of guidance, you may learn a lot, and many transformations can happen; but in the end, if you do not really "leap over" the teacher, then you are not mature. And in a way, the better the teacher is the harder it is to do that. This has been a problem in our Buddhist communities. Whereas it looks to me as though in Christianity, when it is Christ who is really the guide, it is less possible for one to elevate the spiritual director to the point where he or she can actually be a hindrance to the student's maturity. Yet, it is also important to have a mature spiritual teacher or we just wander in our immaturity led by our "jackass" teacher!

BLANCHE HARTMAN: I think the teacher is a great inspiration for a Zen practitioner too, because he or she shows the kind of person that can develop with the practice of *zazen*. A teacher does not tell a student anything. A teacher's function is to help the disciple find out what he or she already knows in his or her deepest being—to find out how limitless we are. There was a student who had finished his work with his Zen Master and was leaving to go on a pilgrimage. The Zen Master asked, "Where are you going?" The student answered, "I don't know." The teacher replied, "Not knowing is nearest." We never get to the point of knowing. But we do—as we become more and more open through practice—discover the boundlessness of who we are and the interconnection with everything. That does result in an overwhelming feeling of gratitude.

LOBSANG TENZIN: The teacher, or guru, in Tibetan Buddhism does not just point out everything to us and solve all our problems. Rather, the purpose of a spiritual teacher is—from the Tantric Buddhist point of view—to give us a glimpse of the real guru which is the fully enlightened or awakened state of mind. The term "guru," or "lama" in Tibetan, means "unsurpassable." Now, the goal of a practitioner is to arrive at that unsurpassable awakened state of mind. If that is the purpose, then to glimpse that unsurpassable experience when one is on the path to achieving that fully awakened state of mind is very helpful. Of course, we might say that it is already there, and we can all agree that it is potentially there. The guru, from the Tantric Buddhist point of view, is seen in a living person who represents that enlightened quality for you. We see that living person not as an ordinary person, but actually as an enlightened being manifested in that form for us. In that respect, the purpose of the spiritual master is to give rise to the experience of the enlightened mind. That is why in Tantric Buddhism you see various forms of guru yoga, where the guru is actually brought into our heart, making us inseparable, purifying our negative and enhancing our positive qualities. That is the main purpose of the guru.

HAVANPOLA RATANASARA: In Theravada Buddhism, the relationship between teacher and student is similar to the relationship of a parent and child. Although as the teachers supervise the students, there is always freedom for the students. The student is not bound on doctrinal points. If there is something in the Buddha's teaching that goes against the teacher's version, then the student is not bound to believe the teacher's views. Our system recognizes the freedom of the individual, the intelligence of the student. Then besides the teacher working with students in the ordinary temple situation, the monk in charge of the temple plays the role of a teacher for the whole community. When people quarrel, when a husband and a wife argue, they come to the monk in the temple. In this way our system is very practical and serves the needs of the broader society outside the monastery or temple.

JOSEPH GOLDSTEIN: For many centuries, the transmission of the Buddhist teachings was held in monasteries. This transmission was preserved and practiced mostly in monasteries by monks and nuns. In this century, especially in Burma, something quite unusual happened. Through the teachings of a few very great masters, meditation practice and the stages of purification were made available on quite a large scale to the lay population. This was a kind of revolution in spiritual practice: the idea that laypeople can actually undergo a course of training and experience the fruits of that transformation. Now, in Burma itself there are hundreds of monasteries where laypeople undergo this training practice. This has had a tremendous import for bringing Buddhism to the West because, at the present time anyway, most of the practitioners in the West are laypeople. Perhaps when there is a sufficient ground of support, some of the great monasteries will also take root in this country as well. But I wanted to emphasize the fact that although undoubtedly it is a great blessing to have the good fortune and the merit to live the monastic life, one need not be a monk or a nun in a monastery to experience the fruit, the very deep and great fruit, of spiritual practice.

KEVIN HUNT: In the Catholic tradition, we speak of the Church as the "Body of Christ," as the social continuation of the existence of Jesus of Nazareth within the world. We also see that as the Body of Christ we are on the road to full realization—not only as individuals—but as community. Does the Buddhist idea of *Sangha* have the same sense of a communal realization?

HIS HOLINESS THE DALAI LAMA: It is said that Buddhas are teachers of refuge, and that the *Dharma*—the realized scriptural doctrine—is the actual refuge. The sisters and brothers helping people to this refuge are the *Sangha*. It is said that the *Sangha* is like nurses and attendants taking care of sick persons. Thus, the *Sangha* is a group that indeed has to work and proceed together in realizing the *Dharma* in the world. Without a *Sangha* that has internalized the practices, the discipline, and so forth, there is no Buddhist teaching. Buddha said that where there is a *Sangha*, a spiritual community that has internalized these practices, then he can feel very relaxed.

Language

DIANA ECK: St. Bernard lived a long time ago and he did not have an opportunity to meet His Holiness the Dalai Lama, the Ven. Ghosananda and our other Buddhist teachers who are with us when he wrote, "When the spiritual light of beauty has filled all the depths of the heart with its abundance, it must necessarily shine outward. It erupts, and its rays appear in the body, reflection of the soul. This beauty spreads through the limbs and senses until the whole body manifests its brilliance." The idea from St. Bernard is that the gifts of the spirit, as we speak of them as Christians, show forth in the lives of people who have gone deeply into the life of prayer or meditation. My question is, what would he have said if he had met a Buddhist glowing with this light?

When I observe the lightening countenance of people who are *not* Christians, it seems strange to say that their lives are filled with what I call the Holy Spirit. Perhaps we need to develop a new language for speaking out of this kind of encounter. Our monks and theologians of the past who expressed the Christian experience in their writings did not have the kind of encounter that we have here. So, perhaps we need a new language, a new theological language that is forged out of *this* dialogue situation so that Christians do not go on discussing the whole world of spiritual reality using just Christian terms that may not express properly the experience of other religious traditions.

GILCHRIST LAVIGNE: I think that there certainly is room for a new interfaith vocabulary in spirituality. But on the other hand, I also feel that we will only speak truly if we speak from our own spiritual idiom, our own spiritual place in the universe. So, as a Christian I have to speak as a Christian. His Holiness the Dalai Lama must speak as a Buddhist. And somehow the meeting in between will be real if we truly express who we really are. When I saw His Holiness yesterday, he was offered a cup of water and he gave the cup of water to someone else. I learned more from that action than from many lectures on compassion. Maybe a new language can be found in our gestures.

NORMAN FISCHER: In the context of spiritual practice, every day certain words and terms become very, very intimate. Through practice they also build up many dimensions of meaning. For example, there are over a thousand years of history behind the word "simplicity" in Christian spirituality. And in Buddhism, every commentator and every practitioner adds and adds layers of meaning to the Buddha's words. As we enter this history, the intimacy and the multidimensionality of these words almost make them into physical objects. That is how concrete and how many relations we have with them, and how many echoes they have in our hearts. So, I think that what happens in an encounter such as this is that by hearing terms from another tradition we bring them into our own tradition. We put another layer of meaning to those same terms. So perhaps rather than creating another terminology, it is a matter of stretching one's own to take in the other's terminology.

BLANCHE HARTMAN: I agree with Norman that we do not need to create new terms. What I think is the wonder of this kind of meeting is that as we begin to understand the words that are used by others and relate what they are saying to our practice, we learn to appreciate more deeply the ways in which our spiritual practice is similar to, and different from, the practice of our Christian brothers and sisters. We can appreciate "simplicity" and we can appreciate "humility" more and more deeply by having this kind of exchange. This is what is so heartening and encouraging to me about our meeting here.

ARMAND VEILLEUX: Our language is used to help others understand what we are speaking about. But we need to have some experience of what the person is speaking about in order to understand him or her. In this spiritual dialogue we are in—whatever are the words we are using—if we are to some extent living the same reality, then through those words we are gradually, mutually being put in touch with *the* reality about which we are talking. And so the words are very relative and not that important in the end. What is important is our living of the spiritual life and our being open to each other's experience of that life.

PIERRE DE BÉTHUNE: I was struck by the fact that in our dialogue we seem to move from a point of great proximity, to another point where there seems to be a lack of understanding. An image comes to my mind that perhaps could express the process we are going through, simply the image of breathing. Dialogue means to receive, to take inside me at the deepest place in myself and to inculturate what I receive. This is breathing in, receiving and assimilating what is given to me. Dialogue is also the exodus, going out of myself and recognizing the differentness of the other. Just as in respiration, dialogue consists in receiving and assimilating something, and then going out and feeling excluded. And I would like to add only two conclusions. We should not try to find some common denominator, some place where we do not feel alien at all. That would be an illusion. The only way to overcome that experience of dualism is deep and full respect for the other *as other*. And I think this image can show us what we have to do: going forward one step at a time through this process of respiration, receiving in and giving out.

Scripture

ARMAND VEILLEUX: Certain words in our tradition, especially those found in scripture, have transformative power for our lives. So, it is regretable that one of the things that people do too often today is to present *lectio divina* as a kind of technique that is distinct from the rest of life. You do your half-hour of *lectio divina* and then you go on to the rest of the day's activities. That is absolutely alien to early monastic tradition. In early Latin literature up to the eleventh or twelfth century, *lectio divina* always meant the divine scripture and not anything we do with it. It is very late that we begin to speak of *lectio divina* as an activity we do with the scripture. For the early monastics, and for early Christians in general, their approach to the scripture was to let themselves be transformed by it in what we call "reading with the heart." For example, when St. Jerome translated the scripture he was doing *lectio divina*, he was being transformed by the texts he was translating.

For a number of centuries, we lost this type of contact with the scripture. While in our time we have found it again, the temptation is to make of it just one more of our observances. That distorts its meaning. What we have rediscovered in this "reading with the ear of the heart," is that it is something we have to do during the whole day, in everything we do, in everything we are. If we are contemplatives, everything that we meet is a contact with God, everything that we do is a contact with God. And if we do not realize this while we are working, while we are talking with people, while we are meeting with people, we will not realize it when we think we are doing *lectio divina*.

NORMAN FISCHER: In our Buddhist monastery, we have a sutra-study time between early morning meditation and meditation later during the morning. We do this all together, and in our monastery we do not have electricity. So it is really wonderful to do this sutra practice with kerosene light in the early morning before there is enough light to see. It is great fun because after all of the sitting practice, the words really enter. As in Christian practice, you listen with the ear of the heart, and this is the great secret about the contemplative life. It is so satisfying to sit after several hours of meditating and just read these words—not necessarily remembering any of it or doing anything with it—but just letting it in and seeing what it feels like all through the body. It is quite wonderful!

JOSEPH GOLDSTEIN: I am reminded of many stories both from the time of the Buddha and also in the present day when people would be hearing a teaching, either from a scripture or from a teacher, and the mind would awaken. In the Buddhist tradition, this is called a moment of enlightenment or awakening. I was curious about what in the Christian tradition would correspond to such a *radical* transformation in the moment—as opposed to the very beneficial resting in the spirit of God.

MARY MARGARET FUNK: We do have conversion stories, for example those of St. Augustine and St. Paul. And many people I have been with tell of a deep, radical conversion such that they cannot return to where they were before. Another sign of this conversion is that they are out of themselves, they are in a new state of consciousness which is usually accompanied by a radical relational dimension with God and with others.

DAVID STEINDL-RAST: St. Augustine's conversion experience was connected with *lectio divina*. He was attuned to hearing a child from over the wall singing in some game, "Take and read! Take and read!" He took this as meaning himself, and he went to the table where there was an open Bible. He read the passage that is there, and that passage really hit his heart and led to his final step of conversion.

KEVIN HUNT: In a certain sense, our *lectio divina* is a form of "mind training," as you refer to it in Buddhism. We do not approach it as the Tibetans do, or perhaps as the Theravadin tradition does, that is from an analytic and philosophical approach. *Lectio divina* means you assume the mind of Christ. As a practical method, the only way that you can do this is by—sitting down and reading. I can remember when I first entered the monastery, my novice master said, "Just take some time." Back in those days Catholics were not well known for their understanding or reading of scripture, so this was a completely new thing to me. I had great problems because my mind would go all over the world. So he said, "Just return to it, just return to it, just return to it." So, gradually this transformation of mind began to take place.

This is truly mind training, but I do not think we Christians have ever thought of it in quite that way. The practical way of doing it that I suggest to people is to take one of the Gospels and just read it from beginning to end. And then when you finish, start again and reread it, and reread it, and reread it, until the particular aspects of the mind of Christ, of what you encounter in the scripture, become part of you. I would like to ask the Zen tradition, do you have something similar to mind training through reading?

ESHIN NISHIMURA: In our medieval Japanese tradition, we have the following poem that Zen people like:

Seeing with ears,
Listening too with eyes,
There is no doubt at all.
A drop of water falling down from the roof,
Returns to itself.

An older poem which Zen people also like very much asks if in the dark night, you can listen to the sound of a not-crying crow. You cannot see the black crow in the dark night. You cannot listen to the sound of a non-crying crow. But if you *can* do that, you will meet your parents before you were born. These poems teach us not to use just our sense organs to see reality. So if you use your sense organs, which are given from your parents, you cannot see reality at all. I remember once a Zen Master's orders: "Play the flute which has no holes! Can you do that?"

JINWOL SUNIM: I can say that I feel there is a common ground, a similarity between our practice of meditation in Zen Buddhism and Christian contemplation. As in your practice of *lectio divina,* we use our sutras in a way that transforms our mind. Also without these scriptures, we could not understand or learn Buddha's intention or teaching. I used to tell my Buddhist congregation to ignore other religions, but I feel very comfortable here, very close. So, I think if we climb up the mountain, maybe at the top—at the peak—we can see each other and get together.

CHUEN PHANGCHAM: I would like to add to what my Korean brother said about different roads. The Buddha said that the different rivers have different colors because they flow through different kinds of soil. The Colorado River has a different color from the Ohio River. But when these rivers reach the ocean, they become one color. The paths may be different, but the heart is the same. We are one.

NORMAN FISCHER: For me one of the wonderful things about this week has been the opportunity to do practice together. I find that even more energizing than all the talking we are doing. And so I was in the church singing the Psalms, and then I was back in my room reading the Psalms. Now the Psalms, as I understand it, are central to the liturgy. But, there are some things in the Psalms that I would find hard to swallow if I were chanting them every day. When it says something like please, Lord, break their jawbones, and trample them under foot, I wonder how you practice with this? How do you work with it?

JULIAN VON DUERBECK: I think one of the ways that Christians deal with negative mental states is in channeling them through prayer. For example, the prayers that Abbot Timothy used in the Sacramentary this morning were about protecting us from people of violence, recognizing that it is there and asking God to destroy weapons of hate. The prayer images of God destroying the enemy are themselves martial images. Sometimes I feel that in the Psalms this gets carried away because we have there reflections by people who are being persecuted by others and are really wanting God to smash in their jaws, etc. But when we do pray those Psalms, we use something called "tropology" which means that we do not think about the individual enemy, but they become symbols of evil, of injustice, of disharmony. In 1989, a group of Tibetan monks came to our abbey where they did the Dance of the Skeleton Lords which presented a frightening destruction of evil. So, I think evil can be addressed through prayer in this way.

DHAMMARAKKHITA: We Buddhist monastics, and you Christian brothers and sisters, have learned from Buddha's teaching and Christ's teaching. Buddha taught the *Dhamma* by his experiences. And I also think that Christ taught his *Dhamma* by his experiences. We can learn much from the experiences of our founders in our scriptures. But you cannot understand by just reading. You must practice the teaching. We Buddhists must practice meditation, and you Christians must pray.

Practice

DIANA ECK: Just a question about the "gift" of prayer. Many young people who are Christians ask about how to pray. I know that in *The Cloud of Unknowing* the author says that if someone asks him how to begin, he will pray that God himself will teach that person. But I know that if I went to a Buddhist center, someone would teach me to sit down in a particular way, and put my hands and my legs in a certain position, and breathe in a certain way, etc. There is a method of practice here that seems absent in the case of Christian prayer. Jesus did not teach us a method of prayer. I think that one of the many reasons so many people go to Buddhist meditation centers is because they provide an avenue, something to work with, a methodology of spiritual practice.

BASIL PENNINGTON: I certainly agree that people are looking for a way of praying, and I think this is one of the challenges our Eastern brothers and sisters have presented to us. We have come to realize that we have not been teaching our spiritual practices in a very practical way. This is what is behind the whole centering-prayer movement. In this movement, we teach both *lectio divina* and meditation, or centering prayer, or prayer of the heart. We do this in very specific steps that anyone can learn and can begin to practice immediately—conscious that this is just a means to open the inner space and the Spirit will do the rest.

For *lectio divina* we tell people to take the sacred text, call upon the Holy Spirit, and come to an awareness of God in that text. Then you listen for a set amount of time since the tendency is to rush through it. We have all been schooled to get things done. So, you say, "All right, for five minutes (or ten or twenty minutes) I am going to just sit and listen." If the Lord really speaks to one in the reading, just stay with that and let it come alive. Then at the end, thank the Lord for being present there and speaking through the text. Finally, choose some word or phrase to carry through the rest of the day.

For centering prayer it is the same thing. You have to get settled comfortably first, and just turn to God who is dwelling in the depths of your being. Then you take up a little word of love, and use that word to stay quietly with God. Whenever you become aware of anything else, just use that little word to come back again. And at the end of the time you can finish with the Lord's Prayer. It is very simple. Anybody can start with it, but it is so simple it leaves a lot of space for the Spirit to lead.

LOBSANG TENZIN: With His Holiness's blessing I would just like to address the question that was raised by our venerable brother with regard to the practice of *lectio divina*. In the Tibetan Buddhist tradition, there are three steps in practice, namely, hearing, contemplation and meditation. The purpose is to tame the wild negative states of mind, and to cultivate the positive states of mind. Through this practice, we experience peace and joy in our lives and bring that peace and joy into our communities for the sake of others. To transform the negative states of mind, it is important that we first know what the process of transforming the mind involves. The first step is to develop a certain experience or understanding through hearing or reading. I think that this hearing is somewhat like *lectio divina*.

The next step, which this hearing leads to, is contemplation. For example, when we have some idea of selflessness, to use a Buddhist principle, then in a very rational and definitive way we determine what that selflessness actually is. When one thus realizes the concept of selflessness, one is at the stage of contemplation. Then the third step is to meditate upon it so that it becomes an intuitive realization, a genuine experience. So, in order to deepen that experience a process of familiarization is emphasized, and that is what the practice of meditation is.

JUDITH SIMMER-BROWN: I am grateful to Geshe Lobsang for talking about these three stages. It took me a long time to understand that when Christians speak of meditation, it is what we Buddhists call contemplation; and when Christians speak of contemplation, it is what we

Buddhists call meditation. In Buddhism, contemplation involves duality, and meditation involves nonduality. In Christianity these are reversed.

Also, while Tibetan Buddhism is very famous for contemplation in an analytic fashion, in the Kagyu tradition in which I have been trained there is also contemplation which is oriented toward devotion. So we do have a devotional element in our spirituality. But my question is do you also have a nondual element in yours? As I understand it, centering prayer is beginning to move toward a sense of nonduality. In Christian contemplation is there ever, finally, a sense of absolute nonduality?

BASIL PENNINGTON: It is a question of trying to put the ineffable into words. I would say very definitely there is an experience of nonduality—I mean you could define it in that way. There is a coming to that point where simply, God is. Here, any sense of oneself is totally gone. I mean, just God is. And I think that is what nonduality means, but when you start with words, it is very hard to work at it. Jesus prayed at the Last Supper that we would be one with him as he is one with the Father. Catholic teaching holds that the Father, Son, and Holy Spirit are absolutely one. So, we are called into and baptized into oneness with Christ, with Christ in God. But, that is beyond any concept of oneness that we can manage with our rational minds. That is why it is more important to leave concepts—all ideas and all images—behind and open ourselves to the experience of what is—and God is.

MARY MARGARET FUNK: Abbot Gerry raised the issue that a person who is struggling in prayer should stay with his prayers rather than search for some technique for meditation. I want to ask our Buddhist friends to respond to that view of practice. The full statement, which is actually by Michael Casey, is: "A monk who is dissatisfied with his prayer needs to make use of that feeling to motivate himself to greater fidelity to grace, rather than to attempt to alleviate his pain by techniques for altering consciousness."

NORMAN FISCHER: I agree with that statement completely because a technique for altering consciousness would be something like a drug that somebody would take to remove a state of mind that one did not like. And this is not, I understand, a characteristic of true meditation practice. Meditation practice would be exactly as it says: to turn *toward* whatever state of mind was present, using that as the way into our life. A greatly misunderstood take on meditation practice is that it is a technique to alter the mind. Of course the mind alters moment after moment. The question is, do we turn deeply *toward* our heart as our path, or do we try to introduce something from the outside?

There is no doubt that some people approach meditation practice as a drug, for stress reduction for example. The first thing I say to such people is, you cannot reduce your stress by introducing something in order to run away from it. The only way to reduce your stress is to move into it, be honest with it, work with it, breathe into it, use it as the doorway to open out into your whole life. So in that sense this is a sound meditation instruction.

JOSEPH GOLDSTEIN: I would like to say something about whether meditation can be used as a drug. While I appreciate and agree with everything that has been said, I also think that sometimes drugs are helpful. For example, there are times when people are going through difficulties and they do not actually have the strength or stability to remain in that difficulty, to investigate it and open to it, even though that would be the most desirable thing. So to do something which actually creates some stability of mind, to move the mind away from the problem for a time in order to gain some strength so that then one can go back and investigate it, I think this could be very helpful.

JOSEPH GERRY: Just a very brief comment. I really think that the point of Casey's observation, and the point I was trying to put across, is how important it is for us to live in the presence, or in the reality, of the God who dwells within us. When you do, I think you will find people who do not think they are getting much out of prayer. But they never stop to ask: "How faithful am I being in responding to God in the daily events of life? How kind am I to others, how forgiving?" The point is that there is tremendous unity and simplicity in a genuine life lived with God. When things are not in harmony, do not blame someone else, or do not look for some new way to pull everything together. Rather, deeply and seriously reflect on what is transpiring in your life.

LEO LEFEBURE: I would like to reflect on the Christian image that the workman is to use all the resources that the master places at his or her disposal. It strikes me that one of the new things that is being used by Christians is the practice of meditation from Buddhism. Many suspicions have been raised about this. What happens when the dialogue is not simply out there between members of different traditions, but also inside when a member of one tradition begins to carry on an internal relationship to another tradition?

During the past ten years, I have practiced—to some degree—insight meditation and Soto Zen meditation. Most recently, I attended an insight meditation retreat with Joseph Goldstein at Conception Abbey in Missouri. I know for myself, as a Catholic priest, it has been a profound enrichment of my life. As Norman has pointed out, Buddhist meditation is not a technique for altering consciousness; it does not do that at all. It has, on the other hand, helped me become much more aware of myself, to let go of many things, and, even more, to let different things come. For myself, my own prayer life and the Liturgy of the Hours have taken on a much greater power in light of my sitting. It is not that I am running away from the Liturgy of the Hours to go to some foreign practice, but the two have come together in what in my life has been very helpful.

JAMES WISEMAN: Your Holiness, please tell us about your own daily practice.

HIS HOLINESS THE DALAI LAMA: I must say that I am a very poor practitioner. Usually I get up at 3:30 in the morning. Then I immediately do some recitations and some chanting. Following this until breakfast, I do meditation, analytical meditation mainly. Then after each analytical meditation, I do single-pointed meditation. The object of my meditation is mainly dependent arising. Because of dependent arising, things are empty. This is according to the Madhyamika philosophy of Nagarjuna and the interpretation of Chandrakirti which is called Prasangika philosophy.

That philosophy is very profound, and, for me, it is really something marvelous. It gives me a kind of conviction about reality—about emptiness—and through that conviction I get the feeling that there is the possibility of eliminating all afflictive emotions. As Nagarjuna says in his *Treatise on the Middle*, by extinguishing contaminated karma and afflictive emotions through wisdom there is liberation. Therefore liberation is a state of having extinguished contaminated actions and afflictive emotions. So then, from what is contaminated karma or contaminated actions produced? Contaminated actions are produced from afflictive emotions. Then from what are afflictive emotions produced? They are produced from improper mental conceptuality, improper mental application. And then from what is that produced? It is produced from conceptual elaborations. Those conceptual elaborations are the elaborations of the mind conceiving objects to exist truly in their own right. These elaborations are ceased through meditating on emptiness.

So, meditating on this gives me a kind of firm conviction of the possibility of cessation. This is one main object of practice. Another is compassion.

So these two are my objects of practice. If you ask me about experience in my practice, I think it is better than zero. On that basis, I can assure you that the mind is always changing, so no matter how strong the afflictive emotion, there is always the possibility of change. Transformation is always possible. So therefore, you see, there is always hope. I think that what is really worthwhile is to make an effort.

Then also, in the Tibetan Buddhist tradition, Buddhist tantrayana is also involved. So you see, a lot of time is also spent on visualization in deity yoga. This includes visualizing the process of death and rebirth. In fact in my daily prayer or practice, I visualize death eight times and rebirth eight times. This is not necessarily the Dalai Lama's reincarnation, but some reincarnation. These practices I feel are very powerful, and very helpful in familiarizing oneself about the process of death. So when death actually comes, one is prepared. Whether these practices of preparation are really going to benefit me at the time of death, I do not know at this moment. I suppose that even with all this preparation for death, I may still be a complete failure! That is also possible. There is another type of meditation which is like praying. Its purpose is to recollect the various levels and stages of the path by going through something that you have memorized and reflecting on each stage.

So from around 3:30 a.m. until 8:30 a.m. I am fully occupied with meditation and prayer, and things like that. During that time I take a few breaks, including my breakfast—which is usually at 5:00 a.m.—and some prostrations. After 8:30 a.m., when my mood is good, I do some physical exercise. One very important thing is that I always listen to the BBC for the news. Then I do office work until noon. And if it is a holiday, I also start reading important texts. Prayer and meditation are usually done without any texts. Then at noon, I have my lunch. Afterward usually I go to the office and do some more work. At 6:00 p.m., I have my evening tea and dinner as a Buddhist monk. Finally, around 8:30 p.m., I go to sleep—my most favorite, peaceful meditation!

Experience

JULIAN VON DUERBECK: This is directed to Sr. GilChrist: when you mentioned different phenomena—visions, clairvoyance and other special phenomena—you said that these experiences are not as important as the virtues of humility, love, compassion, etc. I wanted to ask if you would give some more examples about how compunction and tears of heart function in this regard.

GILCHRIST LAVIGNE: Here are two examples. One person—who at a time in her life realized that perhaps she was doing all the right things but for all the wrong reasons—had a profound experience of her selfishness. It was accompanied by crying for three days. But it was not a crying from psychological guilt, it was a crying from feeling her littleness, you might say, in the face of God. She experienced that God was all-merciful and loved her just the way she was. Her whole life was different after that. The experience brought her to a whole new relationship with God and with other people.

For another person I knew, all the scriptures had become one, they just had welded together. And whenever she read the scriptures she started crying. The experience was that the scriptures touched her, they pierced her heart and opened up something inside of her so that everything came together. Her crying was not from sadness. But her heart was being pierced and broken open so that her coldness of heart evaporated and she was becoming more alive to spiritual realities.

DHAMMARAKKHITA: As for religious experiences, I would like to mention a quotation of Thomas Merton. It says: "At the center of our being is a point of nothingness which is untouched by sin and by illusion, a point of pure truth, a point or spark which belongs entirely to God, which is never at our disposal, from which God disposes of our lives, which is inaccessible to the fantasies of our own mind or the brutalities of our own world." Merton says that this point is like a "pure diamond." In Buddhist scriptures, our pure mind is said to be like a diamond. It is always there, but we cannot see it because of hindrances in our experiences. If we can remove these hindrances, the pure mind appears like a diamond.

GUO-CHOU: Thomas Merton was quoted as saying that the light or the pure glory of God is like a diamond you see in your heart. I wonder how a Buddhist might distinguish that experience from the common use of a certain luminous image in Buddhist meditation practice? And how does a Christian apply what you see, the diamond or the light, to daily life? That is the real point. For instance, a child can clearly see something wonderful, but then go back to fighting with the other children.

DHAMMARAKKHITA: There is a hidden light within us all. In Buddhism, we believe we have the seed of wisdom, we possess this potentiality within ourselves. We must realize this potentiality. Our Christian sisters and brothers realize it by prayer, and we Buddhists do so by meditation. In *vipassana* meditation, I found the hidden light in all phenomena. The whole body becomes light. This is not like a mind-image we use in ordinary practice. Rather, when *samadhi* becomes mature, it becomes like the sun, very bright. At the last stage, we see bright light like a diamond. When we see that light in my meditation class, we direct that light at the top of the head and send loving-kindness thoughts to all directions. This is how it affects our daily life.

BLANCHE HARTMAN: I would like to hear from some of the Christian contemplatives about how you experience God. I think it is essential that God be understood as not separate from ourself, that God is the fundamental ground of our being. Anyhow, that is my understanding, but I would like to hear actually from the Christians. How is God related to your own being?

DAVID STEINDL-RAST: Not that this is the definitive answer but it is an interesting answer to your question in the context here. Thomas Merton made a brief statement which I have always considered one of the deepest theological insights in our century. He simply says, "God is not somebody else."

JAMES WISEMAN: Brother David quoted Thomas Merton as saying that "God is not somebody else." Our spiritual writers often speak of the highest stage of spiritual life as one of most intimate union with God. They often use such language as, "The eye with which God sees me is the eye with which I see God." Or, "I have become one with the very divine light with which I see, and with which I am seen." At times, Christians who have written that way have gotten into some trouble and have even been criticized severely. I think that one always has to keep two ends of the pole in mind. There is a certain tension here, and you find it even in the Gospel. Jesus does indeed say that "The Father and I are one." But you also find in the Gospel Jesus saying that, "The Father is greater than I." Both statements are there, and they are both true. They both have to be kept together.

Now, one of the great spiritual writers in our tradition who indeed speaks very boldly of identity with God—the kind of identity that he would find with God through prayer—also says that, "When I speak about being one with God, I mean through love." That could be read very quickly and one might not make too much of it, but to me it is extremely important. To me, it has become all the more important as I have reflected on the experience of human love, and on what some of our best psychologists have said about the experience of human love. It is noted that often there is a deep experience of fusion of the lover with the beloved. And if you read love letters or love poems you will often find language reflecting that experience. This is also the language of our great mystics. It refers to something real, something very important, but it can also lead to criticisms of them. To me, one of the finest defenses of this language was expressed by Simone Weil, who, toward the middle of this century, said that those who criticize such expressions of oneness with God simply do not realize that the language of the marriage chamber is not the language of the marketplace.

EWERT COUSINS: The highest state of consciousness—or the deepest state which is the goal of the spiritual quest—that some people experience in this life is union with God, or the immediate presence of God. In regard to this mystical experience, I would like to respond to what my Buddhist brother said a few moments ago about light. There are so many examples of the mysticism of light in Christianity. But I would like to highlight one of the greatest, that is, the Hesychast tradition. In this tradition, the monks of Mount Athos practiced deep-breathing exercises and began perceiving a light in the depths of their being. They identified this unchanging light as the light of Mount Tabor—or the light of Christ that was manifested in the great event on Mount Tabor—shining through themselves. This was such a powerful experience that a whole new Christian theology was built by Gregory Palamas in order to express this kind of experience. And then we also have the experience of just the opposite, not only the divine light but the divine darkness, or the divine silence, or the divine emptiness. This experience of "luminous darkness" was given theological expression by the great Pseudo-Dionysius.

KEVIN HUNT: I must admit that I think that we have to get back to the experience of peeling turnips! I think that for most of us a lot of what we describe as mystical experience is not part of our immediate life. But washing and peeling turnips, and scrubbing floors and toilets, things like that, are. It is precisely in these simple daily experiences that we can realize our true self. We can realize who God is and who we are in our ordinary experiences of daily life. I can remember when I was a novice, my novice master saying to me, "Be simple, little brother, be simple."

Discernment

GILCHRIST LAVIGNE: Sr. Donald, related to religious experience I would like to hear a little bit about discernment of spirits because I think it is such an important topic in our tradition.

MARY DONALD CORCORAN: Thomas Aquinas distinguishes a kind of general habit of discernment which he calls discretion. It is a continual inclination of the heart toward God that is like sensitizing the needle on a compass so that it always points north. It seems to me that Benedictine spirituality nourishes this inclining and sensitizing of the heart, and that monastic discernment is largely of this variety. When the Jesuits arose in the sixteenth century, there was more of a need for discernment as a self-conscious process to come to some particular judgment, or some needed decision. St. Ignatius refined a set of rules of discernment that were really a summary of much of the wisdom that had been accumulated over the centuries. Basically, it is a matter of attuning our interior states in order to be in a prayer condition to follow the promptings of the Holy Spirit. Then, of course, a very important way of discernment is to go to someone who is objective and holy, and will give you feedback. We all need someone who can see our motivation clearer than we can.

JUDITH SIMMER-BROWN: I am reminded of material in the yogic literature of Tibet about temporary meditation experiences that can be mistaken for enlightenment. If they are taken in that way, they can become obstacles. So in Tibet, there is a literature that helps you identify these experiences, work with them as promising signs but very seductive obstacles, and then go ahead in practice. The three main experiences of this type are bliss, clarity and nonthought.

JOHANNA BECKER: Sr. Donald and Judith, you have helped to bring to the foreground an impression I have had as I have been listening to the various presentations during the past two days. One of my impressions has been—especially as I have been listening to the Buddhist presentations—that Buddhist teaching is very systematic. There are specific types of meditation, modes of practice and behavior which lead to a deeper insight and a greater profundity of spiritual transformation. And as I was listening, I was thinking that there really is no parallel for this type of procedure in Christianity. Indeed, we do use prayer and meditation, and we do have formal theological training. But more important is the intuition, the inspiration that is so central to the Christian outlook. This you do not arrive at, it seems to me, by systematic practice—although that is recommended as the background against which this can happen. But it is the concept of the Holy Spirit as truly and intimately inspiring and leading you to insight and greater wisdom—and even to good practice and good behavior—that seems to me to distinguish Christian spirituality from the Buddhist practice. I would appreciate anyone else's response to this, recognizing that neither approach is totally black or white.

MARY DONALD CORCORAN: I thank Sr. Johanna for raising this point. As I see the development of Christian spirituality over the centuries, there is an increasing refinement—as far as discernment of interiority—that is today becoming almost "scientific." For me, as a Benedictine and a monastic, to even talk about stages of prayer in the monastic tradition makes me a little bit uncomfortable. It is certainly true that there is a tremendous richness in Buddhist sacred psychology. Their incredible understanding of the ways of the human mind is an enormous well of wisdom for humanity. And yet, there is this something about the Holy Spirit that cannot be pinned down in any systematic understanding of human consciousness.

JUDITH SIMMER-BROWN: My point is almost exactly the same. Many people who try to study something about Tibetan Buddhism, especially through books, begin to encounter incredible intricacies of doctrines and schools and teachings. But one should not mistake the map for the practice—for the journey. When you read texts or doctrines, or practice analytical meditation, you do so to train and refine the mind and to deepen your confidence. But the actual experience of the practitioner is incredibly direct and incredibly immediate. Yes, there are details. I will spend the rest of my life learning more and more details! But, if you think that it is all so serious and so complex, you miss the actuality. When you go through the details, you discover utter simplicity. The logic is so clear and so simple, in actuality you see there is no separation between the logic and the immediacy of one's practice. So, the quality of penetrating insight in Buddhism may appear at times to be only scholastic or analytic, but that is merely the calisthenics of the spiritual path. Along with that is the other part which is sometimes spoken of as compassion, or as "skillful means." It is in the union between wisdom or penetrating insight on the one hand, and compassion or skillful means on the other that one finds true spontaneity.

BASIL PENNINGTON: A way of discerning our spiritual journey is in terms of growth in intimacy with God. This goes back, of course, to our Jewish heritage where the image of a love relationship, of marriage, is presented as the deepest, most intimate form of oneness—when two become one. According to Christian teaching, at baptism we are baptized into Christ; we are raised up and made partakers of the divine nature in life, we are divinized. But it is not enough to have a divine nature; we need the faculties to be able to function at that divine level. And that is precisely what the gifts of the Holy Spirit are. Classically, we speak of seven gifts of the

Holy Spirit: wisdom, understanding, knowledge, piety, fortitude, counsel, and fear of the Lord. The Holy Spirit is given to us as our spirit at baptism, but most Christians leave these gifts, these faculties, on the shelf as it were. What we are doing in meditation or in contemplation is leaving our human, natural level—reason, imagination, memory, and so on—behind, and opening the space for the Spirit to begin to operate through the gifts. This action of the Spirit brings us into the immediate experience of God in an intimate loving relationship.

GILCHRIST LAVIGNE: I would like to share an example of discernment on a community level. Our community does a lot with discernment, not according to Ignatian principles but through the traditional approach of discernment of spirits which has been practiced all through the ages. Some years ago we had a neighbor who had a farm. We always thought we would buy that farm since it was a property right next to ours. But, when the time came and we did a discernment, we realized first of all that the farmer was selling his farm at a very high price and we were the only ones who could afford it. None of the other farmers could afford it, so we were acting like a corporation that could just come in and take something that other people could not afford. People also asked us why we wanted the farm. We wanted to protect our solitude. And people pointed out to us that our reason for buying the farm was based on fear.

Well, this discernment process really awakened our consciousness! We value solitude and silence very much in our community because it is absolutely essential for our life. But we saw that there were also some other things involved that without discernment we would have never realized. So, we did not buy the farm. The people who bought it are good neighbors and there is no problem. This experience was an example of God working in our lives, breaking open our hearts on a new level, and it was done on a community basis. So, it is also important to discern as a community. Our spiritual teacher is still very important, and we use both ways. If I personally have a pattern in my life that is destructive, it helps me to go for help to one person who constantly sees that pattern.

Grace

JAMES WISEMAN: I think I would not be misrepresenting Abbot Gerry if I said that the one major point of his presentation, which I believe is accurate in terms of the Christian understanding of holiness, is that holiness is not ultimately ours but God's. It is a matter of grace, of God or Christ working in us. I think, at least in terminology, that seems not easily to dovetail with the final words of the Buddha: "Be vigilant, work out your own salvation." Yet I also know that some strands of Buddhism do have something approaching what we might call grace in what is called "other power," at least in English translation. Can you help me understand this matter in Buddhism?

JUDITH SIMMER-BROWN: I want to respond to Fr. James's question, and I really want to respond personally. There are a lot of things that could be said academically about the notions of "self power" and "other power" in East Asian Buddhism. And in the Tibetan tradition, there is definitely an aspect of the practice which resembles the Christian notion of grace. There is a sense that when one begins one's practice, effort, exertion and application are required. And that quality of practice continues always. But when one is introduced to Vajrayana practices by one's teacher, there is a very strong sense that one's own power would be insufficient to do the practices thoroughly and completely.

And so in my own experience, part of what occurs is a reliance on what is called "blessings." This has to do with the sacred environment generated by those who are highly realized as well as the lineage of teachers who have gone before and are embodied in one's own teacher. Their blessings create an environment for one's own practice and effort. So, when one exerts oneself—which is always necessary—that exertion is empowered by the blessings of one's teacher and one's lineage. Here, there is no dualism of self power or other power; but there is a kind of magic blend of the two so that one cannot take pride in one's practice even though one must always strive. And so there is a very strong tradition in Vajrayana practice of joining one's own exertion with the support, blessings and empowerment of the lineage, the Buddhas, and the *bodhisattvas* who have gone before.

LOBSANG TENZIN: In response to the question about grace, I just wanted to share a kind of experience or feeling that I had yesterday at the memorial to Thomas Merton. There was a reading that said something to the effect that the *Dharmakaya* is in every phenomenon and everything comes from *Dharmakaya*. This is where I think that the concept of *Dharmakaya* and the concept of a highest superior existence are compatible.

I think that Buddhism is a very large religion. It has many different levels of interpretation, many different techniques, many different ways of seeing things. When it comes to the matter of grace, I think that the core of Tibetan practice is very much in line with "receiving the blessings" as

Judith pointed out. In our Vajrayana practice, a practitioner seeks the blessings or inspirations in order to invoke inner light, inner realization. And the concept behind receiving blessings is very much like igniting fire in straw by using a magnifying glass between the sun and the straw. The sun is always there, but it does not create fire in the straw by itself. If you use a magnifying glass to intensify the heat, then fire is produced. Similarly, the *Dharmakaya* manifests in the form of enlightened beings. If through one's pure faith, appreciation and respect one honestly strives to receive their assistance, the fire of wisdom could be developed within oneself. That is "blessing."

This practice is also based on the very crucial Buddhist principle of dependent arising. Buddhism maintains that everything is dependently arising, therefore the blessing is also dependently arising between ourselves and enlightened beings. We have the potentiality to be Buddha, and how we become Buddha will depend on how we pursue that goal. If with respect, faith and conviction we seek blessings, certainly awakening or realizations develop—and that is the blessing. From our point of view, blessings do not necessarily come from one God, but from higher beings.

JOSEPH GOLDSTEIN: Concerning the point about whether enlightenment or awakening or salvation comes through our own efforts or another power, Krishnamurti said something I find very helpful in addressing this question. He said that it is the truth which liberates, not our efforts to be free. And so it is not our own efforts which result in liberation. Our efforts are to see the truth, or to realize the truth, and it is the truth which actually liberates us. So perhaps we are not so far apart here. But I do have another question. In listening to the language of some of the presentations it often seems that you are speaking of God as a being. And yet my naive understanding is that this is not really a correct understanding. If anybody could help me in this regard, it would be appreciated.

LEO LEFEBURE: No, God is not an entity. In St. Thomas's language, God is *esse ipsum*, "to be," which is a verb. It is the infinite act of unrestricted being which is not *a thing*. Schleiermacher, father of modern theology, had a famous debate. People were accusing him of being a pantheist because he did not believe in a personal God. He responded that if you read the best Fathers of the early tradition, they use as much impersonal as personal language about God. The earlier tradition often used the language of nonbeing for God, because for the Greek mind often "to be" is "to be finite." And so someone like Pseudo-Dionysius will deliberately twist the Greek language and talk about *hyperousia*, *hyper* being "beyond," and *ousia* being "essence." It is an affirmation and a negation, and then a negation of the negation. Dionysius's point is that all our concepts and all our images have to go through this double process of being affirmed and then negated. But we cannot even cling to the negation, we have to let that go too. And precisely in that movement—according to his mystical theology—we can move into a God whom we cannot imagine and whom we cannot conceptually grasp.

PANDITH VAJIRAGNANA: Meditation is the most interesting religious practice throughout the world. Buddhists, Christians, Hindus, people from most every tradition practice meditation. Even doctors now prescribe meditation to those who have mental or emotional problems in order to help them have some peace of mind. And many more people who are not upset have an interest in meditation. Many people feel that they are gaining something through meditation, whether it is Christian meditation or Buddhist meditation. If one really practices meditation genuinely one feels benefitted. From the moment that you start practicing meditation you are gaining something. But it is not a competition, it is not like running a race. It is for happiness, for peace of mind, that we practice meditation.

There are many meditation teachers in the world as the interest is growing in meditation. You can find different teachers who are teaching the same method but their teaching is still different from one another because while they may be following the same method, their experiences are different. In the end, they express and teach their students *their* experience, and these experiences are different from one individual to another. In our meditation or practices, what is our own experience? It is not something that comes from the outside, as the word "grace" implies. In our Theravada Buddhist tradition, we do not have anything like grace as it is understood in the Christian tradition. When we receive blessings, those blessings are not coming from somewhere else. Blessings in Theravada Buddhism come to us from our own deeds—when the deeds are good and we are benefitted by them. We have a special sermon given by the Buddha on blessings. There are thirty-eight factors explained by the Buddha that bring us blessings. For example, the Buddha says that when one abstains from unskillful deeds, it would become a blessing to that person. So to have that blessing, one just has to abstain from unskillful things.

HAVANPOLA RATANASARA: I understand that in Christianity everything depends on God, so our holiness depends on God too. On the Buddhist side, we respect the Buddha as our founder, and it is true that Buddhists give their blessings. It is a gentle, common thing in Theravada Buddhism to give blessings of kindness and compassion for the welfare of all forms of being. But the Buddha, having fulfilled all the ten perfections, achieved the highest attainment which we call Buddhahood. And he taught that it is by the power of *this* truth, the power of the *Dhamma*, that you will be well and happy. See, this is the Buddhist form of giving blessings. So now what I see is that in the religious journey we have two ways of moving ahead. There is no need and it is not possible to bridge this gap. We respect you, and you respect us. Let us respect each other and get together and work for the peace and harmony of humankind.

DIANA ECK: One of the things I have experienced so much from companionship with Buddhists is their expression of gratitude. It seems to be a very strong experience and feeling in many Buddhist people I know. Now, gratitude is a sense of giftedness which is what I mean when I speak of grace. I think the experience of gratitude, of religious gratitude, is something that we all share.

SAMU SUNIM: We have heard about grace—or blessings—from our Tibetan and Theravadin brothers and sisters. I would add something from Zen in Korea. The three main ingredients for meditation are: silence, this very moment, and posture. Posture in the Zen tradition is very important. In the monastery the head monk would shout, "Sit still! Don't wobble!" All the monks understand what that means. In other words, it is just like being a praying mountain, soaring up in majestic silence. Of course the floating clouds hang on top of the mountain but they do not really affect the mountain itself. We just learn to sit. But, for the sake of beginners, one can help by bringing them down to the heart. It has to become a heart matter.

There are five types of meditation. The first type is meditation as healing. In Asia, meditation used to be part of healing regimens. It was always included in a medical treatment. Second, meditation can be a moral discipline for purification. Third, meditation practice can be a type of contemplation or visualization. Fourth, there is formless meditation or meditation with an awakened heart. And fifth, there is *bodhisattva* meditation. Concerning the latter, I would like to say something about self power and other power.

In the Korean tradition, there is a saying that the "Pure Land" is nothing other than our own mind. Here are two stories which illustrate what this means. A Korean Zen Master practicing all by himself in the mountains in the moonlight finally came to freedom. He was so happy that he spent all night dancing. Then he arrived at a temple early in the morning and passed through the gates to face the Buddha Hall. Facing the Buddha Hall, he relieved himself. As he was just doing so, the monks came out from the dining hall. When the monks saw this fellow relieving himself in front of the Buddha Hall, they were shocked and picked up brooms to drive this crazy monk away. Then he said, "You tell me where there are no Buddhas so I can relieve myself there."

In the other story, a Pure Land monk using drums chanted to Amida Buddha with great commitment. This practice is like praying for grace. As this monk chanted, a young Zen monk was passing by and heard this monk chanting all by himself completely oblivious of his surroundings. And so this young monk was moved and he felt at one with the old monk. All of a sudden, the young monk called out and the old monk stopped chanting and turned around. Then the Zen monk asked, "I'm so touched by your chanting, but where is Amida Buddha right now?" And the old monk said, "He's now traveling." "Where is he traveling?" replied the young monk. "He's traveling right here!" came the answer.

DONALD MITCHELL: The question I have about Zen meditation has to do with the following: there is a point in Christian meditation where you move from doing something to having something done to you, you might say. Sometimes we say it is the movement from meditation to contemplation. In contemplation, one feels taken over or in touch with something larger than oneself. This change moves the process of prayer to a deeper level that is very transformative. And I wondered, in *zazen* practice is there a similar point where one is no longer actively meditating from the will, but is in touch with something larger that is transformative from a deeper center or deeper place?

NORMAN FISCHER: Just briefly, in answer to the question that was raised, yes. In Zen meditation, you have to sit there and make an effort, and then—when you really concentrate and are one with your breath and your posture—you do enter into something bigger than will or ego. Sure, I think so, otherwise what are we doing? On the one hand, you better do it, you better make your effort in practice. On the other hand, there is a point when the self "falls off." Otherwise, there is just suffering. So we have to fall off eventually.

BLANCHE HARTMAN: Just a very quick response to Don Mitchell's question. In Dogen's teaching, he says body and mind of themselves will drop away and your original face will be manifest. It is that dropping away, I think, that you are talking about. What is the original face? We have various words with which we try to describe it, but it is not in the realm of words, or thoughts, or descriptions.

JOSEPH GERRY: My days here have been very rewarding, and I have sensed here a great commonality in so many ways. When I spoke of grace, I meant to point out one central aspect of our journey to God. But, in no way does grace do away with the importance of our own effort. My emphasis on grace was meant to point out how primary the reality of God is in our whole journey. Perhaps, though, one of our great faults is that whenever we try to talk about God, the great temptation is to destroy the mystery. I think that has been one of the great failings, shall we say, of theology especially after Cartesianism. Despite the fact that the Church tried not to be limited by Descartes, we became very much attached to the value he placed on the "clear and distinct idea." As a consequence of that, even in my day and age, you never studied theology and fell on your knees to worship. Rather, what you ended up with was almost a complete control, shall we say, of the *idea* of God. Theology led to a world of ideas, not to an *experience* of God. My own experience of God came precisely because I happened to breathe in his reality.

Let me just tell you one very, very simple story. When I was asked to be a bishop, that was on a Tuesday evening, it took me from Tuesday evening to Sunday to respond to the apostolic delegate and tell him that I would accept. And the closest thing I have ever experienced of the "dark night of the soul" was that Tuesday night. The whole bottom went out of my life as I realized that all the people I knew and loved and walked with on my spiritual journey were no longer going to be an intimate part of that journey if I accepted this appointment. I wondered where God was, I wondered where the politics in the whole thing was. It was a tremendous experience for one. And it was only gradually as those days went on that I was able again to put the pieces together.

It seemed to me that the primary reason for becoming a monk was my search for God. That was what it was all about, that I really wanted to know him. In fact, my very attraction to the monastery began when I met a monk when I was a college student. When he spoke of God, you knew he was speaking of someone that he knew and loved—and someone who played an intimate part in his life. And I said, "If that is what the monastery does for him, I would like to discover that same God." So, I understood that my response to being a bishop must be a response to what I believed God was asking of me. My acceptance may have demanded a certain emptiness—a certain abandonment of people I loved dearly—but in the end, it has brought me a tremendous amount of peace. So as I hear my new Buddhist friends speak about detachment and peace, I realize that these are things that I too have been struggling with since I was a youngster in monastic life. Effort, detachment, letting go, finding freedom, purification—all leading to tremendous peace and light—these are realities in my tradition too.

9

Tragedy and Transformation

Behind Gethsemani Abbey there is a cemetery where the graves of the monks are marked with small white metal crosses. This cemetery area sits on a grassy hillside next to a large and impressive ravine. There is nothing that marks the cemetery off from the rest of the hillside—that separates it from the surrounding grassy area. One walks along and suddenly there are dozens of small white crosses. The little white crosses remind one of the ultimate moment we all face, the final measure in light of which all life takes on a precious value. Standing before these crosses, roles and titles are stripped way and suddenly we face our bare and simple humanity, the fragility of our human nature that we all share as human beings. In our little—and sometimes big—crosses, we find a sense of solidarity with all our sisters and brothers, with all humankind and all creation.

The inner spiritual journey leads to the interior cloister where one finds a ground and deep water source that we all share as human beings, indeed as living beings. In that ground of being that holds the spiritual water of life, we find ourselves nourished and refreshed by infinite love and compassion, by eternal joy and empathy in which we are all brothers and sisters. In this realization of our common humanity, suddenly we find ourselves outside the inner cloister walking with our brothers and sisters, sharing their joys and sorrows, sharing life and death. So, it seems natural to walk as fellow pilgrims among the little white crosses with thoughts of sympathy and concern for our whole human family that bears so many tragedies. And it seems natural to search together in our hearts for ways to bring salvation, a "healing salve," to all who suffer.

In our dialogue, we addressed such questions as: How does one practice with the crucified Christ, and with suffering in one's own experience and in the world? What can be said about the martyrdom of the Christian monks in Algeria, the tragic deaths of Buddhist monastics in Tibet and the Buddhist people in Cambodia? What is the place of forgiveness and love of enemies? How do Christians understand the role of Jesus Christ in the struggle to overcome sin, suffering and injustice in ourselves and the world? How do Buddhists seek peace and loving kindness in their hearts and express these values in social action? How can religious tolerance be achieved, and full participation in the religious life be open to everyone? How can interreligious cooperation be fostered in order to build together a more united and peaceful world?

Suffering

NORMAN FISCHER: Now that I am in this monastery, when I see all the crosses with the figure of Jesus on them I find it quite sad. The cross itself I do not find sad, but when there is a figure of Jesus on the cross, I find that quite sad. And so I want to ask the question, and I mean this very sincerely: Do you Christian participants feel sad too when you see this? And how do you practice with this image? I would really be interested to know.

JOHN BORELLI: When I was teaching ten years ago, I taught a course on yoga and meditation. We began each class with 10 minutes of meditation, and one of the meditations we would do was to go up on a hill where there was a large crucifix and sit and meditate on the crucifix. And so, Abbot Fischer, your first observation is very much an observation most people make. They do not want to stare at the crucifix; it is very sad. Many times we Christians do not think about the reality of the crucifix. We think about all that surrounds it, but we do not think about the harsh reality that the crucifix is. In fact, so intense is this reality that it has produced in some people, as with St. Francis of Assisi, the marks of the wounds. But that experience takes us to the reality that makes us Christian, and that is the Incarnation. Shining through this very dreadful moment, there is something of unfathomable depth.

JAMES WISEMAN: Last year, four of us were in Tibet and northern India, and at the last place we stopped, a Buddhist nunnery in Tilokpor, we gave some Christian holy cards to the Buddhist nuns. Some of them showed Jesus as the Good Shepherd, some showed Jesus as a little baby, etc. Each nun, as she got one of those cards, seemed really to like it. And then, without knowing what was next in the deck, I gave a nun a very realistic card depicting Jesus crucified. She drew back in shock.

In a way, that should be the Christian response as well. If it is not, I think it is due to two reasons, one not so important and the other more profound. The less important and maybe somewhat regrettable reason is that we get used to it. But the more profound reason, I believe, is that at least in parts of our scriptures, the crucifixion is depicted and described as really coinciding with Jesus being raised to new life. In John's Gospel, Jesus says, "When I am raised up, I will draw all people to myself." And it is especially in that Gospel that his being lifted up in agony is simultaneously being lifted up to the new life of the resurrection. There is not really a gap or a time span there. And if in looking at the crucifix we see the glory as well, that prevents something of the sadness.

DONALD MITCHELL: Jesus crucified and forsaken was something that surprised me when I became a Christian some years ago. Now when I look at the crucifix, I remember that Jesus on the cross took upon himself all of the sufferings of all humankind past, present and future. Out of love for us, he made himself one with our painful human condition. This means that Jesus forsaken is in all of my sufferings—in the dark and painful moments of my life—sharing the suffering and bringing his consolation. Also since he has made himself one with all who suffer, when I see a person who is suffering, who is tired or sick, I also see the face of Jesus. And the crucifix reminds us of this presence of God in humankind to be embraced and cared for. In this embracement, we move through the suffering into a deeper love for God and our neighbor.

The other day I was watching Ven. Phangcham speaking here in front of the crucifix. He was talking about the need to bring loving kindess into our suffering world. It seemed to me that this was precisely what Jesus crucified was doing. When we look at him we do not see a God who is transcendent from suffering, but a God who enters into all suffering, bringing his transforming love for all humanity. This is a great source of hope, and also shows us how to live compassionately for the benefit of others.

DIANA ECK: I would like to say something about the crucifix as a Methodist, a Protestant. Many Christians do not have the crucifix, do not have Christ on the cross, but have as the focus of our altars an empty cross that conveys the victory of Christ over death, and the resurrection.

However, there is something very powerful, even to a Protestant, about Christ on the cross. It is a reminder that suffering is at the heart of the Christian tradition as well. But, I also might say that for my part there is something troubling about it because in much of our Christian tradition it has come to be a symbol of our sinfulness. And the deep sense of sinfulness has many, many destructive aspects in the way that it has been appropriated in our contemporary culture. Therefore, when I see Christ on the cross, what it means to me is more what some call a "theology of accompaniment"—that Christ is the one who accompanies us in the suffering that we know, in every step of the way. He is not someone who pulls us out of it, or who can take it away. But Christ is a God who deeply experiences and walks with us in the path that all of us as human beings know, which is also a path of suffering.

ESHIN NISHIMURA: My Master always asks, when you meet the horrible situation from which you cannot get out by any way, how do you get out of it? That would be the fundamental *koan*. This is just like the frog falling down into the bottom of a deep well. She has no way to get out from the deep well. So, maybe she could have meditation in the bottom of the well. I think Jesus Christ on the cross, the crucifix, shows us the fact of this terrible situation.

LHUNDUP SOPA: I would like to say one thing in connection with this matter. Buddha first taught the truth of suffering. Without the realization of suffering no one wants to pursue the religious or spiritual goal. The crucifix shows the truth of suffering and leads to the truth of the freedom from suffering: Jesus rises from the suffering. In the Buddhist way, the truth of suffering is first. The root or cause of suffering is second. Third is the total liberation from suffering, called Nirvana. And finally the Path that leads there is fourth.

HAVANPOLA RATANASARA: So much emphasis is being put on suffering. I think there should be no mistake about the Buddhist understanding of suffering. In Buddhism, we seek a realistic understanding of suffering and we seek not to create the causes of suffering. In Buddhism, the suffering we understand and deal with is called *dukkha*. This term means more than just suffering. A better translation is "unsatisfactoriness." People are not satisfied with what they have; they are crying for more. That is the general trend in our human society. No one else can overcome this problem for you. You have to do it for yourself. To be free *from* this condition is liberation, or Nirvana. It is achieved by cultivating the mind. By meditation, one rids the mind of such impurities as jealousy, malice, greed, hatred, delusion and things like that. Free from these negative factors of the mind, you can attain the fourfold sublime way of living: loving kindness, compassion, sympathetic joy and equanimity or peace.

JOSEPH GOLDSTEIN: There have been a few thoughts going through my mind in the course of the discussion. One is just the understanding of some parallels between our two traditions. As has been mentioned, the First Noble Truth of the Buddhist teaching is the truth of suffering. And so it seems like that is really the common ground. In order to awaken, and in order to free ourselves, we need to come to a direct perception of that experience. It is interesting to me that, at least within the Theravada tradition, it is said that the reason enlightenment, or awakening, comes in stages is because we are not able, all at once, to open to the fullness of the suffering that exists. To actually become fully awake, we need to be able to open to suffering in its totality. And that is a major task. It takes a gradual practice of opening. Our ability to open to suffering is very connected to our feeling of compassion, and so the two very much go together.

But this points to something that I feel is very important as we are bringing Buddhist teaching to the West, and it may have its parallels in Christian teaching as well. I refer here to the question of how, in our Western culture, we relate to the suffering to which we open. My experience, both in myself and working with many students, is that there is a tremendous amount of self-judgment in this regard; that as we begin to open to our own suffering, it is often not from a place of compassion but from a place of self-condemnation. And part of the bringing of the Buddhist teachings to the West is very much a matter of addressing this question of how people in their spiritual practice are able to hold the suffering that arises.

SHARON SALZBERG: Like Joseph, I had many thoughts running through my mind this morning. It seems pretty clear that in terms of the Buddha's teaching, he taught both suffering and the end of suffering. He taught dissatisfaction and the end of dissatisfaction. And something that we face a lot as we teach in the West is a somewhat romantic notion about suffering and its redemptive possibility. It seems clear that we all suffer and not everybody is liberated by the suffering itself. We are liberated from the opening—which is a process of love, compassion, and wisdom—to suffering. This opening forms the container for our suffering. It is the opening itself which is vast. Given the immensity of suffering, the opening needs to be as immense and as extraordinary. And I was very curious about what within the Christian tradition forms and sustains that opening?

BASIL PENNINGTON: A year ago last January, I had the privilege of being a part of the burial of Father Sebastian, one of our Chinese monks in China. Sebastian went on a death march in 1947 in which 31 of his brothers were killed and he was thrown into prison. He was released from prison in 1979 because a guard broke Sebastian's back and he was useless. His sister-in-law took him in, and he lay on his bed unable to move from

1979 until he died. All that suffering had meaning to him because he was suffering with Christ. He loved Christ and he felt it was a privilege to be able to suffer with Christ. He found the courage to go on day after day in that suffering because he was suffering with Christ, whom he loved. In those years when he lay on that bed, people with all sorts of sufferings came to him, and he listened, consoled and comforted them all. He was a man of immense compassion. His open compassionate embrace of suffering was in and from Christ whose love is infinite.

When he died he was buried in what was called an underground funeral, with seven thousand mourners marching through three villages in witness to this beautiful man of compassion and love. As I reflected on his life, I realized that was the way I myself faced suffering in my life, though never to that degree. Suffering is meaningful to me because I suffer with Christ and in Christ. I am with my beloved and he is with me in everything. God showed his love to me in Christ's suffering, and I am able to respond and be with him in that love in my own little suffering.

Sacrifice

JUDITH SIMMER-BROWN: When I heard about your Algerian martyrs, I had a question about certain themes in Christianity—martyrdom, sacrifice, tragedy and transformation—which are very difficult to understand. And I guess my question relates to something that Don Mitchell said at the beginning about seeing the face of Christ in others. I can understand the personal transformation that the Algerian monk went through in deciding to stay, but my question is how did their staying express compassion for the aggressors who, from a Buddhist point of view, will reap the karma for lifetimes for murdering them? I guess my question is whether the aggressor is genuinely benefitted by the martyrdom or the sacrifice. And I find it very disturbing and troubling from a Buddhist point of view because compassion seems to be missing. This also seems to relate to the Eucharist and the Christian notion of the body and blood of Christ. Obviously this concerns the central mystery of Christianity, but—and I do not want a theological answer—I would really like to know your experience of this. How does personal transformation and compassion for others come together in this act?

ARMAND VEILLEUX: This is a difficult and beautiful question. In the early Christian literature you often find that the early martyrs desired martyrdom. In this recent case in Algeria you do not find this desire.

Explicitly, they always said they did not want martyrdom, and every time there was a new danger—when some of the missionaries were killed—they reassessed the situation. Each time they had good reasons to believe that they were safe. But they knew they were themselves in some danger and they did not desire to be killed. They desired to live and they loved life. But for them, martyrdom in the Christian sense is a witness. Someone has to be a witness to the way he or she lives, and if as a consequence to being faithful to the Christian life martyrdom comes, then it is accepted—but it is not desired.

Christ saved us by his life, not by his death. But his death is part of his life. It was because he was faithful to being the witness to his Father to the end that he had to accept death as the consequence of this witness. But he did not accept it joyfully. The agony was a tremendous difficulty for a young man who was facing death at thirty-three years of age. Also, if you analyze the New Testament very closely, you see that Jesus puts an end to the practice of sacrifices. The Eucharist is not a sacrifice as in the Old Testament, when we killed lambs. That makes absolutely no sense whatsoever. Christ was not killed as a sacrifice, he was murdered. Because he accepted to be murdered, it is his *life*—including that consequence—that has replaced all the sacrifices. And so in our life, we are not pleasing God by making sacrifices; we are pleasing God by *living* according to his message as Jesus did. And this, *our life*, is the only "sacrifice" that God wants. So when we celebrate the Eucharist, we celebrate the fact that Christ—God incarnated as a human being—has given himself as "food." We are not killing him; we are celebrating his life and the gift of life that he gives us as food—as nourishment—for our life.

DAVID STEINDL-RAST: I would like to speak from my own experience as to what it means to me to receive the blood of Christ. I always say to myself that it is the lifeblood of the risen Christ. So, I am drinking something that pulsates through all humanity—not only through all Christians, or through all humans, but even through the animals and plants—the lifeblood of the cosmic Christ.

MARY MARGARET FUNK: It seemed to me from personally speaking to Fr. Christian from Algeria, that his staying there was both a fidelity to his commitment as a monk in the community, and also an expression of his deep trust in the best in the others. He believed in the others' goodness, maybe more than they did. So I think from a Buddhist point of view, it might help to see that he knew they were good, and so he stayed to make that statement with his life.

JAMES WISEMAN: Of course those monks were not reflecting on the Buddhist notion of karma. But *if* you look at it from that perspective, I think something could be said. First of all, if they had left Algeria on the assumption that they would thereby spare the persons who would murder them any karma that would result from their violent death, obviously those persons would not have simply stopped killing people. Whereas the way these monks died, the testament Fr. Christian gave which surely has been read by his murderers, might well have touched their hearts and have led to a decrease of violence. And even if it did not do so in the case of their particular murderers, I would think that the witness they gave and the beauty of that testament can only work for the increase of peace in the hearts of other people who may have otherwise turned to terrorism. In that sense, I think their remaining there was a very positive step—even from a Buddhist point of view.

BERNARDO OLIVERA: I think that in the question that Judith presented, there was one point that was not answered. I do not mean that I am going to answer your question, but I will try. But first, I want to say something else. The last time I cried was 25 years ago, no, 30 years ago; and I was afraid that Armand was about to cry when he was reading Fr. Christian's testament. And I said, "Well, I hope that he will be able to control himself." Now, I do not know if I am going to be able to control myself, because both of us are very close to the experience of our brethren. Anyhow, this is what I want to say.

When I received the news about the killing of the seven monks of Atlas, the very first idea that moved in my heart was this: I forgive, I give all my pardon to the assassins. And I was absolutely sure that was the intention of Christian, Christopher, Luke, and all the brethren. When I received the testament of Christian in the full text, I saw that he says explicitly that he forgives the man who is going to take his life. So, that is the point. I do not think that the killer is going to go to hell, not at all. My God, and Fr. Christian's God, *the* Christian God, takes very seriously what we say or what we ask of him. And Fr. Christian asked, and I asked, pardon for the killer. So I am absolutely sure that not only is he going to see light and understand what he did; I am almost sure that I am going to meet him at the right hand of the Lord. So, I think that is the only way I can answer your question. Forgiveness, there is no other answer.

CHUEN PHANGCHAM: I am very happy to hear from our brother about forgiving the murderer. Forgiveness is the whole issue that we have to keep in mind. It is very hard for the people to forgive something. So, people kill other people. This we all have experienced. But think about compassion and loving kindness; think about the love that Jesus taught and showed to people. The Buddha too gave the people this idea. King Asoka, the great king of India who lived a few hundred years after the Buddha, was a person who killed a lot of people. But after he listened to the Buddha's *Dharma,* he gave all the weapons away. And he became a "King of the *Dharma.*" He spread out the *Dharma* all over the Indian continent.

So that is loving kindness in action. In the darkness of society today, we also apply loving kindness and compassion from our hearts for everybody. The past has gone, whatever happened is gone, so we try to clear our mind of things that limit our compassion today. Whatever happened, that is all right, we forgive, we understand. The Buddha said that the past has gone, the future has yet to come, so do your best today. How can we get rid of the anger, tension, worry, anxiety and all other kinds of negative thoughts? By cultivating loving kindness to defeat the suffering of human society today. That is the key.

JAMES CONNER: What strikes me in all this is the fact that the ones who are disconcerted either by this story, or by the crucifix, or by the cursing Psalms, are the Buddhists. And the reason I think that the Christians are not disconcerted by this story is because we have taken it so much for granted. Apart from Dom Armand and Dom Bernardo, the one person in this room who has had an opportunity to experience these things in a very existential way would be the one from whom I would like to hear comment, namely, the Ven. Ghosananda, who has experienced this type of thing in Cambodia.

MAHA GHOSANANDA: In Cambodia, we say if you know suffering then you know the *Dharma,* because the Buddha teaches only one thing: suffering and the freedom from suffering. Suffering comes from greediness, anger, and ignorance. On the opposite side we want peace, we want happiness. If we want these things, we have to apply the opposite of what causes suffering: generosity, as the opposite of greediness; loving kindness, as the opposite of hatred; and wisdom, as the opposite of ignorance. Yes, that is the answer.

NORMAN FISCHER: I wanted to say very briefly that I had a really strong experience, and I learned something very important that I would like to share with you. In our discussion—which I thought was so beautiful—of Armand's talk, I realized that the differences that we see among the traditions are really not so much differences as failures to understand. Because I do not understand Christianity, I am not a Christian. If I *really* understood

Christianity, I would be a Christian. And in our discussion, what I really appreciated for the first time, what I found underneath the words, was this. I was so amazed by all of the Christians coming up here and expressing their—this is what I heard in any case—actual passionate love for Jesus Christ. This is a difference between Buddhism and Christianity, and therefore it is something that I do not actually understand. But I certainly got a taste of it and a feeling from it, and I just want to say that it was so incredible to see everybody coming up. And I remember when Fr. Basil said something like, "I suffer with my beloved and my beloved suffers with me." I was astonished by this, not only the words but that he felt this way. This is something I do not understand, but I appreciate it. So maybe our differences are because we do not really understand.

JUDITH SIMMER-BROWN: Obviously this is a very big topic but let me ask one other more specific question. I understand how a person can sacrifice or give his or her life for the benefit of others. But how does the life and death of Jesus Christ acutally save other beings?

ARMAND VEILLEUX: In a few words, I think Christ saves because for us salvation is the transmission of divine life. Divine life is a life of communion, a trinitarian communion in one God. Christ is totally God but also totally human. And when he became man, he did not become simply one man; the whole of humankind is assumed by him and transformed into his divine communion. That is the "Good News," and the root of salvation by Christ.

LEO LEFEBURE: I would like to thank Judith for her very profound and thought-provoking question. I think one way of naming the problem is the conjunction of the sacred and violence. From the earliest records that we have in history, we find societies founded upon the principles of exclusion and violence. Certain groups take power, they dominate others and when rivalries come up the quickest way to get peace again is to target certain individuals or groups, drive them out—at the limit, kill them. Often God was invoked precisely as the justification for violence against our enemy. And I think that one can find sacralized violence in the Bible too.

I think that there are certain texts where we simply have to say, Christians and Jews alike, this is not the God we know. So, how does God really enter a world of systemic exclusion and violence without taking sides? Because if God comes in on one side against the other, we are back in the same problem of sacralized violence. What is most interesting for me in the Hebrew Bible is the emergence of an alternative perspective where God does not take sides, but identifies with all the victims of exclusion and violence. You see this most dramatically in the "suffering servant" poems in the second part of the Book of Isaiah. There God is not on the side of the kings, as in most mythologies, but on the side of the victims.

How God enters the world in the New Testament as the "suffering servant" is one of the most ancient images. When Jesus comes into a world of systemic violence—the Roman Empire was a vicious and brutal world—the whole witness of Jesus' life was to make available the grace of God to all people regardless of their status. He acted this out by having meals with prostitutes and tax collectors, and then telling the people who were presiding over the system that these "despised" people were going to be in the reign of God before them—thus turning the whole system topsy-turvy.

Pontius Pilate, the representative of worldly power, crucified thousands of Jews—lining the streets with their bodies. Jesus enters even into this victimization not because there is anything good in the suffering, but because he is faithful to this witness—the message of God's all-inclusive love. Then as portrayed in the Gospels, even he says from the cross, "My God, my God, why have you abandoned me?," which on one level means that God knows what it is like to feel abandoned by God. This means that no one is ever abandoned by God. Such abandonment for a theist is the absolutely worst position—worse than physical torture, worse than death. Jesus does not save us by changing the mind of God through a sacrifice. He saves us by being the concrete incarnation of the universal will of God to save us, to include all in God's love—even those who performed the act of execution.

ARMAND VEILLEUX: I would like to add one word to this very important topic of the sacred and violence. That was the meaning of all the sacrifices of animals in Israel and in other religions. Humankind found a way of dealing with the violence that we all have in our hearts by directing it toward animals in various sacrifices. Jesus, by putting an end to the economy of sacrifices when he went to the temple, obliged us to face that violence where it is—in our hearts.

CHUEN PHANGCHAM: As for the sacrifice of animals, the Buddha stopped that practice in his time by establishing the precept to not kill any living beings.

LOBSANG TENZIN: First of all I would like to express my deep condolence for what has taken place in Algeria. I had not realized that it happened so recently, and it indeed is a tragedy. At the same time, I admire the courage and the confidence in the truth that the brothers had. That is certainly something to be admired. I have a question about how suffering is elevated. In Buddhist terms, we speak of "afflictive emotions" and karma that have to be purified in order to overcome what results as suffering. In Christian terms, you say that through Jesus Christ the suffering of humanity is elevated. But I have heard through some discussions that original sin has something to do with the crucifixion or the sacrifice of the life of Jesus in elevating the suffering of humanity. So, my question is: what is original sin and how through Jesus Christ is one elevated?

LEO LEFEBURE: I would like to say a few words about this topic of original sin which our venerable brother has brought up. The notion of original sin is an attempt in Christian theology to name what goes awry when people have right intentions, they think, and yet things do not quite work out. In technical Catholic language, original sin is the weakening of our intellect so we cannot see clearly what is good, and the weakening of our will so we cannot do well what we know to be good. We experience this on one level very personally, that no matter how hard I try to get my life all together, somehow something goes awry. We also experience original sin in terms of social systems of sin that are also beyond our power to control and in which we are inevitably involved.

This morning when I went down for lunch there were bananas sitting there. I know that when I eat the banana I am participating in a world economy where cash crops are grown in areas where children under the age of five starve to death every day. There is one large valley in Guatemala that could feed most of Central America. The valley is owned by multinational corporations which use it for cash crops like bananas. So, in my simple act of eating a banana I share in the collective social sin of the world. Original sin is one Christian way of trying to name the sense that, both in our own personal lives and in society, something has gone awry in a way that our own efforts, both personal and collective, are not able to overcome.

The grace of God in Christ "heightens" us, as you say, as we participate in his risen life. This new life brings us a new freedom from sin: the ability to see more clearly and choose more wisely. But we have to cooperate with his grace and use this new freedom to confront and overcome the evil in ourselves and the world in which we live. The heightening is not an event, but a process of discovery and transformation.

Violence

ESHIN NISHIMURA: Some years ago, I visited a Cambodian refugee camp on the Thailand border. It was desolate! People stood, then people sat—they had nothing to do. Then I saw a small Buddhist temple, a hut really.

In the middle of the dirt floor sat a lone monk in meditation. That monk I now realize was you, Maha Ghosananda! My question for you is a Zen question: "What did you do there where there was nothing to do?"

MAHA GHOSANANDA: I was seeking peace in myself so I would have something to give the others.

JOHN BORELLI: In the refugee camps, despite the desolate situation, there is great hope among the people. In the Khmer people who return, you can see that they were nourished by the Buddhist monastic tradition that is alive in each of their camps. But when we look around at the world today—at the conflicts in Sri Lanka, Bosnia, Northern Ireland, the Middle East—very often these conflicts are identified as religious conflicts. We know that sometimes the media are trying to simplify the conflict by reporting them in just religious terms. I think this distortion persists because religious leaders allow this to happen. So, the question is, how should we work within our own communities to disengage our own people and religious leadership from these violent conflicts?

MAHA GHOSANANDA: First, your religious leaders should work at making peaceful persons. A peaceful person makes a peaceful family; a peaceful family makes a peaceful community; a peaceful community makes a peaceful country; a peaceful country makes a peaceful world. Peace begins in yourself. If you are peaceful in your heart, you can always make people become peaceful. The Buddha was a great religious leader. First he found peace in his own heart. Then on the first day he converted only five people. Then he converted 25 more, then 60. Now Buddhism has spread to the whole world. We always start with zero. Before Thomas Merton and the Dalai Lama met there was nothing. But because of these religious leaders, there is something here at Gethsemani today.

HAVANPOLA RATANASARA: I want to dispel any confusion about the violence in Sri Lanka. The media speak of Hindus against Buddhists. But this is not a religious conflict at all! The problem is really a political and economic one. Religiously, the Buddhists, Christians, Hindus and Muslims are living together in a friendly manner.

DAVID STEINDL-RAST: In Ireland it is also not a conflict between Christians, but it is a political matter being masked by religion.

DIANA ECK: We heard yesterday a very moving story of the Trappist monks who were taken from their monastery in Algeria, whose throats were cut, and who were killed. Then we think of the things that the people who came to your refugee camps had seen in Cambodia—so much brutality and murder. You had children who had seen their parents or their brothers or sisters killed, who had seen so many bodies and so much violence, who had these images in their minds, and who had in their heads the emotions that go with that vision of brutality. Against this horrible situation, it sounds very easy to say that we have to make peace in our hearts. I know that is ultimately the only way that peace can begin, but how can you teach this to the children who may react to what they experienced and continue the cycle of violence?

MAHA GHOSANANDA: Teach them with the example of loving kindness. We go to the tents of the Cambodian refugees where people are dying. We go and care for them. And in the hospital we wash them, we clean them when they have diseases. We show the value of peace and love by example. Then, when some monk is seriously sick, the people he served come and take care of him. They learn love and peacefulness by example.

DIANA ECK: And for the many teenagers and children who came and only have weeping and anger in their hearts?

MAHA GHOSANANDA: We tell them what the cause is of what they feel. It is the condition of fighting that comes from the very anger they feel—and they understand. We teach them by example that in order to make peace, we have to cultivate loving kindness in our hearts.

LHUNDUP SOPA: I have just been in your country. Also our Tibetan situation is very tragic and we try to resolve it peacefully—not by violence. But how do you achieve this political peace? We try to inform people about the terrible things that are happening in Tibet. We also speak at the United Nations. We monks do our peaceful prayer to teach peace with our own peacefulness. But you also lead peace marches across Cambodia. Sometimes people interpret these marching monks as showing anger. What do you think? Is marching good, or not?

MAHA GHOSANANDA: We do not "march," we "walk"—and walking is good. We walk peacefully every day in Cambodia. In this manner, we make peace in walking, in every step. We make peace for ourselves and the people follow us. So, they also learn to make peace for themselves and for others.

JOHN BORELLI: What you say reminds me of Selma, Alabama. After the first demonstration for civil rights was met with terrible police brutality, the area was filled with religious leaders doing the peaceful kind of walking meditation that you are talking about. That walking was quite successful in transforming the nation, and in solving the immediate problem there in Selma. I was in my first year of college when that happened, and one of our priests went to Selma to participate. It had a profound effect on him.

JUDITH SIMMER-BROWN: May I ask another question? Several days ago we were talking about anger, and I know how I have been taught by the Tibetan tradition to work with anger in my meditation. Would you tell us about how you advise your students to work with their anger?

MAHA GHOSANANDA: We teach insight meditation so people can see how anger comes from ignorance. Therefore we always ask, "What is the cause, what is the condition of anger?" It is important to see how anger arises through causes and conditions in your heart. When you listen to me, you say, "I am listening to Maha Ghosananda." But what you hear are only the words touching your ear. When you have this auditory impression, feelings arise. Therefore, when I blame you, you feel angry. That is an unpleasant feeling. That feeling of anger then affects your perceptions. Then from the way you perceive things, your thinking is affected and you form certain ideas. These ideas are often negative and hurtful, and can lead to violence against others.

JUDITH SIMMER-BROWN: So, at what point do you move from insight teaching to practicing loving kindness?

MAHA GHOSANANDA: We always do these two practices together.

JAMES WISEMAN: You have seen much death. But you have not only seen other people killed. Often, day by day, your own life has been threatened. When you walk in protest against the land mines, every step might mean you are going to step on a mine. I have no doubt that you have no fear of death, but I think many people walking with you may. What would you tell a young person who wants to walk with you but who is afraid?

MAHA GHOSANANDA: We use meditation on four topics. First we meditate on the Buddha and his loving kindness, compassion, peace, and love. Second, we meditate on loving kindness itself. Third, we meditate on the body in order to overcome thoughts of attachment to the body, and in order to control the body. Last, we focus on vigilance. The Buddha's last words were to the effect that we must be vigilant. So with peace and love, with freedom from fearfulness about ourselves, and with vigilance, we take care in every step.

MARY MARGARET FUNK: Maha Ghosananda, I was wondering if you could tell us what *mantra* you teach to children?

MAHA GHOSANANDA: Just tell them: "Step by step."

DAVID STEINDL-RAST: I hear a beautiful silence in the room. It has been suggested that the Maha Ghosananda would show us how to walk, and lead us out to Thomas Merton's grave.

MAHA GHOSANANDA: Yes, walking is like breathing: breathing in, breathing out. Walking is like breathing: step by step, carefully, watching your step.

Social Action

SAMU SUNIM: There are smiling *bodhisattvas* and unsmiling *bodhisattvas*. Buddhism in the West is more used to smiling *bodhisattvas* who are happy and content. However, there are unsmiling *bodhisattvas* who are not happy and content. With the situation of Buddhism today, particularly in Asia, I sympathize with the unsmiling *bodhisattvas*. So, I would like to speak on behalf of them. Your Holiness, in 1959 you escaped from your country due to the Chinese military occupation of Tibet. Since then, many Tibetans have followed you and have found refuge overseas. Now we have almost ten-thousand Tibetan monks in exile. Since 1979, Your Holiness has traveled in the West giving talks. As a result, thousands of people in the West have discovered Buddhist teachings, and thousands of people have embraced Buddhism in their lives. This would have been impossible without the Chinese invasion of Tibet. It is my opinion that, in this regard, Your Holiness is following the example of the historical Buddha who left his country in order to become a Buddha and a religious teacher.

However, I am also aware that Your Holiness is the head of a Tibetan government in exile in India. You have been seeking a political settlement with China over Tibet, and you oppose any kind of violent struggle for achieving the independence of Tibet. While I appreciate your nonviolent position, there is in Asia a history of Chinese and Japanese imperialism, the legacy of which still survives today. Christians and Buddhists collaborated in this aggression and violence, and often remained silent. The difference is that Western Christians are willing to reflect upon their past wrongdoings and complicity of silence, and to make amends through open apology and reconciliation efforts. How many Chinese and Japanese Buddhists have been willing to confront their failures and reflect upon their shameful past? I am still waiting for overseas Chinese Buddhist leaders, who should have no reason to fear the Chinese government, to come forward and condemn the unjust and brutal military occupation of Tibet. In the past, I have talked to a number of Japanese Buddhist priests about the Japanese war atrocities, and particularly about the Korean and other Asian teenage girls forced by the Japanese military to serve as "comfort women." Their reaction ranged from outright denials to anger. I have found them unrepentant. Buddhist clergy in Asia have failed to make a distinction between Buddhist practice and blind nationalism. This is clearly a case of Buddhism betrayed.

The sad picture of Buddhism in Asia does not end here. In North Korea, Buddhism survives as a propaganda tool for the communist regime. In South Korea, Buddhists leaders supported the military dictators. In Myanmar, the powerful Burmese *Sangha* elders remained silent and turned a blind eye when the democracy movement by students and young monks was brutally suppressed by the military a few years ago. In Thailand the high *Sangha* stayed aloof when world religious leaders, concerned with child prostitution in Bangkok, convened a conference there to bring world attention to the issue. The lack of a social consciousness and the ethical quietism among the Buddhist clergy in Asia is appalling. Your Holiness, there are Buddhists like me who are not happy and content with the situation of Buddhism in the world today. Would you advise us on how to confront social injustice in order to improve this condition of Buddhism?

His Holiness the Dalai Lama: Certainly, I appreciate your concern. At the same time, I think we have to make a distinction between Buddhists and Buddhist institutions. I think that in any religion, once the institution becomes important sometimes some unhealthy things happen. This was true in the past and also today. I do not know what the best method is to address this problem in the short run. In the long run, of course, each Buddhist practitioner should be a genuine Buddhist and should have a wider perspective. Today, the world has become smaller and smaller and everything is now interdependent. In the past, Buddhist practitioners, particularly monks, have remained distant from society in their own small circle. When that is taken to an extreme, there is negligence or indifference about what is happening in the larger society or in the government. There may have been some ground for that isolation in the past. But today things are changing. So I think that the Buddhist clergy and monastics should develop a more sensitive conscience about what is really happening in the world. I think that is important. With such a conscience, eventually a small voice will first come from an individual. Then a group of monks—or a Buddhist community—will express its concern and we can change, we can make some corrections.

Frankly speaking, during the last 37 years in exile, I think that we Tibetan Buddhists, including myself, have developed closer relationships with our Christian brothers and sisters than with our own fellow Buddhists. Although we Tibetans live in India, Thailand, Sri Lanka, Burma, Cambodia and other Asian countries, we only occasionally visit and greet one another. On some occasions, we have had some very useful discussions, but these are entirely on an individual basis. Also, our official visits in these countries are difficult due to political and other reasons. Therefore I think we need to have more regular contact and bigger meetings—like Buddhist conferences—where ideas can be discussed among ourselves. Then, eventually, it will be very possible to develop some kind of concrete method for dealing with issues concerning Buddhism and the modern world. My request or my wish is that within our own Buddhist community—particularly among the monastics and scholars—we should have more international conferences. Such discussions in this current situation would be very, very helpful.

KEVIN HUNT: Part of me is kind of smiling because looking generally at the way we have been discussing things, the Christians are very interested in discussing meditative practices as aids to returning to our spiritual source of prayer and meditation. And the Buddhists seem to express the need for social engagement in their tradition. We seem to have two conversations going on at the same time, which I think is wonderful!

MARY MARGARET FUNK: Your Holiness, I have a practical question about time. The balance between work and prayer has been very difficult for us. I hear that you want your monks to do more work, and we want Christians to get more centered personally through prayer. What advice do you have for both traditions as the one moves further out, and the other one is moving further in?

HIS HOLINESS THE DALAI LAMA: It is true, for many years I have been attracted to those Christian brothers and sisters who are involved in social services—particularly in the fields of education and health care. So, on many occasions since the mid-60's, I told our monks that we have to learn from these Christian brothers and sisters. We should have more activities in the social services.

I think that in both Christianity and Buddhism there are different types of people. Some people can devote their whole time and energy to meditation. Very few people are in this category. We Tibetans have a term for these persons which literally means "those people who are really able to hold up the banner of religious practice." I think that for these people there should be no other activities. And I think we should encourage these people. They bring us to an appreciation of the deeper value of our tradition, and of the value of genuine transformation. However, the majority of monastics need to carry out some form of productive work, not only in monastic institutions, but also in the society at large.

One time when I was in Thailand I raised this issue with the Supreme Patriarch of Buddhism. I told him that Buddhist monks should be more socially engaged in society. Then of course the Patriarch rightly responded to me saying that according to the *suttas*, we monastics must disassociate from the rest of society. That is also true. But now is a time of change. The faith of people today—or, for the Buddhist community, the understanding about the Buddha *Dharma* among the householders—is very essential. To keep a deeper understanding about the Buddha *Dharma* only in the monasteries is, in the long run, not adequate. If in society there is more understanding and experience of the Buddha *Dharma*, then you will find the Buddha *Dharma* atmosphere in the family. As a result, the children who grow up within that kind of atmosphere will be good Buddhists. That is very important. So you see I am always appealing to the Tibetan monks and nuns to carry out more activities in social service, particularly in the field of education.

Now what about time? Sometimes I tell Tibetans we should devote half of our time to religious meditation and things like that, and the other half to worldly work. So the monks and nuns in monasteries, both Buddhists and Christians, should devote a certain period to deep meditation and contemplation, and a certain portion of time to some productive work. Now here at Gethsemani, I think the self-sufficiency system is marvelous!

For Buddhists and Christians alike, there is great value to the practice of spirituality in the early morning. To do so develops an experience or some kind of feeling which can remain the rest of the day. Thereby, when you deal with the worldly activities of the day, these activities, in principle, remain *Dharma* activities, *Dharma* actions. And particularly when you face some problem, sometimes you may need to present some serious sort of argument, or you may need to take some kind of serious counteraction. Spiritual practice coming from deep down sustains or maintains the God-feeling, the love or respect for others, so that you can—according to circumstances—take countermeasures without destroying your peace of mind. This ability very much depends on your early-morning meditation.

JOSEPH GOLDSTEIN: The Buddha gave a great emphasis to Right Speech and, of course, truthfulness is a central piece of it. But the Buddha also taught that we should only say that which is true *and* which is useful. Sometimes something may be true, and it may not be the right time to say it; it may not be useful in that particular context. But I think it is important not to use this teaching as an excuse to hold back from saying the truth when it is difficult *and* useful.

Then with regard to compassion, I feel it is important not to make a hierarchy of compassionate activity. Each one of us—as we develop a more compassionate heart—will express it in our own ways due to a whole variety of conditions. For some, its expression may be very much engaged in social activity. For somebody else, it may be sitting in the cave. I do not think that one is a greater compassionate action than the other. I think we need to embrace the whole range of possibilities.

KEVIN HUNT: I do think that perhaps one part of the Christian tradition that we have failed to emphasize is that our engagement in social activity is very much based on the person of Jesus of Nazareth, and it flows from his own words. In the Gospels, Jesus talks about heaven and hell. To those invited to heaven, he says, "Come into my Kingdom, for when I was hungry, you fed me; when I was thirsty, you gave me to drink." These persons then ask him, "But Lord, when did we feed you when you were hungry? And when did we give you something to drink?" And Jesus answers, "When you did this to the least, you did it to me." So, for Christians, our social engagement is ultimately a self-giving, egoless path of engagement with Jesus Christ.

DAVID STEINDL-RAST: This quote from scripture is worth reading because you will find that those who did the right thing and fed the hungry and visited the prisoners and so forth, did *not* know they were doing it to Christ. This is a parable which goes very much against those who *claim* to be Christian and do not do these things.

JINWOL SUNIM: Just a quick question. What do you mean by heaven and hell?

James Wiseman: For us, heaven is essentially full union with God. It is our expression for the goal of our entire life. The best theologians in the Christian tradition, I believe, have looked upon our entire life as a two-fold movement: coming out from God, and returning to God. The return is to heavenly life, union with God. That is heaven. It is often described in certain books of the Bible as being like a city with twelve gates and all sorts of pearls. Those, of course, are symbols and images trying to convey what is for us ultimate bliss.

Hell, on the other hand, is simply the opposite of that. I think the crucial thing here is that hell is complete isolation. It is being cut off from everyone and everything, completely unloving, full of hate, full of self-absorption, with no capacity for union with God or others. In that sense, anyone in hell has not been put there by God; the person has put himself or herself there. I would add that the Church has never stated that any individual person has been eternally damned. Some ancient and modern writers suggest that God's infinite love will perhaps in some way draw even the worst of sinners back to God's very being.

Tolerance

Havanpola Ratanasara: I am concerned about certain actions being done by evangelical Christian groups in Asia. Samu Sunim has pointed out that such groups are now burning down Buddhist temples in Korea. And they apply so much pressure to Buddhists in the cities—trying to force them to go to their churches—that many Buddhists lock themselves in their houses to escape. Asian people have had this kind of experience for several centuries. Missionaries came to Asia, starting from Portugal, Holland, and Britain, and tried to introduce Christianity in Buddhist countries by force.

When I was rather young, I too had strong feelings against the Christian missionaries. But later on I started to study Christianity and I changed my attitude. So, I started to work together with the Christians in my country. Now, all religious groups meet together from time to time with positive results. However, today these evangelical groups are moving into the rural areas where people are poor and not so educated. They have started to proselytize these people, and this has become a big problem in those areas. They create division among the people. When we ask our Catholic friends about what is going on, they say they are not a party to that. I do not know if this is true. But please, tell your Christian brothers and sisters not to do these kinds of things. They bring disharmony.

SAMU SUNIM: I too have had mixed feelings about Christianity. I am aware that there are no evangelicals present here so their actions are not an issue. However, I think there is something in the Christian teachings that allows its followers to become intolerant to us non-Christians. On the other hand, we also have Buddhists here from countries that have problematic political histories. I am actually more concerned with our Buddhist brothers' and sisters' inability to speak out about such things.

GILCHRIST LAVIGNE: I appreciated what Samu Sunim said, because I think we are all coming toward a moment of truth. In my talk, I spoke about this whole idea of compunction—being sorry for your self-centeredness, being sorry for your sin. So, what I want to say is that I am sorry for any injustice that has been done by my own tradition. Any evil really starts within. So, I am sorry for anything that has happened because of my tradition. And, I am sorry for the evil in my own heart that is the beginning of all injustice.

LEO LEFEBURE: Your Holiness, you have spoken very eloquently of your vision of the community of the world's religions where each religion brings its own tradition to share. What do you look to us Christians to contribute to the community of the world's religions? I pose this question in two parts. First, what can Christians in general contribute? Second, what do you look for from Catholic monks and nuns?

HIS HOLINESS THE DALAI LAMA: One of the most impressive aspects of traditional Christian monasticism is its service to the community or society. That, I feel is one very, very practical contribution. I really feel that Buddhist practitioners make very little practical contributions. Then your discipline and your simplicity are very valuable. Also your gradual initiation process is very good. You give people a long period to think about the monastic life, to practice serious self-examination until they feel sure they can be a good monk or nun. Only then are they ordained. I think that is a very, very good practice. Then also I think your devotion toward God and your unshakable faith is also very impressive and very good. Also, learnedness should not lessen your devotion.

As for Christianity in general, because of your large numbers, and because you are so materially advanced in the West, I think you can be of great spiritual and material help to building world peace. The other day in England, I jokingly told an audience that once they were the greatest imperialist nation and they exploited people around the world. Now the time has come to pay the world back. So, in terms of the promotion of spiritual and material development, I feel you can do more. In parts of

Africa and Asia, many people are struggling just to live. Under those circumstances, there is an urgent need for material aid. In responding to these basic human needs, I think that the advanced Western Christian nations have the potential to initiate a new appreciation of the value of human life. Here, I think, our Christian brothers and sisters can make a great contribution. Also, the most awful weapons, including nuclear weapons, along with the Marxist ideology have come from the West. So in the past, Western nations made some very destructive initiatives in other parts of the world. Now, I think, the time has come to develop more constructive worldwide initiatives. That is my hope and my wish.

Finally let me say that because of the Buddhist-Christian dialogue, we Tibetan Buddhists have developed the best and closest relations with our Christian brothers and sisters. So, dialogue is also one of your great contributions. It builds a healthy spirit of harmony on the basis of mutual understanding. With full knowledge of our differences and our similarities, we have developed mutual respect and mutual understanding. I think this is a good example to other religious traditions. I think you can make a great contribution by showing this to other religious people.

Women's Issues

YIFA: The nuns' Order has grown very much in Taiwan. I would like to ask our Tibetan and Theravadin leaders here about the possibility of reestablishing the nuns' Order.

HAVANPOLA RATANASARA: A burning question in the West is why are women not admitted to the monastic Order—especially in the Theravada tradition. It is true that in Taiwan—and in Korea too—there are now thousands of nuns. The nuns' Order flourished in Sri Lanka during the early days of Buddhism, but later it slowly disappeared. Several centuries have elapsed and certain religious customs have developed that pertain to men and women in the *Sangha*. For example, in Thailand no woman can give anything to a Buddhist monk by hand. However, in Sri Lanka women can offer anything by hand to a monk. These customs cannot be changed overnight. In Sri Lanka, the people are divided now about reestablishing the nuns' Order. But here in the United States things are different. In fact, I myself ordained a Thai woman and admitted her into the Order with the consent of all the Buddhist traditions—both Theravada and Mahayana. After that, three more women have been admitted into the Order. But in general, we need some time to rectify this situation.

These things are being changed, and I hope this issue will be rectified in the near future.

LHUNDUP SOPA: About the nuns' Order in Tibet, we do have nuns but they are not fully ordained because that lineage never reached Tibet. However, His Holiness the Dalai Lama is beginning to examine some other sources for this lineage to enter the Tibetan tradition today. If his initiative is successful, many of our nuns will be able to take full ordination.

PANDITH VAJIRAGNANA: Regarding the question of women's ordination in the nuns' Order, we are one-hundred percent in favor of it. The problem is not with entering the Order of nuns—there are many such nuns in every country. The problem is with the high ordination, making them fully ordained nuns. We have the novice ordination. But in the Theravada tradition, high ordination died out many centuries ago. However, in the seventh century a large number of nuns went to China and established the nuns' high ordination which is said to be continuing up to this day. So, our Theravada nuns are requesting that we bring them back and reintroduce high ordination in our countries. Research is now going on to find out whether that system continues unbroken. If it has, one day it can be brought to Theravada countries and reintroduced. At this very moment, as it so happens, ten women are undergoing training in Sri Lanka. There were about three hundred applications from which ten were selected. When their training is finished, they will be given high ordination in India on December 8, 1996. That ordination will be according to the Korean tradition.

CHUEN PHANGCHAM: Yesterday, His Holiness asked me about my idea concerning the nuns' Order. My idea is to select ten or more women, all with novice ordination, who are willing to join the monastic community in Taiwan, or Korea, or China. There they can be trained for at least five years in order to be fully ordained. After that, they can come back to Thailand and receive another ordination from the monks' Order. This is because according to traditional rules, nuns have to be ordained from both Orders. In this way, we can have fully ordained nuns in Thailand.

JUDITH SIMMER-BROWN: I spent some time in Taiwan, and I was so impressed at how many absolutely articulate and really charismatic Buddhist nuns there are! So, I have two questions. First, how is it that the nuns' Order in Taiwan has been so successful at cultivating *many* remarkable, very well educated and articulate women. And second, is this perceived as a problem in Taiwan since the men are not doing as well at this?

YIFA: I think the idea of humanistic Buddhism—that means being involved in social engagement—is very attractive to women in Taiwan. Besides social engagement, the educational opportunities for nuns are also attractive to many women. As for our relationship with the monks, maybe some monks feel we are a threat but I think our relationship should be one of mutual respect. In my temple we treat each other with respect. I would say that in general my Master feels that Buddhism has to be linked to the public if the *Dharma* is to survive. To propagate Buddhism today, it must be humanistic and applied to daily life for everyone.

DIANA ECK: I also want to make a comment about the women issue. On the Buddhist side, we have lots of monks and nuns, and we have lots of Christian monastics, both women and men. But there is also the whole stream of authority in the ordained ministry of the Christian tradition. And teaching in a Christian theological school as I do, I think it would be important at least for our Buddhist friends to know that it is also true in Christianity that more and more of our candidates for ministry are women. In the 1990s, well over half the students in Christian theological schools and seminaries are women—something that was not true thirty or forty years ago. So, the increased sense of religious vocation among women is not something that we are seeing only in the Buddhist tradition. There is a significant rise in the number of women in positions of religious leadership in Christianity as well. I also might say that this has been a struggle in each and every denomination, in what you might call the various lineages of Christianity.

SAMU SUNIM: I have two questions. Let me say that I have nothing against women becoming female monks, and I am all for it. Actually, I am very happy to see so many Catholic nuns with us attending this event, it is very impressive. There is a *Vinaya* rule which prohibits monks from ordaining women, and there is a *Vinaya* rule against monks and nuns living together. You have Taiwanese Buddhist organizations where the male Master trains and ordains women. I am curious how this came about. That is my first question. And, do the monks and nuns live together?

YIFA: First, about the question concerning monks and nuns living together in our temple, our monks live in one area and our nuns in another area. And I want to say that given my personal experience of working with monks equally, I do not think I could ever develop any attachment to them! As for the *Vinaya* rules about the ordination of nuns, it is a very complex question because different schools have different regulations. I feel that the Buddha was a really wise Master because when he set up the *Vinaya* and a rule was too rigid, he would make an exception.

SAMU SUNIM: Let me just say that you are right, there are major rules that are invariable and minor rules that are variable. However, I think that the rules having to do with ordaining women are among the major rules.

BLANCHE HARTMAN: I am not so familiar with Chinese culture in Taiwan, but I wonder if it was as revolutionary for your teacher to ordain women and give them equal opportunity in the temple as it would be, for example, in Japan? I am more familiar with Japanese tradition, and there I think it would be quite revolutionary and courageous to give women an equal opportunity in practice and study with men. So in general, the way women monastics in Japan have maintained their equal opportunity is to have separate institutions in which they take care of all the activities. Also, I wonder if the emphasis your Master places on social services might be very attractive to women as a way—in a monastic role—to exert their nurturing instincts in the society at large.

YIFA: One thing I want to mention is this: people often think that to become a college dean, as I have done, or to teach, or to do social work, these are secular achievements. But for us such work is part of our spiritual journey. When I first went to the temple for two weeks while I was still a law student, I listened to the Master's teachings and I felt that I was transformed. That feeling is hard to explain, but you feel detached from the world, and fame, reputation, and money are not important to you. And you also feel that the people surrounding you are like aliens; you do not belong to this realm anymore. That is the power from inside me that made me shave my head and become a nun.

I refer to this as a kind of transcendental experience, and this experience has helped me these past seventeen years. After becoming a nun, I spent three years in college, then two years at the University of Hawaii, and finally six years at Yale University. I always lived in the secular world, but this transcendental experience and the joy it brought kept me always a Chinese Buddhist nun. You know, before my Master sent me to the United States a lot of people were worried about me getting lost in the American culture. But these spiritual experiences remind me of who I am and maintain me until today as a Buddhist nun in my secular work.

DAVID STEINDL-RAST: For the information of our Buddhist sisters and brothers, we have one of our earliest texts in the New Testament that says that women should not open their mouths in the assembly. So, it is encouraging to see that we are both dealing with similar problems in our traditions. Also, I might point out that in Taiwan and other countries in which there are now so many Buddhist nuns, there is also an increase in the number of Catholic nuns.

Unity

JINWOL SUNIM: I want to know what you mean by "Kingdom of God." Many different religions use the term "God." So, do you mean that there is only one Kingdom of God for just Christians? Or do each people have their own Kingdom of God? Could you clarify this notion?

EWERT COUSINS: I think we are all in it together. In other words, geography cannot keep us apart any longer. That is obvious. I mean even if we tried it would not work, and I do not think we are going to try, or going to be *able* to try. What was once a geographical and historical separation for humankind has collapsed in our time. So, the new world we are all working for—what we Christians call the Kingdom of God—is something that embraces the whole human community.

HAVANPOLA RATANASARA: I think that the Christian vision of the global situation that was expressed in the Christian talks really takes our hearts! I think my Buddhist friends will agree with me that it is very rare to hear these kinds of large-hearted statements. The vision of global unity will succeed in the future. People are fed up with the terrible things that are happening in the world today.

In Asia, particularly in the Theravada Buddhist countries, we have taken the concept of *dukkha*, suffering, very seriously. We are guided by this principle. Buddha understood human suffering and he provided a way out. However, now the Buddhist communities are not united on how to address this problem on the social, political, and economic levels. Their major focus has been on how to find your own personal way out of suffering. For example, in Thailand people do not want Buddhist monks to get involved in social action. They say that the monks should be in the temple to receive alms and to practice meditation.

But, in spite of this resistance, in Asia the Buddhist *Sangha* has taken into consideration the social needs of the people and has developed social movements where the Buddhist monks and the laity are working in programs for community development. The good news is that people are aware of the bad social conditions and are getting together to address them. This work is not only with the Buddhists, it includes people from other religious groups, especially the Christian communities. We have to look forward, not backward. We have to bring peace and harmony in this world, and therefore prosperity for all people. So let us work together to make this world a habitable place, a sane society.

DHAMMARAKKHITA: I think that in spirituality there are two perspectives: the horizontal perspective and the vertical perspective. From the Christian point of view, these perspectives merge in the "cosmic Christ." This notion includes the vertical depth of God and the horizontal reach of the cosmos. Here is my particular Buddhist point of view. Vertically we seek purity of mind, and horizontally we seek to be of service to others. To attain purity of mind, we need to practice meditation. But as we raise our consciousness to the highest vertical level possible, our mind expands mysteriously like the infinity of space. Therefore, at that stage I instruct all my yogis to send loving-kindness thoughts to all the horizontal directions of the universe. Jesus Christ taught that only love can solve the problems of humanity. So, too, by establishing pure mental energy, we can expand loving kindness to all beings. My aim and object is not just to realize Nirvana, but to solve the problems of humanity. For this we need to build a global spirituality.

DONALD MITCHELL: I am very pleased with Ewert's vision of the Kingdom of God in the broadest sense of the term. He mentioned in discussing it that part of the building of this Kingdom involves reclaiming the tribal sense that we are already one family of humankind. I would just like to underscore that notion. I think that today we are seeing more and more of a sensitivity to that vision of the oneness of humankind. The quotation by Thomas Merton to the effect that we need to realize that we are already one has often been mentioned here.

What Ven. Dhammarakkhita said about the vertical and horizontal dimensions of spirituality reminded me of the F.A.S. Society in Japan. They emphasize that the vertical depth of the Formless Self, or "F," embraces the horizontal breadth of All Humankind, or "A." By realizing this depth and breadth of True Reality, we can build a new history on this spiritual foundation, what they call "super history," or "S." And besides F.A.S., there are other new movements that combine spirituality and social action working for unity in the world. In Buddhism, there is the

Sarvodaya movement in Sri Lanka, the socially engaged Buddhists in Thailand, the Fokuangshan movement in Taiwan, and the Rissho Kosei-kai in Japan. I too belong to a movement called the Focolare which seeks to contribute to a more united and peaceful pluralistic world community by living a spirituality for both personal and social transformation. It is important to note that all of these modern spiritual movements have strong lay and interfaith dimensions.

DIANA ECK: I think it is a fact that we live in a world that is interdependent economically, politically and environmentally. There is no such thing as our own part of the world, or our own religious community. We are all in this together. And yet I think one of the things that is difficult as we look around is that while we can see signs of hope, there also is an increase in tribalism, in minting our religious and ethnic identities in smaller and smaller coins. Why is it that people in this age of expanding global realization feel that they need to cling to a smaller and tighter sense of belonging? Instead of finding their identities by sinking their roots deeper and deeper into the soil of their own spiritual traditions until they actually get to that sort of subsoil waters that nourish all of us, they build higher and higher walls between themselves and others. As religious people we need to ask, What is it in our religious traditions that seems to contribute to this building of walls? Certainly an exclusionist vocabulary contributes to the phenomenon.

EWERT COUSINS: Certainly, Diana, I agree with you and I would say that the need for going down into that rich source in which all the rivers flow together, or however we put it, is one of the reasons why monasticism has a very special role to play in today's world. That has been their traditional role, and today it needs to be played with an interfaith perspective as we are doing here at Gethsemani.

But also I think there is a great fear in any time of transition, a fear that the transition is leading to a loss of identity. That is another reason why some people pull back behind their walls. However, the hope is that we really are in a transformational period in which a new consciousness will be born. That is the whole point, and I think we can see this happening right here as we speak.

LOBSANG TENZIN: I am reminded of a comment by His Holiness the Dalai Lama a few years ago when he was asked what his religion was. He said that loving kindness is his religion. And I think that is one thing that we can all agree with here—not just in principle but as something we can all participate in with our heart. We all need kindness. We all need to be kind toward each other and cultivate love for each other. The reasons may vary, the philosophical reasons may differ, but the fact is that without love and kindness, compassion for each other, our human society cannot survive.

But neither can the earth afford our carelessness and violence. So I think that one thing that our Christian brothers and sisters can think of is that since not only human beings but all living creatures are the creation of God, we should respect them. We should care for them. From the Buddhist point of view, we have been partaking in rebirth from beginningless time, so we are all interconnected in one way or another. Therefore, the Buddhist principle is that all other beings are actually my mother from some lifetime in the past. For these reasons, I think we can all cultivate a feeling of respect for each other—valuing the importance of love and compassion for other. Despite all our differences, love and kindness or caring for each other is, as His Holiness put it, a universal religion. This is something not only for believers. Even nonbelievers need caring, love and compassion, and they accept their value. I hope our dialogue here can somehow convey to the world the importance of compassion in our life.

Epilogue

When you participate in a monastic retreat, you sense that the dynamic of the retreat is something more than dynamics of the participants. There is something more happening to each person and to the group than what is being done by the persons or the group. Often one is so caught up in this dynamic that there is neither the time nor the psychic space to reflect on what is happening. While there may be some moments for reflection during the retreat, it is most often while one is preparing to return home that one reflects on what has taken place.

The schedule of the Gethsemani Encounter was almost as rigorous as the monastic schedule kept by the monks of the Abbey. So, there were only a few times during the week when the participants could sit back and reflect on what was happening. Two such times during the week were at the memorial service for Thomas Merton, and at the final session of the encounter.

For the memorial service, we all gathered in the choir of the church. It seemed to many of us that Merton's spirit had been present throughout the week. His words about spiritual life and experience were often quoted by Buddhists and Christians alike; and his spiritual vision of the future of monasticism and of humankind was always a guidepost for our journey of dialogue together. The memorial included a talk by James Conner, O.C.S.O., who was once an assistant novice master with Merton. His Holiness the Dalai Lama was visibly moved by the memorial for his spiritual friend, and he spontaneously added his own words to the service.

The final encounter session was an opportunity for the Christian monastic observers to share their reflections on the week's dialogue. All of them would be going back to their monastery or convent to share the fruits of the encounter, and to continue its spirit in local intermonastic encounters for years to come. Diana Eck, one of the dialogue participants, gave an opening reflection and invited the observers to share their thoughts with the whole encounter group. At the end of this open sharing,

Br. David Steindl-Rast, who had been the moderator for the dialogue all week, shared his own personal reflections; and Donald Mitchell said a few words on behalf of those who had organized the encounter. Then Abbot Timothy Kelly gave a warm farewell on behalf of the whole Gethsemani community. Finally, the Ven. Havanpola Ratanasara offered an expression of thanksgiving on behalf of the Buddhist participants; and the Ven. Lobsang Tenzin concluded by dedicating the Gethsemani Encounter for the harmony and healing of the world.

A Tribute to Thomas Merton

JAMES CONNER, O.C.S.O

When Thomas Merton became interested in Buddhism, it was not just some esoteric interest which led him. It stemmed precisely from his prevailing interest in the nature of the person. Beginning with his studies at Columbia University and his exposure to Gilson and Maritain, Merton's thought and writing had been directed toward the person. Later when he began studying mysticism, he again returned to this theme in order to explore the relation between the human person and the divine Persons. In a letter to John Wu in 1965 he wrote:

> At every turn we get back to the big question, which is the question of the person as void and not as individual or empirical ego. I know of no one in the West who has treated the person in such a way as to make clear that what is most ourselves is what is least ourself, or better the other way around. It is the void that is our personality, and not our individuality that seems to be concrete and defined and present, etc. It is what is seemingly not present, the void, that is really I. And the "I" that seems to be I is really a void. But the West is so used to identifying the person with the individual and the deeper self with the empirical self that the basic truth is never seen. It is the Not-I that is most of all the I in each of us.[1]

This was written as he began corresponding with Wu in preparation for studying Chuang Tzu. In pursuing this reality of the person, Merton realized he was entering into the heart of his own vocation as a monk and a hermit. For in this he found the totality of God, of other persons and of the whole of reality. He said:

> To give priority to the person means respecting the unique and inalienable value of the *other* person, as well as one's own, for a

> respect that is centered only on one's own individual self to the exclusion of others proves itself to be fraudulent.[2]

This is the key to the whole experience of meditation which we are considering in these days together. Meditation is not an individual affair. It is the way we come into contact with the person that we are, and in so doing come also into contact with others and creation. The tribute that we make to Thomas Merton today is not directed toward him alone. It is a way of acknowledging all that he was, and all that he wrote and taught and lived.

Thomas Merton was the first American Cistercian monk to pursue contact with the East. And gradually he came to recognize the fact that the East has something which we in the West tend to overlook or neglect, and which we need in order to live the life we profess as Christian monks. In the paper he prepared for Calcutta, he said something which we may need to recall at this time:

> This is not just a matter of "research" and of academic conferences, workshops, study groups, or even of new institutional structuring—producing results that may be fed into the general accumulation of new facts about man, society, culture and religion.
>
> I speak as a Western monk who is pre-eminently concerned with his own monastic calling and dedication. I have not left my monastery to come here just as a research scholar or even as an author (which I also happen to be). I come as a pilgrim who is anxious to obtain not just information, not just "facts" about other monastic traditions, but to drink from ancient sources of monastic vision and experience. I seek not only to learn more (quantitatively) about religion and about monastic life, but to become a better and more enlightened monk (qualitatively) myself.[3]

He also showed us the conditions which are necessary for such a pursuit, and which we can see as conditions for this very encounter:

> I am convinced that this exchange must take place under the true monastic conditions of quiet, tranquillity, sobriety, leisureliness, reverence, meditation, and cloistered peace.[4]

He further added:

> I think that we have now reached a stage of (long-overdue) religious maturity at which it may be possible for someone to remain

> perfectly faithful to a Christian and Western monastic commitment, and yet learn in depth from, say, a Buddhist or Hindu discipline or experience. I believe that some of us need to do this in order to improve the quality of our own monastic life and even to help in the task of monastic renewal which has been undertaken in the Western Church.[5]

Merton divided intermonastic dialogue into three levels: preverbal, verbal and postverbal:

> The "preverbal" level is that of the unspoken and indefinable "preparation," the "predisposition" of mind and heart, necessary for all "monastic" experience whatever. . . . [The monk] must be wide open to life and to new experience because he has fully utilized his own tradition and gone beyond it. This will permit him to meet a disciple of another apparently remote and alien tradition, and find a common ground of verbal understanding with him. The "postverbal" level will then, at least ideally, be that on which both meet beyond their own words and their own understanding in the silence of an ultimate experience which might conceivably not have occurred if they had not met and spoken. . . . This I would call "communion." I think it is something that the deepest ground of our being cries out for, and it is something for which a lifetime of striving would not be enough.[6]

This was the kind of communication and communion which Merton was able to attain during his final trip to Asia. It was because of this kind of communion that he was able to have the experience he had at Polonnaruwa ("everything is emptiness, everything is compassion"). Likewise it was because of this kind of communion that he was able to find such a kindred spirit in the Dalai Lama ("I believe that there is a real spiritual bond between us"). It was that "I" which is the "Not-I" which thus entered into a realm of communion with others and with creation in a way that spurred the discovery of that true "I" which can be found only in God.

If our encounter here can bring us even remotely into such a realization, then this time will have been fruitful. On the other hand, if it merely gives us new ideas and concepts, and also new people whom we meet, then we have missed the purpose of this encounter. The greatest tribute that we could make to Thomas Merton is precisely by entering into this path of meditation in a way that brings us closer into the heart of each person here, of all others throughout the world, and of all creation and all reality.

Merton stands as one who lived the same life we live, right here in this very Monastery of Gethsemani. He faced all of the same problems and frustrations of life that any of us experience, if we are honest with ourselves. But he showed us a way by which all of this could lead to that still-point which he experienced at the end of his life. He shows us that "there is no puzzle, no problem, and really no 'mystery.' All problems are resolved and everything is clear, simply because what matters is clear. The rock, all matter, all life is charged with dharmakaya . . . everything is emptiness and everything is compassion."[7]

It is for this reason that he would say to us today the same words he spoke in Calcutta shortly before his death: "My dear brothers and sisters, we are already one. But we imagine that we are not. And what we have to recover is our original unity. What we have to be is what we are."[8]

A Tribute to Thomas Merton

HIS HOLINESS THE DALAI LAMA

I have been moved a great deal today at this memorial or recollection of the life of Thomas Merton, and I am very happy that we have done this. From the point of view of a religious practitioner, and in particular as a monastic, Thomas Merton really is someone that we can look up to. From one point of view, he had the complete qualities of hearing—which means study, contemplating, thinking on the teachings—and of meditation. He also had the qualities of being learned, disciplined and having a good heart. He not only was able to practice himself, but his perspective was very, very broad. Thus it seems to me that in this memorial or recollection of him, we should seek to be following his example that he gave to us. In this way, even though the chapter of his life is over, what he was hoping to do and seeking to do can remain forever. Not only is his wonderful model being followed in this monastery, but it seems to me that if all of us followed this model, it would become very widespread and would be of very great benefit to the world.

As for myself, I always consider myself as one of his Buddhist brothers. So, as a close friend—or as his brother—I always remember him, and I always admire his activities and his life-style. Since my meeting with him, and so often when I examine myself, I really follow some of his examples. Occasionally, just as at this meeting, I really have a deep satisfaction knowing that I have made some contribution regarding his wishes. And so for the rest of my life, the impact of meeting him will remain until my last breath. I really want to state that I make this commitment, and this will remain until my last breath. Thank you very much.

Final Reflections

DIANA ECK: I have been asked to begin our reflections with my own thoughts about this week's extraordinary encounter. I began reading Thomas Merton's books when I came back from India, and I found that so very long ago he had begun to build bridges that I was struggling to find. So during this week, I have often reflected on how remarkable it is that this chapter room at the Abbey of Gethsemani has, for the first time in history, held a congregation of Buddhist and Christian monastics. This has been an historic meeting that certainly would have brought a broad smile to the face of Thomas Merton.

This sustained encounter between Christian and Buddhist monastics has been what Merton called "the dialogue of those who have kept their silences." In the context of this meeting, I think it was wonderful to be reminded by Fr. James Conner the other day—in his tribute to Merton—of the kind of exchange that Merton anticipated: what he called an exchange that must take place under monastic conditions of quiet, tranquility, sobriety, leisureliness, reverence, meditation and cloistered peace. This sort of exchange began to happen this very week. I have attended many dialogues where all the affairs of the world were on the immediate agenda. But never have I seen anything quite like this, where one begins with the realization that Maha Ghosananda has left with us, and repeated so often from the *Dhammapada*, namely, that hatred can never be rooted out by hatred, but can only be transformed by love, by compassion. The many ways that our world counters violence with violence cannot produce the transformation of heart that Maha Ghosananda was speaking of, but can only escalate the level of rage and shame, and become, in fact, factories for further violence. The kind of communion that is beginning to take place here at Gethsemani is terribly important—important for ourselves, important for the world.

I think Merton would have been surprised as well if he could have been in the chapter room this week—not simply because there are so many Buddhists here, but because so many of our Buddhist brothers and sisters are from the United States. Our monastic Buddhist friends here are not only from Asia, but from communities that are in such places as Washington, D.C.; Chicago; Los Angeles; Queens and Barre, Massachusetts. There is something new afoot in the Buddhist tradition: this living water has come from the line of the Buddha to the United States of America. This makes our encounter not only of spiritual significance and of global historic significance, but of deeply important significance for the ongoing religious life of the country in which we live.

The diversity of streams of traditions, the richness of traditions that has flowed from these two teaching sources—Christian and Buddhist—present us with many varieties of monastic life. We see here that they are really living traditions—they are more like rivers than like monuments. They are continuing, alive, and what has happened in their encounter here will be transformative to both of our respective religious traditions. In this coming together, there is the recognition that the qualities of heart that we are seeking to cultivate are matters of practice. They are not simply matters of thought, but require the arts of attention, of stillness, of the "listening of the heart." Just as playing the piano requires practice, spiritual training—whether it is the practice of breathing, of walking, of sitting, or of *lectio divina*—is something we cannot simply take for granted; we do not simply sit down one day and do it. We have many negative habits of mind that all of us have practiced. We have practiced the arts of impatience, if you will, of anger, of self-deception, of pride and of violence. It is instead to the practice of tranquility, of attention, of compassion, of the presence of God that our monastic communities are leading us for real transformation.

We have also talked about the role of the teacher, and we have seen and heard some great examples of teachers this week. Nishimura's example of the teacher bowing to the sleeping student will stay with me forever. We have talked about issues of "ultimate reality." I am so well aware as a Christian—as we bow deeply in the choir and talk about that which is, which was, which ever shall be—that it is precisely that language that our Buddhist brothers and sisters pull out from under our feet, in some way, as they invite us into reflection on change, on the impermanence of the world in which we live, so that we might change it and ourselves for the better.

We have talked about the issue of suffering ever since that first afternoon when Norman Fischer asked, "Isn't there something sad about the cross, about Jesus hanging on the cross?" That opened up into a discussion of the role of suffering in each tradition: how can suffering be the gateway not to self-condemnation, as Joseph Goldstein asked, but to compassion? How can suffering lead not to judgment of ourselves but to opening of ourselves? And we have certainly had examples that will stay with me of the ways in which this practice has been put to the test in the real life of suffering in our communities, such as when Fr. Armand and Fr. Bernardo spoke of the killing of the Trappist monks of Atlas. We have also recognized the way in which practice has been put to the test by Tibetan monks and nuns in captivity, and by Cambodian monks caring for refugees. And there was the issue of forgiveness that was articulated so beautifully by Fr. Bernardo.

Let me simply lift up again the question that Fr. Leo asked yesterday about the dialogue not simply between two different people, but within ourselves. When he invited us to begin to articulate that new phenomenon in the spiritual life, I recalled that Calcutta talk of Merton:

> I think that we have now reached a stage of . . . religious maturity at which it may be possible for someone to remain perfectly faithful to a Christian or Western monastic commitment, and yet learn in depth from . . . a Hindu or Buddhist discipline or experience. . . . Some of us need to do this in order to improve the quality of our own monastic life. . . .

Let me conclude with another quote from Thomas Merton, this time from his writings *Thoughts in Solitude*: "Living is not thinking but the constant adjustment of thought to life, life to thought, in such a way that we are always growing, always experiencing new things in old, old things in new. Life is always new." Life has certainly become new for us in some way this week. Now, I would invite others who have been observing this week of dialogue to share their own reflections.

MACRINA WIEDERKEHR: One of the things I am struggling with is how I am going to be able to share some of this experience with my religious and larger local community. How in the world do you even put this into words? I am a monastic from Arkansas where there is a lot of fear of different traditions. There is a lot of fear even of contemplative sitting, fear of evil getting in. This question comes up so many times concerning meditative practice: when you empty yourself, does this open yourself up to evil? After this week, I realize that the evil is already inside us, like greed, pride, lust, whatever we carry. Perhaps those are the real evils that I need to deal with. Meditation simply helps us see what is already there and needs to be transformed.

FENTON JOHNSON: Something I have also learned across the course of this week is that the root of evil in the world is ignorance, greed and anger. If someone had asked me beforehand what a group like this would discuss, I certainly would have said ignorance. And yet it has struck me that the subject that came up again and again was anger. Why is this such a destructive power in our world today?

JOAN HUNT: The most touching thing to me was to observe the Buddhists' forgiveness for the profound suffering caused to them. Also, I was impressed by the Christians' forgiveness for the murderers of the monks in the Atlas community. For me in everyday life, this is so difficult! I thought of the witness of Jesus on the cross when he said, "Father, forgive them for they know not what they do." Jesus Christ was crucified because of anger coming from ignorance. I see this in my own life. The evil that I do is because of my ignorance. We need to be more aware—and more forgiving.

HAROLD THIBODEAU: I am a monk of the Abbey of Gethsemani, and I do not have too many words. But I must say I am overwhelmed—it is going to take some time to digest. I also feel very honored to be in the presence of all of you who get up so freely and express yourselves so directly, with great freedom. I think that was very important, and held this whole encounter together. Everybody felt very much part of everything.

WILLIAM SKUDLAREK: I am from St. Anselm's Priory in Tokyo, Japan. I have a Zen teacher there who has now asked me twice why I am practicing Zen as a Christian, and I expect he will ask me once more at least. I am very grateful to Nishimura *Sensei* for giving me at least one possible answer. I am doing this because of a radical doubt, and a radical faith.

JEANNE RENEK: I am from the Yankton, South Dakota Benedictines. As I listened this week, I remembered several times Raimundo Panikkar's book, *Blessed Simplicity*, and being very taken by the notion of the "monk archetype" which transcends even world religions. While I have learned many things this week about the Buddhist tradition, and even clarified some things about the Christian tradition, I was most touched by what I would call an archetypal experience that transcends differences and draws one to silence, solitude, meditation and contemplation—regardless of our tradition.

GAIL FITZPATRICK-HOPLER: The one thing that has impressed me the most is the gentleness and utter respect that everyone has had for one another, as well as the attentiveness to one another and the willingness to sit and listen and be open to hear whatever message was spoken, or whatever moved within their own being. It seems to me that this is really where the dialogue begins—at an internal level of silence and openness.

FRANCIS MAZUR: My experience this week was one of people who wanted to come together. The difficulty that I face often is with people who ask, "Why should we come together? Why should I talk to *them*?" whoever "them" may be. There is a tremendous amount of work that needs to be done to get people to move beyond tolerance to dialogue with one another about their faith.

VICTORIA URUBSHUROW: On our first full day, I was sitting next to Sr. Mary Elizabeth Mason, and she said something like, "Well, I sometimes don't remember if a Christian or a Buddhist is talking." That stayed with me the whole time, and I thought, "That's wonderful!"

DOROTHY AUSTIN: I am ordained in the Protestant tradition, and I have for many years been a serious practitioner of *vipassana*, or insight meditation, which has awakened and deepened my appreciation of the teachings of Jesus. It has been a wonderful experience to be here, in what feels like an historic occasion. It seems as if we are on the brink of a huge paradigm shift. I have been moved by experiencing the Buddhist-Christian dialogue as an interior conversation as well as one out here. I have been very moved by the conversations that we have been having about God. The Dalai Lama asked us, "You depend on God, does God depend on you?" I think the answer to that can only be yes. The future of God is truly in our hands.

MARY DONALD CORCORAN: I guess I would have to summarize this week's impact on me by the word *conversion*—some of it is even too personal to share. But I find myself really rededicated profoundly to my commitment to practice and to my vocation to sacred study. I also feel called to the new vision for humanity that Ewert shared. It has been a week that has changed my life!

JONATHAN FASSERO: I am from St. Meinrad Abbey in Indiana. As a result of this marvelous experience, one of the first things I am going to do when I get back is look for my spiritual director and go to confession. That is a way in our tradition of purifying the heart. I feel the need to get rid of my own hindrances, to let go of my selfishness, and this for me will be one more step in doing that. I also feel the need to rededicate myself to prayer. I have seen here during this past week so many examples of compassion, peace and understanding that this has made me ask the question, "How in my life and in my community—especially with the people I live with day in and day out—can I be more compassionate, more sensitive, more understanding?" One thing I have learned is that peace begins here in the heart, and that is where I hope it begins with me. As a result of this, I feel I am moving closer to what we call the Kingdom of God.

LOUISE DOWGIALLO: I am a Benedictine from Virginia. The sisters, as a community, blessed me and sent me here. They have been praying everyday for this whole encounter. Now I am going back as a different person.

MARK DELERY: I am from Holy Cross Abbey in Virginia, and have been practicing Zen for twenty-five years. Every time I pray with all the Buddhist monks, I feel a very, very strong kinship with them—the kinship of prayer. So on that level, I have been very happy sitting in the chapel and also going to choir this week. On another level, I must say that the dialogue has removed a good deal of ignorance. But, we probably have to acknowledge that we can spend the whole of our life having ignorance removed until we end up with our good God in heaven.

AARON RAVERTY: I am from St. John's Abbey. As an anthropologist, I have always been fascinated by the *other*, and by the religions of the *other*. But as a monk, I am also fascinated—and ever more deeply convinced by this meeting—by the ways that the Holy Spirit is present and very active in and through different religious traditions.

DIANE APRILE: I am not a monastic; I am here as a journalist. I came here in my journalist capacity, and I have been just amazed at what has gone on here. Midweek, I wrote a column on anger, which seems to be a recurring theme. And it seemed symbolic that during this same week at the Olympics, the threat of violence from angry people finally erupted just last night. In the Olympics, the idea of self-sacrifice, discipline and suffering in the service of physical perfection is something that we all support and into which we pour money, time and focus. But when we talk about those same activities or values in the service of attention, peace, nonviolence and compassion, somehow the world does not want to support that. I thought about that a lot; that was something I could not get out of my mind.

PATRICK HENRY: I am from the Ecumenical Institute in Collegeville, Minnesota. For me, the question, "What was most surprising here?" had its threshold set by Norman Fischer's remark that he had discovered here how much Christians love Jesus. I found that an extraordinary statement! I too felt that the depth, the sincerity and the persuasion with which people talked about their love of Jesus was something that I have not heard in any Christian setting at that degree in quite a long time.

BENJAMIN TREMMEL: I am a monk of St. Benedict's Abbey in Atchison. When our Buddhist brother got up and spoke about humility and meditating on the earth, I remembered that *humus* is the root from which "humility" comes in Latin. *Humus* is the black dirt under the leaves, the richest of the soil from which all life on this earth grows. When Ven. Ghosananda said that we are the temple, I also thought of our Christian belief that we are living stones built on the cornerstone of Christ.

MATTHEW GREENBLATT: I am just a Jewish guy from Brooklyn! I think the real meaning of Christ or of Buddha today is the fact that the teachings are alive here and now, and that those teachings are reflected in the hearts of everyone here. It has been a great blessing for me to bask in the light of those teachings these last few days. A dear friend of mine was having dinner with Krishnamurti, of all people, and he said: "I read this teaching of yours and I understand it. I finally knew what it meant, and I had this experience." He then described his experience. Krishnamurti was silent for awhile, and then he said, "That's very good, Mr. Salzman. I'm so happy you had that experience; but is it alive now?"

THOMAS BAIMA: I am the Ecumenical Officer of the Archdiocese of Chicago, and I am here representing the Faiths of the World Committee of the National Association of Diocesan Ecumenical Officers. As such, you may not be surprised to learn that I go to a lot of dialogues. I have to say, this is probably the best organized dialogue to which I have ever been. One part of the organization has been especially beneficial in that you have eliminated the in-between. Most dialogues create some kind of safe space that people can go into and talk. But we have come together and practiced together for a week. As a result, I believe the dialogue has moved to a deeper level. One example has been that this week's monastic cycle of Psalms has taken us into the Psalms of violence. There is a temptation, out of embarrassment, to edit that out. But I think that if we had edited those Psalms out, we would never have heard some of the questions from our Buddhist friends that took us to a new depth of dialogue. It shows that what is important is not just finding the right answers, but finding the right questions.

ODETTE BAUMER-DESPEIGNE: I live in Switzerland. When I was seventeen in the boarding school, after three months of talks on the Trinity the chaplain said, "Mademoiselle, now you know everything about God." I took it seriously and I began to cry. I thought, "My goodness, what am I going to do in my life if I already know everything about God?" A few months later I met an abbot and I told him, "You know, I am no longer interested in the Trinity or Jesus Christ. We know everything. So, I want to know how others are going to find the absolute, or God." And he said, "Well, it's not very common. But if it's your way, go." I am only 83 now. So, I must say that here I just felt at home.

ELEANOR ASH: I am a Catholic laywoman, and have throughout my life discerned a vocation to work for the interrelationship of people. The Buffalo Area Metropolitan Ministries, of which I am a member, once had a theme that said, "Harmony amidst Diversity." I feel that this kind of harmony is a calling that each of us can promote in our one-to-one contacts with people of other faiths. Today, we are reflecting on what has happened this week, on people making themselves vulnerable, opening themselves up, and that is very precious and deep. I hope that each of us will always continue to do this on whatever level: personally, in a small group, or in larger communities.

ANDREW LUCZAK: I am a Chicago pastor, and I have three short things to say. First, I realized how important words are, and how unimportant. We *need* to talk to each other, but the unimportance of words was well demonstrated by the walking meditation yesterday. How beautifully the meaning came across just by walking together. We need that kind of presence to each other; it is holy. Second, I would underscore the value of internal dialogue. For those of us who have had experiences with other traditions within ourselves, it is a vital and very creative sign of new and wonderful life in the spirit. Third, as a pastor I am aware that ordinary people are very hungry for the contemplative life. I feel so privileged to be here because I believe that in contemplation and among contemplatives we have the answer for the ordinary world that lives with noise, distraction, hatred and anger.

JOAN MCGUIRE: I am a Dominican Sister from St. Catherine's, which is a few miles from here. At the peace walk yesterday, as we walked through the cemetery and passed Thomas Merton's grave, I thought, "There couldn't be a Thomas Merton without all those other markers of the monks who have gone before him. They are the ground that enabled Thomas Merton to walk." So, I think it says a lot about the need for community, either within our church, or within your Buddhist community, or within the world.

MAURUS ALLEN: I am a Benedictine monastic from Alabama. My experience has been that this is an auspicious historical moment in this chapter room at Gethsemani. I experienced it as a conception, a birthing with deep labor pains, of a cosmic Christ.

GLADYS NOREEN: I am from a monastery in St. Louis. All the words were fine—I like words and listening—but I have to say that the morning meditation period, where all the traditions were present in silence meditating, was the most touching event because we were *doing* what we were saying.

TRICIA DAY: I am a layperson, but I have to admit that some of my best friends are monastics. You are people who try hard to live by what you believe. You have incredible traditions that have given you insight and wisdom to share. My experience is that you are willing to share those traditions and insights. Thank you.

ANDRE BARBEAU: I am the Abbot General's secretary. This morning at five o'clock when we met, he gave me an envelope with all the papers to put in my baggage. So, as usual, we continue our traveling with more and more paper. And I was telling myself, "Well, for sure I will never have the time to read any more of those papers." So, I will not be transformed by the papers. I think I will be transformed more by the face of Ven. Ghosananda, because it shows how one can be transformed when one undergoes a lot of suffering, when one discovers the real truth, when one becomes really oneself. His face was so beautiful for me because it shows that this is possible. Then it helped me to look at other faces here, and I found that not only old people, but also young people can have beautiful faces when they arrive at that same kind of transformation. It is always encouraging to see that this is possible.

PETER FELDMEIER: I want to share with our Buddhist sisters and brothers something I have been dying to say. It is something both theoretical and abstract, but it also connects with my heart. What we seek as Christians, I think, is union with God. This union for us is dependency and relationality, and also absolute identity—all at the same time. And our path is a love which is different from loving kindness—though not opposed to it. It is a love that impels many Christians to love the crucifix. So, I want to share something that I remembered yesterday while talking to Ven. Abbess Blanche Hartman. This is something I wrote six or seven years ago while sitting in the library at the Weston School of Theology:

> And so I am today watching myself, and watching you loving me.
> You hold me, warm me, heal me, overwhelm me; and today you

are destroying me too, annihilating me, tearing me apart. Jesus, I'm hopelessly in love with you, and I desire to be lost in you, but I am so afraid of you. But who am I? Only he who looks like you. And so I am today watching me watching you.

EWERT COUSINS: For years I have glimpsed that interreligious dialogue might be the distinctive collective spiritual journey of our time. I feel that was manifested here extraordinarily, and certainly I feel more than ever that my own spiritual journey is tied up with the spiritual journey of all the other religions of the world in a very concrete way. But there was something very special about the first day of the encounter for me. I already knew that there would be enormous richness and riches made available because this was coming out of the monastic traditions on both sides, and the timing and the planning were so extraordinary. But then I was really surprised—I have never been in an interreligious dialogue when this happened—when on the first day, a treasure chest, as it were, was put on the floor there. The box was completely open, and we could see the gems and the jewels, the shining light, from both traditions. And it is still there! As we see it more profoundly, we discover that what we thought was a Buddhist gem is also ours. And perhaps we have shared some of our gems with our Buddhist brothers and sisters. I think that this treasure chest will always be there, and it will be fuller and fuller as we go on. I want especially to thank our Buddhist brothers and sisters for opening up the mystery of the crucified Christ by just the right question, just the right gesture almost. This has caused all of us to look into that mystery in a way that perhaps we would not have done if we had not been in their presence and with their spiritual energy.

PETER SMITH: I am a reporter with Religion News Service, and I want to thank everyone at Gethsemani for hosting us. There is a growing interest in contemplative prayer and meditation. That may not be a surprise to those of you who teach centering prayer, and those of you who run various Buddhist meditation centers. There is a growing awareness, at least in the news business, that this is something that many people are seeking. Therefore, when I saw some old photos of Gethsemani with its big walls, I thought that it is good that the walls have come down. Today, there is more interplay between laypeople and monastics, and so I think we have to give a whole new meaning to the word *cloistered*.

KATHLEEN GORMAN: I am from a Benedictine monastery in Dayton, Wyoming. For me the most awesome experience was with Maha Ghosananda. I could hardly express what I experienced, but I shall never forget the transparency of his person and of his silence. The other thing—as others have mentioned—is the light thrown on my Christian beliefs by the questions posed by Buddhists: about the crucifix, the body and blood of Jesus, and the Psalms. I relate that to what has been happening with inclusive language in the Catholic Church. Once you become aware of the exclusiveness of certain words, they jump out at you at every point. And so after what has been opened up for me now, I will be aware of every word I say in the prayers that we chant all the time. Finally, this meeting has made me realize that a historic transformation is taking place.

JEAN LAVIN: I am a Benedictine sister from Erie, Pennsylvania. I have experienced this encounter at Gethsemani as love in action. It is for me what Jesus talked about when he said, "I would that they be one, even as you and I are one, Father," Father here being, of course, the absolute. I am a member of the second oldest women's Benedictine community in the United States. Before Vatican II, our ministries were devoted primarily to education. But since Vatican II, we are now devoting our ministries to working with the poor—to helping single-women parents get off welfare. I have a *Zendo* in the inner city which is on the third floor of our former girls' academy where we work with these women. Of course we do not have words for what goes on in there, but the women experience that it is something very special. Because our programs are funded by the government, I cannot teach prayer. So what I do is bring them into the *Zendo* and say, "Now we're going to talk about, and hopefully experience, ways of peace." And it is amazing what happens! Women with very low self-esteem, who have only conceived of themselves as being children-bearers, now realize they have value and are worthwhile. I am convinced that the "prayer" which comes from our center is what envelops them, encourages them and helps them.

SARAH SCHWARTBERG: I am a Benedictine from Missouri. Samu Sunim talked about the need for an apology for the violence committed by the institutional clergy of whatever faith. I have been around enough to know that there is stupidity and ignorance in every faith tradition. I think the only way for people to see the *need* for apology, is to get in touch with the violence and anger within ourselves. And I think that is done through spiritual practice. I think we need to recite and to sing those Psalms until we can come to a recognition of the hatred and violence that exists within each one of us. This has been a very overwhelming experience for me. I am leaving with the sense that we have to access our own traditions and to make them available to the world.

PAT McGUIRE: I am from the Immaculate Conception Monastery in Ferdinand, Indiana. The word that keeps coming to me is *transformation*, and I think that has happened here on many levels. I know that I am not even aware of what it really means to me personally. The experience, as many have expressed, has been overwhelming. I guess I would say that the experience is one of a *seed of unity* that has been planted. I think the seed for this gathering was planted many years ago, and many people have had a hand in it.

ANTHONY DISTEFANO: I am from this abbey. It has been a profound experience for me. What came to mind were two statements of Thomas Merton in his *Asian Journal*. The first was that his going to the East demanded a much deeper purification of his personhood. And the second was when he said, "We're going to have to discover a new language for prayer." This comes out of something that transcends all of our traditions, that arises and comes out of the immediacy of love. The Dalai Lama and others said that having real conviction is most important. For me, the conviction is that at the depths of personhood there is the immediacy of love. To find this depth where true love is present demands purification. We all need to arouse a conviction—yes it is true. Then, purification. Purification of what? Of the conditioning of the ego that hides that deep love. And you know, it is true. From early childhood—how much emotional conditioning we carry! All that anger and violence comes from that. What I find amazing is the wisdom of Buddhism about emotional arisings. These arisings are not indications of who we truly are, but yet we identify so much with them. In our Christian tradition, we know this too and it means that we need a lot of patience. But there is a deep freedom there, you know? Everybody is searching for this.

MARY FEEHAN: I am a Benedictine from Elizabeth, New Jersey. We have been privileged to see such courage and honesty in those who presented among our venerable Buddhist brothers and sisters, and our own Christian speakers. I have never in all my life been in the presence of fire blazing as I was the other afternoon when Fr. Armand and Fr. Bernardo spoke! The depth of the silence that followed that fire, and to hear Abbot Fischer's response to that, touched me to the heart: "If I understood who your Jesus is, I would be a Christian." I have pondered the gift that is mine, the challenge that Abbot Fischer's words were to me, and my desire to be fire. I have always been drawn by that phrase from scripture, "that all may be one." By being fire, I can perhaps help us all move in that direction.

JOAN ANDERSON: I am a Benedictine from Tucson, Arizona. I have a heart full of love and gratitude for everyone here. I think one of the things that struck me was the complete lack of defensiveness. There were many, many challenging questions on both sides, and they were all met with such gentleness, respect and just the desire to be heard and understood. I was moved each time it happened. When the response could have been negative, it was just so gentle and so positive. It was just beautiful.

TIMOTHY KELLY: I am the abbot of St. John's Abbey in Collegeville, Minnesota. I will speak only from my own experience of mystery, a mystery that deepens, a mystery of life, a mystery that is not confined by definitions, documents, or even by organized teachings. It is the reality which is behind all of those things, to which we—following Benedictine tradition—must "listen." And God will speak when he wishes. Therefore, it is very important for me to be a listener to the deepness of the mystery that is life, the mystery that is me, the mystery that is you. It seems to me that what I have heard a little deeper here each time I have really listened is that as I come to that deep center of my own being through meditation, through prayer, I come to the deep center of your being, of all being, and come to know there a little bit more deeply the mystery of life. I have seen that marvelously and wonderfully exhibited this week. I am very, very grateful to all of you for sharing, and for the listening ears of all of us who heard a marvelous message this week.

MIKE FITZPATRICK: I ran out of language on day one, if not before. In fact, in the two weeks leading up to coming here, I kept hearing and anticipating the silence. And during each day, it got deeper and deeper, more profound and scarier, until there were two distinct moments when it became terrifying. I thought, "My God, how can we enter into the depth of that silence?" The musical interludes, or vignettes, that I have performed on the cello during the ritual moments have come out of that silence as they have resolved into that silence. It has been a personal joy to be enveloped in that silence, to echo the sounds of the silence.

DOUGLAS CONLAN: I am a priest from Australia. I would like to thank our Buddhist brothers and sisters for their courage in coming here. My thanks go back 35 years when, as a young man without a religion, I wandered

Asia and joined some Theravada Buddhists in Thailand. That experience was a watershed in my life that led me into the Catholic Church, I am sure of that. My spiritual journey I consider to be the most essential thing about my life. This encounter has been a kind of culmination, and yet also a step in fostering that vision of the future around which we have gathered here this week.

DAVID STEINDL-RAST: I was asked to say a few words to conclude our reflections about our encounter. The word that comes to mind is *gratefulness*. But, even the word *gratefulness* has a new and fuller meaning in this context. I have always known that gratefulness is our full response to the gratuitousness of all that there is. But now I would say that it is a full response to a gratuitousness that immediately echoes with the dependent arising of all. And that full response is precisely our emptying of ourselves in response to that dependently arising fullness. So, we learn new overtones and undertones to our own terms. And that, it seems, was one of the most important fruits of this encounter for me. It is definitely a first. I have attended quite a number of dialogues, but this has been a benchmark in the history of East-West dialogue as far as I can see.

This has been a real *monastic* dialogue. My impression is that the monastic experience as such, the monastic stance, the choice to be a monk, is not the choice to be a super-Buddhist or a super-Christian. But it is a human choice—it is one choice to live your human life. If you happen to live in a Christian country, you will become a Christian monk; and if you happen to live in a Buddhist place, you will become a Buddhist monk. On this monastic level, we can really meet one another as real brothers and sisters. While it is not necessary for *everybody* to meet on that monastic level, everyone can be enriched by our meeting here.

I asked Thomas Merton once whether he could have written the things that he wrote about the Christian faith if it had not been for his exposure to Buddhism. Usually when you asked him a question like that he would just laugh. But on that occasion he really thought for awhile about it; he did not answer right away. And then ten or fifteen minutes later he said, "To come back to this point that you raised, I do not believe that I could understand our Christian faith the way I understand it if it were not for the light of Buddhism." So just as many people who never had the opportunity to meet with Buddhists were influenced by Merton's meeting, many people can also be influenced through our actions, through our being, because we have had this opportunity. And I think that is far more important than our finding some doctrinal agreement, or pointing out the fine points of doctrinal disagreement, and so forth. I really do agree with the Ven. Ratanasara who said, "Don't mix doctrines; but work together for peace."

I am so excited about this encounter not because it was so good, but because it has opened us up for a whole new turn in the road. It has opened up a whole new stretch for us to go. We have come a long way and we have a long way to go. And what should we remember? Before the Christians were called Christians, they were called the followers of the Way. So, it is very good to be *on the way*. Then, what can we take with us from our encounter here as we go ahead together on the way? I leave you with the following image from monastic daily life.

We have lots of mice in our cells, and most of us do not like those mousetraps that kill the mice. So, we have what is called a "Have-a-Heart" trap. It is a little box, and you put some peanut butter in it, and the mouse goes in it but cannot get out. Within two minutes, you can catch the mouse that is in the cell. But then you have the problem of how to get rid of this mouse. So, you take it about a quarter of a mile into the woods—because these mice know very well how to get back into the cell. Somebody even put a little marker on a mouse's ear, and that same mouse came back three times! But now you have got the mouse to the woods, and you want to get her out of this box, and she does not come out. So, you turn it upside down and you shake it. But this little mouse clings with all her little paws to this trap. So, the direction that I would suggest is, let us identify the traps to which we cling, and then let us let loose and go ahead! That is my program for the future, and that is what I take along from our encounter.

DONALD MITCHELL: I have been asked to say a few words on behalf of those of us who have been involved in the organizing of this event for the past two years. In responding to the wishes of His Holiness the Dalai Lama, we intended this week to be a period of time in which there would be a blending of many different voices—Christians and Buddhists—within the silence of this wonderful Abbey of Gethsemani. We invited people who we felt were not only knowledgeable about spirituality, but could also listen with their hearts to other voices, both Christian and Buddhist. And we wanted to enrich our dialogue with the voices of chanting, of liturgy, of ritual, and of monastic living. We also wanted you to hear each other's voices in the quiet times when you could meet as dyads.

All of this made for a tremendously full week of listening, and I wondered how people were going to hold up. I thought that this is more of a *sesshin*, in the Zen sense, than a conference! And it was not a conference, it was really an intense encounter in the history of humankind's spiritual self-understanding. I think people rose to the occasion, as sometimes happens in these situations, and it was a tremendous success. But the word "success" seems out of place, because it was not just a matter of *us* being successful in some endeavor. I felt that there is something at work here that is larger than just us, that we are participating in something happening that is larger than any one of us, or all of us.

We have brought the world into this monastery. We brought the world into our dialogue in a prayerful, heartfelt way that was very touching to me. So what has happened here has meaning not just for ourselves, but for the world. One of the observers said he felt like we were going through labor pains, that something was being born. He used the word, "cosmic Christ." I really do not know what it is that is being born here. But certainly I experienced a labor toward, and a birthing of, a deeper communion, a deeper unity, that many of us felt. I remember that in one moment of meditation this week, Mary Margaret asked us to speak one word that characterizes our experience of this encounter. Geshe Sopa said "unity." Another person said "fellowship." From another person, "harmony."

So what do we take back with us to share with the world? I am reminded of what Ven. Phangcham said at one point. He said, in his soft voice, that we must take loving kindness into the violence, into the darkness, into the anger of the world. So, maybe we can—in our Buddhist way, in our Christian way—take the spirit of loving kindness and unity from our encounter back into the world. Thank you for coming. It has been a truly wonderful week!

TIMOTHY KELLY: As abbot of this monastery, I am a bit embarrassed by all the words of gratitude that have been given to our community—not that I do not think all my brothers deserve it. But we are also most grateful to you for having come to us. We were a bit apprehensive in inviting you, or opening our door to you—such an extraordinary group of people. We wondered if we could supply, if we could be, that support that is so necessary for an encounter like this. So inevitably, as we prepared, we decided we would just be ourselves; and that seems to have been the support that helped the encounter grow. We are most grateful for your presence. It has been a learning experience for each of us; and each of the brothers has been very impressed and encouraged in his own way by seeing the seriousness with which each of you follow your own path. Hopefully in following ours, we can enter more deeply into this whole dialogue. I found it personally very helpful to hear some voices push those boundaries that, in the depths of my own meditation, I sometimes push but am always afraid to speak. So, possibly new courage has been found. It has been a joy having you, and I do hope in some way we can come together again. It has been a real pleasure to open our doors to the Buddhists in a very particular way, and we did learn a great deal. Thank you.

HAVANPOLA RATANASARA: Today, I can tell you that I have gone one step forward! And I am very thankful to the Christian brothers and sisters for appreciating our Buddhist presence at this Catholic monastery. I appreciate your kind words, and we are always ready to join hands and continue this noble work. Thank you very much for your wonderful hospitality.

LOBSANG TENZIN: Three steps are considered very important in Buddhism in general: to set a proper motivation, to do the actual task with proper awareness and mindfulness, and to dedicate whatever positive experience, or positive qualities, came out of the task for the peace and harmony and healing of all sentient beings in the world. So here at Gethsemani we have dialogued with a very positive motivation. The encounter itself has gone very well. Now let us dedicate the experience that we have cultivated in this encounter—the genuine respect and appreciation for each other, the sense of compassion and loving kindness that we have experienced, and the deeper mutual understanding we have achieved. Let it flow through our hearts into the world for healing, peace and harmony.

Notes

PREFACE

1. Naomi Burton, Brother Patrick Hart, and James Laughlin, eds., *The Asian Journal of Thomas Merton* (New York: New Directions, 1973), p. 125.
2. Benoit Billot, *Voyage dans les Monastères Zen* (Paris: Desclée, 1987).
3. A.I.M., *Bulletin of the A.I.M.*, no. 29 (1980):25.
4. A.I.M., *Bulletin of the A.I.M.*, no. 27 (1980):44–45.
5. Merton, p. 143.
6. Jean-Claude Basset, *Le Dialogue Interreligieux, Histoire et Avenir* (Paris: Cerf, 1996), p. 338.
7. Letter from Cardinal Arinze to Pierre de Béthune, 27 July 1991, *N.A.B.E.W.D. Bulletin*, no. 43 (Jan. 1992):15–16.
8. Secretariat for Non-Christians, "Dialogue and Mission," *Bulletin*, no. 56 (1984):35.
9. Merton, p. 308.

Chapter 1. JOURNEY AND DIALOGUE

1. How We Reached This Point: Communication Becoming Communion
PASCALINE COFF, O.S.B.

1. Simon Tonini, "Intermonastic Dialogue: Beginnings and Development," *Pontifical Council for Interreligious Dialogue Bulletin*, 23, no. 1 (1988):12.

2. Dialogue and Unity: A Buddhist Perspective
VEN. DR. HAVANPOLA RATANASARA

1. His Holiness John Paul II, *Crossing the Threshold of Hope* (New York: Alfred A. Knopf, 1994), pp. 147, 149. (Here, I am interpreting the Pope's remarks to apply to interfaith relations. Also, I must note that while I may not agree with everything the Pope says in the book, the points on which we disagree are eclipsed by the points on which a consensus seems attainable, as well as by the breadth of the Pope's vision and his genuine concern for a continuing dialogue with other faiths.)
2. *Nostra Aetate*, "In Our Times," is one of the official documents of Vatican II.
3. The author has been a Co-Chairman of the Los Angeles Buddhist-Catholic Dialogue since its inception.
4. "The Attitude of The Church toward the Followers of Other Religions," in *Handbook for Interreligious Dialogue*, ed. John Borelli (Morristown: Silver, Burdett & Ginn, 1990), pp. 57–64.
5. *Guidelines on Dialogue with People of Living Faiths and Ideologies* (Geneva: WCC Publications, 1990).
6. His Holiness Pope John Paul II, *Crossing the Threshold of Hope*, p. 147. Again, I am quoting somewhat out of context, and can provide no more than the same justification I offered earlier for so doing.

7. *The Collection of the Middle-Length Sayings (Majjhima Nikaya),* vol. III., trans. I. B. Horner (Oxford: The Pali Text Society, 1990), p. 382.

8. *The Book of the Gradual Sayings (Anguttara Nikaya),* vol. 1., trans. F. L. Woodward (Oxford: The Pali Text Society, 1989), pp. 171–172.

9. *The Collection of the Middle-Length Sayings (Majjhima Nikaya),* pp. 173–174.

10. His Holiness John Paul II, *Crossing the Threshold of Hope,* pp. 85–86.

11. *Dhammapada* 17:8.

12. *Guidelines on Dialogue with People of Living Faiths and Ideologies,* p. 2.

13. Ibid.

14. *Dhammapada* 9:10.

15. *The Collection of the Middle-Length Sayings (Majjhima Nikaya),* p. 223.

16. *Dhammapada* 1:3.

17. Ibid., 1:5.

18. Matt. 6:44.

19. Rom. 12:21.

20. As Bhikkhu Buddhadasa has put it: "Buddhism is a universal religion. It can be put into practice by everyone, in every age and era. People everywhere have the same problem: to free themselves from suffering—suffering which is inherent in birth, aging, pain, and death, suffering which stems from desire, from grasping. Everyone without exception, celestial being, human being, or beast, has this same problem, and everyone has the same job to do, namely eliminate completely the desire, the unskillful grasping which is the root cause of that suffering. Thus Buddhism is a universal religion." Buddhadasa Bhikkhu, *Handbook for Mankind* (Bangkok: Mahachula Buddhist University Press, 1975), pp. 76–77.

21. His Holiness Pope John Paul II, *Crossing the Threshold of Hope,* p. 147.

22. Letter to the Buddhist community from the Vatican's Pontifical Council for Interreligious Dialogue, Francis Cardinal Arinze, President, dated April–May, 1996.

23. *Dhammapada* 17:3.

24. His Holiness the Dalai Lama, *A Policy of Kindness: An Anthology of Writings by and about the Dalai Lama,* ed. Sidney Piburn (Ithaca: Snow Lion Publications, 1990), p. 62.

Chapter 2. ULTIMATE REALITY AND SPIRITUALITY

1. Nirvana, Buddhahood and the Spiritual Life
JEFFREY HOPKINS

1. See Swami Dwarikadas Shastri, *Pramanavarttika of Acharya Dharmakirtti* (Varanasi: Bauddha Bharati, 1968), vol. 3, 73.1.

2. God, Creation and the Spiritual Life
DONALD W. MITCHELL

1. St. Augustine, *Confessions* 1.1.

2. Thomas Merton, "Preface," in Ernesto Cardenal, *Love* (New York: Crossroad, 1981), pp. 8–9.

3. Thomas Merton, "A Christian Looks at Zen," in John C. H. Wu, *The Golden Age of Zen* (New York: Doubleday, 1996), p. 18.

4. Thomas Aquinas, "Commentary on the Gospel of John 6:55," Lect. VII, 973.

5. Chiara Lubich, *The Eucharist* (New York: New City Press, 1977), p. 61.

Chapter 3. PRAYER AND MEDITATION

1. Mindfulness and Loving-Kindness Meditation
VEN. DR. DHAMMARAKKHITA

1. The five hindrances are: (1) sensual lust, (2) ill-will, (3) physical and mental torpor and languor, (4) restlessness and worry, and (5) doubt.

2. These four *jhanas,* which are different from the higher "mystical" forms mentioned at the beginning of this talk, include: (1) meditation freed from negative states of mind accompanied by thoughts, joy and happiness; (2) meditation freed from thoughts accompanied by inner tranquility, joy and happiness; (3) meditation freed from joy accompanied by mindful awareness and happiness; (4) meditation freed from happiness and sadness accompanied by pure mindfulness and equanimity.

3. The Four Noble Truths include: (1) the truth of Suffering, (2) the Origin of suffering, (3) the Extinction of suffering, and (4) the eightfold Path leading to the extinction of suffering.

4. The Contemplative Life
JAMES A. WISEMAN, O.S.B.

1. *The Wisdom of the Desert Fathers,* trans. Benedicta Ward (Oxford: SLG Press, 1975), p. 24. Translation slightly modified.

2. Ibid., p. 5. Translation slightly modified.

3. Ibid., p. 59.

4. *Western Asceticism,* ed. Owen Chadwick (Philadelphia: Westminster, 1958), p. 78.

5. St. Basil, "Homilia in Martyrem Julittam," in Migne, *PG* 31:243–44.

6. St. Columba, quoted by Thomas Merton, *Contemplative Prayer* (Garden City, NY: Doubleday, Image Books, 1971), p. 32. Translation slightly modified. The full text of the poem can be found in W. G. Hanson, *Early Monastic Schools of Ireland* (Cambridge, 1927), pp. 21–22.

7. Sheila Cassidy, *Prayer for Pilgrims* (New York: Crossroad, 1982), p. 63.

5. Lectio Divina
MARY MARGARET FUNK, O.S.B.

1. *Rule of Benedict* 48.1, 4, 5, 10, 13; 14.22–23; 49.4. See Timothy Fry, ed., *The Rule of St. Benedict* (Collegeville, MN: Liturgical Press, 1981).

2. See Michael Casey, *Sacred Reading: The Ancient Art of Lectio Divina* (Liguori, MO: Triumph Books, 1996). Thomas Keating, in *Intimacy With God* (New York: Crossroad, 1994) speaks of *lectio* as "Reading, or, more exactly, listening to the book we believe to be divinely inspired. The most ancient method of developing the friendship of Christ, using Scripture texts as topics of conversation with Christ" (p. 164). Also, Thomas Keating writes, "Lectio Divina is the most traditional way of cultivating contemplative prayer. A mainstay of Christian monastic practice from the earliest days, it consists in listening to the texts of the Bible as if one were in conversation with God and God were suggesting the topics for discussion. Those who follow the method of Lectio Divina are cultivating the capacity to listen to the word of God at ever deepening levels of attention. Spontaneous prayer is the normal response to their growing relationship with Christ, and the gift of contemplation is God's normal response to them" (p. 40). The reflective part, the pondering on the words of the sacred text in *lectio divina,* is called *meditatio,* discursive meditation. The spontaneous movement of the will in response to this reflection is called *oratio,* affective prayer. As these reflections and particular acts of the will simplify, one tends toward resting in God or *contemplatio,* contemplation.

3. Ewert Cousins, *Christ of the 21st Century* (New York: Continuum, 1992). This book is helpful for references from the Christian tradition on the spiritual senses, and for contemporary research on altered states of consciousness.

4. Michael Mott, *The Seven Mountains of Thomas Merton* (Boston: Houghton Mifflin Company, 1984), pp. 432–33. Also see Thomas Merton, *The Hidden Ground of Love,* ed. William H. Shannon (New York: Farrar, Straus & Giroux, 1985), p. 364. This is perhaps a more accurate source of this correspondence.

5. *The Cloud of Unknowing,* ed. William Johnston (New York: Image Books, 1973). This little book written in the 14th century by an unknown English author discusses spiritual direction into apophatic prayer. Some sisters at our monasteries use writings from saints such as Teresa of Avila, Gertrude of Helfta, Hildegard or Julian of Norwich. There is a growing interest in women mystics.

6. Thomas Merton, *The Climate of Monastic Prayer* (Kalamazoo: Cistercian Publications, 1969).

7. Consider the following story from the desert Fathers: "A brother in Scete once came to the Abbot Moses seeking a word of exhortation. The old man said to him, 'Why do you come to me to be taught. Go, sit in your cell. Your cell will teach you all things.' " This is profound advice because the monk of that time would have memorized the scriptures and all the texts would be in his heart; when thoughts arose, they would be from scripture.

8. Jean Leclercq, O.S.B., *The Love of Learning and the Desire for God* (New York: Fordham University Press, 1974).

9. Jn. 14:20: "On that day you will realize that I am in my Father and you are in me and I am in you."

10. Guigo II, *The Ladder of Monks and Twelve Meditations* (Kalamazoo: Cistercian Publications, 1981). Written by a Carthusian in the 12th century, this is a classic in Western Christian mysticism.

11. A Monk of the Eastern Church, *A Dialogue with the Saviour*, trans. by a Monk of the Western Church (New York: Desclee Company, 1963).

12. "Institute on the Apophatic Spiritual Heritage in the Christian Tradition," audio tapes available from Contemplative Outreach Ltd., PO Box 737, Butler NJ 07405.

13. See *The Cloud of Unknowing*.

14. See the proceedings from the "Marxism and Monastic Perspectives Asian Monastic Congress," 1968: "What is essential in the monastic life is not embedded in buildings, is not embedded in clothing, is especially not in a rule. It is concerned with the business of total inner transformation. All other things serve that end. I am just saying, in other words, what Cassian said in the first lecture on *puritas cordis*, purity of heart, that every monastic observance tends toward that end" (p.79).

15. See Thomas Keating, *Open Mind, Open Heart* (New York: Continuum, 1991).

16. Thomas Keating, *Intimacy with God* (New York: Crossroad, 1994).

17. John Cassian, *Institutes* and *Conferences*.

18. Evagrius Ponticus, *The Praktikos and Chapters on Prayer*, trans. John Eudes Bamberger, O.C.S.O. (Kalamazoo: Cistercian Publications, 1981). Also see Jeremy Driscoll, *The Mind's Long Journey to the Holy Trinity: The* Ad Monachos *of Evagrius Ponticus* (Collegeville, MN: Liturgical Press, 1993). This is a good commentary on the world view of early antiquity. It is, in addition, a wonderful introduction for someone who wants to do *lectio* with Evagrius. Also see Thomas Spidlik, *Spirituality of the Christian East* (Kalamazoo: Cistercian Publications, 1986). This handbook enables a Western Christian to get a better feel for the rich Eastern tradition.

19. Thomas Merton, *The Wisdom of the Desert* (New York: New Directions, 1960). A charming translation by Thomas Merton with an introduction that gives great energy to the "purity of heart."

20. Matthias Neuman, "The Contemporary Spirituality of the Monastic Lectio," *Review for Religious*, 36 (1977):97–110. By emphasizing conversion, the monastic practice faithfully follows the yet older tradition of Alexandrian patristic exegesis. This manner of explaining the sacred books searches for four different meanings in every text: the "literal" or "historical" meaning, and three kinds of "spiritual" meaning. These spiritual meanings consist of the "allegorical," which found a spiritual reality in each text, that is, some exemplification of a Christian's faith in God; the "tropological," which discerned a moral message for Christian action in each passage; and the "anagogical," which extracted an eschatological significance. The best research on the four senses of scripture to date is Henri de Lubac, *Exégèse Médiévale: les quatre sens de l'Écriture*, vol. 1–4 (Paris: Aubier, 1959–62).

21. Stephen I. Harris, *The New Testament: A Student's Introduction* (London and Toronto: Mayfield Publishing Company, 1995).

22. Bernard McGinn, *The Foundations of Mysticism* and *The Growth of Mysticism* (New York: Crossroad, 1992, 1994). In *Foundations*, there are nine entries and descriptions of the spiritual senses; in *Growth*, there are fifteen entries and descriptions of *lectio divina*.

23. Bruno Barnhart, O.S.B. Cam., *The Good Wine: Reading John from the Center* (New York: Paulist, 1993). This extraordinary book is an experience of reading and interpreting John's Gospel using the spiritual senses.

Chapter 4. GROWTH AND DEVELOPMENT

4. *Prayer as Path*
PIERRE-FRANÇOIS DE BÉTHUNE, O.S.B.

1. *Rule of Benedict* 58, 7; henceforth referred to as *RB*
2. *RB* 7, 30.
3. *Dialogi* II 3, 5.
4. *Dialogi* II, *Exordium*.
5. *Series Alphabetica, Arsenius* 2.
6. *RB* 4, 20.
7. *RB* Prol. 40.
8. *RB* 19, 2ss.
9. *RB* 50, 4.
10. *RB* 7, 50.
11. *RB* 7, 27 and 29, quoting Ps. 13:2.
12. *RB* 4, 10.
13. *Calicem Domini biberunt et amici Dei facti sunt* (antiphon of the feast of the apostles).
14. *RB* 58, 5.
15. *RB* 7, 34 quoting Phil. 2:8.
16. *RB* 7, 43.
17. *RB* 4, 72.
18. *Conlatio* X, 7.
19. *RB* 49, 6.
20. *RB* Prol. 9.
21. *Conlatio* IX, 15.
22. *RB* 7, 67–70.
23. Cf. *RB* Prol. 2.
24. Cf. *RB* 49, 6.
25. *RB* Prol. 49.
26. *Conlatio* IX, 31.
27. *Eveil à soi, éveil à Dieu* (Paris, 1971), p. 147.

5. *Spiritual Experiences on the Path of Prayer*
GILCHRIST LAVIGNE, O.C.S.O.

1. Thomas Merton, *Contemplative Prayer* (New York: Herder & Herder, 1969), p. 94.
2. Barnabas M. Ahern, "Pauline Mysticism," *The Way* 18, no. 1 (1978):3.
3. Timothy Fry, ed., *The Rule of St. Benedict* (Collegeville, MN: Liturgical Press, 1981). Hereafter cited as *RB*.
4. *RB* 58, 7.
5. Irenée Hausherr, SJ, *Penthos* (Kalamazoo: Cistercian Publications, 1982), pp. 89–90.
6. Ibid., p. 93.
7. Ibid., p. 25.
8. Gilbert of Hoyland, *Sermons on the Song of Songs*, II, trans. Lawrence Braceland, S.J. (Kalamazoo: Cistercian Publications, 1982), p. 93.
9. *RB* 7, 31.
10. Dom Bernardo Olivera, O.C.S.O., Workshop given to Novice Directors of the USA Region, Ava, MO, 1996.
11. Roger de Ganck, *Beatrice of Nazareth in Her Context* (Kalamazoo: Cistercian Publications, 1991), p. 271.

12. Gilbert of Hoyland, *Sermons*, II, p. 307.
13. Amandus Bussels, "Saint Lutgard's Mystical Spirituality," in *Hidden Springs, Book One*, ed. Nichols and Shank (Kalamazoo: Cistercian Publications, 1995), p. 217.
14. Miriam Schmitt, O.S.B., "Freed to Run with Expanded Heart: The Writings of Gertrude of Helfta and RB," *Cistercian Studies* 25 (1990):225.
15. Ibid., p. 224.
16. Bernard of Clairvaux, *On the Song of Songs, II* (Kalamazoo: Cistercian Publications, 1976), p. 7.
17. Fra M. Raphael Arnaiz Baron, *To Know How to Wait*, trans. M. Mitchell (Westminster: Newman Press, 1964), p. 255.
18. Merton, *Contemplative Prayer*, pp. 109–110.
19. Ibid., p. 111.
20. Schmitt, "Freed to Run," p. 226.
21. *RB* 7, 35.
22. Ritamary Bradley, "Love and Knowledge in *Seven Manners of Loving*," in *Hidden Springs, Book One*, p. 364.
23. *RB* 7, 67.
24. Charles Dumont, "A Phenomenological Approach to Humility: Chapter VII of the Rule of St. Benedict," *Cistercian Studies* 30 (1995):287.
25. St. Gregory the Great, *Dialogues*, trans. Odo Zimmerman, O.S.B. (Washington, DC: Catholic University of America/Consortium, 1959), p. 105.
26. Hausherr, *Penthos*, p. 50.
27. G.P. Fedotov, *A Treasury of Russian Spirituality* (London: Sheed and Ward, 1952), p. 274.
28. Ibid., p. 256.
29. Miriam Schmitt, "Gertrude of Helfta: Her Monastic Milieu and Her Spirituality," in *Hidden Springs, Book Two* (Kalamazoo: Cistercian Publications, 1995), p. 481.
30. Charles Dumont, "Simplicity as a Principle of Reform in the Writings of Mère Louise de Ballon," in *Hidden Springs, Book Two*, p. 577.
31. Claire Boudreau, O.C.S.O., "Ida of Nivelles," in *Hidden Springs, Book One*, p. 328.
32. Ibid, p. 333.
33. James McPolin, "Johannine Mysticism," *The Way* 18 (1978):33.
34. Thomas Merton, *Conjectures of a Guilty Bystander* (New York: Doubleday, 1966), p. 71.

Chapter 5. COMMUNITY AND GUIDANCE

5. *The Spiritual Guide*

SR. DONALD CORCORAN, O.S.B. CAM.

1. William of St. Thierry, *The Mirror of Faith*, in Migne, *PL* 180:384.
2. Barsanuphius, *Questiones et Responsiones*, 120; in Derwas J. Chitty, *The Desert a City: An Introduction to the Study of Egyptian and Palestinian Monasticism under the Christian Empire* (Oxford: Basil Blackwell, 1966), p. 134.

Chapter 6. SPIRITUALITY AND SOCIETY

2. *Worldly* Bodhisattvas: *Zen Awakening and Social Transformation*

VEN. SAMU SUNIM

1. The "six *paramitas*," or "perfections" of the *bodhisattva* life, include: giving, morality, patience, vigor, meditation and wisdom. The "four divine abodes" include: loving kindness, compassion, joy in others and equanimity toward friend and foe alike.

4. Christian Holiness
JOSEPH GERRY, O.S.B.

1. *Rule of Benedict* 4, 62; henceforth cited as *RB*.
2. *Conferences* 18,V,1 ff.
3. See especially nos. 39–42.
4. *RB* 7, 62–66.
5. Michael Casey, *The Undivided Heart: The Western Monastic Approach to Contemplation* (Petersham, MA: St. Bede's Publications, 1994), p. 20.
6. *RB* 22, 6–8.
7. *RB* 5, 15–16.
8. Prologue 4.
9. *RB* 4, 60.
10. *RB* 7, 70.
11. *RB* Prologue 30–32.
12. *RB* Prologue 50.
13. *RB* 49, 6.
14. *RB* 49, 7.

5. Building the Reign of God
EWERT COUSINS

1. Karl Jaspers, *Vom Ursprung und Ziel der Geschichte* (Zurich: Artemis, 1949), pp. 19–43.
2. Ibid., p. 19; trans. Michael Bullock, *The Origin and Goal of History* (New Haven: Yale University Press, 1953), p. 1. For the ongoing academic discussion of Jaspers's position on the Axial Period, see "Wisdom, Revelation, and Doubt: Perspectives on the First Millennium B.C.," *Daedalus* (Spring, 1975); and *The Origins and Diversity of Axial Age Civilizations*, ed. S.N. Eisenstadt (New York: State University of New York Press, 1989).
3. For a more comprehensive treatment of my concept of the Second Axial Period, see my book *Christ of the 21st Century* (New York: Continuum, 1992).
4. Pierre Teilhard de Chardin, *Le Phénomène humain* (Paris: Editions du Seuil, 1955); see also *L'Activation de l'énergie* (Paris: Editions du Seuil, 1962) and *L'Energie humaine* (Paris: Editions du Seuil, 1962).

EPILOGUE

A Tribute to Thomas Merton
JAMES CONNER, O.C.S.O.

1. Thomas Merton, *The Hidden Ground of Love*, ed. William H. Shannon (New York: Farrar, Straus and Giroux, 1985), p. 627.
2. Thomas Merton, *The Way of Chuang Tzu* (New York: New Directions, 1965), p. 17.
3. Naomi Burton, Brother Patrick Hart, and James Laughlin, eds., *The Asian Journal of Thomas Merton* (New York: New Directions, 1973), pp. 312–313.
4. Ibid., p. 313.
5. Ibid.
6. Ibid., pp. 315–316.
7. Ibid., p. 235.
8. Ibid., p. 308.

List of Participants

ODETTE BAUMER-DESPEIGNE resides in Frauenfeld, Switzerland, and is an advisor for both MID and DIM. She is also Secretary for the Abhishiktananda Society in Europe, and was a close friend of Fr. Henri LeSaux (Abhishiktananda). Mme. Baumer is a leader in interfaith dialogue in Europe, and has participated in dialogues throughout North America, Europe and Asia.

JOHANNA BECKER, O.S.B., is a monastic at the Monastery of St. Benedict in St. Joseph, Minnesota. She is an Asian art historian who has studied in such places as Japan, India, China, Taiwan, Korea and Myanmar. Sr. Becker is a Board Member of MID, and in that capacity she represented MID when His Holiness the Dalai Lama proclaimed the *Universal Declaration on Non-Violence: The Incompatibility of Religion and War* in 1990.

PIERRE-FRANÇOIS DE BÉTHUNE, O.S.B., is Prior of the Priory of Clerlande in Belgium, and is the General Secretary of the MID worldwide. He is a Consultor for the Vatican's Pontifical Council for Interreligious Dialogue. Fr. Béthune has also trained in Zen Buddhist meditation in Japan.

JOHN BORELLI is a member of the Secretariat for Ecumenical and Interreligious Affairs of the National Conference of Catholic Bishops, where he is responsible for interreligious relations with Buddhists. In 1989, he was appointed a Consultor to the Vatican's Pontifical Council for Interreligious Dialogue. Dr. Borelli is also a member of the International Buddhist-Christian Theological Encounter, and is an advisor to MID.

THEOPHANE BOYD, O.C.S.O., is a monk at St. Benedict's Monastery in Snowmass, Colorado. He was trained in Zen practice by Sasaki Roshi, and has also trained in *vipassana* meditation. Fr. Boyd has been engaged in the Buddhist-Christian dialogue since 1976, and has visited Tibetan monasteries in India.

JAMES CONNER, O.C.S.O, is Abbot of Assumption Abbey in Ava, Missouri. He entered Gethsemani Abbey in Kentucky in 1949, and was a student under Thomas Merton. Fr. Conner has served as Editor of the

MID *Bulletin* since 1985, and was President of the International Thomas Merton Society from 1993–95.

PASCALINE COFF, O.S.B., is a Benedictine Sister of Perpetual Adoration, and is foundress and Superior of the monastic *ashram*, Osage+Monastery Forest of Peace in Sand Springs, Oklahoma. One of the founding members of MID, she was Editor of its *Bulletin* for the first ten years. Sr. Coff participated in all the hospitality exchanges with His Holiness the Dalai Lama and his monastics, and has participated in numerous dialogues in Europe, North America and Asia.

MARY DONALD CORCORAN, O.S.B. Cam., is Prioress of Transfiguration Monastery in Windsor, New York. She was Formation Director from 1980 to 1996, when she became Prioress. Sr. Corcoran is a Board Member of MID, and attended an Asian monastic encounter in Sri Lanka in 1980. She is author of *Spiritual Sisters*, her dialogue with a Buddhist nun.

JACQUES CÔTÉ, O.S.B., is a monk of the Abbey of Saint-Benoît-du-Lac in Quebec Province, Canada. He has worked in the Curia of the Benedictine Confederation in Rome under five Abbot Primates, for whom he prepared five congresses of Benedictine Abbots from 1977 to 1996. Fr. Côté specializes in Sacred Theology.

EWERT COUSINS is Professor of Theology at Fordham University. He is the General Editor of the 25-volume *World Spirituality: An Encyclopedic History of the Religious Quest*, and is author of *Global Spirituality: The Meeting of Mystical Paths*. Prof. Cousins has been a Consultor to the Vatican's Pontifical Council for Interreligious Dialogue.

DHAMMARAKKHITA is Director of the Mental Energy Research Centre in Rangoon, Myanmar. Trained in *samatha* and *vipassana* meditation, the Ven. Dr. Dhammarakkhita has published *The Buddhist Way of Mental Culture*.

JULIAN VON DUERBECK, O.S.B., is a monk at St. Procopius Abbey in Lisle, Illinois. At the Abbey, he is a liturgist and coordinator of a very active program in interreligious dialogue. Fr. Duerbeck has also served as an instructor for the monastic novices at St. Procopius.

DIANA L. ECK is Professor of Comparative Religion and Indian Studies at Harvard University where she is also Chair of the Committee on the Study of Religion in the Faculty of Arts and Sciences, and a member of the Faculty of Divinity. Prof. Eck's works include *Banaras, City of Light*, and her most recent book, *Encountering God: A Spiritual Journey from Bozeman to Banaras*, which is in the area of Christian theology and interfaith dialogue.

ZOKETSU NORMAN FISCHER is Co-Abbot of the San Francisco Zen Center, Green Gulch Farm Zen Center and Tassajara Zenshin-ji Monastery. Ordained a Zen Priest in 1980, he is a poet with six books to his credit.

Mary Margaret Funk, O.S.B., is a nun at Our Lady of Grace Monastery in Beech Grove, Indiana, where she served as Prioress from 1985 to 1993. She is a leading figure in the Centering Prayer movement, and has been the Executive Director of MID since 1994. During the summer of 1995, Sr. Funk was part of the Buddhist-Christian Exchange that visited India, Nepal and Tibet.

Joseph J. Gerry, O.S.B., is a member of the Benedictine Community of Saint Anselm Abbey in Manchester, New Hampshire, where he served as Abbot from 1972–1986. Before becoming Bishop of Portland, Maine, he taught philosophy and humanities at Saint Anselm College, and served the College as Academic Dean and Executive Vice President. Since 1988, Bishop Gerry has served at the National Conference of Catholic Bishops' Office for Interreligious Relations. In 1990, he was appointed Consultor to the Vatican's Pontifical Council for Interreligious Dialogue.

Samdech Preah Maha Ghosananda is the Supreme Patriarch of Buddhism in Cambodia. He established temples in each Cambodian refugee camp in Thailand, and in Cambodian resettlement communities around the world. Called the "Gandhi of Cambodia," Maha Ghosananda's peace walks and walks against land mines around Cambodia have earned him recent nominations for the Nobel Peace Prize. He presently directs the Dhammayietra Center for Peace and Nonviolence.

Joseph Goldstein has been leading insight and loving-kindness meditation retreats worldwide since 1974. He is a cofounder of the Insight Meditation Society in Barre, Massachusetts, where he is a Resident Teacher. In 1989, he also helped establish the Barre Center for Buddhist Studies. Goldstein is the author of a number of books including *Insight Meditation: The Practice of Freedom.*

Guo-Chou is currently the Director of the Dharma Drum Mountain Buddhist Association, Vice President of the Ch'an Sitting Group of the Ch'an Meditation Center in Elmhurst, New York, and Resident Teacher at the Chung-Hwa Institute of Buddhist Culture. He is a scholar of Buddhist monastic rules, and has trained extensively in Ch'an meditation practice.

Thien Han is a lay Buddhist practitioner from Myanmar. He is associated with the Pauk Zedi Monastery in Rangoon.

Zenkei Blanche Hartman currently serves as Abbess of the San Francisco Zen Center. In 1977, she was ordained by Zentatsu Richard Baker, and she received *Dharma* Transmission from Sojun Mel Weitsman in 1988. She has participated in and led monastic practice at Tassajara Zen Mountain Center.

P. Jeffrey Hopkins is Professor of Tibetan Buddhist Studies at the University of Virginia, and trained for five years at the Lamaist Buddhist

Monastery of America. From 1979 to 1989, he served as His Holiness the Dalai Lama's chief interpreter into English on lecture tours in North America, Southeast Asia, Australia and Europe. Prof. Hopkins has published over twenty books, the most prominent being *Meditation on Emptiness*.

KEVIN HUNT, O.C.S.O., is a monastic at St. Joseph's Abbey in Spencer, Massachusetts. He trained in Zen Buddhism under Joshu Sasaki Roshi in the early 1970s and has been involved in dialogue with Buddhism since that time. Fr. Hunt is a Board Member for MID, and visited India in 1994 to engage in dialogue with Tibetan Buddhist monastics.

JINWOL SUNIM was fully ordained as a monk at Haein-sa, the largest Buddhist monastery in Korea. He then concentrated on Son (Ch'an/Zen) meditation in the mountains for six years. The Ven. Jinwol Sunim is presently teaching *Dharma* and meditation at the California Buddhist Association at Berkeley, and is an International Advisor for the Society for Buddhist-Christian Studies.

SURASAK JIVANANTO is founder and Abbot of Wat Thai Washington, D.C., and is the founder and Supervisor of the Council of Thai *Bhikkhus* in the United States. Trained in *Dhamma* teaching and meditation practice, he was Director of meditation in both Wat Mahathat, and Wat Thungsathit in Bangkok prior to coming to the United States. The Ven. Jivananto has written over 50 books, and was the recipient of the Award of *Dhamma* Teaching in the West in 1994, and the Mahitala Nusorn Medal Award in 1996.

GILCHRIST LAVIGNE, O.C.S.O., is a nun of the Monastery of Our Lady of the Mississippi in Dubuque, Iowa. Her interest in interreligious dialogue began in 1964, and was heightened at the Petersham meeting in 1976 where she helped to found MID. Sr. GilChrist studied for a period of time under Sasaki Roshi at the Los Angeles Zen Center, and at the Mount Baldy Zen Monastery.

LEO D. LEFEBURE, a priest of the Archdiocese of Chicago, is Dean of the Ecclesiastical Faculty of Theology, and Professor of Systematic Theology at Mundelein Seminary. Lefebure is an advisor to MID, has received training in Zen and *vipassana* meditation, and is the author of *The Buddha and the Christ: Explorations in Buddhist-Christian Dialogue*.

DONALD W. MITCHELL is Professor of Comparative Philosophy at Purdue University where he is also Chair of the Religious Studies Program. He is advisor on Buddhist-Christian dialogue for MID and for the National Conference of Catholic Bishops, and is an Executive Officer of the Society for Buddhist-Christian Studies. Trained in Christian and Zen spiritualities, Prof. Mitchell is author of *Spirituality and Emptiness: The Dynamic of Spiritual Life in Buddhism and Christianity*.

ESHIN NISHIMURA received Rinzai Zen training under Zenkei Shibayama Roshi, Mumon Yamada Roshi and other Zen Masters for about forty years. He qualified as a traditional Rinzai Zen teacher under Matsuki Gessen Roshi. He is presently Head Priest of the Kouhuku-ji Rinzai Zen Temple, Professor of Zen Buddhism and Director of the International Research Institute of Zen Buddhism at Hanazono University in Kyoto, Japan. The Ven. Nishimura is author of *UNSUI: A Diary of Zen Monastic Life*.

SHOHAKU OKUMURA is the Resident Teacher of the Minnesota Zen Meditation Center in Minneapolis. He is an ordained Soto Zen monk trained in monastic life in Kyoto and Ehime, Japan. Since 1988, the Ven. Okumura has been sent by the Headquarters of Soto Zen Buddhism to lecture on Zen at Soto temples throughout the United States.

BERNARDO OLIVERA, O.C.S.O., is Abbot General of the Cistercians of Strict Observance (Trappists). He entered the order at the Abbey of Azul in Argentina where he was Novice Master and then Abbot. As Abbot General since 1990, he resides in Rome and visits Trappist monasteries worldwide. Dom Olivera was responsible for dealing with the death and burial of the seven martyred Trappist monks in Algeria in 1996 because the Mother House of that monastery did not have an Abbot at the time.

CHUEN PHANGCHAM is Resident Teacher of the Midwest Buddhist Meditation Center in Warren, Michigan. He is a *vipassana* meditation instructor at Wat Dhammaram in Chicago, and President of the Buddhist Council of the Midwest. The Ven. Dr. Phangcham is also Co-President of the American Buddhist Congress, and is an official on the Council of Thai *Bhikkhus* in the United States.

BASIL PENNINGTON, O.C.S.O., is now serving his Chinese Trappist brothers at Our Lady of Joy Monastery on Lantau Island, Hong Kong. He has lectured in over twenty countries and has published some forty books. Fr. Pennington is best known for his work on the contemplative life and Centering Prayer.

HAVANPOLA RATANASARA is Chief Patriarch of the Western Hemisphere for the Sri Lankan Siamese Lineage of the Mahasangha. He is President of the Buddhist Sangha Council of Southern California, President of the College of Buddhist Studies in Los Angeles, Executive President of the American Buddhist Congress, and Co-Chair of the Buddhist-Catholic Dialogue in Los Angeles. The Ven. Dr. Ratanasara's most recent work is *A Buddhist Psychological View of Personality, Growth and Development*.

AARON RAVERTY, O.S.B., is a monk at St. John's Abbey in Collegeville, Minnesota. Since 1990, he has been an editor at The Liturgical Press. Br. Raverty is a Board Member of MID, and traveled in 1995 with three other

Board Members to Tibet, Nepal, and northern India as a guest of His Holiness the Dalai Lama.

SHARON SALZBERG has trained with monastic teachers from many countries, including India, Myanmar, Nepal, Bhutan and Tibet. She teaches both intensive awareness practice, and the cultivation of loving kindness and compassion. She is a cofounder of the Insight Meditation Society in Barre, Massachusetts, and the Barre Center for Buddhist Studies. Ms. Salzberg is the author of *Lovingkindness: The Revolutionary Art of Happiness*.

SAMU SUNIM is a Buddhist monastic in the Korean Chogye Order. He is *Dharma* successor to Son Master Solbong Sunim (1890–1969), and is now President of the Buddhist Society for Compassionate Wisdom. The Ven. Samu Sunim is the founder and Master of the Society's three temples in Toronto, Ann Arbor and Chicago.

SHENG-YEN is the only Ch'an Master in the West, and the only holder of both Lin-chi (Rinzai) and Tsao-tung (Soto) lineages. He is Director of Dharma Drum Mountain and Abbot of two monasteries in Taiwan, and he teaches at the Ch'an Meditation Center in Elmhurst, New York. Ven. Dr. Sheng-Yen has written over 60 books, including *Dharma Drum: The Life and Heart of Ch'an Practice*.

JUDITH SIMMER-BROWN is Chair of the Religious Studies Department at the Naropa Institute in Boulder, Colorado. She serves on the Executive Board of the Society for Buddhist-Christian Studies, and is on the Board of Directors of Shambhala International. Prof. Simmer-Brown has been active in Buddhist-Christian dialogue, and is a member of the International Buddhist-Christian Theological Encounter.

LHUNDUP SOPA is Professor of South Asian Studies at the University of Wisconsin. He trained at the Seraje Monastic University in Lhasa, and was an examiner of His Holiness the Dalai Lama. Geshe Sopa was President of the Tibeto-Mongolian Monastery in Farmingdale, New Jersey, and is founder of the Deer Park Buddhist Monastery and Center near Madison, Wisconsin.

DAVID STEINDL-RAST, O.S.B., is a senior member of the Benedictine Monastery of Mount Saviour in New York. He has been engaged in the Buddhist-Christian dialogue since 1965. His Zen teachers were Yasutani Roshi, Suzuki Roshi, Soen Roshi and Eido Roshi. Among Br. Steindl-Rast's publications is *The Ground We Share: Everyday Practice Buddhist and Christian*, coauthored with Robert Aitken Roshi.

LOBSANG TENZIN is Spiritual Director of Losel Shedrup Ling, a Tibetan Buddhist institute in Atlanta, Georgia, where he also teaches at Emory University. He spent eleven years as a member of the Buddhist School of Dialectics, a monastery in Dharamsala, India, under the guidance of His

Holiness the Dalai Lama. Geshe Lobsang also received the Geshe Lharampa degree from Drepung Loseling Monastic University.

TENZIN GYATSO, His Holiness the 14th Dalai Lama, is the spiritual leader of the Tibetan people. Seen as the manifestation of the Bodhisattva Avalokitesvara, His Holiness is now living as the head of the Tibetan Government-in-exile in Dharamsala, India. In recognition for his work for individual and world peace, His Holiness has received numerous humanitarian and human rights awards, and was awarded the 1989 Nobel Peace Prize. Among his many books on such topics as Buddhism, philosophy, religion, and global responsibility, his two autobiographies include: *My Land and My People* and *Freedom in Exile*. His most recent book on Buddhism and Christianity is *The Good Heart: A Buddhist Perspective on the Teachings of Jesus*.

HAROLD THIBODEAU, O.C.S.O., is a monk at the Abbey of Gethsemani and was trained in the monastic life by Thomas Merton. His interest in Buddhism began with Merton's talks on Zen and other Buddhist traditions. Br. Thibodeau visited Tibetan Buddhist monasteries in India in 1992 on a MID-sponsored hospitality exchange, and he is currently a Board Member for MID.

PANDITH M. VAJIRAGNANA was appointed Abbot of the London Buddhist Vihara in 1985, and Sangha Nayake of Great Britain by the Supreme Sangha Council of Sri Lanka in 1990. He is also Vice President of the World Buddhist Sangha Council, the British Representative of the Maha Bodhi Society, and a founder of the British Inter-Faith Network. The Ven. Dr. Vajiragnana has been active in Buddhist-Christian intermonastic dialogue in Europe, and is author of numerous books including *Peace through Buddhism*.

ARMAND VEILLEUX, O.C.S.O., is a member of the General Council, and Procurator General of the Cistercian Order in Rome. He also teaches at the Monastic Institute of Sant'Anselmo in Rome. Fr. Veilleux took part in the Asian monastic encounters in Bangalore in 1973, and in Kandy in 1980. He was a founding member of MID, and is one of its advisors.

JAMES A. WISEMAN, O.S.B., is a member of the Benedictine community of St. Anselm's Abbey in Washington, D.C. He has served as Abbot for an eight-year term, as Novice Master for a further ten years, and is currently Prior of the monastic community. Fr. Wiseman is an Associate Professor of Theology and Chairman of the Department of Theology at the Catholic University of America. He is also in his fourth year as Chair of MID.

YIFA is a nun in the Fokuangshan Buddhist Order in Taiwan. She is a scholar of the Chinese Ch'an monastic rule, and member of the International Buddhist-Christian Theological Encounter. The Ven. Dr. Yifa is presently the Dean of Academic Affairs at Hsi Lai University in Rosemead, California.

Glossary

[Aramaic (A), Chinese (C), Greek (G), Japanese (J), Korean (K), Latin (L), Pali (P), Russian (R), Sanskrit (S), Thai (TI), Tibetan (T)]

Abba (A): father; referring to God; title for early Christian monks who were advanced in years and wisdom.

anatta (P) [*anatman/anatma* (S)]: no-self; the absence of any substantial nature to the self.

Angelus (L): a Christian prayer traditionally said in the morning, at noon, and in the evening.

anicca (P): impermanence; the transiency of all things.

arahant (P): noble one; a holy person who has attained Nirvana and is free from all defilements and ignorance.

Benedictine: a Christian monastic in an Order that follows the sixth-century *Rule of St. Benedict.*

bhavana (P/S): mental cultivation through meditation practice.

bhikkhu (P) [*bhiksu* (S)]: a male Buddhist monastic.

bhikkhuni (P) [*bhiksuni* (S)]: a female Buddhist monastic.

Blessed Sacrament: the consecrated bread and wine in which, Catholics believe, there is a real presence of Jesus Christ.

bodhi (P/S): enlightenment.

bodhisattva (S): one who undertakes the path to Buddhahood for the benefit of all living beings; a future Buddha.

bodhisattvayana (S): another name for Mahayana Buddhism because of its emphasis on the *bodhisattva* ideal.

Buddha (P/S): an enlightened being; title given to the historical Buddha, Gotama Buddha (563–483 B.C.E.); title given to many Buddhas in the Mahayana tradition.

Buddhahood: the goal of Mahayana Buddhism that entails the perfection of wisdom and compassion through the *bodhisattva* path.

Buddha-nature: the essential enlightened nature of all beings; the nature of luminosity and emptiness.

caritas (L) [*agape* (G)]: love or charity; love for God and for neighbor in God that transcends human affection.

Ch'an (C): the name of the Chinese school of Buddhism that is also known by its Japanese name, Zen.

Cistercian: a Christian monastic in the Catholic Order founded at Citeaux, France, in 1098 by Robert de Molesmes, based on the Benedictine Rule.

contemplatio (L): resting in God beyond words or images; a graced state of meditation in the Christian mystical life.

deity yoga: a tantric practice by which one uses visualization to be transformed in accordance with the visualization.

dependent arising: the interdependent process by which things come to be, are sustained, and pass away; the dynamic of emptiness.

devas (S): gods who, according to Buddhism, are within the worlds of dependent arising.

Dhamma (P) [*Dharma* (S)]: Truth; the true nature and law of all existence; the teachings of the Buddha.

Dharmakaya (S): body of the *Dharma*; the eternal essence of Buddhahood.

Divine Office: a set of Christian prayers and readings that are prayed at particular times during the day; the Liturgy of the Hours.

divinization: the process in Christian spirituality by which one participates in the divine character; growth in the divine life.

dukkha (P/S): the "dissatisfactory" condition of human existence.

emptiness [*sunyata* (S)]: the ultimate nature of all phenomena; the absence of an inherent existence of things—all things arise interdependently.

Eucharist (G): thanksgiving, gratitude; the sacrament of the Lord's Supper when the bread and wine are consecrated and shared in holy communion.

Geluk (T): a school of Tibetan Buddhism founded in the 14th century which is led by His Holiness the Dalai Lama.

Geshe (T): a high academic title in Tibetan Buddhism.

Hesychast (G): from the Greek for "hermit;" a sect of mystics in the Eastern Christian Church originating in the 14th century on Mt. Athos.

householder: Buddhist name for married laypeople.

Jesuit: member of the Society of Jesus; a religious order in the Catholic Church founded in 1534 by St. Ignatius Loyola.

Jesus Christ (G): the name of the founder of Christianity; "Jesus" is Greek for the Hebrew "Joshua," meaning "savior;" "Christ" is Greek for the Hebrew "Messiah," meaning "anointed."

jhana (P) [*dhyana* (S)]: high state of meditation.

Kagyu (T): a school of Tibetan Buddhism that was founded in the 11th century.

karma (S) [*kamma* (P)]: human action and the moral effect it produces in the actor.

kenosis (G): self-emptying; the self-emptying of Christ in the Incarnation and cross; an ascetic element in Christian spirituality.

khandhas (P) [*skandhas* (S)]: the "aggregates" that constitute all existence; there are five aggregates to human existence: physical form, sensations, feelings, volitions, and thoughts.

koan (J): a paradoxical saying that can be used in Zen meditation practice.

lama (T) [guru (S)]: exalted one; a Tibetan Buddhist monastic.

lectio divina (L): a prayerful, meditative reading of the Bible or of other spiritual works related to the Bible.

Madhyamika (S): one of the major philosophical schools of Mahayana Buddhism; the Middle Way School, founded by Nagarjuna, that stresses the doctrine of emptiness.

Mahayana (S): the Great Vehicle; one of the two major divisions of Buddhism, the other being Theravada; the form of Buddhism traditionally practiced in Tibet and East Asia.

mantra (S): a prayer word or short phrase repeated in spiritual practice.

Mass: the celebration of the Christian Eucharistic rite.

meditatio (L): a discursive pondering of a sacred text or subject.

mondo (J): a Zen story.

Mulasarvastivada (S): see Sarvastivada.

Nagarjuna: an Indian Buddhist philosopher of the 2nd or 3rd century C.E. who is the founder of the Madhyamika School of Buddhist thought.

Nibbana (P) [Nirvana (S)]: the final state of release following full enlightenment.

Nyingma (T): the oldest school of Tibetan Buddhism traced back to 747 C.E when Buddhism was introduced to Tibet by Padma Sambhava.

oratio (L): prayer; prayerful expression from the heart.

Pali: the language in which the earliest scriptures of Buddhism were recorded; the religious textual language used by Theravada Buddhism.

paramita (S): perfection; virtue; six or ten practices traditionally associated with the *bodhisattva* path.

Paschal Mystery: the Christian belief that Jesus Christ passed through death to new life, and thereby made this new life available to others.

Patimokkha (P) [*Pratimoksha* (S)]: the Buddhist monastic code of precepts for monks and nuns.

perichoresis (G): the trinitarian doctrine that the Father, Son, and Holy Spirit mutually indwell in one another.

Prasangika (S): one of the interpretive schools of Madhyamika philosophy.

Rimpoche (T): precious one; title for a Tibetan Buddhist spiritual master.

Rinzai (J): one of the two main schools of Japanese Zen Buddhism, the other being Soto; uses *koan* practice.

Roshi (J): title for a Zen master.

Sacramentary: the book that contains the prayers used at the celebration of the Mass.

samadhi (P/S): concentration; the eighth step of the Buddha's Eightfold Path.

samatha (P/S): serenity; calming mediation (*samatha bhavana*).

samsara (P/S): the transient world of rebirth.

Sangha (P/S): Buddhist monastic community; community of Buddhists.

Sanskrit: the ancient language of India used by Mahayana Buddhism in writing their scriptures.

Sarvastivada (S): a school of early Buddhism associated with the Theravada tradition.

satori (J): awakening of one's True Self in Zen Buddhism.

Sautrantika (S): one of the early schools of Buddhism associated with Theravada.

sensei (J): teacher.

sesshin (J): an intensive Zen retreat.

sila (P/S): moral precepts to be lived by Buddhists.

skillful means [*upaya* (S)]: means used to bring a being to the state of enlightenment and liberation from suffering.

Son (K): the Korean school of Buddhism that is also known by its Japanese name, Zen.

Soto (J): one of the two main schools of Japanese Zen Buddhism, the other being Rinzai; emphasizes meditation only.

staretz (R) [pl. *startsi*]: an experienced spiritual guide.

Sunim (K): title for a Son master.

sutta (P) [sutra (S)]: scripture; text.

tantra (S): esoteric Indian Mahayana texts used in certain Tibetan Buddhist practices.

tathagata (P/S): Thus Gone One; an epithet for Buddhas.

Theravada (P/S): Way of the Elders; one of the two major divisions of Buddhism, the other being Mahayana; the form of Buddhism traditionally practiced in Sri Lanka and Southeast Asia.

Trappist/Trappistine: a Christian monastic in the reformed Cistercian Order established in 1664 at the monastery of La Trappe in Normandy.

Vaibhashika (S): one of the early schools of Buddhism associated with Theravada.

Vajrayana (S): Thunderbolt Vehicle; refers to Tibetan Buddhist practice based on tantric texts.

Venerable: title given to Buddhist monastics.

vespers: evening prayers; part of the Divine Office.

vijnana (S): consciousness that makes distinctions.

Vinaya (P/S): the collection of early Buddhist scriptures that presents the precepts for monastic life.

vipassana (P): insight; insight meditation (*vipassana bhavana*).

wat (TI): a Buddhist temple or monastery complex.

Yogacara (S): one of the major philosophical schools of Mahayana Buddhism; the Mind-Only School of Mahayana Buddhism.

zafu (J): a cushion used in Zen meditation.

zazen (J): Zen meditation practice.

Zendo (J): a room used for Zen meditation practice.

Index